Feminist Political Theory

Also by Valerie Bryson

Feminist Debates: Issues of Theory and Political Practice

Contemporary Political Concepts: A Critical Introduction
(edited with Georgina Blakely)

Feminist Political Theory

An Introduction

Second Edition

Valerie Bryson

Consultant Editor: Jo Campling

First edition 1992
Reprinted eight times
Second edition 2003

Published by
PALGRAVE MACMILLAN
Houndmills, Basingstoke, Hampshire RG21 6XS and
175 Fifth Avenue, New York, N.Y. 10010
Companies and representatives throughout the world

PALGRAVE MACMILLAN is the global academic imprint of the Palgrave
Macmillan division of St. Martin's Press, LLC and of Palgrave Macmillan Ltd.
Macmillan® is a registered trademark in the United States, United Kingdom
and other countries. Palgrave is a registered trademark in the European
Union and other countries.

ISBN 0–333–94570–0 hardback
ISBN 0–333–94568–9 paperback

This book is printed on paper suitable for recycling and made from fully
managed and sustained forest sources.

A catalogue record for this book is available from the British Library.

A catalog record for this book is available from the Library of Congress.

10   9   8   7   6   5   4   3   2   1
12   11   10   09   08   07   06   05   04   03

Printed and bound in Great Britain by
Creative Print & Design (Wales), Ebbw Vale

Contents

Acknowledgements

I would like to thank the Politics team at Huddersfield University for enabling me to have a sabbatical semester to work on this revised edition and for providing such a supportive academic environment. Thanks too to many of the students on my Women, Politics and Society module for their hard work and enthusiasm.

Thanks to my friends and family for practical, emotional and intellectual support, and for putting up with my neglect as the enormity of the task became apparent and the time available shrank.

And thank you, Alan Pearson.

VALERIE BRYSON

Introduction

For most of its history, western political theory has ignored women. We seldom appear in its analyses of who has or should have power; when it has deigned to notice us it has usually defended our exclusion from public affairs and our confinement to the home; only rarely have we been seen as political animals worthy of serious consideration. Even today, this exclusion of half the human race is frequently either perpetuated or dismissed as a trivial oversight, while the inequalities that may exist between men and women are seen as of little practical importance or theoretical interest. Most feminist political theory, in contrast, sees women and their situation as central to political analysis; it asks why it is that in virtually all known societies men appear to have more power and privilege than women, and how this can be changed. It is therefore *engaged* theory, which seeks to understand society in order to challenge and change it; its goal is not abstract knowledge, but knowledge that can be used to guide and inform feminist political practice.

The term 'feminist' first came into use in English during the 1880s, indicating support for women's equal legal and political rights with men. Its meaning has since evolved and is still hotly debated: in this book I will use it in the most broad and general terms to refer to any theory or theorist that sees the relationship between the sexes as one of inequality, subordination or oppression, that sees this as a problem of political power rather than a fact of nature, and that sees this problem as important for political theory and practice. I will also provisionally use it to include those contemporary writers who are concerned with exploring the meanings attached to 'woman' and the ways in which these are constructed, but who deny that we can talk about 'women' or 'men' as stable political identities.

The following chapters explore something of the history of feminist political theory from medieval times to the present day. They do not claim to be comprehensive, partly because there is not the space to include everything and partly because the rich heritage of feminist thought is still being rediscovered. It is also important to remember that our view of the past and our interest in it are inevitably filtered by our concerns in the present, and that these help determine which tiny fractions of what has gone before are recalled and presented as history. The ideas of the writers discussed in this book are therefore just some of those that have come down to us over time, and some of those that are alive today. This second edition differs from the first in that it gives more space to black feminists, whose early voices are now being re-claimed, and whose insights are becoming increasingly important to feminist thought as a whole. Incorporating recent developments in feminist thought has also meant re-thinking many sections; in particular, discussion of postmodernism cannot be consigned neatly to a final chapter, but casts a backward shadow over the entire book.

Today, any attempt to construct a 'grand narrative' is widely seen as both misguided and old-fashioned, and it has anyway long been clear that feminist ideas cannot be seen in terms of straightforward linear development and cumulative progress. Women writers have often had to struggle particularly hard to be heard and, with no equivalent to the white, middle-class, male 'canon', their ideas have often been written out of history. This means that new generations of feminists have frequently had to start almost from scratch; it also means that although some early writings can appear naive and simplistic, they can at times seem strikingly 'out of time' and relevant to our lives today. They are also frequently written with a passion and wit that sparkle across the centuries and that reflect their basis in women's lived experience: here Mary Wollstonecraft's difficulty in organising her personal life, Elizabeth Cady Stanton's impatience with domesticity or Simone de Beauvoir's rejection of 'respectability' are not simply interesting biographical facts, but may affect both their theories and our perception of them.

The development of feminist thought has not only been uneven, it has also always involved deep theoretical disagreements. These partly reflect the varied needs and perceptions of women in different societies and situations, but also stem from feminism's roots in competing ideological traditions. Although it has become conventional to classify different types of feminism according to their supposed theoretical starting-points, it is also now widely agreed that such attempts to impose order on the rich complexity of feminist thought obscure its fluid, fragmentary and interconnected nature. Nevertheless, it seems that we have to start somewhere and, if classification is handled with care and its limitations acknowledged, it can provide a convenient starting-point into the maze of feminist ideas. The following chapters are therefore based on the provisional identification of a number of broad strands of feminist thought. It must, however, always be remembered that 'reality' cannot be fully represented in this way, and that general patterns are frequently disrupted as ideas pop up in unexpected places and even individual writers often seem to hold contradictory sets of belief at the same time.

Bearing these reservations in mind, we can see that while the earliest expressions of feminist consciousness generally drew on religious traditions to assert women's worth, secular liberal ideas about equal rights were increasingly available from the seventeenth century, and were used by feminists to argue that women have a right to education, employment, political participation and full legal equality. Such claims for equal rights within existing society at first sight seem straightforward. Although strongly opposed in the past, they are largely accepted in the west today, where they act as a kind of 'default setting' for public debate on gender issues. However, women remain disadvantaged despite gaining legal rights and, as we shall see, the logic of their situation has often pushed 'liberal feminist' arguments in much more radical directions.

Since at least the early nineteenth century, some feminists have argued that their goal should not be equal rights within an unequal class society, but that true equality for women requires some kind of socialist society based on co-operation and collectivism rather than competition and individualism. A number have further claimed that the ideas of Karl Marx provide the key to understanding and ending women's oppression and exploitation. Today, although socialism is much less fashionable than in the recent past, the belief that feminist goals cannot be separated from wider socio-economic change remains an important part of feminist thought.

Whilst some feminists have demanded to be included in 'malestream' ideologies, many have also long argued that women are in important respects both different from and superior to men, and that the problem they face is not discrimination or capitalism but male power. From the late 1960s, these ideas were developed into what came to be known as 'radical feminism'. This claimed to be based in women's own experiences and needs, and it used the concept of *patriarchy* to argue that men's power is not confined to the public worlds of economic and political activity, but that it characterises all relationships between the sexes, including the most intimate, and that it is sustained by the whole of our culture. From this perspective, the family is a key site of patriarchal power, which is also maintained through the control of women's sexuality. The insistence that 'the personal is political' involved a major challenge to the assumptions of political theory and has contributed to a general reassessment within feminist thought of the nature of power and politics.

Some of the less cautious exponents of the new radical feminist approach argued that women's experiences cross the boundaries of nation, class, ethnicity and time, uniting them in a common sisterhood. Like much white feminism, this analysis largely ignored or marginalised the experiences of black women. As we shall see, black women themselves have long attempted to address the specificity of their own situation, and in recent years black feminism has emerged as a distinct theoretical approach that seeks to explore the complex ways in which gender, class and 'race'[1] interact. Much as feminism as a whole challenges 'malestream' thought, black feminism has revealed the limitations of many supposedly universal feminist concepts. It shows that 'race' is not just an issue for black people, but one which affects us all.

Black feminism's analysis of differences amongst women is taken to an extreme by feminists drawing on a recent and influential strand in philosophy known as postmodernism. This approach provides a profound challenge to 'common sense' assumptions about the nature of knowledge and the world around us, arguing that 'reality' is created by language and culture rather than simply existing and waiting to be understood. From this perspective, the meaning of being a woman (or a man) is never fixed, and there are no objectively correct answers to political questions. This means that we cannot talk about 'women' or 'men' as stable political identities, let alone claim that women deserve equal opportunities, suffer from patriarchal oppression or will only be free in a socialist society. We can, however, analyse and challenge the ways in which gender identities are constructed. The influence of these ideas on contemporary feminist thought has been profound, and extends well beyond those who would accept a 'postmodernist' label. It has however been fiercely resisted as an elitist, de-politicising and inherently conservative theory that delegitimises any attempt to challenge the status quo; as such, many critics would say that 'postmodern feminism' is a contradiction in terms.

As in the past, feminism today is a site of fierce controversies rather than a body of received truths. Theoretical disagreements are not simply of academic interest, but have implications for feminist political practice. Underlying theoretical perspectives will, for example, influence whether feminists focus their energies on conventional politics, trade unions, anti-racist movements, self-help groups or the deconstruction of literary texts and whether they work with men or in separatist women-only organisations. In this context of on-going debate, earlier writings are not simply 'dead theories', for the issues they engage with are still often unresolved; this means that they are not only fascinating in their own right but relevant to contemporary politics.

Today, western feminism as a whole is often on the defensive, and the stress on complexity and fragmentation which has come to dominate some sections of feminist thought can seem almost overwhelming, making it almost impossible to say anything about anything in a world of fluctuating meanings and precariously shifting identities. Nevertheless, feminism continues to generate exciting ideas, spilling over the boundaries of conventional political debate, challenging its assumptions and forcing new issues onto the agenda. This means that feminist political theory cannot be conveniently 'ghetto-ised', for the issues it raises are of vital importance to any understanding of political power; any political theory that ignores it is inevitably partial and impoverished.

1

Early feminist thought

For most of recorded history, a key aspect of women's subordination has been their exclusion from public debate and the means of written expression. This means that we have little direct access to what they may have thought. Nevertheless, it seems likely that wherever women have been subordinated some have resisted, and it is possible to trace elements of feminist consciousness back to the first written expressions of women's thought in seventh century Europe. As Gerda Lerner has argued, any woman who wrote in this early period, or who claimed the ability to benefit from education or to contribute to theological, philosophical and political debate, was already challenging her society's teaching about women's God-given intellectual inferiority and their propensity for sin. It is therefore unsurprising that an identifiable theme in early writing by women is the attempt to re-interpret the scriptures to challenge such beliefs (Lerner, 1993).

By the beginning of the fifteenth century, there was a European-wide public debate, which came to be known as the *Querrelle des femmes*, over the nature of women and their portrayal in literature. Of the pro-women writers, the best known is the Frenchwoman Christine de Pizan (1365–c.1430), who appealed to the authority of women's own experiences and to the record of 'great women' in history to assert her sex's innate intellectual equality with men and to defend women against the misogyny of contemporary literature and religious authority. Although the work of Pizan and her contemporaries did not produce any kind of political programme or analysis of power, they show that debates over women's role in society that include a recognisably feminist perspective go back much further than has until recently been assumed. While it is important not to impose current preoccupations on earlier periods, it is also possible to identify an early version of the difference/equality debate which recurs throughout this book, as some writers asserted their equal worth with men and others demanded respect for women's alleged sex-specific virtues, such as piety. (For discussion of early feminism and the situation of medieval women, see Lerner, 1993; Akkerman and Stuurman 1998a; Rubin 1998; Rang 1998; Kelly, 1984; Willard, 1975; Shahar, 1983; Power, 1975; King, 1997.)

5

Seventeenth-century feminism in Continental Europe and Britain

The *Querelles* had been primarily concerned with education, morality and manners, and participants frequently based their arguments on interpretations of the bible. Feminist theological arguments were further elaborated in the seventeenth century: for example, some writers used the creation story to argue that Eve was superior to Adam because she was created last, or because she was created out of Adam's rib rather than out of mud and slime (Stuurman, 1998:72). However, some writers also engaged directly with the increasingly secular arguments of mainstream philosophical and political debate, appealing to reason rather than existing authorities when making their claims, and employing concepts and terminology that are still with us today.

The inspiration for these new ways of thinking was the revolution in western philosophy which had been started in the first half of the seventeenth century by Descartes. According to Cartesian philosophy, all people possess reason, and true knowledge, which is based on experience and self-discovery rather than study of the classics or sacred texts, is in principle available to all. This means that traditional authority is rejected in favour of rational analysis and independent thought, and that customs and institutions which are not in accordance with reason should be rejected. Although, as we shall see, the focus on reason has been criticised by some recent feminists, at the time it provided inspiration for many feminist writers, for it implied that women's exclusion from classical education need not also exclude them from philosophy, for what is important is good ideas, and not 'what fanciful people have said about them' (Mary Astell, *A Serious Proposal to the Ladies*, in Ferguson, 1985:188). It also meant that the questioning of authority could be extended to that of men over women, and that 'unreasonable institutions' might include those, such as seventeenth century marriage laws, that perpetuated women's subordination.

Akkerman and Stuurman have described the seventeenth century as the age of 'rationalist feminism' in Europe, as writers such as the Frenchwoman Marie de Gourney and the Dutchwoman Anna Maria von Schurman used Cartesian principles to make increasingly egalitarian claims. Such continental feminism was probably given its most systematic and radical philosophical exposition at this period by the Frenchman François Poulain de la Barre in his three famous treatises on sexual equality, first published in the 1670s. In these, de la Barre not only claimed that, since 'the mind has no sex', women are as capable of reason as men, he also argued that women are as capable as men of gaining the skills and knowledge that would enable them to participate equally in virtually all economic and social activities, including government and military command. Perhaps even more importantly, he suggested that because belief in male superiority was the most basic, widespread and deeply entrenched form of prejudice, a challenge to this could make other forms of prejudice questionable too (de la Barre, 1990; see also Stuurman, 1998).

Early British feminism and the ideas of Mary Astell

The impact of continental debates extended to Britain where, by the second half of the seventeenth century, they had combined with more local influences to produce 'the first sizeable wave of British secular feminist protest' (Ferguson, 1985:15), with significant numbers of women challenging received ideas about their sex in pamphlets and in books.

Any attempt to 'read off' feminist theory from the social situation of women should be approached with extreme caution. However, it does seem that the increased scale and intensity of the debate in Britain stemmed at least in part from changes in gender roles that occurred in its early years of capitalist development, as well as from the political upheavals of this 'century of revolution' (for an overview, see Kent, 1999). Changes in agriculture were creating a new and growing class of wage labourers, and, as the division of labour became more complex and units of production larger, the old system of family-based domestic industry gradually declined, creating for the first time a distinction between the public world of employment and the private world of home and family. Meanwhile, working women were progressively excluded from trades and professions in which they had previously been active, such as brewing, printing and medicine, and aristocratic women, who had formerly played an important role in running their husbands' estates, were increasingly restricted to the domestic sphere. As it became increasingly difficult for women to earn their own living, marriage became an economic necessity and wives became increasingly dependent on their husbands for financial support. Demographic factors were, however, increasing the numbers of 'surplus women' unable to find a husband, while the sixteenth century English reformation meant that the option of entering a convent was no longer available. In this context it is not surprising that the role of women should have been debated. Moreover, it was only now that the public and the private could be clearly distinguished that it made sense to ask about the appropriate sphere of women's activity; this distinction was alien to medieval society, but remains central to many discussions of feminism today.

Politically, the seventeenth century was one of the most turbulent periods of British history, as for a time the country was engulfed by civil war, and all political and religious authority was thrown into question.

It was almost inevitable that many women as well as men would become politicised and, in addition to the traditional 'behind the scenes' involvement, there is evidence of women demonstrating, rioting and petitioning parliament; these activities included a demonstration by 'Shoals of Peace Women' wearing white ribbons, who mobbed Westminster demanding an end to the civil war (Davies, 1998:2). Even more subversively, a number of the radical religious sects that sprang up challenged received notions as to appropriate sexual roles and behaviour: for example, the Ranters preached extreme sexual permissiveness, while the Quakers argued that men and women were not only equal in God's eyes, but were equally eligible for the ministry.

Questions of authority in state and family were, moreover, intimately linked in the political theory of the time. Conservative defenders of absolute monarchical power argued that the authority of the king over his people was sanctioned by God and nature in exactly the same way as that of a father over his family; this meant that 'patriarchy' (the rule of the father) in the home was used as justification for a parallel power in the state. Opponents of such state power, who argued that authority was *not* divinely ordained but must rest on reason and consent, were therefore forced to re-examine arbitrary power within the family as well; logically, it seemed, patriarchy in state and home must stand or fall together. Perhaps unsurprisingly, this logic was not pushed to its conclusion by male writers. Although Hobbes and Locke, the foremost political theorists of the century, did examine relationships within the family at some length, they fell back on arguments of social convenience and men's superior strength to justify the continued subordination of women. This meant that, while they saw men as independent and rational individuals capable of perceiving and pursuing their own self-interest, they saw women as wives and mothers, weak creatures unable to escape the curse of Eve, whose interests were bound up with those of their family, and who therefore had no need for independent political rights.

This at first sight appears to be the kind of inconsistency that a more rigorous application of the underlying principles could rectify; some recent theorists have however suggested that, despite their universalistic pretensions, the basic premises of early liberal writers were inherently biased against women. Here it is argued that they were based on an essentially male view of human nature that ignored human interdependence and attributes such as nurturing that have traditionally been associated with women (Jaggar, 1983). It is further claimed that the whole approach was predicated upon a distinction between the public and private which involved the exclusion of women from the former and a devaluation of the latter (Pateman, 1986a; Arneil, 1999), and that it perpetuated a view of rationality that excluded women, because it defined reason in terms of *overcoming femininity* (identified with nature, particularity, biology, passion and emotion; see Coole, 1993; Lloyd, 1984; Braidotti, 1986; Nye, 1990a; Jones, 1993; Frasier and Lacey, 1993). Similar criticisms have been made of the more fundamental Cartesian revolution in philosophy discussed above, despite Descartes' claim that 'even women' are capable of rational thought. Thus Susan Bordo has attacked his insistence that knowledge can only be achieved through disembodied reason, and describes his refusal to acknowledge the value of subjective, intuitive or 'sympathetic' knowledge as 'an aggressive intellectual *flight* from the female cosmos and "feminine" orientation towards the world' (Bordo, 1994:6; see also Lloyd, 1984; Ferguson, 1985; Perry, 1986; Hill, 1986; Kinnard, 1983; Smith, 1982; Rogers, 1982.; Springborg, 1996; Waters, 2000). These are complex and contested arguments which will recur throughout the book: at this stage it is important to note simply that the extension of traditional theory to include women may not be as unproblematical as it at first sight seems, and that the concepts and assumptions made by male theorists may not be entirely adequate when it comes to expressing female needs and experiences.

As in earlier periods, mainstream political and philosophical debates in the seventeenth century were conducted almost exclusively by men. There were, however, exceptions, of whom the most important is probably Mary Astell (1666–1731). Although she has been written out of histories of political thought, in her lifetime Astell was widely seen as a serious contributor to mainstream political theory; she has also recently been described as 'The First English Feminist' (Hill, 1986, *The First English Feminist: Reflections upon Marriage and other Writings by Mary Astell*) and 'arguably the first systematic feminist theoretician in the west' (Catherine Stimpson, Introduction to Perry, 1986:xi; see also Smith, 1982; Kinnard, 1983; Browne, 1987; Waters, 2000).

In Astell's writings on women, we find the new approach to philosophy and knowledge being used to produce a classic early statement of the core liberal feminist belief that men and women are equally capable of reason, and that therefore they should be equally educated in its use: 'Since God has given to Women as well as Men intelligent Souls, why should they be forbidden to use them?' (*A Serious Proposal to the Ladies*, in Ferguson, 1985:188). Here Astell anticipated the arguments of Mary Wollstonecraft and other later writers, by arguing that although women in the society of her day appeared frivolous and incapable of reason, this was the product of faulty upbringing rather than any natural disability: as such it was evidence of the need for improved female education rather than its impossibility. However, although Astell based her arguments on the liberal idea of rationality, she did not accept the liberal idea of political rights. Like most of the seventeenth-century feminists, she was a staunch Tory and defender of the monarchy; as such, she was more concerned to deny political rights to men than to attempt to extend them to women. Indeed, the logic of her conservatism led her to a seemingly very unfeminist con- clusion: accepting the parallel between authority in the state and in the home, she argued that a wife must obey her husband as a subject must obey the king; when a women enters marriage, she argued, she has chosen a 'monarch for life', and must therefore submit to his authority.

Astell's writings are at times heavily ironic, so that not everything she says should be taken at face value; nevertheless her conservatism does seem genuine enough. It has, however, more radical implications than at first sight appear, and in many ways she is carried beyond liberal feminist demands to a broader analysis of the relations between men and women. Firstly, she insisted that a woman's duty to obey her husband did not involve any recognition of his superiority; indeed there is throughout her writings a marked tone of barely disguised contempt for the male sex (for example, she said that men are not fit to educate children, for 'precepts contradicted by example seldom prove effective'; quoted in Kinnard, 1983:37). Secondly, she argued that submission to male authority could not extend to single women, whether 'poor fatherless maids' like herself or 'widows who have lost their masters' (*Reflections Upon Marriage*, in Ferguson, 1985:195). This meant, thirdly, that an educated woman should choose to reject the domestic slavery involved in marriage, and she therefore advised women to avoid matrimony (while cheerfully admitting that if they all followed her advice, then 'there's an End to the Human Race'; quoted in Perry, 1986:9). From this it followed, fourthly, that women's activities need not be limited by the need to attract a husband, and they could therefore concentrate on improving their minds rather than their beauty: 'Were not a morning more profitably spent at a Book than at a Looking Glass?' (quoted in Perry, 1986:92). Finally, as a practical means of freeing women from marriage and dependence on men, she advocated the establishment of female communities, rather like secular nunneries, where women could live and learn together without men, knowing themselves 'capable of More Things than the pitiful Conquest of some Wretched Heart' (quoted in Perry, 1986:102). This idea excited con- siderable interest; it failed to attract sufficient financial support, not so much because of its feminism, but because of its dangerous associations with Roman Catholicism.

All this means that, despite her political conservatism, Astell's work contains in embryonic form some of the core ideas of recent radical feminism: the idea that man (whether as sexual predator or tyrannous husband) is the natural enemy of woman; the idea that women must be liberated from the need to please men (Perry sees this as an early form of 'consciousness-raising'; Perry, 1986:103); the belief that this liberation can be achieved only if women are enabled to live separately from men; the perception that men have controlled and defined knowledge ('Histories are writ by them, they recount each others great Exploits and have always done so', quoted in Perry, 1986:3); and the understanding that women's experiences can give them a valuable and distinctive perspective on the world (Waters argues that this makes Astell a precursor of late twentieth-century standpoint feminism; Waters, 2000). Underlying all this there is a clear rejection of the whole scale of values in which man is the unquestioned measure of human worth in favour of a celebration of women: it was not for nothing that Astell's major work on education was entitled *A Serious Proposal to the Ladies ... by a Lover of her Sex.*

While Mary Astell may have been the most radical and systematic feminist of her time she was, as has already been said, certainly not an isolated voice. This means that by the early eighteenth century we have a quite widely established perception of women as a group in society whose situation is in need of improvement, and it is this consciousness of women's group identity which Smith thinks distinguishes writers of this period from their predecessors (Smith, 1982). What we do *not* yet find, however, is any direct challenge to women's social and economic positions or to the sexual division of labour, nor do we find any coherent political programme or demand that the rights of male citizens be extended to women. For the most part socially and politically conservative, these early feminists addressed themselves almost exclusively to women of the upper and middle classes and there were few attempts to link the situation of women to other disadvantaged groups in society. For these writers, it was through education and the exercise of reason that women could be made independent of men; it is not until the third quarter of the eighteenth century that feminism was to become associated with wider demands for change.

The Enlightenment and early liberal feminism

In some ways, the middle years of the eighteenth century seem to represent a retreat from feminism, as arguments for women's rationality became less fashionable than belief in their innate weakness and dependence on men, the ideas of Astell and her contemporaries fell into disrepute, and the very names of these early feminists were forgotten. Nevertheless, although there was no systematic analysis of women's situation or organised women's movement, individual complaints about their lot continued, as did discussion of women's abilities and social roles, and Karen Offen has argued that 'there was clearly a full-blown feminist consciousness in existence among some privileged women and men [in Europe], in dialogue with a mounting backlash' (Offen, 1998:98; see also Offen, 2000; Smith, 1982; Ferguson, 1985; Rogers, 1982; Spender, 1983a). In Britain, many women continued to write and publish throughout the period; most famously, the 'bluestocking' group of 'salon intellectuals' debated and wrote on a range of contemporary issues. The bluestockings, whose best known member was Hannah More, have usually been seen as anti-feminist: they stressed the importance of women's domestic role, particularly their responsibility for nurturing virtue within the family, and they argued that, to a greater extent than men, women were motivated by 'sensibility' rather than reason. However, they also argued that if women were to become good wives and mothers they must be educated, while arguments about women's greater emotional sensibility were both positively appraised and used to justify women's involvement in movements for moral and social reform, such as temperance and anti-slavery campaigns. Moreover, the very existence of the bluestockings as a group of intellectual women, publicly discussing and publishing from the 1750s onwards, could be seen as a statement about women's ability and role in society: no longer a silenced majority, women could not be entirely excluded from public debate (see Myers, 1982 and 1986; Midgley, 1995; Caine, 1997; Kent 1999; Stott, 2000; Richardson, 2000). It is in this context that the ideas of the late eighteenth-century feminists must be understood; although there is no *direct* line between them and the writers of Mary Astell's day, their ideas did not explode upon an entirely unsuspecting world.

The second half of the eighteenth century was a period in which the stress on rationality and the questioning of traditional authority which we saw beginning in seventeenth-century philosophy reached its fullest expression. It was also a period dominated by the experiences of the American and French revolutions, and in which philosophical debates on the nature of freedom and human rationality were to take tangible form in the American Declaration of Independence (1776) and the French Declaration of the Rights of Man and Citizen (1789). What united the philosophers of this so-called 'Age of Reason' or 'The Enlightenment' was their optimism and their belief in progress through the onward march of human reason and knowledge; reason replaced God or antiquity as the standard of right or wrong, and no institution or authority was to be exempt from its judgement. Although many of the leading philosophers were in fact socially and politically conservative, the radical implications of these principles are obvious, and they provided the basis for the liberal belief that, as rational beings, individual men have rights that must not be violated by arbitrary power; that therefore any authority must rest upon the consent of the governed; and that individuals should be as far as possible self-determining and free from government control.

Although always expressed in terms of the rights of *man*, it might at first sight seem that this could be understood as a generic term that includes women; for the most part, however, the philosophers of the Enlightenment and the leaders of the revolutions did not simply fail to make this extension, but they denied that it could be made. There was indeed a strikingly widespread consensus amongst leading philosophers that the principles of rational individualism were *not* applicable to women, for it was held that by their very nature women were incapable of the full development of reason; thus we can find in the writings of Voltaire, Diderot, Montesquieu and above all Rousseau, the idea that women are essentially creatures of emotion and passion, who have an important role to play as wives and mothers, but who are biologically unsuited for the public sphere (see Rendall, 1985; Schapiro, 1978; Kennedy and Mendus, 1987; Landes, 1988).

This consensus did not, however, go unchallenged, and by the end of the century there were a number of attempts to show its inconsistency, and to demonstrate that the liberal ideas of the Enlightenment could be applied to women as well as men. The best known of these is Mary Wollstonecraft's *Vindication of the Rights of Women* (1792), but the fame of this work should not be allowed to obscure the extent of other feminist writing at the time (see Offen, 1998). For example, the French writer Condorcet insisted that women *were* capable of reason and should be educated accordingly, that they should therefore have the same political rights as men, and that to deny this was an unacceptable tyranny. In practice he did not anticipate the widespread involvement of women in politics, but this he said was no reason to deny them political rights in principle – indeed he argued that women could no more be logically excluded from politics on the grounds of menstruation or pregnancy than could a man because he was suffering from gout (*On the Admission of Women to the Right of Citizenship*, 1790, and *Sketch for a Historical Future of the Progress of the Human Mind*, 1793, in Baker (ed.) 1976; see also Schapiro, 1978; Vogel, 1986; Landes, 1988). Here we have a direct attempt to confront the inconsistencies of other writers and to claim that liberal principles have a universal application that includes women, so that 'Feminism was ... an integral part of the complete pattern of liberalism that Condorcet so enthusiastically advocated' (Schapiro, 1978). The German writer von Hippel similarly rejected the idea that women's exclusion from civil and political rights could be justified in terms of a biologically given nature; it was men, he claimed, who had made women what they were, and he demanded that men and women be given equal rights and education for citizenship rather than for their traditional sex roles. He went further than other writers of the time in blaming men for women's situation, and in denying that the traditional division of labour between the sexes was sanctioned by reason or nature; it was however, he argued, enlightened *men* who had to act to liberate women, for they themselves had been rendered incapable of independent political action (*On the Civil Improvement of Women*, 1793; see Vogel, 1986).

However, women at this time were themselves far from silent, and their voices were to be heard on both sides of the Atlantic demanding equal treatment with men. Thus in America Abigail Adams (1744–1818) wrote in 1776 to her husband (who later became the second president of the United States), employing the language that he had used against English rule to point out that her sex too needed protection from tyranny and 'will not hold ourselves bound by any laws in which we have no voice or representation'. John Adams' reply that 'As to your extraordinary code of laws, I cannot but laugh...' can have done little to change her opinion that 'all men would be tyrants if they could' (extracts in Schneir, 1972 and Rossi, 1973). Other correspondence of the period suggests that such ideas were commonly discussed by women of Adams's class, while a more systematic analysis was given by Judith Murray (1751–1820) (see Rendall, 1985; Spender, 1983a; Rossi, 1973).

Meanwhile in England the historian Catherine Macaulay (1731–91) was arguing on similar lines. In her *Letters on Education* (1790) she insisted that the differences between the sexes were a product of education and environment and not of nature: she attacked the way in which women's minds and bodies had been distorted to please men, and she demanded that boys and girls be given the same education – and here she went beyond uncritical acceptance of male values to demand that the education of boys too be changed to provide them with traditional female skills. Macaulay's work has been overshadowed by that of her close contemporary Mary Wollstonecraft (1759–97), but at one time her fame extended across two continents: she was in correspondence with George Washington, and Abigail Adams asked a correspondent to find out all he could about her for 'One of my own sex so eminent... naturally raises my curiosity' (Spender, 1983a:127 and 129). Whatever the reason for her rapid disappearance from public memory (an indigestible prose style, the offence caused to polite society by her marriage to a much younger man, and the inability of male historians to cope with the existence of more than one feminist writer at a time have all been suggested – see Spender, 1983a), it is certain that at the time her ideas were widely read and anticipated many of Wollstonecraft's, a fact which the latter readily acknowledged.

By the late eighteenth century, a key source of 'progressive' ideas in England was provided by the Unitarians (Protestant dissenters who saw reason as the basis for religious understanding and social progress). Although their relationship with feminism was not unambiguous, they drew many women as well as men into campaigns against slavery and for education, and they were an important part of the radical circles which Wollstonecraft was to join (Watts, 1998; Gleadle, 1995; Hirsch, 1996).

It was, however, in France that women of this period were to play the most dramatic role: the women of Paris demanding bread, the *tricoteuses* knitting under the guillotine and Charlotte Corday's assassination of Marat have passed into legend, while a number of individual women such as the moderate republican Madame Roland were involved in the struggle for political power. Feminism as such was always marginal to the revolution; demands for improved female education were however included in the first petitions to the National Assembly (the French Parliament), and wider issues of women's rights and representation were soon fiercely debated in pamphlets and the radical press, and in the women's political clubs that sprang up between 1789 and 1793. Like Condorcet, women were arguing that principles of the Enlightenment applied to them too, and that political rights belonged to them as much as to men: Olympe de Gouges' *Declaration of the Rights of Women* (1790, in Riemar and Fout, 1980) is the clearest example of this approach. Such demands can seem a straightforward and 'common sense' application of existing principles. However, as Joan Scott has argued, they were deeply paradoxical, for the claim to equal rights simultaneously denied the relevance of sex difference and affirmed the existence of women as a sexually differentiated group with identifiable interests and needs: '... in order to protest women's exclusion, they had to act on behalf of women and so invoked the very difference they sought to deny' (Scott, 1996:x). As we shall see, this paradox recurs throughout the history of feminism. As the revolution developed, demands were silenced; in an anti-feminist reaction the women's clubs were closed and the most prominent writers and spokeswomen imprisoned or put to death; in the light of her own fate, de Gouges' claim that 'since a woman has the right to mount the Scaffold, she must also have the right to address the House' has a terrible irony (Riemar and Fout, 1980:63). (For discussion of feminism in the revolution, see also Rendall, 1985; Spender, 1983a; Evans, 1977; Tomalin, 1974; Kelly, 1987 and 1992; Ackerman and Stuurman, 1998b; Landes, 1988.)

Although the articulation of feminist demands in the French revolution was short-lived, it had an impact on the public imagination that was to affect popular reaction to feminism in other nations: 'The feeling was that the French were bad, revolution was bad, the French revolution had led to feminism, therefore feminism must be bad' (Rover, 1970:13). It is therefore important to remember that liberal feminism could be seen as a revolutionary ideology in the most literal sense, if we are to understand the reception given to Mary Wollstonecraft's ideas in England; for despite her own revulsion from the extremism and violence of the revolution, 'Viewed through the smoke of the Bastille, Wollstonecraft loomed like a blood-stained Amazon, the high-priestess of loose-tongued liberty' (Taylor, 1983:11; see also Hirsch, 1996). This meant that although her work was less original than both her admirers and detractors have claimed, its effect was maximised by its timing – she wrote it two years after the outbreak of revolution; and it was written with a force and passion which reflected the tumultuous times through which she was living.

Mary Wollstonecraft's Vindication of the Rights of Woman

At one level, the *Vindication of the Rights of Woman* is simply a continuation of the old debate about women's nature and their capacity for reason. Here Wollstonecraft was particularly concerned to refute the ideas of the philosopher Rousseau who, in his work *Emile*, which described the ideal education of a young man, had included a chapter on the very different education of 'Sophy', Emile's future wife. For Rousseau, men's and women's natures and abilities were *not* the same, and these biologically given differences defined their whole role in society, with men becoming citizens and women wives and mothers. This meant that the education of boys and girls must both recognise natural differences in ability and inclination ('Little girls always dislike learning to read and write, but they are always ready to learn to sew', *Emile*:331), and encourage the virtues appropriate to adult life: this involved a training in rational citizenship for boys and lessons in how to please a man and bring up his children for a girl. Rousseau's democratic radicalism had marked him out from the other philosophers of the Enlightenment, and it is partly because she shared his passion for liberty and justice in other spheres that Wollstonecraft was so enraged by his views on women: it is the radical nature of Rousseau's views on politics which give a revolutionary edge to her insistence that girls and boys should be educated alike.

Her quarrel with Rousseau was fourfold. First, like earlier feminists, she refused to accept that women were less capable of reason than men, or that vanity, weakness and frivolity were the natural attributes of her sex ('I have, probably, had an opportunity of observing more girls in their infancy than J.-J. Rousseau', *Vindication*:129): in phrases often strikingly reminiscent of Astell (of whom she had probably never heard) she roundly condemned the mindless vanity of upper-class women of her day, but like Astell saw this 'femininity' as a social construct that distorted rather then reflected women's true ability. Secondly, Wollstonecraft argued that if men and women are equally possessed of reason they must be equally educated in its use: woman is *not* 'specially made for man's delight' (*Emile*:322), but an independent being who is both capable of and entitled to a rational education. This much had, as we have seen, already been asserted by earlier feminists, but Wollstonecraft extended the argument in her third main point of disagreement with Rousseau: as men's and women's common humanity is based on their shared and God-given possession of reason, then *virtue* must be the same for both sexes – that is, it must be based on reason and it must be freely chosen. This meant that for Wollstonecraft the virtues of the good wife and mother could not be seen as 'natural', nor could they be based upon a male-imposed ignorance cunningly disguised as innocence, and she argued forcefully that a woman taught only passive obedience to her husband could never be fit to bring up children. Women must be given knowledge and education so that they can make rational choices, for it is only then that it makes sense to talk of their goodness.

This claim that women's actions must be freely chosen adds a radical new dimension to the debate, for it challenges the whole idea of ascribed social roles, and the rights and duties that accompany them. It is this fourth and final area that distinguishes Wollstonecraft and her contemporaries from the earlier feminists, for the idea of equal *worth* now leads irrevocably to that of equal *rights*. In Astell's time, belief in women's rationality had been combined with political conservatism, but now it was firmly linked to political liberalism, and the principles were established that were to lead to later campaigns for women's suffrage and legal rights and, eventually, to the demand for equal participation with men in the worlds of politics and paid employment.

The systematic articulation of these demands was, however, still very much in the future, and Wollstonecraft was much more concerned to establish the principle than to elaborate a detailed programme for change. She was writing at a time when, although industrialisation was opening up new employment, this was, particularly for women, at very low wages and in appalling conditions, while in the middle ranks of society women's economic dependence on men had grown with the increased separation of home and work. As in Astell's day, employment prospects for middle-class women were almost non-existent, and Wollstonecraft's own experiences showed her how degrading and unsatisfactory were the only available options of teacher, companion and governess. Increasingly, a man's wife was seen as the purely ornamental symbol of his success and not in any sense his partner; this dependency was formalised in Blackstone's famous decree that within marriage 'the very legal existence of the wife is suspended ... or at least is incorporated and consolidated into that of the husband' (quoted in Kramnick, 1978:34). It was in this context that Wollstonecraft insisted that women had an independent right to education, employment, property and the protection of the civil law; this she argued was needed to ensure that women were not forced into marriage through economic necessity, and that wives were not entirely dependent on the goodwill of their husbands. Women therefore needed legal rights in order to make independent rational choices and achieve virtue; a woman who is forced to perform the traditional female roles will do so very badly, but if men

> would ... but snap our chains, and be content with rational fellowship instead of
> slavish obedience, they would find us more observant daughters, more affectionate
> sisters, more faithful wives, more reasonable mothers – in a word, better citizens.
> (*Vindication*:263)

As the above quotation suggests, Wollstonecraft did not expect that education and freedom of choice would lead most women to reject their traditional role, but argued that they would enable them to perform it better. She did not accept the public/private split that runs through liberal thought and which insists on the superiority of the former over the latter; rather she sought to 'envalue' women's domestic responsibilities (Thornton, 1986:88), and to show that domestic duties, properly performed, were a form of rational citizenship: that is, they were to be seen as public responsibilities rather than a source of private satisfaction or tribulation (Vogel, 1986; Sapiro, 1992:182–5).

The problem with this, of course, is that in a world in which domestic duties are unpaid, the economic dependence of a woman upon her husband remains; Wollstonecraft had perceived the dangers of this, but does not follow its implications through. Similarly, her insistence that motherhood is a form of citizenship does not solve the problem of the male monopoly of formal political and legal power, which leaves women dependent on the goodwill of men to 'snap their chains'. Here she did briefly suggest that women should have representatives in government (*Vindication*:260), but this was in no way central to her argument, and although she argued that women must be free to choose a career in business or public life, she never suggested that individual successful women might use their power to benefit their sex as a whole. Carol Pateman has argued that Wollstonecraft was caught in an underlying dilemma which still traps liberal feminists today: she sought to claim citizenship for women on gender-neutral grounds at the same time as recognising their specific qualities and roles, within a framework that allowed women to become full citizens only by being like men (Pateman, 1988b).

Some recent feminist critics of liberalism and the Enlightenment have argued that Wollstonecraft's arguments are further confused by her uncritical acceptance of an inherently male model of rationality which, as discussed above, is bound up with the need to subdue qualities traditionally associated with women, such as passion and emotion, and which sees calculating self-interest rather than sympathy, emotion or imagination as the only legitimate basis for human motivation and conduct. Even Rousseau, who stressed the importance of passion in human affairs, insisted that public life must be ruled solely by reason. He therefore argued that women (the objects of passion) can have no place in politics; his recent feminist critics argue that this exclusion is not simply a regrettable product of Rousseau's personal prejudices, which could be ignored by later theorists, but is basic to a view of rational citizenship which presupposes not only the exclusion of passion from public life, but its containment and expression within the family. This means that, from a Rousseau-ite perspective, if women enter political life they not only disrupt it, they also destroy its domestic foundations (Coole, 1993; Canovan, 1987). Critics argue that such an approach cannot provide an adequate basis for a woman-centred theory or feminist politics. The problem is only compounded if domesticity too is seen as a source of civic responsibility to which the same public standards of rationality apply. Some feminist critics of liberal rationality have therefore criticised Wollestonecraft's apparent denial of any legitimate place to more unruly emotions and desires, and they have attributed her unhappy private life to an unworkable belief that even in marriage passion and love must be subordinated to reason, so that 'In the choice of a husband women should not be led astray by the qualities of a lover' (*Vindication*:224; see Brody, 1983; Caine, 1997).

As Virginia Sapiro has pointed out, a problem with this body of feminist criticism is that it is often based on a caricature of Enlightenment thinking. It also misrepresents Wollstonecraft, who employed the contemporary (and contested) notion of *sensibility* to argue for the legitimacy of both emotion and reason 'so long as emotion was trained by reason and reason tempered by emotion', and whose belief in women's need to control their sexual impulses was simply common sense in an age when lack of reliable contraception or safe childbirth meant that 'Sexuality was – materially and not just conceptually – a life-and-death matter for women' (Sapiro, 1992:xxi and xix). It is also self-evident that unhappy relationships are not confined to liberal feminists, and many a contemporary feminist whose heart or sexual desire refuses to obey the dictates of logic and political correctness will empathise with Wollstonecraft's unhappy love affairs and sympathise with the conflict between love and reason articulated in her private correspondence; many may also envy her eventual marriage to the philosopher Godwin, which appears to have been based on a high degree of mutual respect and independence as well as love (Walters, 1979; Moore, 1999). Ironically, it was the publication of her correspondence by Godwin shortly after her death in childbirth that did most to discredit her ideas for the next generations of women: the association of feminism with 'immorality' effectively banished it from consideration in 'respectable' society.

A further criticism that has frequently been made of liberal feminists is that they fail to recognise any non-sexual forms of oppression or to relate the situation of women to conditions in society as a whole; in particular they are accused of being class-blind, and interested only in the plight of middle-class women. Thus it has been said of Wollstonecraft that 'her feminism was basically a demand for equality with bourgeois man' (Walters, 1979:320), and certainly the *Vindication* does address itself to women of the middle class, and she consistently seems to assume that the existence of servants is necessary if domestic work is to be more than mindless drudgery.

However, the ideas discussed in the radical circles in which Wollstonecraft moved were certainly not confined to the demand for formal legal rights, but encompassed a whole range of social, economic and religious concerns, with a clear overlap between the ideas of early liberal and socialist writers (see Watts, 1998; Gleadle, 1995). If we look beyond the pages of the *Vindication of the Rights of Woman* to Wollstonecraft's earlier *Vindication of the Rights of Man* (1790), we see her rejecting arguments for hierarchy and privilege, and attacking inheritance and property as causes of poverty and misery for working people; her last novel (*The Wrongs of Woman: or Maria*, published posthumously in 1798) was concerned to explore the predicament not only of the middle-class heroine, but also of a servant girl drawn into prostitution. To describe Wollstonecraft as a socialist would be an exaggeration, for her ideas on economics remain latent rather than systematically articulated, but there is in her writings a consistent insistence that a good social order is incompatible with a high degree of inequality: 'From the respect paid to property flow, as from a poisoned fountain, most of the evils and vices which render this world such a dreary place to the contemplative mind' (*Vindication*, p. 252) and 'the more equality there is among men, the more virtue and happiness will reign in society' (*Vindication*:96). Thus she went well beyond the defence of equal property rights normally associated with liberalism, and provides an interesting link with the ideas of the 'utopian socialists' to which we now turn – indeed one of the foremost of these, Robert Owen, was to say that he 'had never met with a person who thought so exactly as he did' (quoted in Rauschenbusch-Clough, 1898:188).

The utopian socialists and feminism

The term 'utopian socialist' was used by Marx and Engels to refer to those who believed that competitive capitalist society should be replaced by a more equitably organised, co-operative and rational one, and that this could be achieved by demonstrating the reasonableness and desirability of reform: persuasion and example, not class conflict and revolution, were to be the agents of social change. The best known of these early socialists were the Frenchmen St Simon (1760–1825) and Fourier (1772–1837), and the British Robert Owen (1772–1837). They do not form a unified group and some of their ideas were eccentric in the extreme; they had, however, an important influence on later writers and, unlike most later socialists, they saw relationships between the sexes and within the family as central issues – changes here were not seen as simply the by-products of social change or class struggle, but were themselves a necessary precondition for the transformation of society. These feminist aspects of their thought were developed by some of their followers and attracted widespread interest and excitement in both Europe and America (Taylor, 1983; Levitas, 1998; Moses 1998, Moses and Rabin, 1993; Gleadle, 2000b). There was lively debate in the press and, while previous generations of feminists had broken ground by going into print, women such as Frances Wright, Anna Wheeler, Frances Morrison and Flora Tristan were now stating their case in public and drawing huge crowds to their lectures and meetings (Taylor, 1983; Eckhardt, 1984). In the numerous but short-lived socialist communities that the movement inspired, the role of women was a central concern (Muncy, 1973), while William Thompson and Anna Wheeler's 1825 *Appeal on Behalf of Women* remains an outstanding contribution to feminist theory.

In this context the ideas of Wollstonecraft and other liberal feminists were but a starting-point and, although socialist feminism was never a coherent movement, a number of key themes emerge. In the first place, the goal was not equal rights within the existing system, but within a radically transformed one in which private property was to be abolished or severely modified, and in which women would have economic as well as legal independence. Secondly, the traditional division of labour between the sexes was widely attacked: not only were women to be given a full place in productive life, but some even suggested that men should share communal responsibility for domestic work. Thirdly, the family as an institution was widely condemned: it was seen as a source of male power, a bastion of selfish individualism incompatible with socialist co-operation, and as a coercive restraint on free choice. Following from this, some stressed, fourthly, the importance of the free expression of sexuality, and argued that 'free love' was the necessary basis of a free society. All this meant that the liberal claim for equal rights was now placed firmly within a social–economic context of which Wollstonecraft had shown only passing awareness, and power relationships were identified within the family as well as in public life. Recent writers have also seen in the new ideas on sexuality a symbolic challenge to the dualism of Western political thought, for reason and virtue no longer seemed to require the denial of passion, but rather its fullest possible expression.

Attempts to put this analysis into practice, however, met with little success. With their faith in reason and human perfectibility the leaders were very much children of the Enlightenment; they therefore expected that education and example would prove the moral and practical superiority of their system, and that capitalist funding would be found to further the cause of social transformation. Perhaps not surprisingly, such support was seldom forthcoming. Thus, although Owen claimed to have shown that benevolence was not incompatible with capitalist self-interest in his famous model factory at New Lanark in Scotland, where improved conditions, health and housing had produced not only a healthy workforce but healthy profits too, other capitalists remained unconvinced that this represented a sound return on investment, and were frightened off the scheme by Owen's increasingly radical ideas on religion and the family. Owen himself came to see the establishment of socialist communities as a speedier means of regenerating society: as with those inspired by Fourier, the idea was not to 'drop out' of existing society, but to change it by force of example; in practice, however, the communities were to prove more of a warning than an inspiration.

America in the nineteenth century had seemed to offer an ideal opportunity for such experiments, and Emerson wrote in 1840 that 'Not a reading man but has a draft of a new community in his waistcoat pocket' (quoted in Muncy, 1973:5). Of the five hundred or so secular and religious communities that were established, about 50 were inspired by Fourier and 16 by Owen (of which the most famous was New Harmony, founded in 1825 by Owen himself); there were also at least 7 Owenite communities in England between 1821 and 1845. However, none of these socialist communities lasted for more than a few years; this was partly because optimism and idealism could not compensate for lack of practical skills and financial resources, and partly because they tended to attract all kinds of opportunists and misfits and were torn by personality clashes and policy disputes; attitudes to women and to the family also seem to have played a crucial role (Lockwood, 1971; Harrison, 1969; Hardy, 1979; Garnett, 1972; Gleadle, 2000b).

For Owen, private property, religion and marriage formed a kind of unholy and inseparable trinity: each was evil in itself, each upheld the others, and none could therefore be eradicated in isolation. Thus, to stop the married woman being treated as the property of her husband, it was necessary to abolish not only marriage but also private property. To abolish private property, it was necessary to remove the major source of individualism and selfish gratification – the family. To do this, it was necessary to attack the cement that bound them together and upheld them both – religion. However, although the three institutions were logically entwined in theory, Owen found himself unable to abolish the family in practice: most of those entering the communities wished to live as couples, communal childrearing and the separation of children from their parents was far too unpopular to carry out, and fear of scandal led him to downplay his attack on marriage (although in fact Owen never advocated promiscuity, but stable relationships based on free consent rather than legal constraint). The need for such caution was shown by the extent of public hostility to the Owenite community that had been established at Nashoba in 1825 by Frances Wright, with the rehabilitation of former slaves as a major aim. Wright's unorthodox views on marriage ('she put an affirmation of sexual experience that no one else in nineteenth-century America would approach', Eckhardt, 1984:156) provoked widespread condemnation and effectively removed any chances of attracting 'respectable' financial support. Fourier's ideas on the liberating effects of sensuality were downplayed for similar reasons: he had advocated extreme sexual permissiveness both as a means of breaking down the ethics of individualism and possessiveness, and because he thought repression was harmful and incompatible with harmonious society; clearly his ideas could all too easily become an excuse for sexual exploitation, but in practice the Fourierite communities largely ignored this aspect of his thought and adopted a relatively conservative attitude to the family (Muncy, 1973:70). This means that although the failure of the communities is often cited as proof of the inadequacy of the utopian socialists' theories, their theories on the family were never in fact put to the test.

As with the family and sexuality, so too with the division of labour, socialist theory was never matched by community practice. Here Fourier's views were again the most radical, for he demanded a total end to all specialisation and the entire division of labour: he argued that work could be fulfilling and creative only if it were freely chosen, and that an ideal community must be organised to allow all individuals to move freely from one occupation to another. He did seem to think that some jobs will naturally be more attractive to women and implied that they should care for very small children, but he also insisted that in any occupation at least some of the workers should be of the sex that does not normally perform it (Robertson, 1982; Grogan, 1992). This meant that no man or woman would be bound to one task for life and that domestic tasks like all other work would be the willingly performed expression of creativity rather than mindless drudgery. In practice, however, Fourier's elaborate ideas were never systematically applied, and, despite the claims of the men to the contrary, it seems that responsibility for domestic life remained firmly with the women in all the communities. In this context it is perhaps not surprising that they should consistently be less enthusiastic in their support than the men; this was often taken as a sign of women's political backwardness, but, as Barbara Taylor has argued, it

> had less to do with any innate partiality for individual wash-tubs than a fear, often justified, of becoming embroiled in a hard life over which they would have too little control, and in which they would bear the brunt of utopian impracticality. (Taylor, 1983:250)

However, as indicated at the beginning of this section, the impact of utopian socialism and its importance for feminist theory was not limited to the experience of the communities, but became linked in the 1830s and 1840s to a revival of interest in feminist issues which although short-lived was international in character. Thus, for example, Frances Wright had contacts in England, France and America, while there were many direct links between Owenites in England and French feminists inspired by the ideas of Fourier and St Simon (Gleadle, 2000b). The ferment of ideas around the time of the revolutions which swept across much of the European continent in 1848 also had a clear impact on the American feminists discussed in the next chapter (Anderson, 1998).

The St Simoniennes (female followers of St Simon) are of particular historical significance, both because they involved unprecedented numbers of working-class women, and because of their affinity with some late twentieth-century feminist thought. As well as firmly identifying the link between sexual and class issues, they rejected liberal arguments based on equal rationality, making their claims for women on the basis of their essential *difference* from men, and they saw sexual repression as central to women's subordination. They also took the unprecedented step of holding women-only meetings and setting up their own newspaper, which only published articles by women. Claire Moses argues that they were, therefore, asserting women's cultural autonomy and establishing what 'was most likely the first consciously separatist women's liberation movement in history' (Moses, 1998:140; see also Moses and Rabin, 1993). Although she too drew on St Simonian ideas to argue that women were both different from and superior to men, Flora Tristan took a rather different line on political activity, arguing that working men must be persuaded both to rise up in protest at their current situation and to liberate working women (Cross, 1996; Moon, 1978; Landes, 1988; Grogan, 1992).

In the early 1840s, Tristan was to be disappointed by most French workers' apparent indifference to both socialism and feminism, whilst even socialists frequently expressed suspicion of feminist concerns. Such tension between socialism and feminism was also apparent in England, where Owenism had by the 1830s built up a considerable basis of working-class support strongly linked to the co-operative and trade union movements. Owenism never became a mass movement on the scale of the Chartist campaign for the vote which reached its peak at about the same period, but its feminism posed problems for working-class supporters at a time when the idea of the male breadwinner and domestic wife was becoming increasingly popular amongst the working class. Women had been widely involved in political activity such as food riots and strikes earlier in the century, but with increased sexual competition for jobs they became excluded from trade union activity, and although they played an active role in both Chartist and Owenite organisations, particularly in the earlier years, this was often in support of male activity and did not necessarily involve any kind of feminist consciousness. By the 1850s political involvement by working-class women had sharply declined and active hostility to feminism had increased (Florent, 1988).

Nevertheless, for a brief period socialism and feminism had been united not only with each other but with the idea that it is only by transforming *personal* life that wider political and socio-economic changes can occur, and that such personal change itself can only succeed in the context of wider social transformation – so that the personal, the political and the socio-economic are inextricably linked and intertwined. Although latent in all utopian socialist theories, especially those of Owen and the St Simoniennes, these interconnections were given their most sustained analysis in the work of Anna Wheeler, a leading socialist feminist lecturer, and her friend William Thompson (1775–1844), a leading Owenite and economist, who gave feminism a centrality lacking in other male writers; their most direct analysis of women's situation is to be found in the splendidly titled *Appeal of One Half of the Human Race, Women, Against the Pretensions of the Other Half, Men, to Retain Them in Political and Thence Civil and Domestic Slavery.*[2]

Wheeler and Thompson's Appeal On Behalf of Women

The *Appeal* was formally a reply to James Mill's *Article on Government* (published 1824) in which Mill had claimed that, because women have no interests separate from those of their husband or father, they have no need for independent political representation. As such, it ridiculed Mill's logic and vigorously restated the liberal case for equal rights; here Wheeler and Thompson went well beyond Wollstonecraft's tentative ideas on representation to insist that women are entitled to full political rights including representation and participation in affairs of state. Women's intellectual capacity is, they argued, at least as great as men's, and biological differences can never be an argument against political rights. At present 'the law has erected the physical organisation into a crime' (*Appeal*:171), but in fact, they asserted, the consequences of female biology are much less incapacitating than the diseases of excess to which male legislators are prone, while

> is it possible to conceive that legislative power lodged exclusively in the hands of women could have produced atrocities and wretchedness equal to those with which exclusive male legislation has desolated the globe? (*Appeal*:131)

However, Wheeler and Thompson were not simply liberal feminists, and although they claimed equal political and legal rights for women, they argued that these could become meaningful only when common ownership and co-operation replaced private property and competition as the basis of social organisation. Until such time, they claimed, women would still be disadvantaged, for formal equality takes no account of actual difference of condition (such as responsibility for childrearing), so that men will in practice be more successful than women and 'superiority in the production or accumulation of individual wealth will ever be whispering into man's ear preposterous notions of his relative importance over woman' (*Appeal*:198). Economic independence for Wheeler and Thompson therefore involved far more than Wollstonecraft's insistence that women have the right to follow a career, for it included the independence of a wife from her husband. This they argued, could only be achieved in a co-operative society in which the full worth of women's contribution would be appreciated, and in which there would be no motives for men to practice injustices or for women to submit to them – for only without the distorting influences of possession and property could men and women relate to each other as free and equal human beings.

However, although women's oppression was therefore seen as a product of capitalism reinforced by unequal laws, Wheeler and Thompson also saw it as based on men's selfishness:

> Whatever system of labour … whatever system of government … under every vicissitude of MAN's condition he has always retained woman his slave. (*Appeal*:196)

This led them to an analysis of the ways in which men have kept women as their slaves which has clear affinities with the radical feminist analysis of patriarchy and oppression in personal relationships discussed in Chapters 10 and 11 below. Thus, they argued that a husband (a man 'who has admitted a woman to the high honour of becoming his involuntary breeding machine and household slave') does not simply use legal or physical coercion to dominate his wife but insists on controlling her mind, demanding her love as well as her obedience and 'exacting from her trained obsequiousness the semblance of a *voluntary* obedience'. They saw the family too as a means of male domination, where women are 'isolated and stultified with their children, with their fire and food-processing processes' and reduced by their despotic husbands 'to a state of stupidity and apathy, rendering them incapable of a greater degree of happiness than that of the brutes' (*Appeal*:63, 66, 180 and 70).

All this is strong stuff, and provides an analysis of power in personal and family relations which is far removed from Wollstonecraft's ideal of the 'domestic citizen'. However it did not lead Wheeler and Thompson to condemn the male sex in perpetuity or to advocate the kind of separatism envisaged by some late twentieth-century radical feminists (and by Mary Astell, see above). Rather, they believed that the true interests of the sexes could be reconciled, for if women were free then men would find the pleasures of equal companionship far outweighed those of despotism; on a larger scale, the ending of relations of dependency and possession in personal life would make possible a new and higher order of society and

> As women's bondage has chained down man to the ignorance and vices of despotism, so will their liberation reward him with knowledge, with freedom and with happiness. (*Appeal*:213)

This conclusion blends liberal, socialist and radical analysis as it shows the interconnections of political, economic and personal power, and as such it has much in common with recent socialist feminist analysis. It also frequently bears a startling resemblance to the ideas put forward by John Stuart Mill (the son of James Mill) in his famous *On the Subjection of Women* some twenty-four years later; and it is based on a philosophy, utilitarianism, which is usually associated with liberal theory but which Wheeler and Thompson use throughout their analysis. The implications of this will be discussed in the next chapter, but at this stage it is important to note that Wheeler and Thompson's use of utilitarian theory suggests that liberal concepts may be more flexible than some feminists have claimed, and not necessarily incompatible with other approaches.

Although the utopian socialists failed to achieve their aims, and they have generally been seen as merely an eccentric footnote to the history books, their ideas represent an important if brief alliance of liberal, socialist and feminist ideals which challenged the distinction between the private and the public and saw the interconnections between legal, political, economic and personal subordination. As we shall see in the next chapter, they also had a direct influence on some later mainstream writers. Nevertheless, for the next 150 years, liberal campaigns for political and legal rights were often separate from socialist preoccupations with the class struggle, while the idea of personal oppression frequently disappeared from the agenda; it was only towards the end of the twentieth century that these strands were to be drawn systematically together again.

2

Liberalism and beyond: mainstream feminism in the mid-nineteenth century

The writers and activists considered in this chapter were essentially 'reformist' in that they did not seek to deny the rule of law, and they did not provide a systematic attack on the socio-economic system, or on marriage and the family. However, their approaches and origins were more diverse than the 'liberal feminist' label which is frequently attached to them suggests. Although many drew on liberal ideas of equal rights, many women also became politically aware through movements for moral reform associated with evangelical Christianity. These were linked to a rapid growth in small-scale women's associations throughout British and free American society in the early years of the century which politicised many women and provided them with the skills and networks which enabled earlier feminist demands to be translated into mainstream political campaigns for educational, legal and political reform. As these campaigns progressed, they developed some analyses of women's collective interests and their oppression in private as well as public life that were remarkably similar to late twentieth-century radical feminist ideas on sisterhood and patriarchy. In addition, some African American women anticipated later black feminist analyses of the limitations of white feminism and of the interconnections of gender, 'race' and class. To label the approach of the nineteenth-century writers and reformers simply as 'equal rights' or 'liberal' feminist is, therefore, to impose an inappropriate classification based on conventional politics, and to obscure its nature and diversity.

This diversity also makes it extraordinarily difficult to gain a clear overview of the development of feminist thought and activity during the period. Any attempt to understand such a complex movement is likely to involve an arbitrary selection of issues and ideas or to risk seeing events from the perspective of middle-class white female historians who have tended to prioritise their own activities and interests and write out other players and participants, much as male historians have ignored the activities of women (Ruiz and Dubois (eds), 1994; Robnett, 1997). As with the first edition of this book, I have attempted to side-step this problem by studying the ideas of outstanding individuals and their interaction with the movement as a whole: here I have chosen to concentrate on Maria Stewart and Elizabeth Cady Stanton in the United States and John Stuart Mill in Britain. This selection involves the exclusion or marginalisation of many notable feminist writers and activists, and may also run the risk of reinforcing an elitist, top-down view of feminist movements and the development of ideas. Nevertheless, it allows for the exploration of issues in more depth than would otherwise be possible, and Stewart, Stanton and Mill between them cover or come into contact with virtually all the ideas of 'mainstream' feminism during the period. Although she only spoke and published for a short time, Stewart is significant as a black woman applying liberal principles to issues of both 'race' and gender. Stanton was not only a highly original writer, but was active in the American woman's movement for over half a century; frequently highly controversial, she cannot be seen as representative even of white American feminism, but she was in touch with all of its aspects. Mill's *Subjection of Women* is frequently seen as the classic statement of liberal feminism, but I will argue that it was both less original and more radical than its reputation suggests; his was not an isolated voice in Victorian Britain, but was bound up with a more general development of feminist ideas.

It is impossible to provide a definitive list of all those writers and activists whom this focus on a few key writers has omitted. Readers wanting to explore the feminist ideas, activities and personalities of this period are referred to the following as good starting-points: Evans, 1977; Banks, 1986; Rendall, 1985; Rendall (ed.) 1987; Rossi, 1973; Sabrovsky, 1979; Spender (ed.) 1983b; Bolt, 1995. On the United States only, they could consult: Dubois, 1979 and 1981; Scott, 1992; Ruiz and Dubois (eds), 1994; Kleinberg, 1999. And on Britain: Levine, 1987; Herstein, 1985; Maynard, 1989; Caine, 1993 and 1997; Akkerman, 1998; Kent, 1999.

Feminism in the United States: Maria Stewart and Elizabeth Cady Stanton

Evangelical Christianity and the temperance and anti-slavery movements

Like many other American feminists, Maria Stewart (1803–79) and Elizabeth Cady Stanton (1815–1902) first developed their ideas in the context of the movements for moral reform that had emerged from the religious revivalism of the early years of the century. For Stewart, the impact of religion was direct. A free black woman, she was orphaned at 5, in service as a young girl, widowed in her twenties and cheated out of her inheritance by unscrupulous white lawyers; shortly afterwards, she publicly dedicated her life to Jesus and the promotion of morality. Like other free black women inspired by the black churches (see Cannon, 1996), she did not see this morality as simply a matter of personal devotion, but a demand for the moral regeneration of her community that would demonstrate its worthiness and entitlement to equal rights and respect. Here, her insistence that all people are equal in the eyes of God was linked with the liberal stress on reason, which she believed God had given to all people equally, and she combined religious rhetoric with the more secular language of the American constitution, placing the demand for black equality firmly in the mainstream of American political thought: 'I am a true born American; your blood flows in my veins, and your spirit fires my breast' ... 'the whites have so long and so proudly proclaimed the theme of equal rights and privileges, that our souls have caught the flames also, ragged as we are' (Stewart, 1987:46 and 47).

For Stewart, black women were not simply included in the movement to gain rights for black Americans, they were central to it. In language that echoes Mary Wollstonecraft's ideas on motherhood as a form of citizenship rather than simply a private responsibility, she argued that it was only through the influence and example of their mothers that children could be instilled with the love of knowledge and virtue, and that such effective motherhood required that women themselves acquire education (Waters, 2000; Richardson, 1987). Like earlier European feminists, she also appealed to the authority of the Bible and cited evidence of eminent women throughout history, and used this to justify her right to speak in public as a woman (during the early 1830s, she had a number of essays published in a leading anti-slavery journal, and she was not only the first black woman to lecture on anti-slavery issues, but probably the first American-born woman to speak publicly to a mixed audience of men and women).

Stewart saw temperance as an essential part of the project of moral reform, and urged black men and women to spend money saved from drinking and gambling on educational projects. Many white women too campaigned against the evils of drink, and their activities rapidly developed a feminist dimension. As in Britain, an American woman surrendered all independent legal rights when she got married; she therefore had no right to protection against her husband if he were violent, and no right to leave him or to keep her own property or earnings. Temperance campaigners soon demanded that women who were on the receiving end of male drunkenness should have legal protection and the opportunity to escape from a violent marriage. This led to demands for the reform of divorce and child custody laws, for women to have the access to education and employment that would give them economic independence, and, by the 1840s, to the first organised political campaign for a married woman's right to her own property.

The movement for the abolition of slavery was also closely linked to the growth of feminist ideas, although not in any straightforward way. The movement was both a moral crusade and a liberal republican campaign, for the institution of slavery could be seen not only as an affront to God, but also as a violation of the spirit of the American constitution. In both cases, the arguments against black slavery was used on behalf of white women, while the frequently cited argument that slavery involved the sexual exploitation of women (both of the female slave by her owner, and of his wronged wife) introduced a gender-specific aspect to the debate. For white women, at a time when a married woman was effectively her husband's possession, there seemed to be a clear analogy between the situation of women and slaves, and the common subjugation of white women and slaves to the male head of household meant that a challenge to one aspect of this had repercussions for the other (Giddens, 1986). For black women, the anti-slavery movement was an obvious priority and free black women led the way in anti-slavery societies in northern cities (Scott, 1992). This does not, however, mean that they were equal partners with white women in a united movement, for some white women's abolition societies refused to accept black women, and others patronised and marginalised them, sometimes while accepting support from prominent black men (Kleinberg, 1999; Beuchler, 1990; Terborg-Penn, 1998; Giddings, 1984). Indeed, the marginalisation of black women was built into the white feminist claim that women's situation was analogous to that of slaves or black men, as this forgot the specific situation of black and slave women. Thus, Stanton's claim that 'the black man and the women are born to shame. The badge of degradation is the skin and the sex – the "scarlet letter" so sadly worn upon the breast' (in Dubois, 1981: 83) lost sight of those women who were not white and denied a voice to women such as Stewart, who faced opposition not only from white people but also from men in her own community (see Yellin, 1989; and Richardson, 1987).

For many women, black and white, it was the hostility of men to their involvement in the anti-slavery campaign that pushed them in a feminist direction. Even the collection of signatures for petitions was often frowned upon, while women's attempts to speak in public were vehemently opposed. This opposition led Stewart to abandon public speaking, and she spent the rest of her life as a teacher. However, it pushed the white anti-slavery campaigners Sarah and Angelina Grimké to a passionate assertion of the rights of women which went beyond the earlier ideas of Mary Wollstonecraft in demanding that women themselves act to secure their political, legal and economic equality with men (Sabrovsky, 1979; Rossi, 1973; Yellin, 1989). Elizabeth Cady Stanton, who, with her husband, had played an active part in the American anti-slavery movement, was incensed to find that she and other women delegates were excluded from an anti-slavery convention held in London in 1840, and that the suggestion of female participation in the proceedings led to an 'excitement and vehemence of protest and denunciation (that) could not have been greater, if the news had come that the French were about to invade England' (quoted in Buhle, 1978:79). It was this experience, coupled with Stanton's personal frustrations with the demands of domesticity, that provided the direct inspiration for the first ever women's rights convention – the Seneca Falls Convention of 1848. Stanton later claimed that this represented 'the inauguration of a rebellion such as the world had never seen' (quoted in Rossi, 1973:144), although later historians have suggested that its significance has been exaggerated (Isenberg, 1998).

The Seneca Falls Convention

At one level the Declaration of Sentiments and the Resolutions resulting from the convention (which were signed by 68 women and 32 men) can be seen as a straightforward demand that the principles of liberal republicanism be applied to women as well as to men. Indeed, the Declaration was deliberately modelled on the 1776 Declaration of Independence, down to its assertion that 'We hold these truths to be self-evident: that all men *and women* are created equal.' (Rossi, 1973:416; my italics); and it used the language of mainstream American politics to demand the rights of women as citizens to the vote, to property, to education, to employment and to public participation in politics and the church. At the same time, the boldness of its tone may reflect links with European feminists and the optimism generated in radical circules by the 1848 revolutions in France and Germany (Anderson, 1998). The Declaration marked an important milestone for liberal feminism: women's rationality and equality with men were now taken as given, and the tentative ideas of earlier writers were brought together in concrete demands for legal change and for collective action to achieve it; the basis was now laid for the emergence of feminism as a political movement as well as a theory.

As discussed in the previous chapter, however, such demands and action can never be as straightforward as they might at first sight seem. As Joan Scott says, the very act of claiming equality with men is always paradoxical, as it involves a recognition of women's distinctive group identity in the name of denying its significance (Scott, 1996). Critics of liberal feminism have also identified a number of other contradictions which they claim were inherent in the position represented by the Convention. Firstly, although it recognised the collective interests of women and their oppression by men, radical critics say that the Convention ignored the vested interests of men in continuing this oppression. Thus, although we find a recognition of male rule which would not seem out of place in a recent radical feminist account of patriarchy ('The history of mankind is a history of repeated injuries and usurpations on the part of man towards women, having in direct object the establishment of absolute tyranny over her' [in Rossi, 1973:416]), this was coupled with an assumption that, by appealing to principles of reason and justice, women and men could work together to change the law and abolish male tyranny. This, critics argue, ignores the fact that a ruling class does not normally surrender power simply because that power is found to be contrary to reason. However, although this position was true of some feminists, Stanton herself became increasingly suspicious of male support, particularly after the feminist cause was set aside by most male abolitionists after the Civil War on the grounds that 'this is the negro's hour'. This betrayal, as she saw it, led her to the belief that women's emancipation must be won primarily by women themselves, and that all men, whatever their 'race' or class, formed an 'aristocracy of sex' with vested interests opposed to women. This belief was one of the issues that separated Stanton from more 'moderate' campaigners, and contributed to a split in the organised women's movement which was not reunited until the 1890s; and it means that in her writings we can find a clear analysis of women as an oppressed class which could only be freed by its own collective struggle.

Another criticism that has been made of liberal feminists in general and of Stanton in particular, is that to demand rights for women as individuals on the same basis as men is to ignore the fact that their domestic situation prevents full exercise of these rights. Stanton had seven children and frequently complained of the problems of combining motherhood and political activity. However, she never really questioned female responsibility for home and children, and Eisenstein says that in wanting women to become citizens without questioning their role in the family, 'Stanton's understanding of how motherhood and woman's domestic responsibility exclude her from public (male) life appears to be forgotten' (Eisenstein, 1981:162). In other words, despite her perception of women as a sex class, her appeal to principles of liberal individualism ignored the collective and sex-specific restrictions on women's lives, and she failed to see that this private oppression could negate the achievements of public equality.

A further problem arises from the implication that the male world of politics and paid employment is a source of fulfilment and 'republican virtue' in a way that women's domestic sphere is not, so that women can only realise their human potential when they enter the public sphere. As we saw earlier, this idea had been rejected by Mary Wollstonecraft, who argued that responsible motherhood could be an important source of citizenship, and the idea of the 'republican mother', nurturing the civic virtues of her family, was influential in American society at the time of the Seneca Falls Convention. Nevertheless, it is difficult to combine respect for domesticity with the liberal elevation of mental over bodily activity – from which perspective all manual and physical work is inferior to a life of reason, and the activities of the middle-class white male are seen as the most truly 'human'. Thus, although Maria Stewart at times seemed to endorse the idea that women's duties lie in frugal housekeeping and bringing up virtuous children, she also saw education as valuable as an end in itself and railed against the limitations of domesticity: 'How long shall the fair daughters of Africa be compelled to bury their minds and talents beneath a load of iron pots and kettles?' (in Richardson, 1987:21).

Stanton too was ambiguous on the matter, and had found motherhood to be a source both of great satisfaction and of intense frustration. At times she suggested that woman's capacity to bear children made her superior to man, and, like Wollstonecraft and Stewart, she argued that good mothering was a public responsibility that must be based on education and the exercise of reason. Here her accounts of her battles with male 'experts' on how to feed and care for her children make for amusing reading: she rejected the contemporary practice of swaddling (which was based on the belief that unbound infant limbs would break under their own weight), and the medical opinion that a baby's stomach could only hold one tablespoonful of milk (an opinion which she held responsible for many infant deaths through malnutrition); when her own childrearing methods proved successful she was congratulated on her 'female instinct', but she preferred to think that her practices were based on reason (Rossi, 1973:396–401). However, she also claimed that motherhood 'calls out only the negative virtues that belong to apathetic classes, such as patience, endurance and self-sacrifice' (*History of Woman Suffrage*, vol. I:22), and in general her writings imply that public life is both more fulfilling and more important than the domestic sphere. Some feminists today argue that such a view is the inevitable outcome of liberal premises, which involve an uncritical adoption of male values and a devaluation of traditional female activity.

However, much of this criticism is to miss the point that for many of the Seneca Falls delegates, and for many activists throughout the century, public rights were demanded not for their own sake, but as a practical means of improving women's daily lives. It was not that these feminists believed that private oppression could be simply legislated away, but it seemed clear that the lot of a woman trapped in a violent marriage would be better if she had the legal right to leave her husband and to achieve economic independence; rights of education and employment were clearly also of practical importance to single women who would otherwise have no role in society or reasonable source of income. The vote itself did not become a central campaigning issue until after the American Civil War, and Stanton consistently argued that women's oppression involved not only the denial of her rights as a citizen but also her sexual exploitation. She further insisted that this was related to her economic situation and to the whole system of social and religious indoctrination: 'The battle is not wholly fought until we stand equal in the church, the world of work, and have an equal code of morals for both sexes' (quoted in Eisenstein, 1981:112).

The analysis of sexual and personal oppression

This claim that women's problems lie not only in the denial of political and legal rights, but also in an oppressive sexual morality goes well beyond traditional liberal concerns, and it was already present at Seneca Falls, where delegates demanded a rejection of the dual standard of morality 'by which delinquencies which exclude women from society, are not only tolerated, but deemed of little account in man' (Rossi, 1973:147). For virtually all the 'mainstream' feminists of the nineteenth century this did not mean that women should be freed from repressive sexual morality but that men should submit to it too; unlike the early socialists, the goal for most feminists was chastity for both sexes. This was in line with the ideas of both the evangelical movement, with its stress on self-discipline and traditional virtues, and the liberal suspicion of the body which tended to equate sexual enjoyment with animal self-indulgence. Although Stanton herself did not deny that sex could be pleasurable to both men and women, and in the late 1860s she worked briefly with Victoria Woodhull, a notorious exponent of free love, she accepted the dominant view that sex was an inferior form of human behaviour and that women were more able than men to control their sexual desires. She also argued that the unrestrained exercise of male sexuality caused great misery and degradation to women. Because a married woman had no legal right to deny her husband's sexual advances, she was at risk from both venereal disease and unwanted pregnancy, and Stanton argued that it was therefore male lust that drove many women to seek abortion (which she opposed on health grounds while refusing to blame the women who had recourse to it); prostitution was a clear consequence of both male sexuality and the unjust economic system that drove some women to such desperate measures; all women, moreover, were united by a fear of rape. Indeed, like some recent radical feminists, Stanton went so far as to see rape as synonymous with the condition of her sex: 'Society, as organised today under the man power, is one grand rape of womanhood, on the highways, in our jails, prisons, asylums, in our homes, alike in the world of fashion and of work' (in Dubois, 1981:123).

All this means that issues of power and domination were identified not only in public political life, but also in the most intimate relationships, and Stanton campaigned publicly to change conditions of family life and marriage. Here she went well beyond existing claims for married women's property rights to attack the institution of marriage itself, seeing it as a form of unpaid prostitution and domestic labour, rather than a religious sacrament based on love and mutual obligation. Her own ideas on this were reinforced by her experience in talking to small women-only groups in the late 1860s; these seem to have been very similar to late twentieth-century consciousness-raising groups (see Chapter 10 below), where personal problems could be explored with other women, and frequently found to reflect a shared situation. A central issue was women's loss of sexual autonomy on marriage, for a wife had no right to deny her husband sexual access to her body; and Stanton increasingly saw this as a root cause of women's oppression: 'Women's degradation is in man's idea of his sexual rights. How this marriage question grows on one. It lies at the very foundation of all progress' (in Rossi, 1973:392–3). In one sense this position can be seen simply as a logical extension of the premises of liberal individualism, whereby the idea that an individual has rights in his or her person gains specific meaning when applied to women. The issue could therefore be expressed using the language of the liberal tradition; thus Lucy Stone, who was generally seen as a more 'moderate' and 'respectable' feminist than Stanton, wrote: 'It is very little to me to have the right to vote, to own property etc. if I may not keep my body, and its uses, in my absolute right' (quoted in Wheeler, 1983:129). However, it also involved a redefinition of power and politics that anticipated the radical feminist claim that 'the personal is political'; private life was seen as an arena in which power is both exercised and can be challenged, and this meant that women's freedom was to be won, not simply by allowing them to enter into public life, but by transforming their situation at home.

Eisenstein has complained that here Stanton failed to match her analysis with an adequate solution: having shown the collective and all-pervasive nature of women's oppression by men, she relied on formal legal and political changes to end it – a solution which falsely 'assumes that all the relations of marriage are embedded in law' (Eisenstein, 1981:159). However, Stanton never argued that these legal changes were sufficient in themselves to bring about the changes she desired: this would require a major shift both in women's and men's consciousness, and in socio-economic conditions. In a sense, the process of demanding change was radical in itself, as it undermined the dominant consciousness by challenging the legitimacy of male power, and placing hitherto unmentioned issues on the public agenda. An assault on the formal collective powers of men therefore brought into question the morality of each individual oppressor. This power was also attacked by challenging conventional as well as legal rights, and it is in this context that we can understand some feminists' insistence on retaining at least part of their own name on marriage, and their experiment with the 'Bloomer costume' in the early 1850s. To refuse to be known as 'Mrs Henry Stanton' and to dress for comfort and convenience rather than male approval was, Stanton believed, to assert her own autonomy and to reject the slave status implied in the loss of name – although the Bloomer costume (a full, calf-length skirt over baggy trousers) attracted so much hostility and ridicule that it distracted from all other issues, and Stanton soon stopped wearing it in public.

Education, religion and The Woman's Bible

Access to education had been one of the earliest feminist demands, both as an end in itself and as a means to decent employment. As so often, Stanton went beyond 'moderate' demands to argue not only that women should be educated, but that the sexes should be educated together. This, she believed, would help change the attitudes of the sexes towards one another: by working and learning together boys and girls would see each other as equals, so that their adult relationships, including marriage, could be based on respect, equality and companionship.

Towards the end of her life, this concern with changing the attitudes that underlie sexual subordination led Stanton to attack what she saw as a major agent of indoctrination: religion. All forms of organised religion were, she argued, hostile to women: the Hindu widow on the funeral pyre, the Turkish woman in the harem, the American mother refusing chloroform in childbirth because she must suffer for Eve's original sin – all were victims of male-dominated religion. Although some individual ministers were supportive, she found the churches in the United States to be an enormously powerful force against her feminist ideas, and as her early evangelicalism turned into agnosticism (although not atheism), she adopted an increasingly anti-clerical position. In the 1890s, she attempted to make the attack on religion a focal point for the organised women's movement; and in 1895 she published, in collaboration with other women, *The Woman's Bible*, a feminist critical commentary which denied that female subordination was divinely ordained, and claimed that men had manipulated religion to legitimise their power (extracts in Dubois, 1981).

However, this 'monument to feminist religious polemical scholarship' (Banner, 1980:164) did not achieve what she had hoped; religious leaders refused to take her arguments seriously, and the new generation of feminist leaders was increasingly reluctant to become involved in any issue other than the suffrage campaign.

Class, 'race' and feminism

Although throughout the century more 'respectable' feminists were anxious to distance themselves from Stanton's attacks on the church and her willingness to debate sexual affairs in public, she was far from alone in seeing women's emancipation as a matter of more than legal and polit-ical change; frequently it was the manner and timing of what she said, rather than its content, that antagonised erstwhile co-workers. On economic matters, however, she sometimes went further from the 'mainstream' position, particularly in the period from 1868 to 1870 when with Susan Anthony she edited a feminist journal, *The Revolution*. This took a decidedly pro-labour, anti-capitalist stand, and made a serious, although unsuccessful, attempt to organise women workers. It is therefore untrue to say of Stanton that she was concerned only with the problems of middle-class women; like Mary Wollstonecraft she consistently criticised economic inequalities, and she showed a keen interest in the ideas of the Utopian socialists. However, she never developed a sustained economic analysis of capitalism; and although she worked in the early 1870s with Victoria Woodhull, who published the first American edition of the *Communist Manifesto*, and who was president of the small American branch of the First International (see Banner, 1980:125–30), she appears to have had no knowledge of Marxist economic theory. Moreover, far from focusing on the problems of the working class as a whole, like many other nineteenth-century feminists Stanton's concern for the situation of working-class women was combined with extreme hostility to working-class *men*. In part, this stemmed from resentment of the fact that the most ignorant man had political rights denied to middle-class women like herself. For Mary Wollstonecraft, writing at a time when most men were denied the vote, the franchise had been a marginal matter (*Vindication*:259), but to a nineteenth century American woman 'to have drunkards, idiots, horse-racing rum-selling rowdies, ignorant foreigners and silly boys fully recog-nised … is too grossly insulting' (Stanton's *Address to the Seneca Falls Convention*, in Dubois, 1981:32). As the century progressed, the feminist movement increasingly preyed upon the class prejudices of middle-class women, and Stanton's original demand for universal suffrage became a call for the 'educated vote' (that is, a literacy qualification for both sexes).

She also maintained that rape was a crime only of working-class men, and towards the end of her life she advocated birth control as a means of limiting the numbers of the working class.

Intertwined with this class hostility was a considerable amount of racism. For some white women, particularly in southern states, this was overt. For many others, it was often unintentional, the unthinking product of a world view that equated the experiences of middle-class white women with those of the whole of their sex. As we have seen, Stanton's claim that the situation of women is like that of black men forgot that some women are themselves black. As many black men both assumed that they could speak for their community and opposed black women who attempted to speak out, the needs of black women were seldom publicly recognised, let alone addressed. The exclusion and marginalisation of black women has been perpetuated by later white feminist and black male historians, who have neglected their distinct history. This history is, however, now being rediscovered by black feminists who are both redefining the concept of political activity from a black perspective and rescuing the ideas of such eminent foremothers as Maria Stewart, Sojourner Truth and Julia Cooper. (See Collins, 1990; Ruiz and Dubois (eds) 1994; Yellin, 1989; Litwak and Meier (eds), 1988; Terborg-Penn, 1998; Giddings, 1984. For a discussion of Cooper, see Chapter 4, below.)

Truth (?1797–1883) was a former slave who travelled the country talking on black and women's issues. Her most famous speech was at a women's rights convention at Akron in 1851 where she poured scorn on the male claim that women were too weak and frail to deserve the vote, with a reminder of the strength and trials of those like herself – 'And ain't I a woman?' (in Schneir, 1972:94–5). This often-quoted refrain is not simply a demand for inclusion, it is also a vivid illustration of the ways in which womanhood is socially constructed, rather than a quality possessed by all female persons, and it also shows the consequences of this for different groups of women, with black women being doubly devalued because they could not conform to a racialised norm of femininity which itself devalued their sex.

Stanton had worked with black campaigners for an end to slavery. However, in the aftermath of the Civil War she refused to support the enfranchisement of black men if the vote were not also given to women; she argued that white women were *more* entitled to the vote than were former slaves and, furious at what she saw as the betrayal of the women's cause by those for whom she had worked, she did not scruple to attempt to 'build feminism on the basis of white women's racism' (Dubois, 1981:92). In contrast, although most black women consistently advocated universal suffrage, many saw racism as the most important source of oppression, and the enfranchisement of black men as an achievable priority. However,

Truth argued against this that 'if the colored men get their rights and not the coloured women theirs, you see the coloured men will be the masters over the women, and it will be just as bad as it was before' (quoted in Giddings, 1984:65; but see Terborg-Penn, 1998 for the suggestion that Truth was often manipulated by white feminists). As the century progressed, black women were increasingly active in a range of clubs and societies and black suffragists began organising locally in the 1880s. However, as racial hostility to black Americans increased, 'Black women were virtually abandoned by most white female suffragists' (Terborg-Penn, 1998:132), and their involvement in mainstream suffrage campaigns was actively discouraged by its white leaders, lest their presence antagonise white women from the south (see Davis, 1982; Spender, 1983a; Bolt, 1995; Giddings, 1984; Taylor, 1998).

The difference/equality debate

Such discrimination on grounds of 'race' seems at odds with the sentiments of individual rights proclaimed at Seneca Falls half a century before. However, as we have seen, the equal rights position itself contained contradictions. Moreover, by the end of the century many American feminists were abandoning equal rights arguments for those based on women's moral superiority – a view of natural difference that could also encompass ideas of racial inequality. According to the increasingly popular cult of 'true womanhood', it was not women's shared rationality but their uniquely female qualities that entitled them to the vote; arguments that had formerly been used against allowing women a role in public life were now used to demand such a role, and to insist that the 'womanly values' of purity, temperance and peace find expression in affairs of state. Although Stanton quite often referred to women's superior qualities, and she was not adverse to using this position in support of her cause, her feminism differed from the later suffragists in that her claims rested much more clearly on liberal ideas of equal rationality leading to equal rights; and despite her analysis of sex, class and the multi-faceted nature of women's oppression, these rights were in the last analysis the rights of each woman *as an individual* (on this, see a famous late essay *The Solitude of Self*, in Dubois, 1981).

Stanton's active political life spanned over half a century and two continents; in the 1880s and early 1890s, she paid three extended visits to Europe and was a key player in a transatlantic network of feminist friends and activists (Holton, 1994). Her output of lectures, essays and letters was enormous, and included an attempt to document the entire course of the feminist struggle in the massive *History of Woman Suffrage* (she co-edited the first two volumes with Susan Anthony and Matilda Gage; the remaining four volumes take the story up to the 1920 Amendment to the American Constitution which gave women the right to vote). By the time of her death in 1902, important gains had been made, and even women who opposed the suffrage campaign could play a public role in a way that would have been unthinkable in Stanton's youth. As her lifelong friend Susan Anthony said, by 1902 all the legal changes demanded at Seneca Falls had been granted, except for the vote (*History of Woman Suffrage*, vol. 4:xiii), and from 1890 the moderate and radical wings of the organised feminist movement had been united, and increasingly concentrated on this one remaining demand. Stanton, however, consistently refused to narrow her interests to this one issue. As we have seen, although she has frequently been labelled a liberal feminist, she did not see women's problems as simply those of political and legal inequality, and throughout her life her own campaigns and interests were quite extraordinarily wide-ranging. The vote and the Bible, property rights and methods of childrearing, trade unions and rational dress, education and rape, employment and marriage – all these were grist to her mill, for she saw male power as all-pervasive, and the public and private spheres as essentially interrelated. Although she never advocated separatism, she was also radical in her insistence that these changes must be fought for by women themselves, conscious of their shared interests and of the contrary interests of men; and she refused to moderate her demands and accusations to what might be considered 'ladylike' or 'respectable' – on the contrary: 'When I think of all the wrongs that have been heaped upon womankind, I am ashamed that I am not forever in a condition of chronic wrath, stark mad, skin and bone, my eyes a fountain of tears, my lips overflowing with curses ...' (quoted in Griffith, 1984:164).

Nevertheless, as we have seen, some critics argue that Stanton's approach was inevitably restricted by its liberal premises, and that this was a general characteristic of American feminism, which grew during her lifetime into a significant, if frequently divided, mass movement. This same kind of combination of radicalism and conservatism was also to be found in British feminist politics and theory, to which we now turn.

Feminism in Britain and Mill's *Subjection of Women*

The spread of feminist ideas

Organised feminism came slightly later to Britain than to America, and discussion of feminist thinking in the mid-nineteenth century has tended to concentrate on the writing of John Stuart Mill, son of the James Mill who provoked Wheeler and Thompson's *Appeal on Behalf of Women*, see Chapter 1 above). However, by 1869, when Mill published his famous *Subjection of Women*, women themselves were far from silent, and his ideas should be approached in the context of wider feminist debate and activity.

In mid-nineteenth century Britain, the situation of women had not really improved since Mary Wollstonecraft's day. As in the United States, a married woman had no more legal status than a child, and Mill was hardly exaggerating when he wrote that 'There remain no legal slaves, except the mistress of every house' (*Subjection*:147). For some 'factory girls', new employment possibilities offered a certain amount of economic independence, but this was lost on marriage (when a husband became legally entitled to his wife's earnings), and often involved appalling conditions of work and pay. There were still no career opportunities for middle-class women, whose only source of economic security was to find a husband. Meanwhile, the increased separation of the worlds of home and paid employment, and the strengthening of the idea of the male breadwinner, helped consolidate the 'separate spheres' ideology. According to this dominant view, woman's role was *naturally* and *essentially* domestic and family-centred, while man's lay in the public world of work and politics – a view summed up in the often-quoted lines from Tennyson's *The Princess*:

> Man for the field and woman for the hearth;
> Man for the sword and for the needle she;
> Man with the head, and woman with the heart:
> Man to command and woman to obey:
> All else confusion.

In practice, this 'ideal' frequently did not correspond to reality. Many working-class households depended on the wife's earnings, and the line between home and work was far from clear, as there remained a considerable amount of domestic industry and many households tasks, such as washing, were still undertaken collectively. It also ignored the large numbers of women who must remain unmarried as there were, quite simply, not enough husbands to go round: the 1851 census found there to be about one third more women than men living in England. However, in a sense reality was less important than *beliefs* about appropriate gender roles; from the perspective of this dominant ideology, unmarried or working women were at best invisible, at worst unnatural failures.

By the mid-nineteenth century, a number of women were challenging their legal subordination and exclusion from the public sphere. Harriet Taylor's *Enfranchisement of Women* (1851) is the most famous feminist work by a woman, but it was certainly not the only one, and many of her arguments had been anticipated in Marion Reid's *A Plea for Woman* (1845). There was a nation-wide growth of debating societies and social clubs in which feminist issues were discussed, and the beginnings of organised campaigns to improve the lives of both single and married women by allowing access to education and employment and reforming marriage, divorce, property and child custody laws; by the 1860s the vote too was a prominent feminist demand. From 1856, much activity centred around the 'Langham Place Group' and *The Englishwoman's Journal*, founded in 1858 by Barbara Leigh Smith Bodichon and Bessie Rayner Parkes in London. Although there was a wide network of groups, feminism did not at this time constitute any kind of united or mass movement (see Levine, 1987; Caine, 1993 and 1997).

Membership of feminist groups was largely middle or upper-middle class, and great stress was placed on the 'respectability' of their activities; unlike the utopian socialists, these ladies had no wish to offend polite society by appearing to attack the family, or by questioning conventional morality. Bodichon herself was illegitimate, although she was extremely well provided for by her father, and this meant that she frequently had to keep a low profile; similarly, the support of the novelist Mary Ann Evans (George Eliot) for feminist campaigns was not publicised because she was known to be 'living in sin'. Moreover, although some women wanted rights in order to enter employment or public life, many saw them as a means of improving conditions at home and fully endorsed both the doctrine of 'separate spheres' and the idea that women have qualities and virtues that distinguish them from men. Perhaps paradoxically, some women who accepted this also sought a public role in order to impose their ideas of 'domestic virtue' and sexual morality on the poor (Rendall, 1987). Others stressed the shared needs of all women to reach quite different conclusions, and the first organised group, the *Woman's Property Committee* (founded 1855), saw the importance for working-class women of the right to keep their own wages.

At times, the stress on moral differences between women and men was linked to a self-conscious seeking out of female company and an assertion of women's superiority which merged with claims about their shared experiences and needs, and the need for protection from men. The idea that women are a group with shared moral values and interests which may be opposed by men is particularly clear in campaigns around sexuality and prostitution. As Levine has pointed out, Victorian attitudes to sexuality were largely based on *fear* (Levine, 1987). This stemmed from an increased public perception of male violence towards women, a widespread concern about the incidence of prostitution (particularly child prostitution), and the related dread of contracting venereal disease. As in the United States, most British feminists therefore advocated greater male chastity rather than the extension of sexual freedom to women and, from the 1850s, some campaigned against the way in which the 'dual standard' of morality was enshrined in the marriage code. By the 1860s, the issues were sufficiently well-aired for a change in the law on prostitution to be met with vigorous opposition. The aim of the notorious Contagious Diseases Acts (of which there were several, the first in 1864) was to reduce the high rate of sexually transmitted disease in the armed forces. The Act decreed that any woman living in a garrison town whom the police believed to be a prostitute could be forced to undergo regular medical examination to discover if she were infected; described at the time as 'medical rape', this examination involved an often brutal and semi-public internal examination. Opponents of the Acts, of whom the most famous leader was Josephine Butler, were appalled at the way in which they condoned male vice, while perpetuating a double standard that decreed that a 'fallen woman' had no rights; some were also prepared to sympathise with the prostitutes, blaming their situation on men's wickedness and on a society that denied them alternative employment. This means that the campaign against the Acts had far-reaching implications. It implied a common interest shared by all women (for the prostitute and the 'innocent' wife infected by her husband were both victims of male lust), and saw this in terms of men's power over women and a highly negative view of male sexuality. It also related women's sexual exploitation to issues of employment and education, and it suggested to many that a woman's control over her own body could not be guaranteed without legal and political rights. The campaign therefore broadened into a more general reform movement which had strong links with the suffrage campaign (Caine, 1993 and 1997; see also Bland, 1995, on the range of arguments involved).

All this means that, as in the United States, mid-nineteenth century British feminism involved a diverse and sometimes contradictory range of aims and assumptions, as liberal notions of equality and individual rights mingled uneasily with religious ideas about 'womanly virtues' and radical ideas of sexual solidarity to produce a widespread, but not necessarily coherent, demand for change (see Caine, 1993 and 1997). Rights might be demanded in order for women to 'be like men', _or_ in order for them to realise their sex-specific virtues (either in the home or by raising the standards of political and intellectual life) _or_ to defend their interests against men; in practice these arguments were often combined. It was similarly unclear whether women were to duplicate, complement or supplant the qualities of men, and whether their alleged political rights were to be seen as an individual entitlement, a means to general social improvement or a necessary weapon for a 'sex class' with interests opposed to those of men. As discussed in previous sections, there were also tensions internal to liberalism, as its stress on women's 'sameness' with men involved a claim for women as an excluded group that itself identified them as 'different' (see Scott, 1996, on this 'paradox').

There were, therefore, a number of contradictions at the heart of Victorian feminism, contradictions from which John Stuart Mill was not exempt. This means that the problems that critics have identified in his work were not unique to him, but reflected more widespread and deep-seated difficulties. It is in this context that we can understand some of the inconsistencies that are to be found in his writings; some others arose from his role as a man writing about and on behalf of women.

John Stuart Mill's Subjection of Women

Mill has been described as 'the only major liberal political philosopher to have set out explicitly to apply the principles of liberalism to women' (Okin, 1980:197). He claimed that his philosophical readings had always convinced him of the need to give women equal rights; however, it was his close friendship with Harriet Taylor, whom he married in 1851 after the death of her husband, that gave an urgency to that intellectual conviction, and inspired his most famous feminist work, *The Subjection of Women* (written in 1861 and first published 1869). Although this book provoked considerable hostility and ridicule in Britain, and some British feminists were lukewarm in their praise (see Caine, 1993 and 1997), it appeared in over a dozen countries in its first few years of publication and it had an enormous worldwide impact (Evans, 1977). In the United States it was received with tremendous enthusiasm: Sarah Grimké (see above) at the age of 79, 'trudged up and down the countryside in Massachusetts' to sell one hundred and fifty copies of the book (Rossi, 1973:296), and Stanton wrote 'I lay down the book with a peace and a joy I never felt before, for it is the first response from any man to show he is capable of seeing and feeling all the nice shades and degrees of woman's wrongs and the central point of her weakness and degradation' (Rossi, 1970:62).

Recent feminist commentary has, however, been generally much less flattering, and Mill's work is often seen more as an example of the inevitable *failings* of the liberal approach to feminism than of its triumphs. Its fame has led to an exaggeration of its originality by both contemporaries and later commentators: had Stanton read the earlier *Appeal on Behalf of Women* (see Chapter 1 above) she would have found an equally perceptive and sympathetic account of women's situation; as discussed above, both Mill's insights and his shortcomings gain a new perspective when his ideas are placed in the context of their time.

Mill's arguments

At one level, Mill's *The Subjection of Women* was simply an extension to women of the Enlightenment belief that an institution can be defended

only if it is in accordance with reason. He argued that women's subordination is a barbarous relic of an earlier historical period; far from being the
inevitable outcome of natural attributes, it originated in force, and was
now sanctified by custom so as to appear 'natural'. He agreed that women
appeared to be in many ways inferior to men, but argued that this was a
consequence of social pressure and faulty education, 'the result of forced
repression in some directions, unnatural stimulation in others'
(*Subjection*:38). Women, therefore, must be given the same opportunities as
men; only then will we know their true abilities, and only then will society reap the full benefit from the talents of all its members. This meant that
legal discrimination against women was wrong in principle; in particular,
women's legal servitude in marriage must be abolished, women must be
allowed free access to education and employment, and they should be
allowed both to vote and to hold political office.

   This gives us a statement of the liberal feminist position that was clear
and forceful, but by the 1860s hardly original; it was, however, qualified
in certain important respects. Mill's initial position on the question of
women's nature and ability was one of agnosticism, but it soon becomes
apparent that the liberal idea that women are probably 'as good as men'
coexisted with the suspicion that they are, in important respects, essentially 'different'. In the first place, he suggested that although women are
like men possessors of reason, their mode of thinking tends to be more
intuitive and 'down to earth', so that 'Women's thoughts are … as useful
in giving reality to those of thinking men, as men's thoughts in giving
width and largeness to those of women' (*Subjection*:109). Some recent
feminists have reacted angrily to this suggestion. For example, Annas says
that in identifying women's thought processes as essentially intuitive, Mill
has fallen for 'the oldest cliché in the book' (Annas, 1977:184), and that this
gives rise to an intellectual hierarchy, in which the man of genius benefits
from the lesser talents of his female research assistant. However, other
recent commentators have denied that the identification of such sexual
difference need involve ideas of superiority and inferiority, and Annas
herself has been accused of an uncritical acceptance of conventional male
values (Thornton, 1986; Mendus, 1989; see also Stafford, 1998). Certainly,
Mill's other writings make it clear that he did not think that rational calculation is the only or the best way of reaching the truth, nor did he simply equate different ways of thinking with differences between the sexes.
Thus he frequently stated that poets and artists have insights denied to a
'mere thinker', and in 1832 he wrote to the historian Carlyle that 'My vocation lies in a humbler sphere; I am rather fitted to be a logical expounder
than an artist … it is the artist alone in whose hands Truth becomes
impressive and a living principle of action' (in Schneewind, 1965:84).
In general, he saw logical and intuitive thought as complementary rather

than antagonistic; this means that the ideal partnership between man and woman was one of 'reciprocal superiority', so that 'each can enjoy the luxury of looking up to the other, and can have alternatively the pleasure of leading and being led in the path of development' (*Subjection*:177). All this suggests that women should be admitted to intellectual life, not because they are in all relevant respects the same as men, but because they are quite probably different. Although this was not a liberal argument as usually understood, it corresponded to a strong strand of Victorian feminism, and it is also echoed in some radical feminist ideas about the superiority of female modes of thinking (see Donner, 1993). However, unlike many feminists of his day, Mill did not extend his argument to identify any *moral* qualities that separate women from men, and he certainly did not think that they might be morally superior.

It is also clear that although Mill gave men and women equal political rights, and insisted that there must be no bar to women's education and employment, in practice he saw the sexes as playing very different roles in society – roles which largely conformed to the ideology of 'separate spheres'. Women, he argued, should be free to follow the career of their choice, and they should not be forced into marriage through economic necessity; if, however, they do choose marriage, then this is their career, and they should accept the responsibilities that it entails. This meant that a married woman should be responsible for running the home, and 'the common arrangement, by which the man earns the income and the wife superintends the domestic expenditure, seems to me in general the most suitable division of labour between the two persons', so that 'it is not ... a desirable custom, that the wife should contribute by her labour to the income of the family' (*Subjection*:87–8). Some recent critics have not been slow to attack this conclusion, accusing Mill of betraying the very principles on which his feminism was based: 'The constraints which Mill believed should be imposed on married women constitute a major exception to his argument for equality of individual freedom between the sexes – an exception so enormous that it threatens to swallow up the whole argument' (Goldstein, 1980:328). His conclusion seems to rest upon the belief that only women can or should perform domestic tasks, so that if a wife goes out to work 'the care which she is herself disabled from taking of the children and the household, nobody else takes' (*Subjection*:88); there is no suggestion that a man could ever share these tasks with his wife. Why self-determining individuals should have their roles prescribed for them in this way is completely unexamined; we can only assume either that Mill was unwilling to antagonise potential supporters of moderate reform or that he saw the point as so self-evident that it did not require discussion. The latter would be surprising in the light of his otherwise consistent insistence that reason, not custom, should regulate human affairs; he was, moreover, well acquainted with and sympathetic towards the ideas of the utopian socialists who, as we saw earlier, did challenge the conventional domestic division of labour.

Mill's conclusions meant that women's opportunities were restricted by marriage in a way that men's were not, that they therefore could not participate equally in employment and politics and that a married woman would be economically dependent upon her husband – here Mill seemed to think that a wife's *potential* ability to earn her own living would be sufficient to earn her husband's respect and ensure her position as an equal partner in the marriage. This conclusion has been vigorously opposed by recent feminists (see for example Brown, 1993), and it also differed from the arguments of Mill's wife, Harriet Taylor, as expressed in the earlier *Enfranchisement of Women* (1851).

There has been some doubt about the authorship of this essay, which was originally published under Mill's name. Mill himself, however, said that he was 'little more than an editor and amanuensis' (Introduction to *The Enfranchisement*:1), and its arguments differed significantly from Mill's in *The Subjection*, confirming the view that it should be regarded as Taylor's work. In it Taylor argued that a married woman *should* contribute to the household income, 'even if the aggregate sum were but little increased by it', as she would then 'be raised from the position of a servant to that of a partner' (*Enfranchisement*:20). This argument is clearly more in line with later feminist thinking than Mill's belief that female liberty is somehow compatible with economic dependency and full domestic responsibility. Nevertheless, Mill's ideas cannot be dismissed as the unthinking or self-interested response of a well-intentioned but essentially chauvinistic male, for they were shared with most feminist women of his day (see Rendall, 1987 and Caine, 1993 and 1997). Marion Reid had in 1845 argued on lines very similar to Mill that women were entitled to civil and political rights, but that married women should stay at home and that 'the best and noblest of women will always find their greatest delight in the cultivation of domestic virtues' (*A Plea for Woman*:16). The problem was, however, compounded for Mill, because he combined his insistence that women take full domestic responsibility with a failure to discuss in any detail the value of domestic work. Reid had argued that the domestic sphere is 'not a mean ignoble one' (*Plea*:21), but is as intellectually demanding as most male occupations. Like Wollstonecraft she insisted on the dignity and worth of women's traditional work and the need for female education if it is to be well performed. Mill on the other hand showed no sign of having such a high regard for domestic work. In an early essay he went so far as to deny that it could be regarded as a serious occupation; and here he argued that in an ideal marriage 'there would be no need that the wife should take part in the mere providing of what is required to *support* life; it will be for the happiness of both that her occupation should rather be to adorn and beautify it' (Rossi, 1970:75). A benign interpretation might dismiss this statement as a product of the young Mill's initial infatuation with Harriet Taylor, whom he had just met; certainly by the time of *The Subjection* he saw domestic work as a serious, if tedious, business. Nevertheless it remains a mystery why Mill thought that a rational woman would freely choose to dedicate herself either to 'adorning and beautifying life' or to the wearying demands of household management; this choice makes sense only if a woman's true fulfilment lies, after all, in service to her husband – an idea which contradicts the main arguments of his book.

Mill and utilitarianism

Thus far, Mill has been criticised for failing to follow his liberal principles to their logical conclusion. Other critics, however, argue that his analysis is flawed not because of an inconsistent application of liberal principles, but because of the limitations of these principles themselves. For some, this starts with his use of utilitarian theory. As originally propounded by Jeremy Bentham, a close friend of John Stuart Mill's father, James Mill, this stated that laws and moralities should be judged, not according to some abstract idea of right and wrong, but according to whether or not they increase the sum total of human happiness (*Introduction to the Principles of Morals and Legislation*, in Warnock (ed.), 1966). In calculating this (and Bentham provided complex guidelines as to how this should be done), it is assumed that all individuals seek to maximise their own pleasure, and that each person's happiness carries equal weight. This has obvious egalitarian implications, which has led Boralevi to claim that utilitarianism has a strong theoretical link with feminism, despite the unfeminist conclusions reached by James Mill and, at times, by Bentham (Boralevi, 1987; see also Ball, 1980). For some feminists, on the other hand, the assumption that people are to be understood as calculating, competitive, hedonistic and autonomous individuals is highly suspect, a paradigm based on male thinking and modes of behaviour, and one that ignores female nurturing and human interdependence. From this perspective, classic utilitarianism involves a denial of female qualities, and cannot be the basis of an adequate feminist theory.

Mill, however, did not support this paradigm. He consistently denied that there is such a fixed, eternally-given human essence, arguing that human character is a variable product of society rather than a constant fact of nature (see *Logic*, Book 6). He also stressed the interconnectedness of human pleasures, arguing that in a properly organised society each individual would find happiness in the pleasure of others, so that 'a direct impulse to promote the general good may be in every individual one of the habitual motives of action' (*What Utilitarianism Is* in Williams (ed.), 1985:129). As Coole has pointed out (Coole, 1993:123), similar qualifications had already been made by Wheeler and Thompson, whose *Appeal* used this modified utilitarian theory to demand political and legal rights for women. Here, therefore, Mill was not taking any original philosophical step, and there are striking similarities between his arguments and those in the *Appeal*, while he described Thompson as 'a very estimable man, with whom I was well acquainted' (*Autobiography*:75). Both works argued that women must be included in the utilitarian calculation of happiness, and that they required full legal and political rights to defend their interests and the opportunity to express themselves in whatever sphere of life they chose. Both argued that men too would benefit if women became their equals, for the pleasures of intellectual companionship are far greater than those of despotism and men will gain when they no longer 'surrender the delights of equality ... for the vulgar pleasures of command' (*Appeal*:70). Finally, both argued that the whole of society would benefit if relations between the sexes were based on justice and equality (although this is more explicit in Mill's work). Mill's arguments here were complex. The most important were, firstly, that the pool of talent available to society would be doubled, with obvious benefits for social prosperity and progress. Secondly, political life would improve as the family became 'the real school of the virtues of freedom' (*Subjection*:80), where citizens would learn the democratic virtues of self-reliance and mutual help and respect. Thirdly, the character of both men and women would improve, as 'All the selfish propensities, the self-worship, the unjust self-preference, which exist among mankind, have their source and root in, and derive their principle nourishment from, the present constitution of the relation between man and woman' (*Subjection*:148). Mill further argued in other writings that if women had an alternative to marriage then this would go far to curb the evils of overpopulation (*Principles of Political Economy*:459) – and population control was, for Mill and many other liberal economists, a prerequisite of economic prosperity.

Coole has argued that in thus stressing the benefits to men and to society, Mill had partly moved away from the stronger case that can be based on equal rights arguments. She claims that his utilitarian position opens the door to compromise, for if it could be shown that sex equality were *not* a means to the greatest happiness, then logically it would have to be abandoned, for 'Rights are now means to social well-being rather than absolute ends intrinsic in every individual' (Coole, 1993:115). Here it could be that Mill's position was primarily intended to persuade the unconverted, rather than an integral part of his approach. However, as discussed above, he simply did not think that means and ends do ultimately conflict in this way; if they appear to, then this is a reflection of poor social arrangements and lack of education. A true child of the Enlightenment, be believed that the just society could be achieved through the advance of reason; there was no place in his thought for the possibility that the interests of one group or class in society could clash irrevocably with another; a harmonious society was, he believed, in the interests of all.

The 'animal instinct' of sex

Another aspect of Mill's theory that has troubled some later feminists arises from a further qualification that he made to Bentham's utilitarian theory, by which he insisted that all pleasures are *not* equal, but that some are clearly superior to others; and here he argued that the 'higher' pleasures are those of the mind rather than the body. Critics say that this attitude devalues women's reproductive activity and denies the legitimacy of sexual enjoyment, and that it involves a concept of reason based on a rejection of all that has traditionally been associated with the female, so that 'the truly equal woman is she who eliminates all trace of femaleness' (Cook, 1988:153). Certainly, Mill never suggested that women's nurturing role might be a cause for celebration: on the contrary, he shared the negative view of Taylor that 'There is no inherent reason or necessity that all women shall voluntarily choose to devote their lives to one animal function and its consequences' (*Enfranchisement*:18). Sex too could not be liberating or genuinely fulfilling, but must be strictly controlled; he wrote that there could be no great improvement in human life so long as 'the animal instinct of sex occupies the absurdly disproportionate place it does therein' (quoted in Mendus, 1989:178–9). His own friendship with Harriet Taylor caused considerable public scandal, but was almost certainly not sexual; his friend Thomas Carlyle wrote: 'His *Platonica* and he are constant as ever: innocent I do believe as sucking doves, and yet suffering the clack of tongues, worst penalty of guilt' (Hayek (ed.), 1951:86): Mill himself wrote 'We disdained … the abject notion that the strongest and tenderest friendship cannot exist between a man and a woman without a sensual relation' (*Autobiography*:137).

Mendus has argued that this attitude gave Mill an impoverished view of human nature, and she finds his ideal of marriage – that is, marriage of minds and not of flesh – and the accompanying image of women 'deeply depressing and distorted' (Mendus, 1989:172). However, as so often, Mill's views here were not merely idiosyncratic. As we have seen, the campaign against the Contagious Diseases Acts, which developed in quite radical directions, rested on a similarly negative view of sex, suggesting that Mill's views cannot be dismissed simply as the outdated prejudices of a prudish Victorian intellectual, for they may be compatible with quite radical feminist analysis.

Mill himself was particularly concerned with male violence within marriage, and with a wife's loss of sexual autonomy:

> however brutal a tyrant she may be unfortunately chained to – though she may know that he hates her, though it may be his daily pleasure to torture her, and though she may feel it impossible not to loathe him – he can claim from her and enforce the lowest degradation of a human being, that of being made the instrument of an animal function contrary to her inclinations. (*Subjection*:57)

This meant that, like many American and British feminists, Mill did not see women's subordination as lying only in their exclusion from public life: it was rooted in relationship within the family, as it is there that men are free to act as petty despots, and many 'indulge the utmost habits of excesses of bodily violence towards the unhappy wife' (*Subjection*:63). Again like other nineteenth-century feminists, he saw legislative change as an important way of ending this private oppression. For women to be free from domestic tyranny they needed access to education and employment, so that economic need would not force them into marriage; they also needed the full protection of the law, and this included political rights.

Politics and education

Although Mill was far from the first writer to argue that women should have the vote, he was the first politician to make a serious attempt to achieve this. For a short period he was himself a member of parliament, and he introduced an Amendment to the 1867 Reform Bill (which gave the vote to most of the urban working class) which sought to enfranchise women on the same basis as men. This was supported by a petition signed by nearly 1500 women; although defeated by 123 votes in the House of Commons, a not insubstantial 73 were cast in Mill's support, and similar reforms were introduced by other members in many subsequent sessions. Mill's arguments in favour of his Amendment make it clear that he was not simply demanding public political rights as a matter of abstract justice; rather, he saw the franchise as a way of improving women's conditions in the private sphere. He denied that a woman's interests could be incorporated in her husband's, and he insisted that the myth of male protection be exposed – he therefore demanded that 'a return be laid before this House of women who are annually beaten to death, kicked to death, or trampled to death by their own protectors' (in Kamm, 1977:160).

This belief that domestic tyranny can be tackled by granting women legal and political rights was very similar to Stanton's, and has been attacked on similar grounds. However, like Stanton, Mill insisted that legal and political reforms were *not* in themselves sufficient to ensure the ending of female subordination; for this, a more fundamental change in men and women's consciousness and their perception of each other was required. Here Mill argued persuasively that male dominance was maintained not only by the obvious methods of coercion and denial of rights, but also by a more subtle and insidious control of women's *minds*. Thus the whole of a woman's experience and education instilled ideas of dependence and voluntary submission; they were trained not only to obey, but to love their masters, for 'Men do not want solely the obedience of women, they want their sentiments ... They have therefore put everything in practice to enslave their minds' (*Subjection*:26–7). Although often overlooked by critics, the sections in which Mill developed these ideas were perhaps the most perceptive in *The Subjection*, and may well have been those that so delighted Stanton; these ideas were, however, not original, for very similar points had been made earlier by Wheeler and Thompson.

Mill therefore saw education as an essential part of the process of emancipation, not simply because it would provide women with career opportunities, but because it could help change their self-perception so that attracting a man would cease to be the prime goal of a woman's life. Throughout his philosophy, education in its widest sense was a key means to social improvement, and, as we saw earlier, he believed that women's position within the family was integrally linked to progress in other areas: as public rights improved women's situation and status at home, so the family would become a place where the lessons of despotism and submission were replaced by those of partnership and equality, and the democratic family would thus become a training-ground for democratic citizens.

Class

A further criticism that is often made of liberal feminists is that they are concerned only with the needs and interests of middle-class women. Clearly Mill empathised strongly with the intellectual frustrations facing educated woman such as Harriet Taylor. Although he supported Butler's campaign against the Contagious Diseases Acts and he was very much concerned with working-class victims of male violence, he never saw prostitutes or working-class women as potential fellow campaigners; like other Victorian feminists, he saw them simply as the beneficiaries of campaigns on their behalf.

Nevertheless, Mill was no apologist for the socio-economic status quo, which he saw as one in which the wealthiest were the most idle, while those who worked hardest were little better-off than slaves. His goal was not equality between the sexes within the existing unequal society, but within one in which both political and economic life had become significantly more egalitarian and democratic. Mill showed considerable sympathy for the ideas of the utopian socialists, and in comparing their proposals with existing society he concluded that 'The restraints of communism would be freedom in comparison with the present condition of the majority of the human race' (*Principles of Political Economy*:129). However, his preferred solution was not communism, but a reformed private property system in which rights of inheritance were strictly controlled and workers' co-operatives and profit-sharing schemes would be encouraged. Although he believed that this would break down class divisions, it left intact the underlying principles of a society based upon competition and the pursuit of profit; from the perspective of the Marxist ideas discussed in the next chapter, this means that Mill was really only offering women the right to become a wage slave or the dependent of a male wage slave, rather than genuine freedom (see Brown, 1993). Unlike Wheeler and Thompson, Mill never developed an analysis of the ways in which the capitalist system systematically disadvantaged women, nor was there any room in his theory for the possibility of substantive conflict of interest between classes or between women and men.

There is a sense in which Mill's feminism is significant not because of what he said but because of who he was. As Josephine Butler said, his views on women were not specially advanced, but rather 'the somewhat tardy expression of a conviction which has been growing in society for the last twenty years' (quoted in Caine, 1993:34), for virtually all of the points that he made in *The Subjection* had been made earlier by Wheeler and Thompson; many had also been made by Marion Reid, Harriet Taylor and the American feminists. Because of his fame, however, Mill has attracted more than his share of both praise and critical commentary, and he has been widely criticised both for failing to follow his principles of liberal individualism to their logical conclusion, and for failing to understand the limitations of these principles. Like the American feminists he failed to explore the critical questions of economic dependency and the division of labour, nor did he really examine the interrelationships of class and sex oppression, or see that the institutions of society might not be neutral, but might be systematically biased in favour of one class or sex. His repressive attitude to sex also finds little sympathy from contemporary feminists. Nevertheless, like so many nineteenth-century feminists his concerns were not as narrowly formal and legalistic as the 'liberal feminist' label suggests; at times his ideas have a surprising affinity with some strands of later radical feminism. In terms of both his insights and his limitations he would seem to be a typical Victorian feminist; despite the attention which his work has received he did not produce any new theoretical insights.

Britain and the United States were not the only nations in which feminism developed in the nineteenth century. There was a clear international dimension to the growth of feminist ideas and, although the timing and nature of feminist ideas and movements varied, Evans has claimed that there was a common pattern of development throughout the industrialising world, whereby initial claims for property, education and employment rights became fused with campaigns for moral reform, and led eventually to the demand for the vote (Evans, 1977). The nineteenth century cannot, however, be seen simply as a time when the justice of mainstream feminist demands was gradually accepted. As we shall see in the following chapters, the success of feminist movements varied widely. Although many men and women came to believe that women should have legal rights, when it came to the vote and more substantive change many others agreed with Queen Victoria who wrote in 1872 that: 'The Queen is most anxious to enlist every one who can speak or write to join in checking this mad, wicked folly of 'Women's Rights' ... It is a subject which makes the Queen so furious that she cannot contain herself. God created men and women different – then let them remain each in their own position' (quoted in Kamm, 1977:179).

3

The contribution of Marx and Engels

It is at first sight odd to include a section on classic Marxism in a work on feminist political theory, because Karl Marx was not a feminist. This does not mean that he was hostile to female liberation but simply that, unlike Mill or Thompson, he did not see issues of sexual oppression as interesting or important in their own right, and he never made them the subject of detailed empirical or theoretical investigation. It is true that he several times stated that the condition of women can be taken as an index of social progress; however by the mid-nineteenth century this idea was commonplace (see Mill's *Subjection*:38), and it certainly cannot be taken as evidence of feminist insight. Indeed, recent writers have suggested that, far from providing a feminist view of history, it gave women an essentially *passive* role, seeing them as the sufferers or beneficiaries from man-made history (Coole, 1993; Barrett, 1987); cynics might also draw support from Marx's least frequently quoted formulation of the approach: 'Social progress can be measured exactly by the social position of the fair sex (the ugly ones included)' (1868 letter, quoted in Draper, 1972:88; see also Lee-Lampshire, 1994). Nevertheless, although Marx himself had little to say directly about women, his theory claimed to provide a comprehensive analysis of human history and society, and later writers have attempted to apply it to feminist issues. This means that to understand much recent feminist debate, it is necessary to have some knowledge of Marx's original ideas, for his theory provides a perspective completely different from the feminist ideas we have discussed so far; it is to a brief account of his theory that we therefore now turn.

Classic Marxist theory

The ideas that Marx and Engels developed were extremely complex, and they have been interpreted in very many different ways. However, at their core was a view of history and society that saw the world as constantly changing and progressing, and that insisted that liberal ideas of individual rights, justice and human nature were not universal principles, but the product of a particular period of human history. The key to understanding the process of historical development lay, they argued, not in the ideas that people may hold, but in their physical productive activity: it was the first co-operative act of production that formed the basis of the earliest primitive society and the beginnings of human history, for

> life involves before everything else eating and drinking, a habitation, clothing and many other things. The first historical act is thus the production of the means to satisfy these needs, the production of material life itself. (*German Ideology*:48)

As methods of production gradually became more complex, so too did the division of labour and the form of social organisation based upon it. With the production of a surplus came the institution of private property, the division of society into classes and, corresponding to and reinforcing these, the development of laws, states and systems of belief, for 'The mode of production of material life conditions the social, political and intellectual life process in general. It is not the consciousness of men that determine their being, but, on the contrary, their social being that determines their consciousness' (*Preface to the Critique of Political Economy*, Selected Works:182). The process of historical development was neither random nor smooth, but was expressed through class conflict and revolution, for although human history was the study of man's progressive mastery over nature, so far this had taken place within a framework of ever-increasing alienation and exploitation. Nineteenth-century capitalism was not however the final form of human society, for the conditions were developing within it that would give birth to the final proletarian revolution. It was only through this that man could gain full control over the whole productive process, and only then that a classless communist society could develop in which full human freedom could eventually be achieved and 'the narrow horizon of bourgeois right be crossed in its entirety and society inscribe on its banners: From each according to his ability, to each according to his needs!' (*Critique of the Gotha Programme*:17).

The extent to which all this implies a theory of technological or economic determinism is a matter of intense political and scholarly debate, but it seems clear that in seeking to understand social, political and legal systems and the beliefs that people have about them, Marx said that we must look first at the economic system on which they rest. It also means that the possibilities for change will be fairly strictly limited by socio-economic conditions, rather than being a simple product of people's intentions – for 'Men make their own history, but they do not make it just as they please; they do not make it under circumstances chosen by themselves, but under circumstances directly encountered, given and transmitted from the past' (*The Eighteenth Brumaire of Louis Bonaparte*, in *Selected Works*:97).

The implications of this whole approach for feminist theory are profound. In the first place, the family and sexual relationships are, like other forms of social organisation, placed in a historical context: neither eternally given nor consciously planned, they are the product of a particular historical situation and therefore open to change in the future. Secondly, however, this change will not be brought about by appeals to reason or to principles of justice, but only as part of changes in conditions of production; unlike the utopian socialists, Marx and Engels believed that the 'good society' could not be achieved at will, but only at a particular stage of historical development.

Engels' *The Origin of the Family, Private Property and the State*

It was essentially these ideas that formed the basis of Engels' analysis in *The Origin of the Family, Private Property and the State*. Here he drew heavily on the work of the nineteenth-century anthropologist Lewis Morgan to trace the supposed evolution of the family from the earliest savage society to the present day. He totally rejected the claim that the modern family is somehow 'natural': indeed, he argued that in the earliest societies sexual relationships had been totally promiscuous and unregulated, and that they gradually evolved to take the form of the 'pairing family' which characterised later forms of primitive society. The force behind this evolution was in the first instance natural selection (which ensured that those tribes prohibiting incest were stronger), and then the wishes of women, who increasingly found group marriage 'oppressive and humiliating' and longed for 'the right of chastity, of temporary or permanent marriage with one man only as a way of release' (*Origin*:60). Primitive societies also differed from modern society in that relations between the sexes were based on *equality*; there was a sexual division of labour whereby women were responsible for domestic work and men for agriculture and husbandry, but even in the pairing family (which was not the same as strict monogamy), this did not involve subordination; the women reigned supreme in the home, and descent was calculated through the female line (Engels called this 'mother right').

This egalitarian situation was changed by the development of a new source of wealth in the male sphere of activity, through the domestication of animals and the breeding of herds. As some men gained property and power over others, their position within the family was strengthened, and they wanted to pass their property to their children; to do this they had to overthrow the traditional order of inheritance and ensure strict monogamy on the part of each woman, who became the mere possession of her husband, the means of producing heirs. In Engels' vivid phase, 'The overthrow of mother right was the *world historical defeat of the female sex*. The man took command in the home also; the woman was degraded and reduced to servitude; she became the slave of his lust and a mere instrument for the production of children.' This means that the subordination of women coincided with the first private property and class society, for it was then that women lost control in the home and became economically dependent upon men; it also means that female oppression has no other material cause – it is a part of class society, but not a necessary or permanent feature of human relationships. From this it follows that the abolition of private property will mean an end to sex oppression, for men will no longer have any motive to exploit women: 'The supremacy of the man in marriage is the simple consequence of his economic supremacy, and with the abolition of the latter will disappear of itself' (*Origin*:65 and 95).

The basis for new and equal relations between the sexes was, Engels argued, already developing within capitalist society, for modern industry's increasing reliance on the labour of women and children in factory production was having a profound effect upon the balance of power within the family. Nearly forty years earlier in his *The Condition of the Working Class in England* (1845) he had been greatly concerned about such employment, noting the appalling effects upon family life and describing as an 'insane state of things' the not infrequent situation in which a woman was in paid employment and her husband 'condemned to domestic occupations' – this, he argued, 'unsexes the man and takes from the woman all true womanliness', and he commented that 'It is easy to imagine the wrath aroused among the working men by this reversal of all relations within the family' (*Conditions*:184). However, his concern that working women were neglecting their home and children takes on a new dimension when we remember the condition and nature of early factory employment and the particular problems faced by women, who had to work throughout pregnancy (even on occasion giving birth amongst the factory machines), and who often had to return to work less than a week after giving birth; they also faced problems of sexual harassment and exploitation by the male factory-owner. Engels' descriptions were largely based on analysis of government reports and official statistics, and they remain a searing indictment of mid-nineteenth-century conditions: 'Women made unfit for childbearing, children deformed, men enfeebled, limbs crushed, whole generations wrecked, afflicted with disease and infirmity, purely to fill the purses of the bourgeoisie' (*Conditions*:198, 187 and 203).

Although of course he retained his opposition to capitalist exploitation, by 1884 Engels saw female paid employment as a progressive force.

The bourgeois woman was, he argued, still a mere breeding machine and provider of sexual services who 'only differs from the ordinary courtesan in that she does not let out her body on piece-work as a wage earner, but sells it once and for all into slavery'; her economic dependence on her husband meant that 'within the family he is the bourgeois and the wife represents the proletariat'. However, the proletarian marriage was not based on property, and because the wife was frequently a wage earner 'the last remnants of male supremacy in the proletarian household are deprived of all foundation'. This meant that, paradoxically, the proletarian wife was less oppressed as a woman than her bourgeois counterpart (although she remained oppressed as a worker), and that 'the first condition for the liberation of women is to bring the whole female sex back into public industry' (*Origin*:82, 85 and 86).

The second condition for liberation was the social revolution that Engels believed would soon occur, and which would replace the capitalist economic system with one based on common ownership. As private property disappeared, so too would men's motive to produce heirs and their ability to 'buy' women, whether as wives or prostitutes. At the same time, women's productive labour would no longer involve neglect of home and family, for 'Private housekeeping is transformed into a social industry. The care and education of the children becomes a public affair; society looks after all children alike, whether they are born of wedlock or not.' Marriage ('that compound of sentimentality and domestic strife') and sexual relations would also be transformed as they ceased to be based on economic needs. Engels claimed that present arrangements were characterised above all by hypocrisy; enforced monogamy for women was accompanied by sexual licence for men, while adultery and prostitution rather than fidelity and love were the basis of modern bourgeois marriage. He thought that this would be replaced not by promiscuity but by 'individual sex love', which he believed already characterised relationships amongst the proletariat. However, he refused to speculate in detail about future sexual relations, arguing that these will only be known

> when a new generation has grown up; a generation of men who never in their lives have known what it is to buy a woman's surrender with money or any other social instrument of power; a generation of women who have never known what it is to give themselves to a man from any other consideration than real love, or to refuse to give themselves to their lover from fear of the economic consequences. (*Origin*:87, 87–8, 66 and 96)

All this gives us a theory that sees the changing condition of women as a product of economic processes: the subordination of women began with private property and class society; amongst the propertyless classes it has already lost its economic foundations; with the impending socialist revolution it will disappear in its entirety. For non-Marxists the apparent reduction of all social questions to an economic cause makes Engels's approach unacceptable, as does his belief in the imminent replacement of capitalism by socialism; many late twentieth-century Marxist feminists have also been highly critical of Engels's ideas, and he has been attacked at a number of levels.

Recent criticisms of Engels

Obvious problems arise from Engels' reliance on anthropological findings that are at best highly dubious (for discussion of this, see for example Lane, 1976; Maconachie, 1987). The assumption that there was a universal pattern of family development from the first human societies is questionable, as is the claim that there was an original condition of sex equality; early man's desire to leave property to his heirs was also assumed rather than explained. Engels' belief that it must have been men who created the first wealth has also been challenged, for it seems likely that women were the first cultivators who both provided subsistence and produced the first surplus (Mies, 1998): this has led some writers to suggest that for men to assert control over this wealth, sexual oppression must have *pre-dated* class society (Humphries, 1987). More serious in its implications for future developments is Engels' assumption that there was an original and natural division of labour between the sexes, an assumption that is also to be found in his and Marx's early writings (see *The German Ideology*:44 and 51). This meant that although he said that in socialist society housework and childcare would be collectivised, he never thought it necessary to discuss which sex should perform these tasks; given his other remarks, the implication is that they would be done by women, an interpretation that was certainly assumed by many later Marxists.

The assumption that women are naturally responsible for home and family also obscured Engels' understanding of contemporary society and led him to ignore the labour performed by women in pre-capitalist economies. He saw the problems a woman faced in trying to combine paid work with domestic responsibility, but he never really analysed the implications of this 'dual oppression', or suggested that it could be alleviated with male help. Similarly, his approach allowed little room for understanding the sex-specific oppression of women *as workers*; in particular, he failed to show why women were paid so much less than men. He also failed to explore the implications of male opposition to female labour; his belief that capitalist development would continue to draw more women into employment ignored the success of some parts of the workforce in achieving the 'family wage' (that is, a wage sufficiently high to maintain a dependent wife and children).

Engels has been further criticised for his views on human sexuality (see Evans, 1987; Jaggar, 1983; Millett, 1985). Like the mainstream feminists discussed earlier, he rejected the hypocrisy of the double standard of morality that praised chastity in women while condoning widespread prostitution, and his suggestion that morality may be dependent on economic needs offers an advance on earlier analyses. However, he consistently assumed that men's sexual needs are *naturally* greater than women's, without questioning whether this too might be a reflection of social and economic conditions: thus he assumed that it was women and not men who originally found group marriage 'degrading', and he consistently wrote of a woman 'giving herself' or 'surrendering' to a man – a use of language that would seem to exclude the idea of sexual activity based on equality and reciprocal enjoyment. He also assumed that sexual activity is naturally heterosexual; he described homosexuality as an 'abominable practice', and it is clear that it would have no place in socialist society. At the same time, his stress on economic motivation often led to an oversimplification of sexual morality and behaviour. For example, he thought that in socialist society, when children are the responsibility of the whole community, there will no longer be 'the anxiety about the "consequences" which today prevents a girl from giving herself completely to the man she loves' (*Origin*:88); the possibility that effective contraception might also remove this anxiety, or that a 'girl' might simply not wish to become pregnant, seems not to have crossed his mind. Similarly, while the family may serve an important economic function, to *reduce* it to this function is highly dubious; at the very least, it ignores important psychological functions, and, as we have seen, it denies the possibility of oppression within the proletarian family. This economic reductionism also ignores the enduring results of the different sexual needs that Engels assumed to be 'natural'. He described how girls were abducted and 'sexually used' in the later stages of primitive society (*Origin*:51), but he did not see that this contradicted his claim that such societies were based on equality between the sexes, nor did he question its implications for the future; the possibility that male sexuality might continue to pose a threat to women in socialist society was never raised; unlike many contemporary feminists, neither Engels nor Marx ever saw rape as a source of men's power over women.

This point is related to Engel's failure to acknowledge that the proletarian family might also be a source of oppression and sexual exploitation rather than equality. He had remarkably little to say on the problem of domestic violence which received widespread publicity in the nineteenth century and which, as we saw, was a central concern of many feminists in both Britain and America; his only comment on the issue is a half-sentence that refers to 'a leftover piece of the brutality towards women that has become deep-rooted since the introduction of monogamy' (*Origin*:83). In general he held a very romanticised view of proletarian marriage which he saw as the freely chosen result of love and sexual attraction; here male brutality could not last long as it no longer had an economic foundation, and the wife was free to leave. This rosy view ignored the reality of many women's lives and the fact that they were often *not* free to leave a violent marriage; quite apart from the fear of violent revenge, many women were unwilling to abandon their children, and few could earn enough to support themselves, let alone their children too; as we have seen, Engels ignored the causes and implications of women's low pay, and he also ignored the benefits that a husband might gain from his wife's sexual and domestic services, irrespective of whether his marriage continued to be based on love.

The relevance of Marxist concepts

To some extent these problems may be relatively superficial, a product of Engels' personal limitations and prejudices rather than the underlying methodology. However, there remains the problem of whether Marxism is really able to see or understand any non-economic sources of oppression, and this is related to its underlying theory of history. In the *German Ideology* Marx and Engels saw both production and reproduction as the basis of society: 'The production of life, both of one's own in labour and of fresh life in procreation, now appears as a double relationship: on the one hand as a natural, on the other as a social relationship' (*German Ideology*:50). Engels expanded this position in his Preface to *The Origin*:

> According to the materialist conception, the determining factor in history is, in the final instance, the production and reproduction of immediate life. This, again, is of a twofold character. On the one side, the production of the means of subsistence, of food, clothing and shelter and the tools necessary for that production; on the other side, the production of human beings themselves, the propagation of the species. The social institutions under which the people of a particular historical epoch and a particular country live are conditioned by both kinds of production: by the stage of development of labour on the one hand and of the family on the other. (*The Origin*:4)

Despite these formulations, neither Marx nor Engels gave production and reproduction equal roles in the productive process. As we have seen, Engels did say that the family developed autonomously in the earliest human societies, but he argued that this independent development ceased when it reached the stage of the 'pairing marriage', and that 'Unless new *social* forces came into play, there was no reason why a new form of family should arise from the single pair' (*The Origin*:60). He further argued that such social forces did arise in Europe, with the introduction of private property, but that in America they did not, so that the indigenous American family remained in its early form. This means that it was only in pre-class societies that the family and sexual relationships developed under their own momentum; for most of recorded history their form was dependent upon the development of production. Marx never said anything so specific, but it is quite clear that although he saw reproduction as a part of the material basis of society, it was in no way an independent source of change; in general, therefore, he found the oppression of women to be theoretically uninteresting, a product of class society rather than something worth understanding in its own right.

This theoretical perspective meant that Marx and Engels never explored in any detail the ways in which sexual relationships and family organisation have changed over time. It also meant that in terms of practical politics the whole question of women's oppression tended to disappear. Marx did say that 'of course' women could join the First International Workingmen's Association and he proposed the establishment of women's branches within it (see Vogel, 1983:71); however, the idea that women as a group might have shared interests that cut across class lines, and that these might be in opposition to men's interests, never arose. For some later Marxists, this approach has been explicitly interpreted as meaning that all problems of relations between the sexes can be postponed until 'after the revolution', and that any attempts to improve the situation of women in the short term are at best a bourgeois irrelevance and at worst a ploy to divide the working class and distract it from the class struggle. As we shall see in later chapters, this kind of assumption that if we 'take care of the class struggle then feminism will take care of itself' has been attacked by some recent feminists, who reject the idea that Marxism need involve a crude reductionism whereby there is a one-to-one causal relationship between economic organisation and the situation of women. For such Marxist feminists, reproduction is a key part of the material base which must be incorporated into a correct understanding of society; this opens up the possibility of a causal interaction between production and reproduction, which in turn implies the interaction of class and sex struggles – and in practical terms this means that the sexism of men in left-wing organisations or the working class can legitimately be challenged.

Despite this kind of attempt to 'rescue' Marxism for feminism, some critics have argued that the key concepts of Marxist theory are not gender-neutral ones which Marx happened not to apply to women, but that (like liberal ideas of reason, autonomy and competition) they are based on a male view of the world that excludes women's needs and experiences. Thus the concepts of 'productive labour' and 'praxis' (self-conscious, creative, rational and unalienated activity) are said to be based on a paradigm of male activity that not only fails to encompass women's reproductive and domestic labour but depends upon it; by treating this work as 'natural', it renders it invisible and places it outside of history (see Lee-Lampshire, 1994). Others claim that the whole view of history as a process through which men increase their mastery over nature reflects an essentially male view that is responsible for our current ecological crisis; the drive to subdue or conquer nature is contrasted with the female method of working with and understanding it.

Defenders of Marxism, however, argue that despite their apparent limitations its concepts offer genuine insights. Thus Lise Vogel has claimed that, although Marx never developed their feminist implications, his economic categories point the way to an understanding of domestic labour and of the role of women in the capitalist economy. She argues that, properly applied, they allow us to develop an understanding of how the proletarian family and the sexual divisions within it serve the needs of capitalism by 'reproducing the labour force'; this means that although Engels may have been wrong in seeing the transfer of property as the prime economic function of the family, and in failing to see sexual oppression within the working class, the form of the family and sexual oppression can still be seen as rooted in material conditions (Vogel, 1983 and Chapter 13 below).

Michelle Barrett has identified a similarly embryonic feminist theory in Marx's concept of *ideology*. For Marx and Engels, ideas were not unchanging or ahistorical, but the product of men's actual lives and experiences; an ideology is a set of such beliefs that purports to explain the world but which, because it is rooted in particular class relationships, offers only a partial understanding of reality. In general, the dominant economic class will be able to impose its view of reality upon the whole society; ideology therefore becomes an important means by which the dominant class maintains its power, and 'The ideas of the ruling class are in every epoch the ruling ideas' (*German Ideology*:64). As Barrett says, the implications of this for the ways in which men have maintained control over women through their control over ideas are very interesting; however she warns against a too easy transfer of the concept to the realm of sexual politics, which may not be based on economic relationships in the same way. As we shall see in Chapter 14, other feminists have developed related arguments around the claim that women's material situation gives them a different, and better, understanding of the world or 'standpoint'.

The concept of alienation, which was particularly important in Marx's early writings, may similarly provide potential feminist insights, but certainly not a ready-made feminist theory. Originating in Hegelian philosophy, the concept is a very complex one, centring upon the idea of man's *loss of control* over what he himself has created. As we have seen, Marx saw man's productive life as a driving force in human history; however, as man's productive powers have increased, his ability to control or understand the whole process has become lost, and what was an expression of human creativity has become a mere means to the end of making money. This means that production has become an alien imposed activity, and the worker has lost all control over the products of his own labour; moreover, the more he produces the more his own poverty is increased. This process has reached its final form under capitalist production, under which the extreme division of labour removes all vestiges of creativity or job satisfaction, and poverty becomes absolute while wealth is vastly increased. At the same time, however, the process of alienation also creates the conditions for a new and higher form of society, in which men will enjoy all the benefits of technological advance and co-operative production: thus 'Communism is the *positive* abolition of *private property*, of *human self-alienation*, and thus the real *appropriation* of *human* nature through and for man' (*Economic and Philosophical Manuscripts*:155).

Some recent feminists have argued that the concept provides an important basis for feminist understanding (see Jaggar, 1983; Foreman, 1978; Bryson, 1995; Barrett, 1987). It may provide insights into women's parallel loss of control over the *reproductive* process, whereby developments in contraception and reproductive technology have become a means of controlling rather than liberating women; some have also argued that woman has become a packaged, feminised, marketable commodity, and has thus become alienated from her own self and her own sexuality. The concept is also bound up with the division of labour in society: this has reached an extreme form under capitalism, but Marx believed that it would be ended or greatly reduced in future communist society, in which work could be freely chosen and fulfilling. Although he was not concerned with the *sexual* division of labour, many feminists today see this as a central issue and argue that men and women can only realise their full humanity when domestic responsibilities as well as productive work are shared by all. Barrett has developed a rather different argument to claim that the concept helps us to understand how people can create the conditions of their own oppression, seen 'not as an arbitrary imposition, but as a process involving the oppressed' (Barrett, 1987:51). Here, the implications for women's role in maintaining patriarchy, particularly through the family and the socialisation of children, are interesting but remain unexplored.

In general, although the concept of alienation seems relevant, no recent writer has applied it systematically. Some, moreover, are highly critical. Thus Wendy Lee-Lampshire has argued that because the concept arises from a male paradigm which treats women's domestic and reproductive labour as natural, such activities cannot be simply encompassed in his theory of alienation and its transcendence: 'excluded in principle from the potential for self-realization through praxis, women, in effect, represent alienation in its most totalizing form; a self which cannot be realized is a self which cannot be lost' (Lee-Lampshire, 1994:194).

Lee-Lampshire's quarrel with Marx includes the claim that he perpetuated the dualism of Victorian ideology, equating men with conscious, rational activity and women with 'the unconscious, the irrational and the affective' (Lee-Lampshire, 1994:195). However, in his early writings Marx rejected the liberal idea that it is men's rationality that is the defining characteristic of humanity, in favour of a view of man as *creator*, whose purposeful and planned productive activity differentiates him from the animals, for unlike them 'man produces when he is free from physical need, and only truly produces in freedom from such need' (*Economic and Philosophical Manuscripts*:128). Later, Marx dismissed the idea that there is any kind of eternally given 'human essence', arguing that man is simply the product of society. However, as we have seen, it is man's productive activity that creates this society, so that he becomes in effect his own self-creator; therefore although men may exhibit different characteristics at different historical periods, the centrality of productive activity remains constant.

As discussed earlier, Marx did not seem to include women's domestic and reproductive work in this paradigm of creative, productive activity. Nevertheless, there seems no reason why this could not be included in principle. Because the idea of conscious creativity escapes the kind of dualism that pervades much of liberal thought, and which elevates mental above physical activity, there is then no reason why women's work should be seen as inherently inferior to men's. This rejection of dualism also suggests that, from a Marxist perspective, sexuality could be recognised as a fully human activity, something which as we saw earlier John Stuart Mill and other liberal feminists had denied. Thus in 1844 Marx wrote that although for the alienated worker sex had been reduced to an animal function, 'Eating, drinking and procreating are of course also genuine human functions' (*Economic and Philosophical Manuscripts*:125); while Engels, despite his questionable ideas about sex difference, saw 'individual sex love' rather than Mill's 'marriage of minds' as the highest form of relationship between man and woman. Unlike liberalism, Marxism therefore provides no theoretical basis for fear of sexuality or suspicion of sensual pleasure.

As Barrett has pointed out, some of the ideas expressed in Marx's early essay *On the Jewish Question* (1843) also offer insights that may be useful to feminist theory; the essay also helps pinpoint the ways in which a Marxist feminist analysis could differ from a liberal feminist one. In it, Marx made a clear distinction between political emancipation and human emancipation: the former declared that all men are equal as citizens, but it left untouched the real inequalities existing in society. Although the state 'decrees that birth, social rank, education, occupation are non-political distinctions', 'Far from *abolishing* these *effective* differences, it only exists in so far as they are presupposed' (*On the Jewish Question*:12). Formal equality for all men as citizens therefore only disguises the real inequalities on which the state is based; real human emancipation requires a transformation of society so that such differences are denied their material basis, and the artificial distinction between state and society, citizen and private individual, disappears. Marx applied these ideas specifically to the Jews, whom he thought could not be emancipated simply by abolishing religion as a basis for political rights; in the same way, they imply that women's subordination will not be ended when sex ceases to be a political and legal distinction – from this perspective it is not equal rights that are important, so much as the transformation of the economic and social conditions upon which subordination is based. This gives us the crucial distinction between Marxist and liberal feminism; it also has affinities with the radical feminist idea of the ubiquity of power, and the artificiality of the public/private distinction. However, the extent to which the state may have a degree of autonomy or may itself be an 'arena of conflict' has been fiercely debated by later Marxist theoreticians, so that the theory does not necessarily imply that the struggle for political and legal rights is without importance. Although these rights are only likely to be achieved at particular historical periods and they are not the final goal, they can therefore both represent significant stages in reaching that goal and valuable gains in their own right.

Marxism is an extremely complex theory, and although it offers feminists a number of suggestive insights, it is not some kind of 'lucky dip' from which concepts can be extracted at will; ideas that Marx developed in relation to class and economic processes *may* be applicable to an analysis of relations between the sexes, but they cannot be automatically transferred. Nevertheless, it does claim to be a comprehensive theory, and a number of key points emerge which must form the basis of any coherent Marxist feminist position. In the first place, it is quite clear that for Marxists questions of sex equality cannot be understood in terms of abstract principles, but only in a historical context. Secondly, opposition to women's emancipation is not simply a result of injustice; rather it reflects material interests and the structured economic needs of society. Thirdly, for women as for any other oppressed group, emancipation is not equated with political and legal rights, but can only be won by restructuring the whole of society to give full economic equality. Fourthly, the material conditions for such changes are already developing within existing society; successful change requires both these objective circumstances and self-conscious revolutionary will and organisation. Fifthly, the struggle for sex equality is integrally connected to the economic class struggle; full freedom for women, as for men, requires the replacement of capitalism by communism. Finally, and more specifically, if women are to become equal to men they must achieve full economic independence; for this to be a source of liberation, housework and childcare must be reorganised on a collective basis.

These are the 'positive' ways in which Marxism may contribute to feminist theory. On the 'negative' side, it cannot allow for the possibility of oppression without an economic foundation, and this means that the very possibility of a non-economic conflict of interests between the sexes is denied, as is the possibility that patriarchy could exist outside of class society. Contemporary feminists who wish to use Marxist theory in a less reductionist way are therefore left with the problem of how to understand the interrelationships of sex and class, patriarchy and capitalism; as we shall see in subsequent chapters, this is an area that has generated much debate.

4

Mainstream feminism: the vote and after, 1880s–1939

The situation of women in the late nineteenth century

By the end of the nineteenth century, many of the demands made by earlier feminists had been met in both the United States and Britain. In particular, although opportunities were still far from equal, education for girls and women had expanded at all levels and in all social groups; this in turn generated a demand for teachers that gave middle-class women a new source of employment, as did the 'typewriter revolution' and the great expansion of office work that had taken place by the 1890s. However, improved education for women did not in itself challenge their traditional role in society, for the elementary education that was all that most girls received stressed domestic skills rather than attempting to broaden their horizons, and the women's colleges sought to produce educated wives and mothers rather than independent women. Similarly, new forms of employment did not necessarily mean female liberation, but frequently involved new forms of exploitation. Few women succeeded in the professions, and for most of those who entered paid work, economic independence meant bare survival rather than fulfilment; in general, new opportunities arose 'less because of the demands of feminists ... than in response to the needs of business, the professions and government for docile, well-educated and cheap labour' (Rubinstein, 1986:x; see also Caine, 1997). It is also important to remember that at this time the single largest occupation for women in both countries remained domestic service. In the United States, a majority of black southern women still worked in the fields and, although a significant minority of black women now entered college and the professions, most were still confined to the most menial and badly paid work of all (Kleinberg, 1999; Cannon, 1996; Giddings, 1984).

Nevertheless, it could be argued that the key demands of Mary Wollstonecraft and other early feminists had been achieved: the world of learning was no longer an exclusively male monopoly, education was seen as a requisite for responsible motherhood, and middle-class women who could not or would not marry at last had some respectable alternatives. Moreover, once women's rationality and capacity for learning had been conceded in principle, an important argument against giving them full legal and political rights had been removed, whilst improved education increasingly gave women the skills and confidence with which to demand and campaign for these rights.

In the legal sphere too, many feminist demands had met with success. By the end of the century, women in both Britain and the United States had won a significant degree of legal independence: a married woman could now own her own property and keep her own earnings, she had new rights concerning the custody and welfare of her children, and she had some degree of protection against physical abuse from her husband. The divorce laws still enshrined the 'double standard' of morality (so that 'simple' adultery was grounds for divorcing a wife but not a husband), but a woman now had the legal right to leave her husband. Similarly, although a husband still had sexual rights over his wife in the sense that rape within marriage was not a crime, he had lost the legal means of enforcing these rights. Men's sexual rights over women were also challenged by the repeal of the Contagious Diseases Acts in Britain (see Chapter 2 above), and by the raising of the age of consent for girls (to 16 in England and 18 in some American states). In general, therefore, although women by 1900 certainly did not enjoy full legal equality with men, the most glaring legal violations of their rights as individuals had been removed; as in the field of education, the principle had been conceded that women could be treated as rational and autonomous individuals, albeit as individuals who might need protection from men.

These formal changes were accompanied by changes in social behaviour and expectations, particularly on the part of middle-class white women, and the 'new woman' of the 1890s was portrayed in the press and novels of the time as the free-thinking, economically independent product of higher education. Although she was usually presented as a pathetic creature, losing her femininity in a ridiculous attempt to ape the achievements of men, she could also be seen as a heroine by those who sought some role in society beyond the capture of a husband, and who believed themselves, like Mary Astell two centuries earlier, to be 'capable of More Things than the pitiful Conquest of some Wretched Heart' (see Chapter 1 above). Such independence was also valued by black American women such as Julia Cooper, a prominent campaigner from the south, whose mother was a slave and whose father her owner. In *A Voice from the South*, written in 1892, she claimed that the poet Byron's claim that 'Man's love is of man's life a thing apart, Tis woman's whole existence' was no longer true, as women increasingly had their own interests and resources. However, she did not think that educated women would reject men, and in response to those who thought that strong-minded women would put off potential husbands, she commented acidly: 'I have been told that strong-minded women could be, when they thought it worth their while, quite endurable, and, judging from the number of female names I find in college catalogues among the alumnae with double patronymics, I surmise that quite a number of men are willing to put up with them' (Cooper, 1988:72).

Parallel to the emergence of the 'new woman' was the much discussed 'revolt of the daughters', whereby young women increasingly refused to abide by the rigid social constraints that custom and their parents decreed. This was epitomised by the cycling craze of the 1890s which gave such young women an unprecedented freedom; as Rubinstein comments: 'It is unlikely that the Chaperone Cyclists' Association formed in 1896 had many clients' (Rubinstein, 1986:216). This increased freedom was not accompanied by any general move towards sexual permissiveness, for 'free love' and birth control were largely seen as sources of sexual exploitation rather than liberation for women. However, there was a greater degree of openness in discussion of sexual matters, and although many 'respectable' young women were still quite unaware of the 'facts of life', ignorance was less widespread than hitherto. Josephine Butler's campaign against the Contagious Diseases Acts and Ibsen's play *Ghosts* (1881), which dealt with the effects of congenital syphilis, represented a gradual shift to a society in which 'respectable' women were allowed to know that such things as prostitution, venereal disease and indeed sex itself did exist, and in which feminists could begin to identify and challenge the power relationships involved in sexual relationships (see Kent, 1990; Bland, 1995).

At the same time, women were entering public life on an unprecedented scale. In the United States, there was a rapid growth of women's clubs and societies which, as earlier in the century, drew on an extended view of women's domestic role to justify their involvement in movements for moral and social reform. Such activity was particularly important for those middle-class black American women who, like Maria Stewart in the 1830s, argued that women had a key role to play in the elevation of their community, and helped establish schools and welfare support (Gordon, 1994 and Gilmore, 1996). In 1896, black women's clubs and associations were co-ordinated into the National Association of Colored Women which in less than twenty years represented 50,000 women in over 1,000 clubs. As legal segregation and racial violence against black people increased, particularly in the southern states, a number of black women also played a prominent role in anti-lynching campaigns (Giddings, 1984; Taylor, 1998; Terborg-Penn, 1998).

For many middle-class white women, public activity was an extension of traditional charitable work: in both Britain and the United States there was a growth of the 'settlement' movement whereby middle-class women sought to reform and improve the conditions of the working class by living amongst them. In England, women were from the 1870s active on School Boards and in administering the Poor Law, and increased numbers participated in local government (Caine, 1997). In the United States many were active in the growing temperance movement, which was particularly concerned with regulating the behaviour of new immigrants (Beuchler, 1990; Staggenborg, 1998; Akkerman, 1998).

Working women themselves were also beginning to organise both independently and in mixed organisations with men – for example, in England the Women's Co-operative Guild had over 14,000 members by the early twentieth century (Gleadle, 2000a). Women's trade unionism still involved only a minority of women, as it faced not only the hostility of employers, but often that of working men as well; domestic responsibilities also obviously made active participation by women very difficult. Nevertheless, with the gradual growth of organised labour, some women were involved in strikes and trade union activity, and the needs of women workers were finding a place on the political agenda.

All this means that by the end of the century women were no longer totally excluded from public life and political debate, and many were not only demanding but also achieving a role outside the home. Most of the clubs and organisations that had grown up were not self-consciously feminist, and women were frequently divided by class, generation, ethnicity and beliefs. Nevertheless, there now existed a significant number of women with experience in campaigning, organising, fund-raising and public speaking. For such women, the right to vote, which Mary Wollstonecraft had only hinted at, and which had seemed such a revolutionary demand at Seneca Falls in 1848, now often appeared both as an obvious entitlement and the one key right they lacked; in this context, the suffrage campaigns came to dominate the women's movement in both Britain and the United States 'not as their dominant concern, but as the demand which men were not willing to concede' (Levine, 1987:57).

The suffrage campaign

The following discussion concentrates on Britain and the United States. Although feminist ideas were extending beyond national boundaries, it is important to realise that campaigns for women's suffrage in other parts of the world had an independent dynamic, often linked with nationalist struggles for independence, so that 'there was no simple celebration of global sisterhood, no universal strategies upon which women could rely for their individual struggles, but rather a slippery and constantly negotiated set of exchanges embracing both rejections of and collusions with colonialism and with differing forms of nationalism' (Fletcher, Mayhall and Levine, 2000:xiv). Even in the west, the campaign was based on a number of apparently contradictory assumptions. This means that although for some women the suffrage campaign was an end in itself, for others it was but a means, or part of a wider goal. 'Votes for women' was therefore a deceptively simple slogan that concealed a number of very different political perspectives. It is to the disentangling of some of these that we now turn.

Equality or difference?

As earlier chapters have shown, the demand for the vote could clearly be derived from liberal principles: thus it had been argued by such as Mary Wollstonecraft, Elizabeth Cady Stanton and John Stuart Mill that women are, like men, rational and autonomous individuals, and that they are therefore entitled to full and equal political rights. However, early writers had also allowed for the possibility of natural difference between the sexes, and the claim that men and women are morally and intellectually equal had coexisted with the idea that women were the custodians of sexual purity, temperance and traditional values. By the end of the century, the idea that women were the potential saviours of the nation, who must be given political rights to reform and purify the conduct of public affairs, had come to dominate some sections of the suffrage movement; from this perspective it was not women's rationality but their sex-specific virtues that were seen as important (Kleinberg, 1999). An important aspect of sex difference was said to lie in women's inherent pacifism, which was contrasted to men's predisposition to war, and strong links developed between feminist and pacifist analyses, with militarism being seen as both cause and consequence of women's oppression; the image of woman the nurturer and giver of life opposing man the destroyer is one that remains powerful today (see Chapter 11 below on such 'ecofeminist' claims).

Claims about women's moral superiority were not confined to the white suffrage movement, but were also important for many black women in the United States, who agreed with Maria Stewart and Julia Cooper that the fate of both their country and their 'race' depended on black women. Unlike white women, black women had to assert their virtue in the face of dominant racist beliefs about their natural promiscuity and immorality; unlike black men, they also faced opposition to their claims within their own community from men who 'when they strike the woman question ... drop back to sixteenth-century logic' (Cooper, 1988:28).

Belief in 'womanly virtues' was linked to a celebration of women's traditional role, rather than the claim that women should be treated the same as men. In practice, many suffrage campaigners attempted to combine this 'difference' position both with liberal ideas of natural rights and sex equality and with more radical ideas about women's collective interests and their need to defend these against men. However, once the vote was won, the incompatibility between a position that asserted the equal worth of men and women and one that stressed their essential difference and/or conflicting interests was to become apparent, and to split the feminist movement.

The retreat from liberal arguments also involved a shift away from the idea that the vote was an individual entitlement, and towards utilitarian arguments about its beneficial social consequences. Although Mill had primarily argued from an equal rights position, he had also claimed that men and society, as well as women, stood to gain from women's enfranchisement, and a very similar position was later held by Millicent Garrett Fawcett (1847–1929), the leader until 1919 of the National Union of Women's Suffrage Societies (NUWSS), the main constitutional suffragist organisation in England. Like Mill, Fawcett combined equal rights and utilitarian arguments, and she called her suffragist paper the *Common Cause* because 'It was the cause of men, women and children. We believe that men cannot be truly free so long as women are held in political subjection' (quoted in Oakley, 1983:191; see also Akkerman, 1998). In the United States, the natural rights arguments that had been so prominent half a century before at Seneca Falls had by 1900 been largely dropped, to be replaced rather than combined with claims about the desirable consequences of enfranchising women. This new approach meant that, increasingly, 'Expediency and interest replaced right and justice in the feminist vocabulary' (Evans, 1977:204; see also Kraditor, 1965). It also meant that utilitarian arguments could be used not only to claim political rights for women, but also to deny them to other groups in society.

Anti-democratic strands in the suffrage campaign

The shift away from liberal 'equal rights' arguments came therefore to be linked with a profoundly anti-democratic strand in the ideas of the suffrage movements; although particularly strong in the United States, this was also important in England. It seems at first sight surprising that a movement to extend political rights could be seen as anti-democratic; but whereas a strict and consistent application of equal rights arguments would seem irrevocably linked to ideas of political equality, utilitarian arguments could be used to justify the exclusion of 'unfit' groups from political power at the same time as enfranchising women – thus Carrie Chapman Catt (1858–1947), the leader of the American suffragist movement, demanded: 'Cut off the vote from the slums, and give it to women' (quoted in Evans, 1977:204). The germ of this idea had already been present in earlier writers, for Mill expressed fear of tyranny by the ignorant majority, and shared with Stanton the view that the vote should be confined to those who could read and write; by the end of the century a much more overt elitism found powerful expression within the suffrage movement.

In England, the campaign for women's suffrage had begun at a time when most men were still denied the vote, and although of course many rejected a property-based franchise for women as an unacceptable betrayal of the working class, and others accepted it only as a staging post on the road to full adult suffrage, some middle-class women saw a limited franchise as desirable precisely *because* of its class basis – as such, it was seen as a way of defending property and conservative values against the ignorant masses. By the end of the century, the vote had been won by many more working-class men, so that women's enfranchisement on the same terms would in fact have increased the voting strength of the working class; nevertheless, the demand for anything less than full universal suffrage was still frequently seen by both opponents and proponents as a class-based claim for the 'ladies' vote'. This view was reinforced by the largely middle-class background of both the constitutional suffragists and the militant suffragettes in the Women's Social and Political Union (WSPU).[3] Fawcett supported the employers in the famous 1889 Bryant and May 'matchgirls' strike' for an improvement in appalling working conditions and poverty-level pay (she was herself a shareholder in the company; Caine, 1997). The WSPU, under the leadership of Emmeline Pankhurst (1858–1929) and her daughter Christabel (1880–1958), began in 1903 as a democratic and pro-labour campaign based in the north-west of England; however, it rapidly jettisoned attempts to win the support of working-class women in favour of attracting wealthy and hopefully influential patrons, and it became a highly autocratic and undemocratic organisation. For some suffragettes, hostility towards men merged with a more general hostility towards the working class, so that the suspicion of many within the labour movement that the suffrage campaign was simply a movement of middle-class ladies indifferent to other social needs was not entirely without foundation.

In the United States, this anti-democratic strand was far more dominant, and here 'race' took the place of property as the key issue. As we saw in the previous chapter, although the American women's movement had been born out of the campaign against slavery, some of its white founders were not averse to harnessing racist prejudices to their cause and, as the campaign for women's suffrage became a mass movement and a mainstream rather than a radical fringe demand, it attracted the support of women who were in all other respects highly conservative. By the end of the century, the economic situation of many former slaves had sharply deteriorated, legal segregation was firmly in place in the south and racist violence against them had reached new heights. Far from campaigning for racial justice, many white women leaders promoted women's suffrage as a means of *maintaining* white supremacy; indeed, this become the main argument for the women's cause in the southern states. From 1903 the demand for the 'educated vote' dominated the campaign; this sought to combine the enfranchisement of most women with the disenfranchisement of 'unfit' men, thus shifting the balance of voting power away from black people and immigrants and in favour of the 'respectable' middle classes; it meant in effect that 'votes for women, which had once been an expression of equal rights, became an issue of social privilege' (Banks, 1986:141; see also Kleinberg, 1999; Taylor, 1998; Davis, 1982; Terborg-Penn, 1998; Kraditor, 1965; Gilmore, 1996).

Socialism, black feminism and the suffrage campaign

Of course, not all middle-class suffrage campaigners accepted this kind of conservative and racist position, nor did they all see the vote as a goal in itself, a means of slotting women into a system which remained itself unchallenged. As discussed in the next chapter, Sylvia Pankhurst (1882–1960) refused to toe the 'party line' laid down by her mother and sister, and concentrated her efforts on campaigning with working-class men and women in the East End of London; she worked closely with the male-led labour movement, and saw feminism as part of a wider movement for socialist change. Working-class women themselves were far more involved in the suffrage campaigns than conventional accounts, which have concentrated on the London leadership, suggest. Activity was particularly strong in the north-west of England, where women did not prioritise the vote for their own sex, but were more concerned with achieving full adult suffrage for all, seeing this as a means to social and economic reform (Liddington and Norris, 1978; Mitchell, 1977; Hannan, 2000; Frances, 2000). Working-class women were also involved in semi-autonomous organisations in Scotland, Ireland and Wales (Bolt, 2000; Hannan, 2000; Smith, 1998).

In the United States, some sections of the main suffrage campaign did attempt to involve working-class, black and immigrant women, and Harriet Stanton Blatch (friend of Sylvia Pankhurst and daughter of Elizabeth Cady Stanton) argued that the experiences of working-class women meant that they were better informed than middle-class women on many issues, and in more need of the vote (Dubois, 1994). Although the main leadership did not take this line, and retreated from the broader issues that Stanton had earlier espoused, others continued to insist that feminism could be a source of wider social change, and argued that to succeed it must be linked to socialist goals (see Cott, 1987, and Chapter 5 below).

Meanwhile, black women in the United States were increasingly organising separately to campaign for their right to vote, and some were developing distinctive arguments which anticipate elements of recent black feminist analysis. Some were beginning to argue that black women needed the vote not simply as women and black people but *as black women*: that is, as people whose labour was most exploited, whose children were sent to inferior schools and who were particularly vulnerable to sexual abuse, but whose specific needs were not recognised either by white women or by black men. Although she was primarily concerned with women's cultural and educative role, this sense of a specific but unrecognised identity was most vividly articulated by Julia Cooper:

> Only the BLACK WOMAN can say 'when and where I enter, in the quiet, undisputed dignity of my womanhood, without violence and without suing or special patronage, then and there the whole *Negro race enters with me*'. (italics in original)

and

> our train stops at a dilapidated station ... I see two dingy little rooms with FOR LADIES swinging over one and FOR COLORED PEOPLE over the other; while wondering under which head I come.

Cooper argued in 1892 that the voices of black women needed to be heard because only they were 'confronted by both a woman question and a race problem' (Cooper, 1988:31, 96 and 134; see also Washington, 1988; Terborg-Penn, 1998; Giddings, 1984: Waters, 2000). However, she did not really extend her analysis to class issues, and, along with many women in the black club movement, she has been accused of speaking from a narrowly middle-class perspective, seeing working-class black women as beneficiaries of altruism rather than equal partners (see Washington, 1988; Taylor, 1998; but see also Gordon, 1994).

In mainland Europe, class issues were much more to the fore, and the fight for women's suffrage was spearheaded by the new mass socialist parties rather than middle-class feminist organisations. In Germany, a Marxist feminist analysis was developed which saw political rights for women as an important weapon in the revolutionary struggle and which, in contrast to the 'bourgeois feminist' position, insisted that women's oppression would only be ended with the overthrow of capitalism.

The whole question of the relationship between socialism and feminism is a highly complex one which will be explored further in the next chapters; here it is sufficient to note that any kind of socialist feminist position within the suffrage movement tended to see the vote in utilitarian terms, that is, as a means to a social goal rather than an individual right; it also refused to accept that the suffrage issue transcended all others, or that divisions of class or 'race' could be dismissed as insignificant squabbles amongst men. This position was diametrically opposed to the radical feminist analysis that was developing within some sections of the movement, and which was particularly explicit in the ideas of Christabel Pankhurst.

Christabel Pankhurst

The political involvement of all the Pankhursts began well to the left of British politics, and Sylvia Pankhurst described her childhood home as 'a centre for many gatherings of Socialists, Fabians, Anarchists, Suffragists, Free Thinkers, Radicals and Humanitarians of all schools' (Pankhurst, 1977:90). It was both their own observation of the situation of working-class women and the male chauvinism and selfishness of many men within supposedly 'progressive' groups that led the Pankhursts to see feminism as a key issue. For Christabel Pankhurst, this developed into an analysis that saw women's oppression as basic to the whole of society, underlying and determining all other aspects of life. Like recent radical feminists she thought that 'the subjection of women as a group, to men as a group, was the fundamental determinant of all other aspects of social life' (Sarah, 1983:270); and like them she saw this subjection as all-pervasive, involving not just political power, but also ideological, economic and sexual control.

This analysis meant that the struggle for the vote was part of a struggle against all forms of male control, while the *methods* she chose could be seen as liberating in themselves, quite apart from their likelihood of success. Hitherto the suffragists had played according to the rules of the game, conforming to received notions of respectable womanhood and ladylike behaviour; when the suffragettes began to march, to demonstrate, to interrupt, to storm the Houses of Parliament and to court arrest and imprisonment, they were challenging basic assumptions about gender roles and attributes, and, according to a recent commentator, they were 'taking one of the most important steps in the history of women' which 'split assunder patriarchal cultural hegemony by interrupting men's discourse with each other' (Marcus, 1987:9). The courage of the suffragettes in facing the dangers of hunger-strikes and force-feeding (experienced by over a thousand women; see Marcus, 1987, and Morrell, 1980) meant that they could certainly not be seen as frail and timid creatures in need of male protection.

Moreover, the tactics used by their opponents, particularly the explicitly sexual violence sometimes used by the police, exposed the reality of this 'protection' in practice (see Rosen, 1974:158–60). The challenge to conventional views was completed by the brief but famous period of active militancy in the years immediately before the First World War, when an outright war on property (but not on life) was declared: arson and window-breaking are hardly the traditional activities of 'ladies', and so 'The suffragettes smashed the image of woman as a passive, dependent creature as effectively as they smashed the plate-glass windows of Regent Street' (Rover, 1967:20).

Although such militant tactics were not widely used in other western countries, they attracted world wide publicity, and there were limited attempts to emulate the methods of the suffragettes in Germany, Hungary and France. In the United States, the main suffrage organisation stressed respectability above all else; however, even here large public demonstrations and parades came to be a widely accepted form of political protest, and the smaller Women's Party adopted a policy of deliberate confrontation, leading to arrests and hunger strikes, although on a much smaller scale than in Britain (see Evans, 1977:192–7). Here again, as Christabel Pankhurst saw, the knowledge that women could act in such ways was significant not only for its direct effect on the franchise campaign, but for its impact on the prevailing ideology.

For Christabel Pankhurst, as for earlier feminists, another important aspect of women's subordination was their economic dependence upon men; she therefore insisted that all women be enabled to compete freely and equally on the labour market, and 'Equal Pay for Equal Work' became a slogan of the Women's Party which she co-founded in 1917. Although she advocated increased involvement by fathers in childrearing, she did not seriously challenge women's responsibility for domestic work; unlike most earlier feminists, however, she did not ignore the implications of this for women's economic situation. Housekeeping as it was currently organised was, she argued, an intolerable burden on married women, and a waste of their time and economic energies; it was also unpaid and largely unrecognised. If, however, it were organised on a more efficient and co-operative basis, then productivity would be increased as women were freed from unnecessary labour. She therefore advocated 'Co-operative Housekeeping' (in particular, the central production and distribution of food by expert cooks and nutritionists, and the provision of laundries) as a more rational and equitable use of resources, which would also recognise the value of domestic work. This has some affinities with Engels' ideas on the collectivisation of housework as discussed in the previous chapter, but unlike Engels she did not see it as dependent on wider socio-economic changes, and she never really explored the economic basis of her proposed reforms, or explained in any detail how they could be financed. Despite her early involvement with the Independent Labour Party, she refused to see socialism as the solution to women's problems, and she insisted that sex interests transcend those of class: 'Why are women expected to have such confidence in the Labour Party? Working men are just as unjust to women as are those of other classes' (quoted in Rosen, 1974:29); in general her politics moved steadily in a conservative direction.

Women's lack of political and economic rights were not for Christabel Pankhurst simply facets of female subordination, but were causally related to what she increasingly saw as the central aspect of oppression – their sexual exploitation by men. Here she argued that if a woman is unable to sell her labour to earn a living then she is forced to sell her body (either temporarily as a prostitute or permanently as a wife), and that men denied women the vote primarily as a means of covering up sexual vice. As we saw in the previous chapter, fear of male sexuality had been a dominant strand in nineteenth-century feminism in both Britain and the United States, and this fear found its most powerful expression in Pankhurst's pamphlet *The Great Scourge and How to End It* (first published in 1913). In this she claimed that 75–80 per cent of men were infected with gonorrhoea and many others with syphilis, that marriage was therefore 'a matter of appalling danger to women' and that venereal disease was so rampant that 'race suicide' was imminent (in Marcus, 1987:210, and *passim*). Men *can*, she argued, be as pure as women, but they will never be so voluntarily; the cure was therefore 'Votes for Women; Chastity for Men', as the former would give women the power to enforce the latter. Much subsequent commentary has dismissed this as the irrational and hysterical outburst of a frigid, man-hating virago, and has tended to concentrate on Pankhurst's exaggerated statistics rather than on the arguments behind them. However the problem with which she was concerned was very real, and some recent radical feminists have hailed her pamphlet as an important step forward for feminist theory. In particular, it is claimed that in seeing sexuality as an arena of struggle, where subordination can be both reinforced and challenged, Pankhurst expanded our perception of sexual politics to the private and personal, so that *The Great Scourge* represents 'a sustained challenge to the organisation of sexuality in the interests of men and a cogent analysis of the relationship between male control of sexuality and the subjection of women in general' (Sarah, 1983:260; see also Jeffries, 1982; Kent, 1990; and Bland, 1995).

In fact, Pankhurst's analysis was less original than such comment suggests, for, as we saw in the last chapter, the oppressive effects of male sexual behaviour had been of major concern to earlier nineteenth-century feminists, who similarly saw chastity for both sexes as the solution; it was also widely discussed in popular novels of the day (Bland, 1987).

Nevertheless it does mean that the campaign for the vote could have far wider implications than the 'liberal feminist' label so often attached to it suggests, and that for some it was a radical feminist demand that certainly did not see women's subordination as beginning and ending with their lack of political rights. However, Pankhurst's analysis remains unsatisfactory for those who deny that political change can bring about a transformation of private, sexual relationships, and many recent radical feminists would consider her concentration on public political rights to be a distraction from more fundamental inequalities, rather than a means of ending them.

A further implication of Pankhurst's analysis, and one shared by some recent radical feminists, is that the struggle for women's rights is part of a sex war in which, unless they offer total and unconditional support, all men are to be considered the enemy. Alliance with existing parties was therefore rejected, and although she suspended all suffragette activity in 1914 to work with men in support of the war effort, the 1917 manifesto of her short-lived Women's Party stated that 'it is felt that women can best serve the nation by keeping clear of men's party machinery and traditions, which, by universal consent, leave so much to be desired' (*The Britannia*, 2 November 1917). However, unlike some later radical feminists, Pankhurst did not extend her hostility to male sexuality, politics and institutions to advocate extreme separatism or lesbianism as a solution; commentators have speculated about her own sexual orientation, but it is probable that she accepted the widespread view that any form of sexual activity is an inferior form of human behaviour which, in the interests of both mental and physical health, should as far as possible be avoided by both men and women.

All this gives us an analysis of women's oppression and the role of the vote in ending it that is very different from the conventional view of the suffrage campaign, and which encompassed not only formal rights but the whole of political, economic and personal life. It is also an analysis that denies the liberal premise that reform can be achieved through reason and persuasion; for Christabel Pankhurst and the militant suffragettes, it was less the justice of their cause than the demonstrable strength of women that would ensure their victory. Although much less clearly formulated than in later theories, this position may have links with those feminists who have recently questioned the whole concept of 'rationality' as a part of male ideology that denies or denigrates other forms of knowledge such as intuition or empathy. It has also led some commentators to suggest that the militant suffrage campaign became an increasingly irrational movement devoted to 'the politics of the apocalypse' (Rosen, 1974), and that as it became characterised by authoritarianism, anti-socialism, hysteria and a cult of violence it was in fact moving in the direction of fascism (Evans, 1977). Fascism is of course anathema to most contemporary feminists, but in the inter-war years supposedly feminist groups were to support both Hitler and Mussolini, whose ideas on women's role and virtues could be reconciled with some aspects of a feminism based on belief in essential sex difference; as we have seen, some feminists also held profoundly anti-democratic and racist views.

Accusations of irrationality also gain some support from Christabel Pankhurst's own later activities. Earlier, she had condemned war as a senseless manifestation of male aggression, 'the tragic result of the unnatural system of government by men only' (quoted in Sarah, 1983:279), but in late 1914 this pacifism was transformed overnight into a nationalistic militarism. Rejecting any idea of a negotiated peace, she and her mother changed the name of their newspaper from *The Suffragette* to *The Britannia*, and suffragettes were the first to hand out white feathers (the symbol of cowardice) to men in civilian clothing. In 1919 (the first election in which women were able to stand or vote), she unsuccessfully opposed labour on a nationalistic and anti-Bolshevik platform; following a religious conversion she later abandoned politics, and from 1921 she devoted her life to preaching the imminence of Christ's Second Coming. Of course, such facts do not mean that either radical feminism or the broader suffrage campaign can be dismissed as essentially irrational or inherently fascistic; however, they illustrate well the very different directions in which feminist beliefs can lead, and the conclusions to which individual feminists may be drawn. They therefore show the dangers of assuming that any movement, individual or idea that has been labelled 'feminist' can automatically be seen as 'progressive'; historically, feminism has most often been associated with humanitarian, liberal or socialist beliefs, but in some forms it has the potential for development in a right-wing direction.

Subsequent commentary has on the whole failed to recognise the diversity of beliefs underlying the suffrage campaigns. It should, however, now be clear that, contrary to popular belief, this was not a quintessentially 'liberal feminist' demand, and apparent unity as to the goal obscured the very different assumptions and values held by different sections of the movement. At the same time, there were frequent disagreements over methods and tactics, and the clash between Marxist and 'bourgeois' analyses was already clear in many European countries; when the vote was finally won, the practical irreconcilability of the various positions became apparent, and mainstream feminism dissolved more clearly into its constituent parts.

After the vote: the re-emergence of contradictions

The first country in the world to give women the vote was New Zealand in 1894, shortly followed by Australia; in Europe, Finland and Norway both enfranchised women before 1914, and most other countries did so shortly after the war (here France provided a notable exception). In Britain, the suffrage campaigns finally met with limited success in 1918, when the vote was given to women over 30 who were also local government ratepayers, wives of local ratepayers, or university graduates (for details, see Smith, 1998). This had the effect of enfranchising slightly over 50 per cent of the adult female population in a year in which virtually all men were given the vote; it was not until 1928 that it was granted to women on the same terms as men. In the United States, women had won the vote as early as 1869 and 1870 in the states of Wyoming and Utah; in 1920 the Nineteenth Amendment to the American Constitution, enfranchising all adult American women, was finally ratified.

The reasons for this enfranchisement were extremely complex, and varied from country to country; they frequently owed more to political expediency than to any mass conversion of politicians to the feminist cause. Thus in Britain, the issue became entangled in the convoluted logic of party politics and politicians' manoeuverings for position over the question of Irish independence. Increasingly too, ruling groups came to see women as a stabilising force that could be used against the threat of unrest and disruption; in this sense, therefore, their enfranchisement was a conservative rather than a radical step, designed to counteract the potential power of new immigrant groups in Australasia, immigrants and blacks in the United States, and the working class in Europe (see Evans, 1977). Fear of renewed suffragette militancy (which had been suspended for the duration) was also important, as were the changes in social attitudes, behaviour and expectations generated during the war years (although these changes were complex and did not all work in women's favour; see Kent, 1993).

Whatever the mix of reasons, in many nations a seemingly critical feminist battle had now been won. However, this victory was not followed by any further rapid advance, and historians of the women's movement have often been very negative about the inter-war period, seeing it as one of in-fighting, loss of direction and, in some cases, uncritical adaptation to an essentially anti-feminist ideological environment through which institutional barriers to women's progress were replaced by psychological ones (see for example Kent, 1993; Pugh, 2000; and Bouchier, 1983).

Certainly, those who had hoped that politics would be morally transformed by the enfranchisement of women was soon to be disappointed. Despite the fears of the liquor industry (which had vehemently opposed women's suffrage in the United States), many women actively opposed prohibition (see Cott, 1987:263–4), and female enfranchisement seems to have had little overall effect on the issue. Internationally, some feminists opposed militarism in 1914, and in 1915 the Women's

International League for Peace and Freedom, a pacifist organisation that still exists today, was founded with the support of women from both sides of the war (see Bussey and Tims, 1980; Evans, 1987; Florence *et al.*, 1987; Wiltsher, 1985). However, most suffrage leaders, like most women, had supported the war effort, and although some continued to be active in pacifist organisations after the war, they remained a minority with little significant effect on government policies.

More generally, any hopes or fears that women would vote as a united group proved unfounded; like men, women voted according to their class, religion and family traditions rather than on feminist issues, whilst in the United States white women were not prepared to support black women who were rapidly disenfranchised by racist voting regulations in the southern states. There was, moreover, no great rush of women waiting to stand for public office. Although a few women were elected to both local and national governments, party differences and the hostility of party leaders made it difficult for them to act as a united group, even if they had wanted to; their small numbers also meant that they were dependent on male support for any action on feminist issues.

Nevertheless, in the years immediately after they won the vote, women made some further legal gains (mainly concerning marriage, child custody and entry into the professions), and some concessions were made on women's welfare issues. Although the nervousness that induced politicians to make such changes soon evaporated, politicians could no longer simply bin letters from women's organisations. In Britain, women members of parliament developed links with women's organisations and were in general more inclined to address issues such as equal pay and family welfare than their male colleagues. Moreover, whilst some women dropped out of political activity after the vote was won, many others were involved in a wide range of single issue campaigns at both local and national level, and it is certainly an over-simplification to see these as the 'silent years' of feminism, or a retreat by women into the private sphere. It was, however, a period of intense ideological disagreements amongst feminists, as the contradictory nature of the assumptions behind the suffrage campaign became apparent.

Equal rights v. welfare feminism in the United States

A key source of conflict arose from the tension between the demand that women be treated the same as men and the claim that their specific qualities and roles should be recognised and supported. This meant that liberal assumptions that women should be seen primarily as individuals rather than as members of a sex group, that they should be free to compete with men in whatever sphere they chose and that state intervention is to be avoided wherever possible clashed head-on with those that stressed women's sex-specific needs and attributes, that insisted on the primacy of their role as wives and mothers, and that sought collective interventionist solutions to the problems of women's welfare.

A central issue at the time was the question of protective legislation, which was aimed at protecting women from the worst effects of danger-ous and unhealthy occupations and long working hours (see Crystal Eastman in Cook (ed.), 1978, for an excellent contemporary account of the debate, and Cott, 1987, and Tobias, 1997 for more recent analyses). Some saw protection simply as a desirable first step towards improving work-ing hours and conditions for both men and women rather than as a specif-ically women's issue: in general, however, feminist opinion was divided between the majority who advocated protection as a real and necessary improvement to the lives of working women and a minority who argued that it would only confirm women's subordinate situation and perpetuate the traditional division of labour.

This minority position was defended by the small *Women's Party* which every year from 1923 managed to secure the introduction of an Equal Rights Amendment before Congress. The approach of this group was based on a fierce rejection of traditional ideas of sex difference and women's role, and in insisting on a married woman's right to a career and economic independence it pushed liberal feminism to the logical conclu-sion that J. S. Mill and most nineteenth-century American feminists had avoided. However, in seeing a career as a source of fulfilment it ignored the fact that for the vast majority of women paid employment was an added burden rather than a source of liberation. It also failed to acknowl-edge the role of black women and refused to help black women in the south to register to vote, on the grounds that this was a racial rather than a feminist matter (Bolt, 1995:40) As Cott says, this kind of feminism appealed primarily to those 'who belonged to and were privileged by the dominant culture in every way except that they were female' (Cott, 1987:76), and it contributed to the widespread perception of American feminism as a movement of and for the white middle classes. It is therefore unsurprising that former black suffragists chose to organise separately and developed international links, such as the International Council of Women of the Darker Races (Terborg-Penn, 1998).

Another problem with this kind of equal rights feminism arose from its attempt to combine liberal principles with a much more radical analysis of women's oppression. Here some claimed that artificially-created sexual division is the 'primary antagonism' in society which towers above 'the petty quarrels of religious creeds, above the rivalries of class, above the slaughterings of nations, above the sinister enmity of races' (quoted in

Cott, 1987:76). Not only do the proposed legal solutions seem inadequate, given the immensity of the problem that has been identified, but, as Eisenstein has pointed out, the perception of women as a sex-class, united in their struggle against men, runs counter to the liberal insistence that, once they are given equal political and legal rights, it is up to *individuals* to change their situation (Eisenstein, 1981; see also Scott, 1996). Cott has therefore argued that those few women who in inter-war America achieved success in the male world were unable to work for the wider interests of their sex, for to succeed they had to accept the existing rules of the game, and if they were to draw attention to the disadvantages faced by other women they would in effect be drawing attention to their own inferiority (Cott, 1987:281; see also Scott, 1996).

In general, the feminist label in the United States in the inter-war years tended to become restricted to these equal rights campaigners, whose position was increasingly seen as both old-fashioned and narrowly elitist. Thus Cott reports that whereas in 1913 an enthusiastic proponent could describe feminism as 'something so new it isn't in the dictionaries', by 1919 some 'progressive' women were referring to their position as 'post-feminist' (Cott, 1987:13 and 282). Nevertheless, many other groups continued to work for the needs and interests of women as they saw them. This involved both charitable work by and for women, and political campaigns to improve their living conditions. The main suffrage organisation became the *League of Women Voters*, and although, as we saw, women did not tend to vote on sex lines, this acted as a pressure group, particularly concerned with the welfare of children and their mothers. Although the League enjoyed some early successes when politicians were still nervous of women's supposed political power, the 'Red Scare' that followed the 1917 Bolshevik revolution meant that collectivist or interventionist policies had no hope of reaching the statute book, while the (unfounded) accusation that many of the leading women's organisations were part of an international Bolshevik conspiracy further discredited their cause (see Cott, 1987:242 for the 'Spider Web Chart' of 1924 that purported to show these links).

To a large extent, this kind of 'welfare feminism' stemmed from nineteenth-century ideas about women's moral superiority as carers and nurturers, and it certainly did not involve any challenge to traditional sex roles; critics of this approach accuse it of equating motherhood with the condition of *all* females and, by stressing biological difference, of denying freedom of choice to both men and women. During the Depression, this attitude led many women to agree that the preservation of jobs for male breadwinners should be a priority, and demands for equal pay and opportunity were replaced by campaigns to allow women to perform their traditional roles under the best possible conditions.

Many campaigners for welfare reform were themselves middle-class, and inclined to favour means-tested benefits which could be combined with a measure of social control, and they also often failed to recognise that many women simply could not afford to stay at home (within the black community there may have been less distance between helper and helped; see Gordon, 1994). Nevertheless, it was such middle-class groups that were largely responsible for keeping the whole idea of state responsibility for the welfare of its citizens on the political agenda at a time when this was rejected not only by business interests and the main political parties, but also by organised labour. The tradition of welfare feminism continued into the 1930s, when a network of influential women led by Eleanor Roosevelt, the President's wife, were able to make an important contribution to the planning and administration of the New Deal. As we shall see in Chapter 8, the resulting welfare provision was both gendered and racialised in its assumptions and effects. Nevertheless, women's needs were not entirely ignored, and Ware claims therefore that 'It is in the 1930s that many of women's expectations beyond suffrage finally found fulfilment' (Ware, 1981: 2).

Equal rights v. welfare feminism in Britain

The split between equal rights and welfare feminists became explicit rather later in Britain than in the United States, partly because the suffrage campaign continued until 1928, when women were finally given voting rights on an equal basis with men. The situation in Britain was also very different because welfare feminists were not politically isolated as in the United States, but could frequently make common cause with the new Labour Party.

Some women had long been involved in charitable work, and a number of studies carried out in the first decades of the century increased public awareness of the particular problems faced by women, revealing an appalling catalogue of chronic poor health, bad housing and malnutrition (Davies, 1978; Reeves, 1979). Organisations such as the Women's Co-operative Guild argued that these problems were the products of poverty rather than of ignorance or bad housekeeping, and they insisted that the solution lay in state provision rather than individual self-help or charity. The inter-war years were therefore characterised by campaigns for improved maternal and infant health provision, for the inclusion of women in the developing system of national insurance, and for economic assistance to women through maternity benefits or child allowances (Dale and Foster, 1986). All this was a far cry from the laissez-faire individualism of older feminists such as Fawcett, and meant that 'the notion, of the feminist as a middle-class women in pursuit of a job was radically overturned', so that 'feminism's identification with middle-class professional women had been shattered, and the working-class mother had emerged as the new symbol of oppressed womanhood' (Phillips, 1987:98 and 102). This ideological shift has been criticised by some recent commentators as an uncritical acceptance of separate spheres ideology, and Susan Kinsgley Kent has argued that 'By the end of the 1920s, "new" feminists found themselves in a conceptual bind that trapped women in "traditional" domestic and maternal roles and limited their ability to advocate equality and justice for women' (Kent, 1993:7; see also Pugh, 2000 and Banks, 1993). However, it was in line with the general trend in British politics away from liberal ideas of laissez-faire and towards a greater degree of state intervention that was eventually to produce the Welfare State; thus Banks has claimed that 'to a large extent we may see the Welfare State in Britain as a product of an alliance between welfare feminism and the Labour Party' (Banks, 1986:174).

As in the United States, welfare feminism had the advantage of addressing the real needs of large numbers of women, and in this it contrasted favourably with the equal rights feminists who seemed largely concerned with the needs of middle-class women. It was also seen by some as a step towards improved conditions for all. However, again as in the United States, in stressing the needs of women as wives and mothers, it sometimes seemed to deny them the option of being anything else, and in concentrating on the welfare of women in the home it tended to ignore the exploitation of those in paid employment – and in the aftermath of the First World War the number of 'surplus women' rose dramatically, so that nearly one third of women had no choice but to be economically self-supporting. With the ending of the war, the large numbers of women who had been substituting for men in all kinds of occupations were replaced by returning soldiers; for welfare feminists this was a welcome return to the natural order of things, rather than a blow to their cause, but for many individual women it meant extreme hardship.

Eleanor Rathbone and the family allowance campaign

Perhaps paradoxically, the one campaign that might have served the needs of both single and married women was the demand for family allowances, led by Eleanor Rathbone, a long-time suffrage campaigner and social reformer who succeeded Fawcett as President of the NUWSS in 1917 and was elected as an Independent member of parliament in 1929. Rathbone claimed to represent a 'new feminism' based on women's real and specific needs and differences from men, rather than on the abstract rights claimed by older liberal feminists; nevertheless, she was also concerned with questions of equal pay and freedom of choice, and aimed at economic independence for all women.

Her main demand was for a policy of 'family endowments' to be paid directly to women, for she insisted that the task of bringing up children must receive financial recognition in order to alleviate poverty, to give women financial independence, and to recognise the importance of their maternal role – and here she was scathing about those who claimed to revere motherhood while refusing to act to alleviate the squalor and poverty it so often involved:

> The sentimentalist, who has taken motherhood under his special protection, is shocked at the base suggestion that anything so sordid as remuneration, anything so prosaic as the adjustment of means to ends, should be introduced into the sacred institution of the family and applied to the profession of motherhood. (Rathbone, 1927:66)

This was clearly in line with the ideas of welfare feminism, but anathema to liberal feminists like Fawcett, who believed that parents should take responsibility for their own children rather than relying on the state, and who described family allowances as a 'Socialist nightmare of abolishing the ordinary responsibilities of marriage and substituting them with State salaries for mothers' (quoted in Akkerman, 1998:169). However, although her prime concern was with the welfare of mothers and children and she did not challenge the traditional division of labour, Rathbone was not attempting to 'force women back into the home', as some critics have suggested. Rather, she sought to give *all* women a *choice*: women would no longer be forced into the labour market through financial necessity, but if they wished to pursue a career they could use their family endowment to purchase domestic help. She also believed that her proposals could lead to equal pay for men and women. At present, she argued, a man's wages were based on the assumption that he had a non-earning wife and children to support, whereas in fact over half of working men over the age of 20 had no dependent children at all; once mothers and children were provided for by the state, a man's pay could, like a woman's, reflect the work which he as an individual had performed, rather that covering frequently non-existent family responsibilities; with this removal of the 'family wage', the need for wage differentials between men and women would disappear.

In practice, when family allowances were introduced after the Second World War (for second and subsequent children), they were at a level far below that which would give women financial independence or undermine the idea of the male breadwinner. In this sense they had become a means of alleviating poverty and encouraging population growth rather than of shifting social and economic power in the direction of women, and later feminists have criticised the policy's nationalistic implications. Nevertheless, it was feminists such as Rathbone who ensured that the allowance was paid directly to mothers. Later feminists have therefore seen the defence of family allowances as both an important practical issue and a part of an ideological struggle to have women's work fully recognised; recently, the Wages for Housework group has attempted to fuse earlier arguments with a Marxist analysis of women's domestic labour, and has resurrected Rathbone as a heroine for its cause (see Chapter 13 below).

Birth control

An area which spanned the concerns of both equal rights and welfare feminists was the issue of birth control. This had formerly been largely regarded as a source of sexual enslavement rather than liberation, and nineteenth-century proponents such as Annie Besant had received little support from the suffrage leaders. There was, however, a gradual change in attitudes towards sexuality, which came to be seen as an important source of human pleasure rather than a sin or a purely animal activity: as the American activist Crystal Eastman said, 'Feminists are not nuns' (in Cook, 1978:47). However, as Sheila Jeffries has pointed out in *The Spinster and Her Enemies*, the new 'scientific' recognition of women's sexual pleasure by sexologists and psychologists was not necessarily liberating, as it usually involved a narrow insistence on the importance of marriage for a 'healthy' life, which ruled out celibacy or lesbianism and challenged earlier feminist ideas of the possibility of independence from men (Jeffries, 1985). Although in both Britain and the United States after the First World War a few women took freedom of choice to mean sexual permissiveness and to advocate 'bachelor motherhood', such deliberate flouting of convention, although widely reported, was rare (Rowbotham, 1973a).

The main reason for the increased acceptance of birth control was not so much a new awareness of women's sexual needs, as the recognition by social reformers of the appalling effects on women's health of repeated pregnancies; this led to the demand that contraceptive knowledge be made available to working-class women; in Britain this involved not only the establishment of charitable clinics to provide such information, but also a demand for state funding. Although there was much support for such welfare feminist measures within the British Labour party, there was also a sometimes well-founded suspicion of the motives of reformers; for example, Marie Stopes, the author of *Married Love* (1928), was motivated not only by compassion for the plight of working-class women, but by fears that unchecked breeding by the impoverished working class would lead to 'race deterioration'. For some working-class men and women, therefore, the birth control movement was seen as a sinister move towards controlling the working class rather than a means of liberating women; it was also seen as a way of blaming poverty on feckless over-breeding rather than on capitalist exploitation. Similar well-founded suspicions were shared by many black people in the United States. Nevertheless, a woman's ability to control her own fertility came to be a key feminist demand which could be advocated by equal rights campaigners, by those welfare feminists who saw family planning as an essential prerequisite for responsible motherhood and by black women opposing both the 'white bigots' and the male black leaders who 'found common cause in the assertion of male authority over women's decisions regarding reproduction' (Ross, 1993:151). During this inter-war period, feminists concentrated largely on contraception (Banks, 1986:192–4; but see also Rowbotham on the pro-abortionist Stella Browne [Rowbotham, 1977]); their arguments recur, however, in contemporary debates about abortion and reproductive technology, which many feminists now see as a key issue (see Chapter 11 below).

In general, feminism at this time moved away from liberal individualism, equal rights and laissez-faire, and towards more collectivist and interventionist solutions. It also tended to concentrate on the short-term interests of women and to aim at improving the conditions under which they performed their traditional roles, rather than challenging the traditional division of labour and the confinement of women to the private sphere. This approach was often based on an insistence on the high value of domestic work and the belief that, although men and women might differ in their natural attributes, women were in no way inferior. However, as the family allowance arguments show, to 'envalue' women's traditional activities is not necessarily to deny them the right to choose an alternative role; as J. S. Mill said in 1881, it is only when women have freedom of choice that we can know what their 'natural' abilities are. It may be, therefore, that the conflict between 'equal rights' and 'welfare' feminism is less absolute than it at first sight appears, so that acceptance of the proposals of one need not involve rejection of all the principles of the other, and women's choices need not be restricted by an artificial dichotomy (for further discussion, see Chapters 9 and 14 below).

For some critics, a problem with both equal rights and welfare feminism is their relationship to other forms of social change. Thus it is argued that the former ignores oppression within the home, and that although it advocates equal rights for men and women in the public sphere, this is within an unequal and hierarchical society in which most must be losers. The latter, on the other hand, tends to assume that state machinery can be used benevolently to redistribute resources and improve the situation of women, whereas, critics say, the state is not some neutral tool, but a reflection or instrument of prevailing patriarchal or capitalist class interests. From the perspective of such radical, socialist or Marxist critics, real change must involve more fundamental social transformation.

During the inter-war years there was little development of radical feminist theory, indeed much earlier analysis of the all-pervasive nature of male power seems to have become largely forgotten, not to be rediscovered until the 1960s. The entire period of this chapter was, however, a time when socialist and Marxist feminist ideas were being developed and, some believed, being put into practice. It is with these developments that the next chapters are concerned.

5

Socialist feminism in Britain and the United States

In many European countries there seemed by the end of the nineteenth century to be a sharp split between 'mainstream feminists' with their demands for equal political and legal rights, and Marxist socialists with their talk of class war and revolution. In both Britain and the United States, however, there was much more of a continuum, as the social concerns that had long characterised sections of the women's movement merged with a more radical critique of existing society which led some to socialism as well as feminism. For most, this socialism was based on humanitarian ideals or a pragmatic response to poverty and the conditions of working-class life, and owed little to Marxist ideology. As such, it favoured gradual and piecemeal reform rather than revolution, and it could seem readily compatible with a feminism based on ideas of social justice rather than on an analysis of patriarchy; from this perspective, socialism and feminism could be seen as complementary, promising equality and an end to exploitation for all.

Britain

Although many male socialists may have shared this perspective in theory, in practice socialist organisations in both countries tended to combine formal commitment to a degree of sex equality with a marginalisation of 'women's issues', discriminatory practice and a frequently unthinking sexism that permeated all levels of political and personal life. Thus in England, Hannah Mitchell, a working-class socialist and suffrage campaigner from the north of the country complained:

> I soon found that a lot of the Socialist talk about freedom was only talk, and these Socialist young men expected Sunday dinners and huge teas with home-made cakes, potted meat and pies, exactly like their reactionary fellows.

and

> Most of us who were married found that 'Votes for Women' were of less interest to
> our husbands than their own dinners. (Mitchell, 1977:96 and 149)

At a more general level, different priorities often produced a clash
between the methods and aspirations of socialists and feminists. Although
some leading Labour Party members, most notably Keir Hardie and
George Lansbury, were consistently and actively supportive, the party for
a time refused to support the suffrage campaign for women's enfranchisement on the terms that already existed for men, on the grounds that
this would only strengthen the voting power of the middle class; the
response of some women to this 'betrayal' was to follow Emmeline and
Christabel Pankhurst out of the party, and to form their own militant and
independent organisation (see Chapter 4 above). However, such polarisa-
tion at the level of national organisation concealed a widespread continuity at the grass roots, as many women were active both in suffrage groups
and in the mainstream of trade unions and such organisations as the
Labour Party, the Fabian Society and the Co-operative Guild
(Rowbotham, 1977; see also Walker, 1984; Rowan, 1982; Hannan, 2000; and
Frances, 2000). Although many men in these groups saw feminism as a
middle-class movement and women's issues 'at best irrelevant, at worst a
dangerous distraction' (Bolt, 1993:36), there seemed to be a widespread
feeling amongst socialist women that the shortcomings of socialist organisations were merely contingent, and that there was no need to reject
socialism as inherently patriarchal or hostile to the interests of women.
This meant that there was within the mainstream of the British socialist
movement no theoretical confrontation of the 'divided loyalties', the
'dilemmas of sex and class' (Phillips, 1987a, *Divided Loyalties: Dilemmas of
Sex and Class*) that might be faced by socialist feminists. As we saw in the
previous section, the Labour Party's programme generally meshed well
with the demands of a welfare feminism that preferred reformism to
either sex or class warfare and which made no real attempt to investigate
the sexual division of labour or issues of power between women and men.

Perhaps surprisingly, major theoretical analysis of the relationships
between socialism and feminism was also absent in Britain's first Marxist
party, the small Social Democratic Federation. As Karen Hunt has shown,
the official party line that only economic issues are directly relevant to
socialist politics, so that other matters are a question of individual
conscience, enabled it to avoid confrontation by adopting a 'no policy'
position on women's issues. In practice, this meant that although feminist
views were expressed in the party press, anti-feminist and misogynist
views were seen as equally legitimate, and indeed set the tone for
the debate (see Davis, 1999). Therefore, although many women did see

themselves as facing sex-specific problems, and tensions became acute over such issues as the vote and women's work, in principle feminism 'remained an optional extra for socialists' which the male leadership could ignore (Hunt, 1988:475).

Sylvia Pankhurst

This male domination of socialist politics was challenged by Sylvia Pankhurst (1882–1960), for whom feminism and socialism were always inseparable. Although best remembered as a militant suffragette, she always saw the struggle for the vote as part of a wider move to a more equal society in which the emancipation of women would be linked to that of the working class, and she became a key British player in the revolutionary political movements that erupted around Europe at the end of the first world war. Unlike her mother and sister in the WSPU (see Chapter 4 above), who were more interested in attracting middle-class supporters, she concentrated her efforts in the East End of London, where she lived and campaigned from 1912–24, and she refused to see working-class men as an undifferentiated enemy rather than as potential allies and fellow victims of an exploitative economic system. Despite her early belief in the transformative power of the vote, by the end of the First World War she had rejected parliamentary politics, which she saw as inescapably corrupt and de-radicalising, in favour of the self-emancipation of the working-class through community-based soviets. Here, she insisted both on the importance of grass-roots democracy and on the inclusion of women, arguing that housewives and unemployed and elderly people as well as workers should be represented. Like both her sister and most Marxist feminists she argued for the collectivisation of housework; she also condemned marriage as an economic relationship which made women financially dependent on men, and argued in favour of open relationships based on love.

Pankhurst was not an armchair thinker but an active campaigner at local, national and international levels who was founder-editor and founder-leader of a series of radical newspapers and organisations and 'lived her politics, especially her feminism' (Davis, 1999:120). She immersed herself in the life of the East End poor, and tried to set up support services, including 'two cost-price restaurants, four baby clinics, a day nursery and a toy factory' (Dodd, 1993:17). Her involvement in suffrage militancy meant that she was frequently in prison, where she risked her life and ruined her health through hunger strikes and consequent forcible feeding. In 1919 she made a dangerous tour of revolutionary Europe which included crossing the Alps on foot, and the next year made an equally hazardous visit to Moscow. In accordance with her beliefs, and to the dismay of her mother and sister, she did not marry when she gave birth to her son, at the age of 45.

Pankhurst was a life-long defender of the rights of the oppressed, and certainly did not see herself as some kind of 'lady bountiful' ministering to their needs; although the pressure of immediate destitution led her to fund-raise and provide some immediate help for her East-End neighbours during the war years, she argued both that the skills and energies of poor people themselves should be harnessed to improve conditions and that 'no private effort could cope with the vast misery around us, it was the responsibility of the Community, of the State' (in Dodd (ed.), 1993:91). Although she too was concerned with supporting working-class women in their domestic roles, her ideas go far beyond the kind of 'welfare feminism' discussed in the previous chapter, as her call for collective responsibility was combined with suspicion of the state and the surveillance that state provision might involve – hence her preference for community-based democracy. She soon became highly critical of the centralising tendencies in the Soviet Union, and was one of the first European socialists to identify and oppose the dangers of fascism. Consistently anti-racist and anti-colonial, she campaigned against the invasion of the Ethiopa (the last independent African state) by Mussolini, and she spent her final years in Ethiopia.

Contrary to many accounts, Pankhurst was not an isolated political eccentric, but part of a left-wing European movement and a libertarian strand in socialism that in 1917 believed that radical social change was both possible and imminent. She was in contact with the European Marxist feminists discussed in the following chapters, and Mary Davis claims that by 1917 she 'had adopted, albeit unsystematically, a Marxist analysis which postulated that the roots of women's oppression lay within the capitalist mode of production which, through its extraction of surplus value, exploited all workers' (Davis, 1999:58–9). However, like the other Marxist feminists, she failed to discuss the sexual division of labour and its implications: although she included women in soviet democracy through household or workplace soviets, she assumed that these were exclusively for women, and she never explored the consequences of women's double (domestic and workplace) responsibilities.

The United States

In the United States at this period there was a complex and often uneasy intermingling of the 'orthodox Marxism' imported by German refugees facing Bismark's anti-socialist laws in the 1880s, and a home-grown socialism (see Buhle, 1981). This latter form of socialism was essentially a moral movement which owed much of its inspiration to Edward Bellamy's *Looking Backward* (1888) and led to a form of socialist feminism that was in the tradition of earlier abolitionist, temperance and anti-prostitution campaigns. Frances Willard, the temperance leader, came to embody this approach, as she increasingly saw drunkenness as a product not a cause of poverty, and the solution as lying in Christian socialism rather than individual restraint or class conflict; similarly, the anti-prostitution campaign had by the early twentieth century developed a distinctive socialist dimension: 'If the mainstream woman's movement of the nineteenth century had named man as the potential debaucher, socialists had substituted capitalism and its masters as the curse of maidenly virtue' (Buhle, 1981:253). Such socialist feminists based their arguments on the ideas of woman's moral superiority and her potential role as regenerator and reformer of a corrupt society that, as we saw, had come to dominate mainstream campaigns in the United States; for many, this was accompanied by the sanctification of traditional family life and a commitment to the ideal of woman as homemaker rather than producer in the public sphere.

Charlotte Perkins Gilman

The idea of female superiority was also important for the woman who has been described as 'the leading intellectual' in the women's movement in the United States at the beginning of the century: Charlotte Perkins Gilman (1860–1935) (see Rossi, 1973:568); in her theory, however, it gained a new significance and led to very different conclusions. Although she was not really involved with the organised feminist movement, Gilman enjoyed widespread if temporary fame in the years before the First World War, and her views were expounded in fiction, journalism and highly popular public lectures, as well as in theoretical works. In all of these she developed a woman-centred view of the world that linked female values with human progress and socialism, which she saw as the inevitable product of a particular stage of human history. Although she said she disagreed 'with both theory and method as advanced by the followers of Marx' (quoted in Hill, 1980:283), this last point has clear affinities with a basic tenet of Marxism, as has Gilman's insistence that economic conditions are basic to human development, that human nature is not fixed but the constantly evolving product of society, and that work is a basic human need which in future society can be liberated from economic compulsion and freely performed for the general good. Like Marx, she saw society's economic development leading it beyond selfish individualism, exploitation and the profit motive and towards human freedom, co-operation and equality. Unlike him, however, she did not think this would come about through class conflict and revolution, but by the gradual and peaceful continuation of tendencies already present in modern society.

This kind of analysis was by the end of the nineteenth century not strikingly original; what gave Gilman's ideas a dramatic novelty was her combination of such socialism with a wholeheartedly woman-centred approach to history and society. According to Gilman, sex relations are not simply a by-product of economic development but a basic force. Originally, she argued, women were the first producers, for while man was 'gallantly pursuing the buffalo … acting merely as an animal under direct stimulation of hunger and the visible beast before him', women were thinking ahead and sowing grain for themselves and their children (*Human Work*:207). They were, moreover, the first educators, and 'the woman, the mother, is the first co-ordinator, legislator, administrator and executive' (*the Man Made World*:198). These and the essentially human attributes of caring, loving and protecting, stemmed originally from women's maternal role, but have to be *learned* by men who have no such natural virtues, for 'To violently oppose, to fight, to trample to the earth, to triumph in loud bellowings of savage joy – these are the primitive male instincts' (*World*:189). History was therefore the process by which men became fully human and developed production and other originally maternal functions such as legislation to their highest form. In the past, men's strength had enabled them to subordinate and exclude women, but now increased specialisation and the division of labour were enabling women to enter industrial production. These economic developments were also increasing the organic nature of society, so that selfishness, competitiveness and individualism ('the spirit of the predacious male', *World*:197) would soon become outmoded in a new era which would be characterised by such 'womanly' qualities as collectivism and socialist co-operation in the interests of all.

All this gives a history of sexual relations and a promise of their trans-formation in the future which, however shaky its anthropological foundation, gave women a sense of power and optimism; this was accompanied by trenchant condemnation of present arrangements. Central to this was Gilman's insistence that woman must become economically independent from man; far from being 'natural', her present dependency meant that she was the only animal for whom the sexual relationship was also an eco-nomic one, for her exclusion from production meant that her survival depended upon her ability to attract a mate. This meant that not only were women denied expression of their productive nature, but they were forced to compete with each other in the marriage market, a particularly demean-ing state of affairs as women are both compelled to marry, but also obliged to pretend indifference rather than actively pursuing a man: 'Although marriage is a means of livelihood, it is not honest employment where one can offer one's labour without shame' (*Economics*:89). Like earlier writers, she also claimed that this marketing of women in marriage meant that it was essentially the same as prostitution: 'The transient trade we think evil. The bargain for life we think good.' She added that the revulsion that 'respectable' women felt for prostitution was therefore simply 'the hatred of the trade-unionist for scab labour' (*Economics*:64 and 100). Not only did this universal commercialism of sex demean women, but it led to an exaggeration of sexual differences and the encouragement in women of inferior qualities such as frailty and weakness; these qualities would, she believed, be passed on to children, both boys and girls, leading to a decline in the quality of the whole human race.

Women must therefore be given economic independence both for their own sake and for the benefit of humanity; this independence would also transform the existing oppressive family structure, leading to a higher form of relationship that was not based on economic need. Here Gilman parted company with most feminists of her day, and forcefully attacked the traditional family: far from being the cosy world of popular sentiment, she saw it as a place of degrading toil and exploitation, where women slaved for no reward, and where their unnatural confinement led to frustration, anger and, all too often, madness. It was, moreover, an exceptionally inefficient way of performing functions essential for society's survival: she argued that cooking, cleaning and childrearing were complex skills requiring expert and scientific knowledge; the present system whereby they were performed by all women inevitably meant unhealthy, malnourished and ignorant children growing up in tension-ridden homes. Professionalisation of such tasks was therefore for Gilman the key to both the liberation of women and a better society; it was also a process that was already underway, as laundry, cooking and much of childcare were passing out of the home and into the hands of infinitely more efficient specialists. Against those who attempted to resist this trend, and who claimed that it would destroy the family and monogamous marriage, she argued that it was only the oppressive aspects of these that would disappear. Thus the relentless hard work now involved in motherhood would be removed, and parent–child relations would be based on genuine love rather than jealous exclusivity and possessiveness, and the home would become a place of love and rest for women and men alike.

These ideas clearly owed much to Gilman's own unhappy experiences of domestic life; she suffered acute depression after the birth of her daughter, and she was widely vilified when she entrusted the child to the care of her former husband and his second wife, who was and remained her own good friend. For her, the worlds of private and public oppression and liberation were inextricably linked, and the key to liberation lay in a general move to a society in which 'womanly values' of peace, love and co-operation were no longer confined to the home, but were the basis of the whole social order. In this context the differences between men and women would become less important than their potential shared humanity (she therefore described herself as a humanist rather than a feminist), and men too would benefit immeasurably from the ending of female subordination. Like class exploitation, sex oppression could therefore be ended in the interests of all, without the need for conflict, revolution or revenge.

Although Gilman's period of popularity and influence was short-lived and it is only recently that her ideas have been rediscovered, she provided an important and pioneering analysis of the inter-relations of the political, cultural, economic and personal dimensions of life that anticipates some key strands in the recent women's movement. Unlike much later feminism, however, her analysis of personal life remained within relatively conventional bounds, and she had little to say about sexuality; in this she was quite unlike her less respectable contemporary, the anarchist Emma Goldman (1869–1940).

Emma Goldman's anarchist feminism

Anarchism contains many different strands, but all push liberalism's stress on freedom, self-expression and suspicion of the state to an extreme. Communist anarchism departs furthest from liberalism, as it rejects liberalism's view of individuals as competitive property owners and its acceptance of hierarchical relations of domination and subordination in the market economy (Brown, 1993). Most early anarchists were not feminists. However, anarchism's insistence on human individuality and freedom can readily be given a feminist dimension, while the idea of a society based on trust and co-operation rather than exploitation and force finds echoes in many sections of the women's movement (Marsh, 1981). In the hands of Emma Goldman, the most prominent of the anarchist feminists in the United States in the early twentieth century, communist anarchism led to an analysis of the sexual and familial bases of women's oppression that, as many writers have commented, is in many ways remarkably close to late twentieth-century radical feminism.

According to Goldman, it was not women's right to vote or to work that was liberating, but personal autonomy expressed through free love and psychological independence: 'True emancipation begins neither at the polls nor in the courts. It begins in woman's soul' (quoted in Shulman, 1983:227). 'Democracy', she argued, was a facade that left the structures of oppression standing, while employment was simply a new form of exploitation; for a minority of 'emancipated women' it might appear liberating, but such women lost more than they gained: sacrificing all to their careers, fearful of love and childbirth, they had become 'professional automatons' cut off from 'life's essence' (in Shulman, 1979:137). The state, private property and the wage system were therefore for Goldman all interrelated systems of oppression that must be destroyed, not negotiated with; and this familiar anarchist critique was extended to attack the home, motherhood, the family and conventional morality as the core oppressors of women.

Although the utopian socialists had attacked the traditional family and sexual morality, nearly all later feminists had abjured free love and embraced respectability; for 'Red Emma', however, the free expression of sexuality became a dramatically central issue. At present, she argued, a woman is condemned to be 'a celibate, a prostitute, or a reckless, incessant breeder of hapless children', and of these three the celibate is the most unfortunate: 'There is nothing more pathetic, nothing more terrible, than this grey-grown victim of a grey-grown Morality' (in Shulman, 1979:129 and 132). Sexual liberation is not, however, simply a means of individual fulfilment, critically important though this is, but it is connected to the wider social morality to which exploitation and private property are central, and women are but one form of possession. Love and passion must therefore, she argued, be freed from ideas of ownership, fidelity and control; however, like Mary Wollstonecraft, with whom she identified (see Chapter 1 above), she often found that her heart could not always follow where reason led, and that jealousy and possessiveness were more easily eradicated in theory than in practice. Her letters show her love affairs to have brought her agonies of jealousy as well as ecstasy, as she found that 'sex is like a double-edged sword, it releases our spirit and binds it with a thousand threads' (quoted in Wexler, 1984:278–9).

Goldman's sexual radicalism and her active involvement in revolutionary politics both gained her extreme notoriety and meant that she had little influence outside the narrow circle of anarchist politics. However, Marsh argues that she faced up to fundamental issues ignored by the mainstream women's movement: 'In the short run, the organized suffragists seemed to have been following the most assured path to equality. In the long run, however, American society still struggles with the issues abandoned by them but kept alive by the unsuccessful, unpragmatic anarchist feminists' (Marsh, 1981:64; for another positive view see Brown, 1993). Against this, Spender suggests that Goldman's analysis failed because although she pinpointed the elements of personal oppression being explored by feminists today, she lacked any awareness of sex oppression or patriarchy: 'For one who is against everything, she is significantly silent on the abuse of women by men'; this failure to analyse or indict male power is combined, Spender says, with a failure to identify the potential collective power of women, so that 'sisterhood' is a concept absent from Goldman's political vocabulary, and it is left to the individual woman to assert her will against the forces of oppression (Spender, 1983a:504). Nevertheless, although she does stress the individual responsibility or women (and men) to resist power, Goldman did not isolate personal change from wider social transformation. Unlike some feminists today, she did not ignore the realities of class oppression, for she believed that true freedom for men or women could never be achieved within capitalist society, but only in a socialist society based on co-operation and the elimination of all forms of domination.

Mary Inman and American communism

Orthodox Marxists of course agreed with the last part of this analysis, while rejecting the anarchists' belief that revolution could be the product of a spontaneous act of will rather than of objective economic circumstances, long-term political organisation and class struggle. The small Communist party that survived in the United States after the First World War generally followed the 'official line' emanating from Moscow, which treated feminist issues as marginal and diversionary. Nevertheless, during the 1930s a handful of women reached relatively high positions in the organisation and from 1919 a growing sensitivity to issues of ethnicity and 'race' paved the way for a later concern with gender (Morton, 2001). This was reflected in the party press, where women were at times enabled to express their concerns; and debates on feminist issues gave rise to sophisticated theoretical developments in the work of Mary Inman.

Although Inman rejected the 'socialist feminist' label and claimed to be writing in the Marxist–Leninist tradition, the ideas expressed in her book *In Woman's Defence* (1936) go well beyond the usual orthodoxies, as she examined the ideological construction of femininity through childrearing practices, education, the media and culture (she listed ninety-nine derogatory names for women, and challenged her readers to find more than a couple for men. Weigland, 2001). She also extended her analysis beyond the conventionally defined boundaries of economics and politics to analyse oppression in the home and through the sexual double standard (which she referred to as 'fascism in the bedroom'; quoted in Shaffer, 1979:292). She claimed that *all* women are oppressed in these areas of life, and insisted that the working-class man could himself be an oppressor of his wife – she called this 'male domination under class rule' (Shaffer, 1979:85). Like some recent Marxist feminists, she attempted to extend Marxist economic categories to include women's domestic labour and to show the functional necessity of housework for capitalism as the process by which labour power is reproduced and maintained; this enabled her to argue that women as housewives could agitate and organise for changes in their working conditions rather than seeing trade union activity as the only valid form of struggle. However, although she therefore called for unity between *all* women, she was enough of a Marxist to claim that this could only be as part of the class struggle, and that the real interests of working-class men are also served by sex equality, rather than the illusory domination that is all they can enjoy under capitalism.

Inman's ideas at times have a startlingly later feel, anticipating recent debates on domestic labour and on the politics of personal life. Although they were largely rejected by the communist leadership (see Landy, 1943), Kate Weigland has recently argued that this was less sexist and intolerant than she suggested, and the Party did keep alive debates on women's issues which fed into wider 'progressive' circles in the 1940s and 50s. Although subsequent anti-communism forced many to deny any such links, Weigland argues that such debates had an effect on the children of left-wing parents (so-called 'red-diaper babies'), some of whom were to become active in the Women's Liberation Movement; there is also evidence that they had an indirect influence on the equal rights campaigner Betty Friedan (see Weigland, 2001; Horowitz, 1998; and Chapters 9 and 10 below).

No doubt during this period there were also many unsung heroines who 'washed up for socialism' (Walker, 1984:71) while thinking subversive feminist thoughts; there were, too, many other socialist feminist women famous at the time such as Crystal Eastman (Spender, 1983a, Cook, 1978), Olive Schreiner (Spender, 1983a; First and Scott, 1980; Stanley, 1983), and Dora Russell (Spender, 1983a), and others who played an important role at grass-roots level but who have only recently been rescued from oblivion, such as Selina Cooper (Liddington, 1984), Stella Browne (Rowbotham, 1977) and Hannah Mitchell (Mitchell, 1977). The insights of these women were often important at the time; however, the marginalisation of women's issues within socialism meant that their ideas seemed to die with them.

For Marxist feminism, the process has been rather different, as organised Marxism's tendency to insist that there must be a 'correct' position on all issues has meant that there has been no shortage of 'classic texts' and 'party lines'; emphasis on these, however, obscures the debates that took place, and ignores those contributions that were not officially sanctioned. As we shall see in the next two chapters, the 'Woman Question' did at times force itself onto the Marxist agenda, and became an important theoretical and practical issue for European Marxism in the late nineteenth and early twentieth centuries, where debate centred first upon the German Social Democratic party, and then upon events in Russia.

6
Marxist feminism in Germany

Before the First World War, the German socialist movement was the largest and most successful in the world; as such, it had a dominating position with the Second International (1889–1914), and debates within the German Social Democratic party (SPD) had a far-reaching influence. The SPD itself was formed in 1875 as the result of an uneasy coalition between reformist and Marxist socialists, but by the 1890s it was, under the leadership of August Bebel, fully committed, in theory at least, to a thoroughgoing Marxist position, complete with the rhetoric of class war, revolution and the inevitable victory of socialism; it was also, despite anti-socialist legislation during the 1880s, now the largest party in the German parliament. This shift in a Marxist direction was accompanied by a shift in attitudes over the role of women, as the debate between those traditionalists who thought woman's destiny lay in the home and those who welcomed her entry into the labour force was resolved in favour of the latter. However, as elsewhere in Europe, traditional ideas abut women's domestic responsibilities and men's leadership role were never really abandoned, so that there was a contradiction between 'the ideal of gender equality and ingrained notions of gender difference and hierarchy' (Gruber and Graves, 1998:9). Moreover, both at the level of general politics and on women's issues, there appeared to be growing contradictions between the party's formal commitment to the long-term goals decreed by Marxist orthodoxy and its more pragmatic pursuit of short-term reforms and parliamentary success. The ensuing debate between 'orthodox Marxists', 'radicals' and 'revisionists' was reflected in arguments over the so-called 'Woman Question' which were never really resolved.

Bebel's contribution

The single most important work in establishing the official party line on this question was Bebel's *Woman Under Socialism* (also published as *Woman in the Past, Present and Future*). First published in 1878, it went into numerous editions and was rapidly translated into many languages. As the book most frequently borrowed from workers' libraries in

Germany, it was enormously popular, and it had a much wider and more immediate impact than Engels' *The Origins of the Family, Private Property and the State* (1884), although it is the latter that is now generally regarded as the classic Marxist text on women.

Bebel agreed with Engels that women's oppression is a product of class society that will only be ended when proletarian revolution brings about a socialist society in which women will have full economic independence, and domestic work and childcare will be collectivised. However, he went beyond Engels in a number of ways, and he gave women's issues a centrality quite lacking in Marx's own writings, insisting that socialism could not succeed without the active participation of women and that 'there can be no emancipation of humanity without the social independence and equality of the sexes' (*Woman*:6). Unlike Engels, he saw that the working-class woman in paid employment was oppressed as a woman as well as exploited as a worker. He argued that under conditions of capitalist competition she could not earn as much as a man and that she was additionally worn down by domestic toil: while her husband 'avails himself of the freedom that accident gives him of having been born a man' and seeks refuge in drink and gambling, the wife 'sits up, and sews and patches deep into the night … she must work like a dray-horse; for her there is no rest or recreation' (*Woman*:103). He also identified non-economic sources of oppression such as the double standard of sexual morality and the restrictive effects of conventional female dress. This led him to argue that all women, regardless of class, have some interests in common and might unite on some demands: he therefore saw female suffrage not only as a means of furthering the class struggle but as an individual entitlement based on women's contribution to society and a weapon needed by women *as a group* to defend their interests.

Despite all this, Bebel's analysis has found little favour with recent feminists (see Vogel, 1983; Coole, 1988; Hunt, 1986 and 1988; Boxer and Quataert, 1978; but see also Draper and Lipow, 1976, for a more positive view). In particular, it is argued that, although he was very aware of non-economic issues, his over-rigid loyalty to the Marxist tradition meant that he could not really confront or explain them. The solution for women could ultimately only be to join the fight against capitalism; the proletarian man and woman must realise that they were both 'tugging at the same rope' and there would be no need for an autonomous struggle against patriarchy, for this would necessarily disappear under socialism. As we shall see in Chapter 13, the problem of whether patriarchy has an independent existence and how it can be confronted within left-wing movements is one that Marxist feminists are struggling with today; it was also one faced but never really acknowledged by those women in the Second International who attempted to put Bebel's ideas into practice.

Clara Zetkin

The foremost of these was Clara Zetkin (1857–1933). Her name has since been eclipsed by that of her contemporary Rosa Luxemburg (1871–1919) and to a lesser extent by Eleanor Marx Aveling, Karl Marx's daughter; at the time, however, she was effectively 'the leading woman of European socialism' (Foner, 1984:42). Unlike Luxemburg, she concentrated her energies on women's issues, and as editor of the SPD's women's journal *Die Gleichheit* ('Equality') she addressed the theoretical and practical problems involved in recruiting women to the socialist cause. She had a considerable measure of success in ensuring that the 'Woman Question' remained on the agenda of international socialism (even if official policy was not always matched by genuine commitment), and it was largely due to her efforts that Germany had by 1900 'a large, well-organised, and extremely militant socialist women's movement' (Vogel, 1983:107). However, although by the mid-1890s she held a leading position in the SPD, she increasingly found herself in conflict with the other party leaders both on women's issues and on the whole question of whether socialism could be brought about by piecemeal reform and parliamentary methods. Here Zetkin's determinedly radical position isolated her not only from the party leadership, but from a new generation of women party members who were concerned more with welfare and children than with challenging the power structure or achieving wider social change, for 'The transformation of Social Democracy into a state-supportive reform party had its parallel in the metamorphosis of the proletarian women's movement into a training ground for social angels' (Thonnessen, 1973:9). In 1917 Zetkin left the party, in 1919 she was elected to the German parliament as a member of the newly-formed Communist party and she spent most of her later years in the Soviet Union. As Evans has pointed out (Evans, 1987), Zetkin was a figure of opposition rather than orthodoxy within the international communist movement; as the expression of views contrary to the Stalinist party line became increasingly difficult, any independent discussion of the 'Woman Question' was effectively silenced.

Hostility to bourgeois feminism

For Zetkin, as for many other socialist women, Bebel's book had been an inspirational starting-point: 'It was more than a book, it was an event, a great deed' (quoted in Foner, 1984:22). She accepted wholeheartedly his central thesis of the necessary interconnections between the aspirations of women and the achievement of socialism; indeed, she went even further than Bebel in her insistence on the primacy of class over gender interests and her denial that middle-class and proletarian women could ever share a common goal. This meant that in practice she was extremely hostile to 'bourgeois feminists' with their demands for improved education, employment prospects and legal status, and she refused point-blank to co-operate with them in their campaigns for the vote. This position was backed up by a materialist analysis of the modern women's movement which argued that it was composed of three separate strands based on three opposing class positions: the 'Upper Ten Thousand' were concerned with freeing property rights from their last feudal restrictions by granting them to women; women of the petty bourgeoisie and intelligentsia needed economic independence at a time of capitalist crisis when many men could no longer afford to maintain a wife; and working-class women were struggling alongside their men to bring about an end to capitalism. Like Luxemburg, whose diatribes against bourgeois women were even more vitriolic (she called them 'parasites of the parasites of the social body'), she believed therefore that there could be no common ground, and that class loyalties would reassert themselves as soon as legal and political rights were won. Proletarian women therefore needed political and legal rights only as part of their fight against capitalism, and there could be no common front with 'bourgeois feminists' involved in a superficial struggle against men.

Her analysis also meant that the very possibility of sex oppression within the working class was ruled out of order. Like Engels and Bebel, she argued that the lack of property in the working class and the entry of proletarian women into industry meant that there was no material basis or motivation for the continuation of gender inequality. In practice, of course, she was well aware that all was not rosy in the proletarian garden, and that even in the SPD the most old-fashioned chauvinism still flourished. Not only was there still a strong strand that believed that the role of a socialist woman could only lie in providing a secure domestic base for her husband, while others were able to concede the principle of more active participation only if this were not at the expense of their own hot dinners, but women's issues were repeatedly marginalised, trivialised and removed from the mainstream agenda; like other women leaders, she was also the subject of cruel sexist jokes. Until 1908, women could not join the SPD officially, as the law in many German states still forbade women to join political organisations or to attend public meetings; they could therefore become involved only by joining the semi-autonomous women's section. Although Zetkin opposed separatism, she came to see the advantages of such a distinct women's group within the party where, in a supportive atmosphere, women could develop the skills that would enable them to participate in the wider movement and, by building up a firm understanding of their own interests, maximise their influence and ensure that their needs were not swept aside. Zetkin's views were not, however, acceptable to the party leadership, and the resulting integration of women into the mainstream after 1908 effectively meant the marginalisation of radical women such as herself and the silencing of an independent women's voice.

Zetkin's methodological framework did not, however, enable her to confront such problems theoretically, nor did she expand her analysis to explore the problems of sexuality and domestic responsibility that had been raised by Bebel. Here again she was certainly not unaware of the issues involved. In her speeches she could easily draw applause by references to the problem of husbands who expect to be waited upon by their wives, and in conversation with Lenin in 1920 (recalled by Zetkin in 1924) she acknowledged his complaint that 'at the meetings arranged for reading and discussion with working women, sex and marriage problems come first. They are said to be the main objects of interest in your political instruction and educational work'. She attempted to justify herself by claiming that such discussions could lead to an understanding of the different historical forms of the family and their dependence on economics: 'All roads lead to Rome. Every truly Marxist analysis of an important part of the ideological superstructure of society … had to lead to an analysis of bourgeois society and its foundations, private property.' However, when Lenin expressed doubts as to whether such analysis actually occurred, she agreed and said that she had therefore ensured that personal matters were no longer the focal point of discussion (in Lenin, 1977:102–3). The problem here was that for Zetkin such issues could only be seen as part of the ideological superstructure rather than as subjects in their own right. This reduction of the most intimate problems to an economic basis is one which many feminists today find unsatisfactory, for removing male oppression from the political agenda did not mean that it disappeared in the home, the party or in society as a whole; it means, however, that it could not be confronted, and that while patriarchy remained unnamed by Marxist feminists it could not effectively be challenged.

Although the 'bourgeois feminists' (or 'women's righters' as they were often called) were sometimes more able to identify instances of sex oppression, their liberal individualist perspective did not allow for the possibility of the systematic domination of women by men, or for the ways in which such oppression might serve the needs of capitalism. Some of course did criticise social inequality, but many were in most respects highly conservative, and few were prepared to work with or join a party which was still formally committed to class war and revolution and which refused to allow the reality of any cross-class gender interests. As elsewhere in Europe, German socialist leaders were also opposed to cross-party alliances with non-socialist women (Guer and Graves, 1998).

Therefore, although by 1900 Marxists and feminists shared common demands, the women's movement remained irretrievably split at the level of both theory and practical political activity. Many commentators have suggested that this split was responsible for German women's lack of success in achieving the legal rights won earlier in many other European countries, but this failure has to be seen in the more general context of the weakness of liberalism in the German political system (see Evans, 1980).

Lily Braun and the revisionist debate

Nevertheless a few feminists did join the SPD. Of these, the most notable was Lily Braun (1865–1916), and the ensuing battle between her and Zetkin over the correct socialist solution to the 'Woman Question' reflected a wider debate over the future direction of the party and the nature of socialism itself. By the end of the century, it seemed to many that the electoral success of the SPD meant that it was becoming a part of the very system it was dedicated to overthrowing, and that its increasing preoccupation with short-term goals and attracting votes meant that it was no longer a revolutionary party. For the 'revisionists' led by Eduard Bernstein, these changes were to be welcomed. In *Evolutionary Socialism* (1899) he argued against an approach to socialism based on economic determinism, and he demanded that the party's official ideology be revised to accept that capitalism was neither on the point of collapse nor leading to the impoverishment of the working class. On the contrary, he claimed, gradual reform was leading to a general improvement in living conditions and class conflict was losing its significance; from this perspective, achievable short-term gains were more important than a mythical predetermined goal, and socialism was transformed from the inevitable product of economic forces to an ethical ideal, for which all men of good-will could work. This opened the door to co-operation across class lines, and it meant that feminist goals, like other benefits of socialism, need not be postponed until 'after the revolution' but could be achieved as part of the gradual process of social change; in this context, legal and political rights were not to be seen as weapons enabling proletarian women to participate more fully in the class struggle, but as valuable ends in themselves. This kind of approach was attractive to feminists like Braun, who also argued for the establishment of co-operative living arrangements, which would both relieve women of the burden of household toil and encourage the growth of the co-operative feelings that would be required in a socialist society. Luxemburg had long rejected co-operatives as a misguided attempt to return to a pre-capitalist lifestyle that could never lead to socialism, and Zetkin condemned Braun's ideas as 'the last blossoming of utopianism in its most dangerous, opportunistic form' (quoted in Quataert, 1978:130). She argued that such experiments would be a diversionary luxury affordable only by the affluent and that, because they concerned only patterns of consumption, leaving production quite unchallenged, they could never become an agent of social transformation. She also rejected Braun's interest in birth control and the call by some socialists for a 'birth strike' which it was said would both ease the burdens of working-class women and deprive capitalism of its next generation of soldiers. This, Zetkin argued, was a dangerous distraction from the real problems that falsely blamed poverty on over-breeding rather than capitalist exploitation; it might help individual women, but by reducing the size of the working class it could only harm its long-term class prospects.

Although the ideas of the revisionists were never formally accepted by the party, the 'orthodox' line became increasingly out of kilter with political reality, as the SPD combined formal loyalty to Marxist dogma with increasingly reformist practice; this rightward move was symbolised when in 1914 all but one of the SPD members of parliament voted to support Germany's war effort. Like Luxemburg, Zetkin vigorously opposed the war, and in 1915 she organised an international conference of socialist women to campaign against it. Whereas some mainstream feminists also attempted to co-ordinate international activity against the war, they tended to see it as a manifestation of male aggression that must be countered by female pacifism (see Chapter 4 above). Zetkin, however, true to her materialist approach, saw it as a product of capitalist imperialism; the campaign against the war was therefore part of the international socialist attack on capitalism in which women, because they did not face conscription, were able to play a major role.

Modification of Zetkin's position

Although Zetkin frequently opposed the SPD's drift to reformism and its prioritisation of electoral popularity, she herself may not have been immune to such pressures, and some of her ideas were significantly modified over time. In particular, her early analysis of the family as an oppressive institution and her insistence on the importance of women's participation in trade union and political activity gave way to the reassurance that under socialism the family would remain as a moral unit. She insisted that 'It is out of the question that the task of socialist women's activity should be to alienate proletarian women from their duties as wives and mothers', and that 'Many a wife and many a mother who imbues her husband and children with class-consciousness accomplishes just as much as the women comrades whom we see at our meetings'

(Draper and Lipow, 1976:199 and 120). This shift was reflected in Zetkin's editorship of the SPD women's journal *Die Gleichheit*. She originally saw this as an important theoretical publication, providing information on trade unions, strikes, wage levels and working conditions and aimed at the most 'advanced' women workers. In practice, however, although female party membership grew rapidly (to reach over 16 per cent of total membership by 1914), most of the new recruits were not, as had been expected, factory workers but the non-working wives of male party members. Zetkin was persuaded to aim much more of her material at these new members, and *Die Gleichheit* came to include practical household tips as well as ideas on how to instill socialist values in children and a general reassurance that, in keeping the home fires burning, women were making an important contribution to the socialist cause. Evans has defended this move: 'Zetkin's increasing tendency to appeal to the proletarian women as wives and mothers rather than as workers was no more than a gradual recognition that this was what, in their own consciousness and that of their husbands, they were' (Evans, 1987:26). However, while failure to challenge this consciousness might lead to political popularity in the short run, in the long run it could only mean that women were marginalised in the decision-making processes and that power relationships between men and women remained unexamined.

In 1903, Zetkin wrote: '[Marx's] materialist concept of history has not supplied us with any ready-made formulas concerning the women's question, yet it has done something much more important: it has given us the correct unerring method to comprehend that question' (in Foner, 1984:93). Her own attempts to put this method into practice gave her a new perspective on the women's movement by enabling her to disentangle some of the class interests involved, but it led her to a too-easy rejection of any idea of shared gender interests across class lines and it prevented her from identifying or challenging patriarchial practices and beliefs at a theoretical level. It also meant that she came to defend a position whereby women played an essentially supportive role in a socialist movement dominated by men and in which their concerns were seen as trivial or diversionary; despite her own undoubted commitment to sex equality, it seems therefore that her methods could not lead her to her goal.

Some critics of Marxism would argue that such shortcomings are the inevitable product of an inadequate theory which, in seeking to reduce everything to an economic cause, is quite unable to grasp the all-encompassing nature of patriarchal power and its manifestation in personal as well as public life. Certainly, for some later Marxists the legacy of Zetkin and the Second International has been a crude economic determinism and a hostility to feminism as a diversionary and divisive movement of middle-class women. Today, Marxist feminists are however attempting to show that Marxism can provide the basis for a more sophisticated approach. The adequacy of the Marxist approach to the 'Woman Question' was also of course explored in Russia, where from late 1917 state power was in the hands of Marxists; although all kinds of problems arose in putting theory into practice and many gains were lost with Stalinist repression, it was here that the first serious attempt to extend Marxist analysis to questions of sex, morality and family life was made by Alexandra Kollontai.

7

Marxist feminism in Russia

Although the Russian revolution has often been seen as a testing-ground for Marxist theory, it must be stressed that for Marx himself communism was essentially the product of industrial capitalism, in which technology could be used to liberate men from drudgery, and problems of scarcity would be ended. He also believed that, as capitalism was becoming a worldwide system, communism would replace it on a world scale. Neither of these conditions was in place when the Russian Bolsheviks seized power at the end of 1917. Although Russia had been industrialising rapidly it was still basically a peasant society, and the war with Germany had had a devastating effect on the economy, while events in Russia did not spark off successful proletarian revolutions in the more advanced European nations, but were followed by both civil war and foreign invasion. Many western defenders of Marxism would therefore argue that the material preconditions for a successful communist revolution simply did not exist in Russia in the early twentieth century, and that failure was inevitable. From the point of view of the 'Woman Question', the resources needed to liberate women were not available: Engels, Bebel and Zetkin had all argued that women in communist society would be freed from domestic toil, but the provision of adequate public facilities was a luxury unattainable in a society fighting for its very survival. Nevertheless, partly because significant numbers of women were involved in revolutionary activity, the issue was not simply set aside in the immediate aftermath of revolution. Indeed, the resulting social dislocation and questioning of all traditional arrangements and values meant that relationships between men and women were fiercely debated and some serious attempts were made to put Marxist theory into practice; although of course the Soviet Union did not solve the 'Woman Question', the ideas and experiences of these early years may still have relevance for feminists today.

Early Russian feminism

The earlier history of feminism in Russia was in some ways similar to that in Western Europe, as from the mid-nineteenth century middle-class women increasingly demanded the right to education, to a career, to full legal equality and the vote. As in Germany, this was in the context of a society in which liberalism was weak and only left-wing organisations seemed prepared to treat women's issues seriously. Therefore, although many feminists remained true to their class, others came to link feminist concerns with ideas of wider political, economic and social change. Unlike Germany, however, the parliamentary road to socialism was firmly closed, and significant numbers of women came to be involved in more radical and revolutionary political movements – indeed, 'the vocation of revolutionary was the only one open to women which would greet her as an equal, allow her talents freely to unfold, and permit her to rise to the top' (Stites, 1978: 153).

Radical involvement ranged from outright terrorism (it was a woman who assassinated the Tsar in 1881) to the mass Populist movement 'to the people' in the 1870s, when thousands of young people attempted to bring ideas of socialist revolution to the peasants. Female involvement in subversive movements was by the early twentieth century so great that the authorities had to build a new women's prison. The early revolutionaries were generally intellectuals rather than peasants or workers; as such they were able to support feminist ideals at an abstract level 'unencumbered by the need to compromise with political reality or take account of the anti-feminist prejudices of a working-class following' (Evans, 1977:179), and in some circles quite radical notions of gender identity and the need for female autonomy were discussed (Engel, 1978). From the 1850s, some were also influenced by the nihilist idea of immediate personal liberation through total moral, sexual and intellectual freedom. This left Russia with a heritage of sexual radicalism and experimentation which had been quite lacking in German left-wing culture, and which was to surface in the years following the revolution.

Such individualistic solutions were, however, anathema to orthodox Marxist analysis and, as the influence of Marxism increased towards the end of the nineteenth century, any idea that sexual questions might be seen as an autonomous problem disappeared; as in Germany the 'Woman Question' came to be seen as an aspect of the wider 'Social Question' which would automatically be resolved in future socialist society. Although there were significant numbers of women Bolsheviks, most toed the party line and 'did not fundamentally challenge gender roles but tended to justify what they did by reference to their traditional domestic resonsibilities' (McDermid and Hillyar, 1999:200–1). These 'Bolshevichkni' were, however, more inclined than male activists to see the need for immediate and practical action to address women's situation after the revolution (Clements, 1997).

The first serious attempt to apply orthodox Marxism to the situation of Russian women was probably made in 1900 by Nadezhda Krupskaya

(Lenin's wife). In her pamphlet *The Woman Worker* she described the appalling conditions of work facing Russian women in both town and country, but she followed the line already laid down by Engels, Bebel and Zetkin in arguing that women's participation in the labour force was ultimately progressive and that liberation could only come about through participation in the class struggle. Although her analysis was not original, her pamphlet enjoyed considerable popularity and helped ensure that women's demands for full legal and political equality were from 1903 included in the party programme (see Stites, 1978:239–43). She also went further than other Marxists in challenging traditional gender roles: in a 1910 article, she argued that under socialism boys as well as girls should be taught 'how to sew, knit, and darn clothes' and to do 'everything which cannot be avoided in life and an ignorance of which makes a person helpless in life and dependent on others' (quoted in Attwood, 1999:9; see also McDermid and Hillyar, 1999).

Lenin himself did not display the indifference or hostility to women's demands that Krupskaya complained of in other men. In particular, he went beyond the usual platitudes about legal rights and future equality to an insistence on the need to liberate women from domestic drudgery which Vogel claims was 'unique in the Marxist literature' (Vogel, 1983:121). Not only did he argue that women would be liberated by technology and public provision, but he demanded that the old male 'slave-owners point of view' be rooted out, and he roundly condemned 'the common sight of a man calmly watching a woman wear herself out with trivial, monotonous, strength- and time-consuming work ... and watching her spirit shrinking, her mind growing dull, her heartbeat growing fainter, and her will growing slack' (in Lenin, 1977:115 and 111). He also agreed that, because of their specific needs and problems, separate organisations and methods might be needed to recruit women and involve them in revolutionary politics; he therefore approved the publication of a separate women's newspaper from 1913, and supported the establishment of a special women's department (the Zhenotdel) in 1919.

Women's issues were not, however, a political priority for Lenin, and he saw the Zhenotdel more as a way of educating women in socialism than responding to their views. Despite his frequently quoted comments on housework, he never really questioned whether or how men could be persuaded to change their attitudes and, like most other Marxists he seemed to have assumed that socialised housework would remain the responsibility of women (Attwood notes that there is no record of Krupskaya challenging him on this. Attwood, 1999). In general, Lenin refused to treat problems of sex and marriage as serious political issues, regarding them as a frivolous distraction at a time of revolutionary crisis. Trotsky, in contrast, claimed that such neglect of the social and personal dimensions of women's oppression led to a too-narrow concept of liberation. He argued that equality within the family was infinitely harder to achieve than political or workplace equality, he saw male attitudes as a major problem and he saw changes within the home as central for the success of communism: 'From the enslavement of women grew prejudices and superstitions which shaped the children of the new generation ... Freeing the mother means cutting the last umbilical cord linking the people with the dark and superstitious past' (*Women and the Family*, 1970: 34–5, written 1924–5; see also *Problems of Life*, 1924). However, although he identified areas of concern, Trotsky too failed to give such ideas more than lip service or to make them the focus of his political activity. In general, therefore, although their sympathies may have been genuine, the male communist leaders failed to take on board the serious practical and theoretical issues involved if women were to achieve full equality with men; from their perspective, it was an issue for which Marxism already provided clear answers, and which therefore need not involve any questioning of orthodox theory or political priorities. It was left to a handful of women activists, of whom Alexandra Kollontai (1873–1952) was the most theoretically innovative, to explore the implications of the quest for equality, and to discover that the solution of the 'Woman Question' was perhaps more complex than orthodox theory suggested (on her contemporary, Inessa Armand, who was the first head of the Zhenotdel, see Elwood, 1992).

The ideas of Alexandra Kollontai

Kollontai once claimed that 'Women, and their fate, have occupied my whole life. It was their lot which pushed me into socialism' (quoted in Stites, 1978:250). In fact, however, the reverse appears to have been true, as Kollontai's early commitment to socialism showed no awareness of the special needs of women; on the contrary, it was what she saw as the feminist threat to the socialist movement that first drew her attention to women's issues. At first she simply upheld Marxist orthodoxy as interpreted by Zetkin, and campaigned vigorously against what she saw as a selfish, egotistic bourgeois women's movement, demanding that this be replaced by the class-based solidarity of proletarian men and women. Soon, however, she became much more critical of socialist practice, and aware of the ways in which women's needs were marginalised by the male-dominated party hierarchy; she therefore demanded that separate women's organisations be established within the party, and fought vigorously for women's issues to be kept to the forefront of the political agenda.

Practical achievements

The provisional government set up after the February revolution had given women civil and political rights, and when in October 1917 Kollontai became the first woman in modern history to hold Cabinet office as Commissar (Minister) of Social Welfare, her first task was to complete the process by giving women full legal independence and equality within marriage, legalising abortion, ending illegitimacy as a legal category and establishing the principle of equal pay. She also laid the legal foundations for state provision of maternity and child health care and succeeded in committing the party to the principle of communal housework, childcare and eating facilities (a pledge withdrawn by the party in the early 1920s). Although lack of resources often meant that such decrees could only represent statements of intent, they were quite an extraordinary achievement given the chaotic conditions and demands being made on the new government. They reflected both the determination of individual women like Kollontai and a more general shift in attitudes that had taken place since Marx's time; this in turn was a result both of the impact of feminism and of the increased strength and organisation of the female workforce.

However, the Marxist solution to the 'Woman Question' had promised more than legal equality and welfare rights, for these were already being won in capitalist societies; rather it claimed that women's economic independence, based on full participation in production and liberation from domestic toil, would transform the whole of private life, as morality, the family and relationships between men and women would be based on free choice and equality rather than dependence and exploitation. As we have seen, Engels, Bebel and Zetkin interpreted all this in a fairly conservative way, for they saw freely-chosen monogamy as the likely form of future sexual relationships, and Zetkin in particular came to stress that the family would continue as a social and moral unit even when it ceased to serve an economic function. Kollontai, however, was much more radical; she was also much less prepared to agree that the attitudes underlying existing gender relations would automatically change with economic progress. Rather, she argued that they must be tackled in their own right, and that the ideological superstructure is not *only* a reflection of the economic base but can also itself play a role in social transformation.

In practical terms, this meant that the situation of women could not simply be changed by state enactment or provision, but must also involve a change of consciousness; this in turn would be both cause and result of changing circumstances and women's full participation in the building of socialism. It was this principle that Kollontai tried to put into practice in her brief period as head of the women's department (Zhenotdel) in 1920–1. Although she has recently been accused of being out of touch with ordinary Soviet women (McDermid and Hillyar 1999), Kollontai saw activity within the Zhenotdel as a two-way process, by which women would be educated and informed of their rights and enabled to bring their needs to the attention of the party; she also sought to combine practical help with theoretical discussion and challenges to traditional patriarchal attitudes. Organisationally, the Zhenotdel operated both nationally and at grass-roots level, where there was a loose federation of discussion and self-help groups. The idea was that women should be involved in their own emancipation and that they themselves should, with state help, organise the nurseries, laundries and educational campaigns that would liberate them. It was also intended that experience in separate groups would give women the skill and confidence to assert their own interests and to work together with men in mixed trade union and party organisations. Certainly women's political participation did increase, particularly at local level, and the Zhenotdel penetrated even the distant Muslim areas of the Soviet Union. This was, however, the period of 'war communism', when the country was fighting for its very survival: with widespread famine, the economy in ruins, transport almost non-existent and steel production less than five per cent of the pre-war level, nursery provision and women's education were hardly going to be seen as priorities, and in practice material conditions for most women – as for most men – deteriorated sharply. It was also a period in which the whole idea of the kind of 'revolution from below' favoured by Kollontai was viewed with increasing suspicion by the party leaders; indeed her support for an opposition group and her attack on what she saw as increased centralisation and bureaucratisation within the party were seen by Lenin as a threat to party discipline and unity. At a secret session of the 10th Party Congress in 1921 a resolution was passed banning factions, and in 1922 Kollontai was effectively removed from the centre of political debate and influence by being sent on a minor diplomatic mission to Norway. With her fall from power, the officially sanctioned attack on patriarchy ended, and the Zhenotdel concentrated on more low-key welfare issues; in 1929 it was abolished by Stalin on the grounds that the 'Woman Question' had been solved.

Sexual morality and communism

Despite her failure to achieve the kind of radical transformation for which she hoped, Kollontai's work remains of major theoretical importance. She is best remembered (and frequently misunderstood) for her views on sexuality, but these can only be understood in the wider context of her vision of communism as a form of society developed by the people themselves and in which selfish competition and individualism are replaced by loving comradeship and co-operation. Communism for Kollontai was therefore not simply about redistribution of economic resources or public ownership of the means of production, but about changing the very nature of men and women. Such changed people would relate to each other in ways very different from those which we know today, and their behaviour would be based on a new, higher form of morality; this morality however would not simply be the automatic by-product of economic change, for struggles in the ideological superstructure would themselves help bring about material change: 'The new morality is created by a new economy, but we will not build a new economy without the support of a new morality' (in Holt, 1977:270). From this perspective, changes in sexual morality were not simply important in their own right, but part of the process of creating good socialist men and women. They were also central to challenging men's power over women, and here Kollontai made an important step in identifying the political significance of areas of life conventionally defined as 'private', and in attempting to extend Marxist analysis to morality, sexuality and the family without simply reducing these to passive reflectors of the economic base.

Kollontai agreed with earlier Marxist writers that bourgeois morality was based on hypocrisy, inequality and possession, but she extended this to argue that no one in capitalist society could escape its effects and that it generated unequal power relations in the most intimate areas of life, even when these were not based upon economic dependence. 'True love' in capitalist society was therefore an impossibility for the working proletarian woman and the 'career girl' as much for the dependent bourgeois wife, for sex and marriage had come to be based upon emotional and psychological as well as economic inequality. This meant that Engels' solution of economic independence for women could not on its own lead to true sexual equality, which requires a 'radical reform of the human psyche'; this in turn, however, could only come about as part of the general communist transformation of society.

It was on the nature of the desirable form of future proletarian morality that Kollontai parted company with earlier writers most decisively, for while they tended to see genuine monogamy as the ideal form of sexual relationship, she was much more concerned with the dangers of sexual exclusiveness, which she suggested might be contrary both to the interests of women and to the welfare of society as a whole. On this she has been much misrepresented and misunderstood, as her enemies portrayed her as both preacher and practitioner of casual promiscuity and the 'glass of water' theory of sex that saw it as a simple physical need that should be satisfied as readily as thirst. In fact, her own sexual activities would probably have passed unnoticed in a man (she married twice and had two other recorded affairs), and she certainly never advocated promiscuity. She did however hold the view, then thought shocking in a woman, that sex was neither sinful nor shameful, but that it could be a high form of human activity, and she showed sympathetic tolerance for the sexual experimentation that characterised the chaotic post-revolutionary years, in which rejection of bourgeois values was equated by some with rejection of all sexual restraint. Here she differed markedly from Lenin, who spoke with contempt and disgust of those 'yellow-beaked fledglings newly hatched from their bourgeois-tainted eggs' who preached casual sexual gratification: 'To be sure, thirst has to be quenched. But would a normal person lie down in the gutter and drink from a puddle? Or even from a glass whose edge has been greased by many lips?' (Lenin, 1977:104–5). However, although she saw such excesses as excusable or even inevitable at a time of social upheaval, Kollontai did not think them desirable. She saw that for women, sexual 'liberation' all too often meant 'liberty, equality and maternity' (Stites, 1978:360); she also objected to the reduction of human sexuality to an animal activity, and saw promiscuity as an anti-social form of behaviour that both endangered the health of the workers and distracted them from more serious tasks.

Nevertheless, the solution for Kollontai could not be as simple as Engels' basically monogamous 'individual sex love'. Earlier in her life she had believed in the possibility of one 'great love' (and the permissibility of other relationships before this was found), but by the 1920s she believed such all-consuming passion should have no place in communist society: 'proletarian ideology cannot accept exclusiveness and "all-embracing love"' (in Holt, 1977:288). It was not simply the idea of ownership involved, or the fact that the woman in such a relationship would still inevitably give more of herself than the man; rather she believed that such intense love between two individuals was essentially anti-social, isolating the couple from the wider community and reducing their interest in the general social good. Such relationships would, she believed, in fact become *unnecessary*, for they were a response to the isolation engendered by capitalist society, in which love and closeness could be experienced in no other way. Communist society would, however, be based on companionship and solidarity, so that intimacy and emotional comfort would not be confined to the family or sexual relationships, and sexual love (Eros) would become part of an expanded human capacity for love: 'In the new and collective society, where interpersonal relations develop against a background of joyful unity and companionship, Eros will develop an honourable place as an emotional experience multiplying human happiness' (in Holt, 1977:290).

For some critics, this seems a rather cold-blooded insistence on the joys of collective solidarity rather than individual love and passion ('The old idea was "all for the loved one", communist morality demands all for the collective', in Holt, 1977:231), but Kollontai, who had by the 1920s read western writers on sexuality such as Havelock Ellis and probably Freud, was seeking to transform rather than to deny the role of the erotic in future society. In this context, she argued that sexual love would not be a simple animal activity based on physical attraction alone (which she called 'Wingless Eros'), but would also involve the sensitive and comradely love of equals, in which the partners would retain both their personal integrity (there would be no 'slavish dissolution of personality') and their commitment to the collective. It is here, when she expands on the joys of 'Winged Eros' that other critics have accused her of flowery romanticism and a woolly utopianism that could have little basis in reality; from a radical feminist perspective, her failure to consider the possibility of homosexuality as a valid form of relationship or strategy for change might also be a problem. As McDermid and Hillyar have recently noted, her views were also alien to 'ordinary' Soviet women, who had more immediate and practical concerns (McDermid and Hillyar, 1999). However, the importance of Kollontai's ideas perhaps lay less in the precise nature of her views on future relationships than in her perception of how such apparently private matters intersect with wider questions of social morality. The 'correct' form of interpersonal relationships was not for her something that would be automatically discovered in the future, but was an issue that must be fought for as part of the class struggle. Ideology was therefore not a straightforward reflection of class interests, but itself an arena of conflict; here Kollontai's ideas anticipate those of the Italian Marxist Antonio Gramsci and those later Marxists who argued for a degree of 'superstructural autonomy'.

The family, childcare and motherhood

Changes in the nature and role of the family were for Kollontai similarly both effect and cause of wider social change. As we have seen, Engels thought that collective housekeeping and childcare were essential for the liberation of women, and although Zetkin downplayed the latter, public provision of such services as laundry, cooking and cleaning were by the early twentieth century clearly-established Marxist principles, which were firmly endorsed by both Lenin and Kollontai. Immediately after the revolution, some steps were taken to put these ideas into practice (and also to ensure that people got fed at a time of acute shortages), and it has been estimated that in 1921 93 per cent of Moscow residents ate in public dining halls (Elwood, 1992:249). However, such provision was not usually on anything like the scale required, and the standard of collective facilities was appalling; as Trotsky reported, many early experiments ended in dirt and chaos, and 'the communal houses were often grim and depressing, the shared kitchens chaotic and the creches makeshift' (quoted in Rowbotham, 1972:148). Kollontai never abandoned the goal of good public services based on the perceived needs and co-operation of those who used them, while Trotsky came to favour small-scale experiments in collective housekeeping until such time as mass public provision could be afforded; however, as Stalin consolidated his power during the 1920s such views were effectively silenced.

Childcare was a much more complex and emotive issue than housework, and here again Kollontai was more radical than some more cautious Marxists, stressing the anti-social aspects of the traditional family which, she claimed, was not only inefficient and oppressive but an important means of transmitting and perpetuating old bourgeois values. She therefore argued strongly in favour of communal childrearing, through which 'the new generation will, from the earliest years, learn to value the beauties of solidarity and sociability, and become accustomed to looking at the world through the prism of the collective and not through his own selfish ego' (quoted in Stites, 1978:267). Communal childrearing would also mean that women would no longer have to sacrifice everything for motherhood, and would never have to make the kind of agonising decision that Kollontai herself made when she chose to leave her young daughter in the care of her former husband in order to dedicate herself to revolutionary activity. Her proposals did not mean, she insisted, that children would be forcibly removed from their mothers. Indeed she stressed the importance of the maternal instinct and the joys of motherhood that could be experienced once the drudgery, poverty and ill-health that surrounded it were removed; she claimed that the mother could be 'relieved of the cross of motherhood and be left with the smile of joy which arises from the contact of the woman with her child' (in Holt, 1977:143). However, in the context of a caring communist society, the maternal instinct would have a wider meaning and higher social value than at present: 'Of course the maternal instinct is strong, and there is no need to stifle it. But why should this instinct be narrowly limited to the love and care of one's own child? ... [in communist society] the woman not only cares for her own children, but has a genuine affection for all children' (in Holt, 1977:144). Here again we have the idea of a reciprocal interaction between economic base and superstructure: communism provides both the material conditions and the sense of shared responsibility and affection that make collective childcare possible; collective childcare promotes the values that will enable communist economic relations to work, and it also allows women to enter social production, where they learn the good socialist values that they can feed back to their children. From this perspective, the question of childcare was not simply a woman's issue, a kind of 'optional extra' to be provided when times were good, but an integral part of the process of establishing a communist society.

Recent feminists have not found all this entirely satisfactory. Thus Diana Coole is highly suspicious of her idea that elements of personal life should be assessed in terms of their social consequences, for she sees this as opening the door to a Stalinist type manipulation of ideas, the family and sexuality (Coole, 1993). However, Kollontai was not saying that sexual and familial relationships *should* not be seen as purely private, but that they *cannot* be, for the attitudes and experiences they engender inevitably have an influence beyond the individuals immediately involved. The desirability of particular forms of manipulation (or, from a more benign point of view, education) may therefore be questioned, but this does not in itself invalidate her analysis. Other critics dislike Kollontai's stress on the maternal instinct and her glorification of the potential joys of motherhood. Such emphasis on sexual difference inevitably falls foul of the liberal feminist stress on equality. Although others share her attempt to 'envalue' the role of motherhood (which has interesting affinities with Mary Wollstonecraft'c claim that good citizens require good mothering, see Chapter 1 above), they criticise her failure to examine the role of fathers, or to question the sexual division of labour in any kind of detail. It seems that, for Kollontai, as for nearly all Marxist and socialist feminists of her day, women are to be enabled to be both mothers and producers but men are to be only producers; the idea that men might, through parenting, increase their capacity for sensitivity, caring and co-operation (values which Kollontai saw as central in a communist society) is never explored. Moreover, while women were mothering, collectively or otherwise, they could not be contributing equally to decision-making in the public arena; it would therefore tend to be men who would decide on political and economic priorities – including, presumably, the level of provision for childcare facilities.

It is, however, Kollontai's views on the social responsibilities attached to motherhood that are most out of line with recent feminist thought. Here she argued that in communist society, where the community cares for the pregnant mother and her child, maternity is no longer a matter of individual choice but a question of social duty. This meant that in communist society there would be no need for abortion and that a pregnant woman must, as a responsible member of society, care for her foetus by looking after her own health, for 'in these months she no longer belongs to herself; she is serving the collective, "producing" from her own flesh and blood a new social unit of labor, a new member of the labor republic' (in Holt, 1977:144); it also meant that she had a duty to breast-feed her baby as long as this might be necessary. Kollontai therefore totally denied women any abstract or absolute right to control their own reproduction and treat their bodies as they pleased. Reproduction was as much a social matter as production was; it was therefore an area of legitimate social concern that could be subject to collective planning rather than individual choice. For a generation of feminists for whom 'a woman's right to choose' is often a cardinal principle of faith, such views seem startlingly retrogressive and dangerously close to the forced motherhood policies of Stalin and, more recently, Ceausescu of Romania. Kollontai did not, however, argue that such responsibilities should be forced on women in an unequal, oppressive or selfish society, but saw them as arising naturally out of the wider and more generous social relationships that she thought would characterise mature communist society. In this context the idea that childbearing might involve duties as well as rights takes on a very different significance; until such time, however, women could not be expected to see motherhood as a social responsibility rather than an individual burden, and Kollontai therefore supported the legalisation of abortion in 1917 (a right revoked by Stalin in 1936).

After 1923, Kollontai had no real influence on events in the Soviet Union, and her views on the family were officially declared erroneous. The remainder of her political life was largely spent outside the country in a series of diplomatic posts, and she kept silent on Stalin's policies, although these were the antithesis of everything she had ever worked for. Alix Holt has however argued that her work 'represents the most important contribution of the period to the development of the relationship between the women's movement and the socialist programme, and her contribution to this long-neglected area of Marxist theory deserves to be more widely known and appreciated' (Holt, 1977:27). As we have seen, Kollontai attempted to extend Marxist analysis to areas of life that had previously been seen as theoretically uninteresting and practically unimportant. She developed a looser form of Marxism that was very different from the simplistic determinism that too often characterised debates within the Second International and that enabled her to allow some autonomy and reciprocal causality to elements of the superstructure. This meant that, although she did not really have a systematic theory of patriarchy as a unifying system of domination, she was able to identify power relations in morality, sexuality and the family, and to insist that these, as well as the economic world, be seen as key areas of struggle for communist men and women. Although at the time her ideas were not developed and they did not become part of any ongoing Marxist or feminist debate, they raised issues that have only recently been seriously addressed.

8

Feminism after the Second World War

The situation of women in the mid-twentieth century

By 1945, women in most western democracies had won a high degree of political and legal equality with men. No longer were they excluded from political participation, education and employment and no longer did they lose all autonomy upon marriage; even in France, where the earlier feminist movement had been particularly unsuccessful, women were finally enfranchised in 1944, and the Code Napoleon, which explicitly subordinated women to their husbands, was gradually modified.

As discussed in Chapter 4 above, 'welfare feminism' had gained in influence in the inter-war years and helped ensure that women's needs received some recognition in the developing welfare states. Welfare benefits for women were primarily based on their maternal role, as in Britain where, following the 1942 Beveridge Report, a small state allowance was paid to mothers for their second and subsequent children. In most nations, entitlement to other state benefits, including pensions, was based on employment contributions, and it was assumed that women's main duties were domestic and that they would normally be provided for by a male breadwinner (see Sommerville, 2000). As recent feminists have argued, these assumptions meant that ideas of equal citizenship rights were in practice highly gendered (see for example Lister, 1997; and Gordon (ed.) 1990). Welfare provision also sometimes operated as a means of social control and marginalised or pathologised the needs of minority ethnic women (Mink, 1995). Nevertheless, in the short term the expansion of welfare provision did much to ease the burdens of ill-health and poverty for many women.

In the field of employment too, important changes had occurred in many western states. During the war, women had worked outside the home in unprecedented numbers, sometimes in skilled and high status jobs for which their sex had previously been thought unfit. Although women's wartime employment was generally seen as a temporary measure which did not challenge their 'normal' domestic role, and many returned to the home in 1945, the shortage of manpower and the need to restructure the economy ensured that the upward trend to paid employment continued into the 1950s in both Britain and the United States. By this time, many of the women who stayed at home were benefiting from a general rise in living standards and a greater availability of consumer goods; the combination of increasingly sophisticated household appliances with a long-term decline in family size meant that domestic work no longer needed to involve ceaseless toil and that the housewife could devote herself more to the needs of her children. It seemed therefore to many that a new age had begun, and that most women could find true fulfilment in a domesticity from which drudgery had been removed, while the minority who preferred to follow a career could do so freely.

In this context feminism had little appeal, for it was associated with battles long-won or with values that found little support in the pro-family and increasingly hedonistic atmosphere of the post-war years. Thus Sheila Rowbotham recalls that to her feminism 'was all very prim and stiff and mainly concerned with keeping you away from boys', while 'emancipated women' were 'frightening people in tweed suits and horn-rimmed glasses with stern buns at the backs of their heads' (Rowbotham, 1973b:12). In contrast to earlier years, no significant group was interested in challenging male power within the home, or in questioning the idealised version of family life that was assumed to be the norm. Those who insisted on a woman's right to a career saw this as an alternative to marriage and motherhood rather than something that could be combined with it, while most communists followed the Stalinist line that earlier socialist attacks on the family had been mistaken, and that women's true fulfilment lay in motherhood.

However, although there was no mass feminist movement, some campaigns continued, for women's formal equality masked a high degree of inequality in practice. Women remained a small minority at all levels of political life, they were strikingly absent from high professional positions, they were discriminated against in all areas of employment, they were paid less than men, and many women certainly did not share the benefits of their newly affluent society. During the war years, some feminist groups had campaigned to try to ensure that women's contributions were adequately paid and acknowledged: for example British groups successfully worked with women members of parliament to ensure that women received the same compensation as men for war injuries and in 1943 an Equal Pay Committee was established (Caine, 1997). In the post-war years in both Britain and the United States there were increasing pressures, particularly from professional women, for equal pay and an end to discrimination in employment. There were also less readily articulated problems and discontents. Many working-class women had always been in paid employment, but the growing numbers of 'working wives' were increasingly burdened with guilt as economic necessity and the demand for their labour clashed head on with the cult of domesticity, the belief that the husband should be the sole breadwinner and the discovery of the supposedly harmful effects of 'maternal deprivation' on young children. On the domestic front, liberation from housework was an ever-receding mirage, as standards and expectations seemed to rise as fast as household gadgets multiplied; later events were to show that many suburban housewives living the 'American dream' were in fact far from happy, but the idealisation of their role precluded the idea of a career as an alternative form of fulfilment.

Wilson has therefore argued that the harmony and consensus of the period were in fact deceptive, that discontents and protests were isolated and silenced rather than eliminated and that 'women's liberation has been in part a reaction against that silence (Wilson, 1980:187). It is also likely that there was more feminist activity than conventional analysis has suggested: in particular, there were important debates on feminist issues in 'progressive' circles in the United States loosely linked to the Communist Party, which developed the ideas of earlier writers such as Mary Inman (see Chapter 5 above) and anticipated later feminist arguments about consciousness-raising, exploitation and the specific situation of black women (Weigland, 2001). Such ideas were, however, always confined to a small minority, and effectively disappeared with the anti-communist scare of the late 1950s. For most young women growing up after the war there was no ready access to feminist debates and few knew anything of feminist history, for many of the ideas that have been discussed in this volume have only been rediscovered since the 1970s. It is in this context that we must understand the importance of the book to be considered in the next section, for Simone de Beauvoir's *The Second Sex*, first published in 1949, was for a generation of women the only available feminist text.

Simone de Beauvoir and *The Second Sex*

France in the mid-twentieth century was in many ways a particularly unlikely source of new feminist theory. Women had been slow to gain the legal and political rights won earlier in other western democracies, and the entire political culture was dominated by strong patriarchal assumptions; from anti-Republican Catholics on the right to socialists on the left, the consensus was that women's place lay strictly in the home. There was no strong tradition of 'mainstream feminism', which was by 1945 'the monopoly of a handful of upper-class women' (McMillan, 1981:187). Although the socialist party had long been theoretically committed to women's rights, it remained influenced by the anti-feminist ideas of the nineteenth-century anarchist writer Proudhon (who said the women could have only two possible roles – that of housewife or harlot; see McMillan, 1981), and it accepted the standard view that feminism was a middle-class distraction from more important class issues and that all women's problems would be solved under socialism; later, there was little questioning on the left of Soviet claims that full equality for women had in fact been achieved in the Soviet Union (see Sowervine, 1982). Therefore, although there had been exceptional women such as Madame Pelletier, who developed a far-reaching analysis of women's position and fought for the feminist cause within the socialist party (see Mitchell, 1989 and Scott, 1996), or Viola Klein, who attempted a scientific investigation of 'The Feminine Character' (Klein, 1946), there was no significant women's movement or public discussion of women's issues; for a young Frenchwoman growing up between the wars, feminism was simply not on the available political or philosophical agenda.

Simone de Beauvoir (1908–86) always insisted that she herself never suffered because of her sex: 'Far from suffering from my femininity, I have, on the contrary, from the age of twenty on, accumulated the advantages of both sexes' (*Force of Circumstances*, 1968:199). Born into a conservative petty-bourgeois family, she was able to escape her background through academic success, and she consistently rejected domesticity and conventional female roles. The central relationship of her life was with the existentialist philosopher Jean-Paul Sartre, but they never married or shared a home; their relationship was not based on sexual exclusiveness, and she had a number of other affairs (although significantly fewer than Sartre). She had no children, she lived most of her life in hotels, and in effect she lived very like a man in the male world of the French intelligentsia; it was not until she was nearly 40 and about to embark on her autobiography that, following a suggestion from Sartre, she decided that in order to understand herself she must also understand what it meant to be a woman.

The result of de Beauvoir's investigations was the massive *The Second Sex*, first published in 1949. This drew upon a vast range of philosophical, psychological, anthropological, historical, literary and anecdotal material to argue that the most important obstacle to a woman's freedom was not her biology, or the political and legal constraints placed upon her, or even her economic situation; rather it was the whole process by which femininity is manufactured in society. In her celebrated phrase 'One is not born but rather becomes a woman' (*Second Sex*:297), and her discussion of the ways in which girls are forced into certain paths and denied expression of their full humanity led her to an examination of the experiences of girls and women that included discussion of hitherto taboo areas of female life such as menstruation and sexuality, which she discussed with a frankness unprecedented in a serious academic work. This meant that, like later radical feminists, de Beauvoir saw the ways in which apparently non-political areas of life such as the family tied in with wider power structures. However, like Marxist feminists, she did not see the liberation of women as an ahistorical act, for it was only under modern conditions of production that women could realise their potential for free and autonomous action.

Existentialism applied to women

An understanding of what de Beauvoir meant by freedom requires some knowledge of her philosophical framework: existentialist theory as developed by Sartre. Central to existentialism was a questioning of existing customs, values and beliefs and a rejection of the idea that an individual's fate is irrevocably predetermined, whether this be by conventional expectations, early childhood experiences or economic conditions. It therefore opposed the assumptions of both Freudian psychoanalysis and the kind of crude Marxism that characterised communist parties at the time, and stressed instead an individual's total freedom and responsibility for his own life. For Sartre, the only 'authentic' way of living was one that recognised this freedom; such freedom is not, however, easily accepted, for it involves an overwhelming responsibility and sense of aloneness. For many, the recognition of human freedom is quite simply unbearable and is therefore denied; the individual lapses into 'bad faith' and blames circumstances for his own actions and character rather than accepting responsibility. At the same time, the individual's freedom seems unacceptably limited by the very existence of other people, for whom he is but an object; here Sartre argued that there is a conflict at the most basic level of human consciousness, as each individual seeks domination by asserting himself as subject and the 'Other' as object. Later, he was to suggest that an individual's acceptance of freedom involved responsibility for the freedom of others also, and to see the exercise of freedom in terms of collective class action and conscious revolutionary activity; at the time of *The Second Sex*, however, he seemed to see this conflict as basic to the human condition, and solutions as basically individualistic; in this context the task of philosophy was essentially to reveal to people the possibility of freedom, and to show that man can freely choose and create his own future.

In *The Second Sex*, de Beauvoir argued both that such freedom and responsibility could be achieved by women as well as men, and that historically it had been denied to them. Here it was the concept of the

'Other' that provided her with a starting-point. For Sartre, the sex of the potentially autonomous individual was not an issue, but de Beauvoir argued that it was all-important, as for most of human history man has successfully relegated woman to the status of permanent Other, excluded from the realm of true humanity, never an equal and so never a threat:

> She is defined and differentiated with reference to man and not he with reference to her; she is the incidental, the inessential as opposed to the essential. He is the Subject, he is the Absolute – she is the Other. (*Second Sex*:16)

This was originally possible, de Beauvoir argued, because women's lack of strength and their childbearing role excluded them from the productive process; this did not, though, mean that a biological or materialist explanation on its own could account for women's subordination, for this required the original drive to dominate, the 'imperialism of human consciousness' posited by Sartre (*Second Sex*:89). Now, however, modern technology and contraception meant that women's subordination was no longer based on physical necessity; the only thing preventing women from seeing themselves as subjects in their own right was the artificial idea of womanhood engendered by society, which still saw women as secondary objects, acquiring meaning only in relation to men. If women were to be free, they must therefore be freed from this prevailing idea, and enabled to take responsibility for their own lives, rather than accepting the security of dependence or the 'bad faith' represented by conformity to the feminine ideal. The aim of *The Second Sex* was therefore to reveal the artificial nature of womanhood, in order that this might be rejected, for

> No biological, psychological or economic fate determines the figure that the human female presents in society; it is civilisation as a whole that produces this creation, intermediate between male and eunuch who is described as female. (*Second Sex*:295)

Feminist responses to The Second Sex

When *The Second Sex* was first published, it was both shocking and inspiring, and de Beauvoir herself was amazed at both the hostility and the support it generated. Above all, it broke the silence that surrounded women's experiences, and it enabled some women to see the world in a different light. As such, 'In the darkness of the Fifties and Sixties, *The Second Sex* was like a secret code that we emerging women used to send messages to each other', so that 'The book is part of some women's personal history, and part of the history of feminism' (Schwarzer, 1984:13; Okely, 1986:70).

Its role in the history of feminism is, however, not straightforward. Its appeal in the United States was always less than in Europe (see Dietz, 1992) and, as new feminist theories and activities exploded into political life from the mid-1960s, de Beauvoir's ideas could seem inappropriate and outdated. In particular, some of the radical feminist approaches discussed in the following chapters claimed that any theory based in male philosophy must inevitably be limited and partial, and, as we shall see, de Beauvoir has been heavily criticised for failing to recognise or address the patriarchal foundations of existing systems of knowledge. More recently, however, feminists influenced by postmodern theories (see Chapter 14, below), have self-consciously 're-read' de Beauvoir to argue that her insights open up far more radically subversive possibilities than her critics allow and that, far from being bound by an outdated existentialist framework, her philosophy is strikingly 'untimely' and characterised by 'the uncanny recurrence of preoccupations that supposedly arose after it was written', so that it '... in many ways prefigures and anticipates postmodern feminism' (Ruth Evans, 1998:3; and Vintgnes, 1998:214). These competing assessments of de Beauvoir by later feminists are explored in the following sections.

A negative view of women?

According to some critics, de Beauvoir's rejection of femininity depended upon an unquestioning acceptance of male values and assumptions which meant that she failed to explore how masculinity might also be artificially created or to consider the positive aspects of characteristics or qualities associated with women. At the most basic level, in the course of discussing what it means to be a woman, de Beauvoir provided a detailed account of women's biology that seems to be entirely negative. Ignoring any possibility that some aspects of male biology might also be unpleasant or problematic, she described the processes of menstruation, pregnancy, childbirth and lactation with extreme disgust, seeing women trapped in their bodies, victims of the reproductive needs of the species. Although she did not accept that these biological handicaps need any longer determine woman's position in society or 'her ovaries condemn her to live for ever on her knees' (*Second Sex*:736), she insisted that it is only by *overcoming* their biology that women can become 'fully human'. She also completely rejected the idea that maternity, marriage or domesticity could be sources of fulfilment or pleasure, and while for many commentators her descriptions of the trials and tribulations of marriage and maternity were a much needed corrective to the prevailing syrupy view of domestic bliss, her denial that motherhood (or fatherhood) could be a source of positive values seems a too-easy rejection of a whole area of human experience.

Here, it may be that de Beauvoir's perceptions were limited by her own experiences as a token woman who functioned as an honorary man. Although her own life has often been portrayed as the ideal of independent womanhood, some radical feminists refuse to accept this as a model both because it seems to be based on a rejection of traditional female qualities and because in practice her relationships with men were not entirely equal; some also criticise her failure to recognise the intellectual, emotional and sexual importance of her own relationships with other women. At a deeper philosophical level, critics have claimed that her whole stress on rationality, autonomy and self-affirmation involved an uncritical acceptance of a male paradigm that places reason above emotion, mind above body and culture above nature, and which equates man with the former and women with the latter. This paradigm both devalues traditionally female qualities such as caring, intuition and emotion and implies that it is only by *denying* her female-ness that a woman can achieve humanity, while the psychological assumptions of existentialist philosophy take as given the drive to dominate, and rule out the possibility of an equivalent drive to co-operation, nurturing, mutuality or sharing (see Mary Evans, 1985 and 1996; Heath, 1989; Moi, 1987 and 1990; Leighton, 1975; Walters, 1979; Lloyd, 1984 and the discussions in Dietz, 1992; Moi, 1994; Pilardi, 1995; and Simons (ed.) 1995).

In response to such criticisms, Karen Vintges has employed postmodernist perspectives to argue both that de Beauvoir developed a new version of existentialism 'in which solidarity with fellow human beings, corporality and emotion had a very great place' and that her negative portrayal of women's bodily functions was intended to reflect existing social and cultural practices and attitudes rather than necessary facts of female existence: in other words, to view a woman's body with disgust does not mean that it is inherently disgusting, but that it has been made so by society. According to Vintges, this means that de Beauvoir believed that 'If women gain active control over their own lives they will also experience their bodily functions including menstruation, pregnancy and labour in different ways' (Vintges, 1998:205 and 209). Such a view perhaps gains credence from de Beauvoir's statement in *The Second Sex* that 'It is the social context that makes menstruation a curse' (*Second Sex*:340) and from interviews towards the end of her life in which she said that it was good that women were ceasing to be ashamed of their bodies (Schwarzer, 1984). It is, however, far from clear that she consciously intended all of her earlier negative depictions to be seen as culturally specific rather than inherent an inevitable product of biology.

What is clear is that de Beauvoir had no truck with the view that was being expressed by some radical feminists in the 1970s that female biology could be a positive cause for celebration, and she denied that it could be a source of superior qualities or understandings:

> One should not believe that the female body gives one a new view of the world. That
> would be ridiculous and absurd. That would mean turning it into a counter-penis.
> (Quoted in Schwarzer, 1984:79)

It is this very refusal to recognise any essential female identity or
'name the category of woman' that some postmodern feminists see as truly
radical (see Butler, 1998; Ruth Evans, 1998 and the discussions in Simons
(ed.), 1995, especially the chapter by Pilardi). For these writers, her uncou-
pling of sex and gender not only means that there may be no necessary link
between biological sex and being a man or a woman, but it opens up ways
of thinking and becoming that move beyond a binary male/female gender
system and towards the possibility of a fluid multiplicity of genders
(for further discussion of these ideas, see Chapter 14 below).

Women and collective action

As we shall see in Chapter 14, a standard critique of postmodern feminism
is that its insistence on the fluid and provisional nature of gender identities seems to rule out the possibility of collective action by women. Similar
criticisms have been made of de Beauvoir, and it has been said that she
offers only individualistic solutions to women's collective oppression.

It is certainly the case that *The Second Sex* never argued for united action
by women to improve their position. However, de Beauvoir's intention
was not simply to describe and bewail the lot of her sex. Rather, her intention was to expose and identify the social and cultural processes through
which femininity was constructed in order to demystify and challenge
them: having recognised the artificial nature of the restrictions placed
upon them, women would be free to realise their true potential. As Judith
Butler argued in an influential essay, first published in 1986, de Beauvoir's
insight that 'becoming a woman' is an active and on-going process enables
us to see that women's gender is not simply imposed upon them but also
has to be accepted, for

> Oppression is not a self-contained system which either confronts individuals as a
> theoretical object or generates them as its cultural pawns. It is a dialectical force
> which requires individual participation on a large scale in order to maintain its
> malignant life. (Butler, 1998:35)

This means that women are not simply passive victims but also agents;
according to Butler this also opens up the possibility that, despite the constraints under which they live, individuals can to some extent 'choose'
their gender identity. Some critics think that de Beauvoir was blaming

women for 'choosing' to remain oppressed. However, she never saw free choice as an easy option; although she was an optimist and believed that changes in education, culture and morality were all working in women's favour, she recognised that things might be very hard for individual pioneers (and she said later that she had underestimated the problems still facing women in 1949).

To some extent, de Beauvoir's failure to consider the possibilities of collective action by women in *The Second Sex* simply reflected the time in which she was writing, when there was no large-scale women's movement and she had little contact with other feminist women. The whole idea of collective female identity and 'sisterhood' developed by some later radical feminists may also be ruled out at a deeper level by her denial that there was any inherent female 'essence'. However, as Toril Moi has argued, collective feminist action need not presuppose a theory of female identity, and Margaret Simons has further claimed that the logic of de Beauvoir's arguments means that '[her] feminism is activist: the only recourse for women is the *collective* struggle for their own liberation' (Moi, 1994 and Simons, 1995:247, my italics). Certainly, when the women's movement developed in France after 1968, de Beauvoir was an active participant and convert to the idea of female solidarity; for the first time she started to call herself a feminist, she was to the forefront of campaigns to legalise abortion, she defended the need for separate women's organisations free from the threat of male domination, and her earlier apparent contempt for women was replaced by a new stress on the value of female friendship (see Schwarzer, 1984). Nevertheless, Toril Moi thinks that she continued to underestimate the potential political impact of an independent women's movement and that in rejecting all claims based in female identity she 'fail[s] to grasp the progressive potential of "femininity" as a political discourse' and 'seriously underestimates the *strategic* value of a politics of difference' (Moi, 1994: 211 and 213). She also failed to engage with later radical feminist analyses of patriarchy and the argument that, because men have emotional, psychological, sexual, domestic and economic interests in maintaining women's subordination, they are likely to oppose real change. Although by the 1970s de Beauvoir had come to agree that men should be treated 'with suspicion', she therefore never accepted an analysis of patriarchy that saw them as 'the enemy' (Schwarzer, 1984).

Letters and journals published after de Beauvoir's death show that she was sexually involved with a number of women. However, she never identified herself as a lesbian and, unlike some later radical feminists, she never discussed the political significance or liberatory potential of lesbianism or challenged the primary importance for women of their sexual and emotional relationships with men. She has therefore been criticised both for taking heterosexuality as a given norm and for concealing her own sexuality. Margaret Simons has, however, argued that not only were there often sound practical (employment-related) reasons for her to conceal her lesbian relationships, but that de Beauvoir's refusal to accept a lesbian identity was part of a more general rejection of essentialist conceptions which, as discussed above, opens up more fluid and open possibilities for gender relationships than those suggested by conventional labels (Simons, 1992).

Women and class

Although de Beauvoir clearly rejected essentialist notions of womanhood, critics have asserted that she too readily equated the situation of women with women of her own background, and that she ignored the needs and priorities of working-class, peasant and/or non European women. It is true that in her descriptions in 1949 of how femininity is constructed and maintained she drew largely on the experiences of middle-class French women, and her proposed solution, which saw women as independent, fulfilled and liberated through their careers, could have little meaning outside her own class. However, she herself recognised this limitation and, although she shared with earlier Marxist feminists the belief that women's entry into the paid labour force and their achievement of economic independence were far more important than legal or political rights, she was more realistic than many of them in seeing that for a working-class woman faced with domestic responsibilities, paid labour could only be an additional source of drudgery and exploitation rather than a road to liberation; for such women, the price of independence would at present simply be too high. Meanwhile, she argued that even for the professional woman there would be all kinds of problems from which her male counterpart would be immune; as the demands of her career clashed with traditional assumptions about her domestic and sexual life, she too would be tempted to abandon the struggle and sacrifice her autonomy for the sake of security. Here de Beauvoir was not so much blaming women for lapsing into 'bad faith' as seeking to understand the temptations and pressures that might be involved. Rather than abstracting gender from other social forces, she was also anticipating some later feminist analyses of the complex ways in which gender, class and ethnicity can interconnect, for her basic claim that gender is artificial allows for the possibility (or even the likelihood) that it could vary with its social context.

At the same time, de Beauvoir shared the Marxist belief that women's liberation was only becoming possible because of modern methods of production, as modern machines now made physical strength irrelevant to the processes of production and effective methods of contraception enabled women to avoid endless childbearing. In later writings she placed even more stress on a materialist explanation of women's situation (see *Force of Circumstances*:197; *All Said and Done*:449). She also seems consistently to have assumed that true freedom for all women would be impossible without socialism (which she said had *not* yet been achieved in the USSR, although she was for a time enthusiastic about China). Late in life she admitted that she did not know the exact connection between capitalist and patriarchal oppressions, but argued that for feminism to succeed it must be part of the class struggle (Schwarzer, 1984).

De Beauvoir's life and influence

De Beauvoir's personal life has often been seen as a playing out of the values she asserted as a feminist writer, and as such it has been appraised both positively and negatively. She lived in a manner dramatically more independent than most women of her time. Today's changed circumstances present young women with a much wider range of alternatives, and the attractiveness of her life as a role model has diminished; for an earlier generation, however, it suggested exciting new possibilities and the beginning of a new era in which 'The free woman is just being born' (*Second Sex*:723). Above all, her life showed that women *could* make choices, they *could* reject their traditional roles and they could, apparently, find happiness and fulfilment in so doing; as such, it was 'a symbol of the possibility, despite everything, of living one's life the way one wants to, for oneself, free from conventions and prejudices, even as a woman' (Schwarzer, 1984:3).

As discussed above, however, some writers have seen her rejection of domesticity and motherhood as a rejection of female values. Although her relationship with Sartre, which she claimed was based on love, absolute trust and equality but not possession or exclusiveness, has been seen by some as a model of equal partnership, radical feminists have seen this central relationship as encapsulating the inequality and female dependency she was supposed to have rejected. At a basic level, although de Beauvoir succeeded in liberating herself from most household tasks, she still performed more domestic duties than Sartre, and it seems clear both that Sartre took far more advantage of the 'open' nature of their relationship than she did, and that she suffered far more from jealousy; it is also likely that despite the alleged honesty of their relationship, Sartre did not scruple to lie to her about his affairs (see Winegarten, 1988:30). Others have attacked the whole attempt to intellectualise and rationally plan sexual behaviour; this could give rise to a cold-blooded approach that, as de Beauvoir admitted, caused great pain to other people, and it reflects her general mistrust of passion and emotion and her over-enthusiasm for a life of reason. She is also said to have allowed herself to be intellectually dominated by Sartre (much less well known than the fact that she came second to him in their final philosophy examinations is the fact that he had failed them the year before), although some recent commentators have claimed that she was more philosophically independent than critics suggest (see Kruks, 1992 and Vintgnes, 1998).

In terms of her intellectual reputation, there is no universal agreement with Toril Moi's claim that, despite her limitations, de Beauvoir was 'the greatest feminist theorist of our [the twentieth] century' (Moi, 1994:3). However, even those who disagree with her usually temper their criticisms with praise for her pioneering insights, while some postmodern feminists claim that these insights are richer and more profound than is generally realised, and are claiming her as one of their own. Today, it is probably true that de Beauvoir is 'much worshipped, often quoted and little read' (Dietz, 1992:78). Nevertheless, those who take the trouble to read her will discover that her claim that 'One is not born but rather becomes a woman' is not a platitude, but a central starting-point for questions which feminists are still debating today.

9

Liberalism and beyond: feminism and equal rights from the 1960s

During the 1970s, it became quite widely accepted that different kinds of contemporary feminisms could be classified as liberal, radical or socialist/Marxist. As ideas and practices developed, many other categories were identified, including black and postmodern feminisms. Although some feminists today see such classification as at best naïve and at worst dangerously misleading, it provides the starting-point for discussion in this and the following chapters. This classification is however only a starting-point: it is not intended to suggest either that it is the only possible way of approaching recent feminisms[4] or that ideas can be neatly packaged into competing bodies of thought.

Although sometimes entangled with contradictory assumptions, feminist demands for equal rights have usually started from the claims that women are 'as good as men', that they are entitled to full human rights, and that they should be free to explore their full potential in equal competition with men. These are liberal arguments and, as we have seen, they were used by earlier feminists to demand legal and political equality. During the inter-war years, feminism based on equal rights arguments had been in abeyance, as 'mainstream' feminist activities concentrated on supporting women in their traditional roles rather than on challenging their remaining legal inequalities. However, as discussed in the previous chapter, the years after the Second World War contained the seeds of the discontents that were to explode in a 'Second Wave' of mass feminist activity in the 1960s. Although this activity had a number of sources and developed rapidly in several very different directions, it began in the United States as an essentially liberal protest against the failure of that society to deliver to women the promises of independence, self-expression and fulfilment that seemed central to the 'American dream'.

By the 1960s, this kind of feminism was not usually expressed as a self-conscious political theory, but as a 'common sense' application of pre-existing values to women's situation. As other feminist theories developed, a somewhat one-sided theoretical debate emerged, with critics of liberal feminism attacking positions that had never been fully articulated and perhaps at times creating and demolishing a liberal feminist 'straw woman' who did not really exist. However, uncovering and examining the assumptions behind campaigns and debates is central to the development of effective feminist politics; the fact that liberal assumptions are seldom consciously propounded or defended may indeed make the task more urgent, as these assumptions continue to be the largely unquestioned starting-point for much public political debate in the west.

Betty Friedan and the politics of NOW

The clearest and most famous expression of such 'common sense' liberal feminism is to be found in Betty Friedan's *The Feminine Mystique* (first published 1963; references to the 1986 edition). Friedan argued that, in the United States since the Second World War, earlier feminist dreams of education and independence had been displaced by an all-pervasive 'feminine mystique', through which women had been manipulated and persuaded into the belief that their only fulfilment lay in domesticity. She claimed that this mystique, which taught that 'the highest value and the only commitment for women is the fulfilment of their own femininity' was more dangerous and insidious than earlier traditional values, because it was supported by pseudoscientific theories (particularly vulgarised Freudian analysis and functionalist sociology) and reinforced by women's magazines and the entire advertising industry. This meant that the whole of an American woman's life was geared towards attracting and keeping a husband and serving the needs of him and his children; denied the expression of her own humanity, she was forced to live her life vicariously, parasitic upon the activities of her husband in the 'real world' outside her home. Such a life, Friedan claimed, could not lead to happiness, for no multiplicity of consumer goods could compensate for the inner emptiness involved; at best it could lead to passivity, at worst to bleak despair. This despair could not however be articulated, for its existence was denied by the feminine mystique, which interpreted women's unhappiness in terms of their own failure to 'adapt' to their sexual role; isolated in her 'comfortable concentration camp', each individual suburban housewife was therefore 'so ashamed to show her dissatisfaction that she never knew how many other women shared it'. The cause of this 'problem that has no name' was, Friedan said, simply the fact that American women were denied any opportunity for independence or self-development; its most dramatic effects were the rise in mental illness, alcoholism and suicide among women, but it also had a highly damaging effect upon the next generation, indeed:

> If we continue to produce millions of young mothers who stop their growth and education short of identity, without a strong core of human values to pass on to their children, we are committing, quite simply, genocide, starting with the mass burial of American women and ending with the progressive dehumanization of their sons and daughters. (*Mystique*:38, 245, 17 and 318)

This meant that the interests of society and the needs of women demanded that women be freed from the feminine mystique and enabled to 'say "No" to the housewife image'. Like Simone de Beauvoir, Friedan believed that the crucial issue was to reveal to women the possibilities of freedom and fulfilment outside the home and the artificial nature of the restrictions that currently confined them; here she saw education as the key to widening women's horizons and therefore called for 'a national education programme, similar to the G. I. Bill' (which had been introduced for returning soldiers in 1945). Unlike de Beauvoir, however, she unequivocally rejected any attack on conventional morality and family life. With the help of maternity leave and workplace nurseries she believed that women could *combine* long-term career plans with their family responsibilities; like Margaret Thatcher, who wrote in 1954 that with efficient organisation 'as well as being a housewife it is possible to put in eight hours work a day besides', she said that women must 'see housework for what it is – not a career, but something that must be done as quickly and efficiently as possible'. Her goal therefore was to allow women to live for themselves as well as for others by being educated to their full potential and enabled to follow a career outside the home; she believed that this would also create new possibilities for love with men, which could now be based on shared work and values rather than inequality (*Mystique*:270, 323, 297; Thatcher, 1954).

Whatever its shortcomings and exaggerations, *The Feminine Mystique* clearly struck a chord with many women. By 1970 it had sold over a million copies in the United States and Britain; many readers claimed that it had changed their lives, and one wrote to Friedan saying that after reading it she wanted to rush into the streets and cry 'To arms, sisters! You have nothing to lose but your vacuum cleaners!' (quoted in Horowitz, 1998:203. For an excellent 'insider's' view of events at the time, see Tobias, 1997). Such reactions were, however, not simply a reaction to the effectiveness of Friedan's prose style for, whereas in the 1950s de Beauvoir's *The Second Sex* had been a bolt from the blue, *The Feminine Mystique* crystallised ideas that were already very much in the air (see Horowitz, 1998). As women continued to enter paid work in increasing numbers, pressure for improved pay and conditions was building up and support for an Equal Rights Amendment to the constitution had been gradually growing for some years. Partly with the hope of deflecting such support, President Kennedy set up a Commission on the Status of Women which reported in 1963, the year *The Feminine Mystique* was published. The report documented the discrimination still faced by women in many areas of life and, along with the fifty state commissions which were shortly established, it had the unintended effects of providing a forum for debate, radicalising the professional women involved in its investigations, helping to create a network of politically informed and active women and contributing to a climate in which it was once again acceptable to talk about women's rights (see Buechler, 1990 and Davis, 1999). In 1963 an Equal Pay Act was also passed, and in 1964 a clause prohibiting discrimination by sex was added to the Civil Rights Act. The addition of this clause to an Act concerned with racial discrimination was at least in part a last-ditch attempt to block the whole issue (see Tobias, 1997:284 n.22), but it was the subsequent failure of the authorities to implement the sexual equality aspects of the Act that led many women to see the need for a national pressure group to promote their cause. The result was the formation of the National Organisation for Women (NOW), which was founded in 1966 with Friedan as its president, and which rapidly became the world's largest feminist organisation.

According to its founding statement, the aim of NOW was

> To take action to bring women into full participation in the mainstream of American society *now*, exercising all the privileges and responsibilities thereof in truly equal partnership with men.

Here we have the logical culmination of the demands that had been developing over the centuries and a total rejection of the 'separate spheres' argument: no longer confined to the home, women were to use their hard-won legal rights to join men in economic, social and political life, and Friedan's arguments about women's need for fulfilment outside the family were taken as a self-evident starting point. No further subversion or criticism of society was intended, for the democratic institutions of the United States were seen as a means to the well-being of all its citizens, and the traditional family still seemed the lynchpin of the good society. It was agreed that, as argued in *The Feminine Mystique*, the long-term interests of men and society as a whole would be served by sexual equality; although it was assumed that women would be most active in pursuing their own interests, support from men was therefore welcomed, and in its early days about 10 per cent of NOW's members were men. The strategy was to establish a pressure group organised on conventionally hierarchical lines, that would use the law and existing political processes to seek an end to discrimination and to achieve full equality of opportunity in all areas of life; following Friedan's arguments about the artificial nature of conventional femininity, NOW also challenged the prevailing gender ideology, particularly by demanding changes in education and in the media portrayal of women.

Subsequent developments

At some levels, NOW's campaigns have met with considerable success. It gained some early legal victories on employment law, during the 1970s it spear-headed a massive campaign to amend the United States constitution to give women equal rights which very nearly succeeded,[5] and it has been a major force in changing attitudes to women in education, employment and the media. NOW was the first national organisation to campaign for the legalisation of abortion, and today it campaigns for the right of all women to make their own reproductive choices. It has both helped inspire numerous other campaigns for women's rights and become a key political player in its own right: by 1988, when it successfully campaigned for the selection of Geraldine Ferraro as the Democrats' vice-presidential candidate, it 'was being taken seriously as part of the Democratic party's decision-making process' (Frankovic, 1988:123), and since the early 1990s it has played an important role in increasing the number of feminist women (and some feminist men) elected to political office. At the beginning of the early twenty-first century it remains the largest organisation of feminist activists in the United States, with over 500,000 contributing members.

The impact of the kind of equal rights feminism epitomised by Friedan and NOW has been felt worldwide. For example, although there was no similar large-scale movement for equal rights in Britain, it was similar 'common sense' ideas about justice and the needs of society that helped inspire the Equal Pay and Sex Discrimination Acts of the 1970s and the setting up of the Equal Opportunities Commission (although Britain's impending membership of the European Common Market was also a factor). In most western nations there are now far fewer formal barriers to full equality with men than in the 1960s, increasing numbers are in well-paid senior positions and elected political office, and the full-time housewives whose distress was identified by Friedan seem to be on the verge of extinction.

From 'backlash' to 'power feminism'

Despite apparent gains, however, it is clear that profound economic, social, political and cultural inequalities between women and men remain in every country of the world, and that the movement of women into paid employment has largely been into poorly-paid and insecure jobs and in response to economic forces rather than feminist campaigns. It is also clear that, in comparison with other western nations, the United States has a particularly bad record in terms of the pay gap between women and men, the growth of poverty amongst women and the numbers of women in elected political office. Nevertheless, as Susan Faludi has argued in *Backlash: The Undeclared War Against Women*, by the 1980s there was a widespread perception in the United States that women had indeed achieved equality – or even that men were now the oppressed sex. As the New Right gained in ascendancy, feminism was increasingly attacked as the source of a wide range of social ills: not only did it seem threatening to many men, but it was blamed for the break-up of the family and a rise in juvenile crime and drug-taking, while 'all that equality' was allegedly damaging to women themselves, who were widely portrayed in the media as lonely, exhausted, stressed and depressed (Faludi, 1992).

For right-wing anti-feminists, feminism was the problem. In contrast, as we shall see in later sections, many feminists have employed other perspectives to identify the liberal starting-point of equal rights feminism as the source of its failure to achieve its own stated aims. However, many equal rights feminists have not questioned their goals and methods, but have argued that they should be pursued and employed more vigorously. Although from an early stage NOW broadened its remit to include more 'private' issues, including reproductive rights, domestic and sexual violence against women and the rights of lesbians, its first 'official priority' today is to win economic equality and secure it with an Equal Rights Amendment to the constitution. Faludi herself re-stated and defended the basic claim that women should be treated as full members of the human race 'just as deserving of rights and opportunities, just as capable of participating in the world's events' as the male half of the population (Faludi, 1992:18). Like many liberal feminists before her, she argued that men could benefit too from genuine equality and, although she has been accused of understating women's gains in a 'supremely depressing read' (Somerville, 2000:200), she argued that women could defend and build on the rights that had already been won.

In 1993, equal rights feminism was the basis for a rallying call from another young American writer. In the best-selling *Fire with Fire*, Naomi Wolf described feminism as 'a humanistic movement for social justice' which men as well as women could support, and she argued that while the 1980s may have been the era of the backlash, the 1990s were to be the era of 'power feminism' and a 'genderquake' 'in which the meaning of being a woman is changed for ever' (Wolf, 1993:152 and xiv). Rather than endlessly bemoaning their status as victims, she argued that women should celebrate their achievements and overcome their fear of success to realise their potential strength and compete on equal terms with men. More recently, the young British writer Natasha Walter has similarly argued that the history of feminism is not one of ongoing oppression but increased freedom: 'a great story, a happy, triumphant story'. She claims that a new generation of assertive, independent young women are ready to fulfil their potential in a world in which Margaret Thatcher 'normalised female success' (although she does concede that Thatcher did not help other women or openly acknowledge her own debt to feminism), and she sees success in the workplace as the starting-point for improving women's situation in other areas of life (Walter, 1998:50 and 175; see also Walter (ed.) 1999).

At first sight, all of this sounds simply like an updated affirmation of Friedan's earlier demands. Along with a number of other writers such as Christina Hoff Sommers, Camille Paglia and Kate Roiphe (see Cole, 2000 and, on young Dutch feminists, Bussemaker, 1998), Wolf and Walter are particularly anxious to distance themselves from some of the radical feminist ideas discussed in Chapters 10 and 11 below, which they see as 'victim feminism', characterised by a hostility to men, an obsession with sexual violence and the pursuit of drab, poverty-stricken separatism rather than economic or political success. Nevertheless, their approach shows the influence of radical ideas, and Wolf and Walter go beyond Freidan's initially narrow focus on success in the public sphere in three key ways. Firstly, they recognise the political significance of coercive sex and the need to act against it; secondly, they do not simply want to join men in the workplace, but to change conditions of employment to make them more compatible with family life; and thirdly, they want men to play a much greater role within the home (Wolf says that her ideas on the family were radicalised by her own experience of becoming mother. Wolf, 2001; Viner, 2001). Friedan herself has moved towards a similar position on family–work issues, and has called for an increased role for the state in promoting gender equality through education, employment legislation and childcare provision (Friedan, 1970 and 1981). More recently, she has called for a 'new paradigm' in social policy which places more stress on family and community values than short-term profitability and involves 'new thinking about competitiveness, ... new thinking about work in terms of time and family, and new definitions of success' (Friedan, 1981:46 and 1997:19). As we shall see in later sections, these shifts in feminist thinking involve a challenge to key liberal assumptions about the public/private distinction, the role of the state and the market, and the terms on which equality is granted.

Richards, Okin and a feminist theory of justice

Friedan, Faludi, Wolf and Walter are journalists and activitists rather than theoreticians and, as I said at the beginning of this chapter, most recent equal rights feminism has been expressed in terms of political action and campaigns, with little attempt to identify or defend its theoretical premises. Attempts to provide an updated theory based on a relatively critical application of liberal ideas have however been made by Wolgast (1980) and Midgley and Hughes (1983); rather more innovative contributions have been made by Janet Radcliffe Richards (1982) and Susan Moller Okin (1980, 1987, 1989 and 1990).

In *The Sceptical Feminist* Richards provided a robust defence of liberal feminism against both anti-feminists and radical feminist 'extremists'. She said that her prime concern was with justice, which she saw as bound up with an individual's freedom to pursue his or her own destiny, and which she believed women were still systematically denied. Like Okin, she used the ideas of the contract theorist, John Rawls, to provide a model of the just society in which women would be as free to explore their own potential as men.

In *A Theory of Justice* (1971) Rawls had discussed the kind of society that might have been planned by individuals who did not know in advance which social positions they were to occupy. He argued that the only kind of inequality that would be agreed to by those behind this 'veil of ignorance' would be that which in fact benefited the *least* well off members of society; this 'difference principle' was the principle for the just distribution of resources in society and meant that inequality could not be defended in terms of the needs or merits of those already advantaged. Pateman has forcefully criticised all contract theory including Rawls' as a patriarchal device designed to conceal the realities of sex oppression behind a spurious equality (Pateman, 1988). Certainly in its original form Rawls' theory supported her accusations, for he assumed that his anonymous individuals were in fact the male heads of households (*Justice*:128), and that justice within the family already existed. However, Richards argued that a more consistent application of Rawls' principle, according to which knowledge of one's sex would also be firmly behind the 'veil of ignorance' and family structures could be questioned, would lead to a fundamental challenge to the gender divisions in society. She argued in particular that a sexually just society would require both measures of affirmative action in the workplace, and a radical restructuring of work and childcare arrangements that would increase the choices available to women and ensure that the benefits and burdens of having children were shared more equally between the sexes.

In *Justice, Gender and the Family*, Okin too argued that Rawls' ideas could be extended to the family, and she claimed that this was essential if the interests of women and children were to be defended. At present, she said, women were systematically disadvantaged in all areas of life, and 'Underlying all these inequalities is the unequal distribution of the unpaid labour of the family'. Her ideal was therefore a society in which childrearing and domestic work were shared equally; this equality within the home would make possible gender equality in all other areas of life, so that 'A just future would be one without gender. In its social structures and practices, one's sex would have no more relevance than one's eye colour or the length of one's toes.' In order to achieve such a future, she advocated the introduction of both state-subsidised nurseries and much greater flexibility in employment patterns, so that paid work and nurturing could be readily combined by both men and women. In accordance with Rawls' principle that all interests must be considered when planning the just society, she also argued that those who choose to continue to base family life on traditional patterns must be protected. She therefore suggested that both partners should have an equal legal entitlement to all earnings coming into the household and that neither should be disproportionately disadvantaged in the event of divorce (*Justice*:25 and 171).

As with the more practically oriented demands of recent equal rights feminists discussed above, Richards' and Okin's proposals involved an important step away from the classic liberal insistence on the non-political nature of the family and a shift in the understanding of what genuine equality might mean. However, they rejected radical feminist or Marxist ideas about conflicting sex or class interests, and retained the liberal belief that people of goodwill can, through reason, establish the principles of a just society that is in the interest of all.

Critical analysis and debate

Equal rights feminism has been a progressive force, and few feminists today would want to lose the legal and political rights that have been won. However, the apparently simple claim for equal rights is also deeply problematic, and critics have argued that the failure to achieve more substantive equality is an inevitable consequence of liberal assumptions which, despite their claim to universality, are inherently partial and hostile to women at practical, epistemological and ontological levels.[6] The arguments and principles involved are complex and will be developed further in later chapters; here I will consider them around the inter-connected headings of *equality, power and the state, the public/private distinction, individualism* and *reason*.

Equality

Beyond the equality/difference debate

As we have seen in previous chapters, the demand for full legal equality for women is much less straightforward than it at first sight seems; indeed, Joan Scott has argued that it is inherently paradoxical, as a claim to equal rights simultaneously denies the relevance of sex difference and affirms the existence of women as a sexually differentiated group (Scott, 1996). Unless it is combined with more radical analysis, the call for equality also leads to what Carole Pateman has called 'Wollstonecraft's dilemma': that is, it enables women to be treated and valued equally only to the extent that they can behave like men, ignoring the ways in which women's domestic responsibilities restrict their ability to compete; at the same time, any attempt to acknowledge or value these responsibilities is seen as a recognition of women's 'difference' from men, and therefore a sign of inferiority that justifies unequal outcomes (Pateman, 1988).

It is therefore unsurprising that the demand for full legal equality has led to many immediate practical difficulties and unintended consequences. For example, gender-neutral divorce laws ignore inequalities in the job market produced by marriage and childrearing; while equal citizenship rights and responsibilities have been based on a male paradigm which largely ignores the needs and important contributions associated with women's traditional roles (Davis, 1999; Lister, 1997). Major difficulties also arise when women are given workplace rights on terms which have already been set by men, as these are likely to depend upon definitions of 'merit' which are biased in men's favour and they do not recognise practical family responsibilities or reproductive needs. These difficulties have been particularly acute in the United States, where uncritical use of equal rights discourse has made it difficult for feminists to campaign for maternity rights and benefits, as this can seem like special treatment for women – although some constructed tortuous arguments to justify giving maternity rights to 'pregnant persons'. (For an overview of the arguments, see Bryson, 1999). By 1982, when the Equal Rights Amendment fell, such difficulties meant that some former feminist supporters were expressing doubts about demanding full legal equality, and recognising that in practice gender-neutral laws could often be damaging to women. For many feminist critics, this explains why maternity and childcare provision in the United States are so poor and why gender inequalities in earnings and political power are significantly higher than in most other western democracies; some therefore no longer support the demand for an Equal Rights Amendment (see Hewlett, 1988; Mansbridge, 1986; Davis, 1999; and Somerville, 2000).

As we have seen, some earlier feminists had rejected the argument that women were essentially the same as men, and demanded rights so that their *different* qualities, experiences and needs could be expressed, represented or protected. Recently, the claim that women are different from and superior to men has most often been associated with the radical feminist ideas discussed in the following chapters. There is also an increasingly widespread perception that, rather than accepting standards laid down by men we should value qualities and roles traditionally associated with women, treating caring responsibilities as a basis for citizenship entitlements such as pensions, and ensuring that they do not disadvantage women in the competitive employment market. In the United States Mary Mason, a former campaigner for the ERA, has argued that genuine equality of opportunity 'would not have stressed equal competition, but would address the issues of government-subsidized child care, paid maternity leave, a higher minimum wage ... rights for part-time workers, affirmative action and re-entry rights' (Mason, 1988:41).

Some writers are concerned that if such provisions are seen as rights for women workers only, they will confirm their domestic responsibilities and re-establish their 'natural' difference from men. Here Ruth Lister has argued that we need to move beyond the difference/equality debate and to remember that in fact the opposite of equality is not difference but *inequality*: 'To posit it as difference disguises the relations of subordination, hierarchy and consequent disadvantage, which underlie the dichotomy, and serves to distort the political choices open to us' (Lister, 1997:96). She argues both that it is essential to recognise and reward the qualities and roles associated with women (particularly as mothers and carers) and that these should not be seen either as essential attributes of womanhood or the sole basis of women's claims to rights. She therefore calls for a reconceptualisation of equality that by-passes arguments about difference and sameness to recognise human interdependence and acknowledge the diversity of individual circumstances (for related arguments, see Bacchi, 1990). As we have seen, some high profile equal rights campaigners are also moving in this direction and demanding changes in employment practices that recognise the family responsibilities of male as well as female workers. Such recognition has gone furthest in the Scandinavian nations (see Bryson, 1999), but even in the United States there is now a limited right to unpaid parental leave for men as well as women. Although this right is fenced round with restrictions, it marks an important step away from earlier 'common sense' assumptions based on male experience, and offers some recognition of the work that is still largely done by women without assuming that it has to be their responsibility.

Such arguments allow for a resolution of the difference/equality debate at a practical policy level. As we shall see in Chapter 14, they are also in line with postmodernism, which rejects binary thinking and seeks to de-stabilise, displace and go beyond apparent dichotomies.

Affirmative action: employment and political representation

The conflict between 'common sense' understanding of equality and feminist demands for more meaningful change is even more acute when these are extended to affirmative action programmes to improve women's workplace situation or increase their political representation (see Bacchi, 1996 and Eisenstein, 1994). Such programmes include women-only train-ing schemes and target-setting as well as formal quotas, and are widely seen as a form of charity for the underprivileged or as a form of unjustifi-able discrimination against men. However, affirmative action is supported by NOW as a way of promoting genuine equality of opportunity on the grounds that existing procedures still frequently favour white men even when they appear to be neutral, as they reflect subjective and gender-biased assumptions about 'merit'. Although NOW does not go so far as to support quotas, this marks a step towards the radical feminist view that 'virtually every quality that distinguishes men from women is already affirmatively compensated in this society' (Catherine MacKinnon, quoted in Jaggar, 1994:56). Arguments for affirmative action also bring out clearly the tension between the liberal feminist demand that women be given rights as *individuals* and the recognition of their shared subordination and needs as *women*; as such, they help reveal structural patterns of privilege and oppression and the biases that underlie the apparent neutrality of existing practices. Iris Young has therefore argued that affirmative action programmes 'challenge principles of liberal equality more than many proponents are willing to admit'; she maintains that they *do* discriminate, but argues that discrimination against the privileged is just:

> If discrimination serves the purpose of undermining the oppression of a group, it may be not only permitted, but morally required. (Young, 1990:192 and 197; see also Richards, 1982)

Debates around affirmative action become even more complex when applied to political representation, as this involves not only the claims of aspiring candidates but issues around group representation and what Anne Phillips has called the 'politics of presence' (Phillips, 1995). As Phillips notes, liberal democratic theory has generally seen political representation in terms of opinions and ideas, and treats the social or physical attributes of elected members as irrelevant. However, some earlier feminists claimed that women have distinct interests that should be represented and/or attributes that can improve political life, and debates around difference and equality have re-surfaced in demands for positive action to increase the number of women in elected office. Such debates were expressed particularly clearly in France in the mid 1990s, when the 'parity movement' successfully campaigned for laws obliging political parties to field equal numbers of male and female candidates (Gaspard, 2001; Lambert, 2001). Although some parity campaigners used essentialist arguments, advocacy of quotas need not depend on this, and many argue that quotas are only needed because women have been subordinated – that is, for historically specific and contingent reasons (see for example Mansbridge, 2001). Phillips herself rejects essentialism but argues in favour of quotas on the grounds that the needs of a politically excluded community, such as women, are unlikely to be adequately represented unless members of the group are actually present, and that the under-representation of women means that important areas of human experience are likely to be excluded from political debate. She does not claim that all women share the same interests or that an increase in female representation will *necessarily* benefit women. It is however clear that interests are gendered (for example, although not all women become pregnant, childbirth and abortion are not gender-neutral experiences), and Phillips believes that a move towards gender parity is at least *likely* to produce more balanced politics, so that 'Changing the gender composition of elected assemblies is a major, and necessary, challenge to the social arrangements which have systematically placed women in a subordinate position' (Phillips, 1995:82).

As in other areas of employment, such equality of outcome is unlikely to be produced without some kind of deliberate action. In their 'Introduction' to an edited volume that compares the use of such methods in Europe and the United States, Jytte Klausen and Charles Maier have recently argued that in this sense liberal democracy has failed women (Klausen and Maier, 2001). Certainly, the more collectivist political culture of many European nations has made the use of quotas and related measures more acceptable than in the United States. Although Klausen and Maier suggest that in practice liberalism may ultimately prove flexible enough to allow the use of quotas to promote equality, this would run counter to liberal ideas of the state discussed below; and their claim that welfare measures in the Depression of the 1930s sets a precedent for state action to overcome inequality fails to see that provision in the United Sates was aimed at mitigating the most extreme effects of poverty rather than narrowing the gap between rich and poor.

What kind of equality? equality with whom?

The demand for equality raises the question of 'what kind of equality?' and 'equality with whom?' Here equal rights feminists are often accused of a narrow focus on formal legal and political rights which ignores economic, cultural and sexual exploitation and oppression. They are also said to reflect only the concerns of middle-class white women who are privileged in every way other than their sex, and of ignoring the inequalities amongst men and the realities of class and 'race' oppression. Such criticisms over-simplify a complex movement for, as we have seen, recent writers within the equal rights tradition acknowledge the 'private' and domestic bases of public inequalities and are going some way towards challenging the terms on which equality is granted. Nevertheless, the liberal writers discussed in this chapter show little awareness of the needs and experiences of black and/or working-class women. In the late 1940s and early 1950s, before she herself became a suburban housewife, Betty Friedan had been involved in left-wing organisations and union activity, and, as a labour journalist, had addressed the situation of working-class women (Horowitz, 1998). However, *The Feminine Mystique* was clearly aimed at middle-class women for whom employment could be a means of fulfilment rather than an economic necessity; indeed, Friedan said that it would be worth doing even if the former housewife had to spend most of her earnings on a cleaning woman (*Mystique*:303) The needs of the cleaning woman, along with those of all the other women who have always had to work in monotonous, badly paid jobs rather than interesting careers, were, however, completely ignored. Elitist assumptions are similarly found in Naomi Wolf's suggestion that women form 'power groups' with twenty to thirty members, which can meet once a month at parties with wine and music to support each other by sharing information, resources, contacts and plans (Wolf, 1993), as she seems quite unaware that this can appeal only to those women whose houses are big enough to host such events, who have time free from caring or workplace responsibilities and who are members of a cultural group which approves the use of alcohol.

Following the rise of the New Right in western democracies and the collapse of communism in Eastern Europe, socialist critiques of the capitalist economic system have recently declined in influence, and issues of economic inequality are strikingly absent from today's political agenda (see Phillips, 1999). In this context, it is unsurprising that equal rights feminism generally fails to question the logic of a hierarchical, competitive society in which most men and women can only be losers, and in which 'Women who enter the competitive marketplace do not become free, but rather simply join men in chains' (Brown, 1993:69). This means that although some equal rights feminists today are concerned with broader aspects of equality (for example, NOW campaigns vigorously on a range of poverty-related issues) and, as we have seen, many are broadening their concerns to demand radical changes in conditions of employment, there is little analysis of the implications of this for the underlying logic of an economic system driven by the pursuit of profit.

Power and the state

Critics of liberal feminism have argued both that feminist demands for equal rights inevitably push the state in a non-liberal direction and that they are often based on a naïve approach that fails to understand the nature of state power. Classical liberal theory was highly suspicious of the state, which it saw as a threat to individual freedom; from this perspective its role was simply to provide the legal framework and security that enables individuals to pursue their own ends. For much of the twentieth century, there was a gradual trend within liberal thought away from this classic laissez-faire position and towards a greater degree of state responsibility for the economy and general social welfare. Welfare provision was, however, far more limited in the United States than in Europe, where more collectivist ideologies were stronger, and, since the 1980s, neo-liberal ideas of individual self-reliance and freedom from state intervention have been far more influential.

Today, there is a clear tension between the New Right call to 'roll back the state' and feminist demands for active policies to combat discrimination against women, particularly if these involve 'social engineering' to encourage people into non-traditional gender roles, or the uses of quotas. This tension is also acute if equal opportunities for women are thought to include the provision of adequate childcare, or if the terms of equal rights are changed to enable both men and women to combine paid work with family responsibilities. From a liberal perspective, such policies constitute a dangerously high level of state intervention in the workings of the free market which reduces profitability, requires heavier taxation and reduce individual choice – hence opposition from the 1988–92 Bush administration and Conservative governments in Britain in the early 1990s to measures providing a right to unpaid parental leave (very limited rights were approved in the United States by Clinton in 1992 and in Britain by Blair in 1997).

As we have seen in this chapter, many equal rights feminists now see state intervention as a means rather than a threat to individual freedom, and are moving in what could be described as a 'social democratic' direction. However, some radical and Marxist feminist critics see such approaches as naïve. In contrast to liberal theorists, their arguments are based on the belief that the state is *not* neutral between competing groups in society, but is structured around class and/or male interests; this means that the state is not some kind of neutral tool that women can use for feminist ends, for it is inherently opposed to their needs (see MacKinnon, 1983). Some argue that, although state provision and intervention may free women from dependence on individual men, it increases their dependence on the patriarchal state, and that state provision of services may operate as a means of social control – for example by increased surveillance of women's sexual behaviour or their childrearing practices (for discussion of whether the state is inherently patriarchal, see Borchorst and Siim, 1987; Pateman, 1988; Smart, 1989; Hernes, 1988; Siim, 1991 and Chapter 12 below). From this perspective, equal rights campaigners fail to see the gendered and/or class nature of state power and the vested interests that may obstruct women's progress; they are therefore taken by surprise when apparently reasonable and just demands are met with vigorous opposition, or when legislation fails to produce the results that they intended. For example, although Friedan described the ways in which the cult of domesticity serves the needs of the capitalist economy (*Mystique*:181) and is now calling for less stress on short-term profitability (Friedan, 1997:19), she seems to assume that once the injustices of women's position have been pointed out, then capitalists will make the necessary sacrifices and adjustments; similarly it does not seem to have occurred to her that many men might be reluctant to surrender public power and economic superiority in order to participate more fully in family life. Wolf too acknowledges the ways in which the market economy damages women's lives, but believes 'in equipping women so that they're not disempowered in the market economy' (quoted in Viner, 2001) without analysing what this might mean in practice.

Similar issues arise from the analyses of Okin and Richards. Although these were more theoretically based, they made no real attempt to explain *why* women were still treated unjustly, or to understand the forces that militated against their proposed changes. In an earlier book Okin did acknowledge the problem: she expected her proposals 'to be resisted strongly by those with economic power and an interest in maintaining the status quo', and she questioned whether they were achievable within the structures of capitalism (Okin, 1980:303). However, she never explored the implications of this statement. Richards seemed even less aware of such considerations. For her, the prime task was to demonstrate the philosophical requirements of justice, and her main enemies were therefore careless thinking and faulty logic. The possibility of opposition to her proposals based on self-interest was not even considered, and she made no attempt to explore the very real motives that powerful groups may have in perpetuating injustice. This means that her approach failed to see that 'the terms of moral debate do not exist in a remote philosopher's heaven' (Grimshaw, 1982:6), but in a world characterised by gender, 'race' and class divisions and in which outcomes are likely to be determined by power, rather than by the sweet voice of reason.

Here then we have one of the major problems of liberal feminism: that in trying to discover through reason a universally valid concept of justice, it cannot understand the realities of social existence and the power relations of society. For many critics, this does not necessarily mean that the task of identifying goals is meaningless, but that unless it is combined with an attempt to understand the history and causes of women's oppression and the very real forces opposing liberation, feminist proposals will remain merely utopian, academic exercises incapable of realisation. As we shall see in later sections, however, some feminists today also question the whole idea of objectively discoverable justice and/or the use of reason to discover it.

The public/private distinction

Many feminists have argued that the use of a liberal framework in the pursuit of equality also produces a related set of problems stemming from its distinction between the 'public' and the 'private'[7] (for recent feminist discussions, see Lister, 1997 and 2000; Landes (ed.) 1998; Eisenstein, 1984 and 1996; Okin, 1990; Phillips, 1991 and 1993; Young, 1990; Pateman, 1986a, 1987 and 1989; Allen, 1996; Fraser, 1998; Ackelsberg and Shanley, 1996). From a liberal democratic perspective, politics must be kept out of private life if freedom is to survive; this perspective also sees the public sphere as one in which the particularities and personal differences of private life can be transcended, so that all adults are treated as equal citizens under the law, irrespective of their sex, skin colour, economic resources or other differences. This promise of universal citizenship is in many ways very attractive. However, while the underlying public/private distinction sets itself up as a universal principle, it is culturally and historically specific. It is also heavily gendered, with women associated with the private and men the public. Not only does the distinction devalue the qualities and activities associated with private life and women, but some argue that it is premised on their exclusion, as the public world of dispassionate, impersonal, disembodied rights and reason is seen as rising above the messy particularities of emotion, caring, subjectivity and physical needs. The distinction also makes it difficult to see that such apparently 'private' areas of life as the family or sexuality may in fact be the site of sexual politics or oppression and that women's private responsibilities affect their ability to compete with men in the public sphere.

The public/private distinction does therefore seem to pose major problems for feminists; indeed, as we shall see in the next chapters, some radical feminists have argued both that the distinction is itself a patriarchal device, designed to conceal the private bases of women's oppression, and that no area of life can be outside politics. However, many feminists today defend the principle that we have a right to some form of privacy, arguing against the ways that the public/private distinction has been constructed and used rather than against the principle of distinction itself.

From this perspective, a key task of feminist theory is to reveal the political and essentially contested nature of the current categories and their gendered and subordinating nature, so that the distinction can no longer be used to exclude issues from public discussion, and the ways in which privileged groups have established the boundaries in their own favour can be identified and resisted. The aim here need not be to establish new, definitive boundaries, but to recognise that these can be both fluid and context-dependent (for application of these issues to the Clarence Thomas hearings in the United States, see Fraser, 1998; and Ackelsberg and Shanley, 1996). As with the reconceptualisation of the difference/equality debate discussed above, this kind of movement beyond rigid, dichotomous thinking is both a product both of practical considerations and a reflection of the influence of the postmodern ideas discussed in Chapter 14.

Individualism and individual rights

For many feminists, a more adequate conception of equality and a re-drawing of public/private distinctions require a modification of liberal assumptions about the very meaning of what it is to be human. Most liberal thinkers have treated the individual for whom rights are claimed as essentially pre-social, disembodied and autonomous, possessed of rationality but no more particular characteristics; many also see individuals as inherently competitive and egotistical. Some feminist critics argue that this approach, which Alison Jaggar has labelled 'political solipsism', ignores the emotion, nurturing, co-operation and mutual support that are an essential basis for human society, and that have historically been central to women's lives (Jaggar, 1983; see also Pateman, 1986a; Wolgast, 1980; and Frazer and Lacey, 1993).

The liberal paradigm of 'the individual' produces a number of interrelated problems for feminists at the level of both ontology and political practice. Nancy Hirschmann has drawn on feminist psychoanalytic theory to argue that its view of the self as fundamentally separate is based upon a psychic need to reject women which is itself an inevitable product of woman-only childrearing practices, as these mean that a small boy can achieve adult male identity only by rejecting 'the mother' and the ideas of connectedness that she represents (Hirschmann, 1992). From this perspective, liberalism's historic exclusion of women from fully human status is no accident, and they can never be fully assimilated on existing liberal terms. Secondly, and rather more tangibly, if liberalism is based on a partial and incomplete view of human nature, it cannot provide an adequate understanding of human motivation and behaviour; this means that it will be unable to predict political outcomes or provide a workable political strategy. Thirdly, even if the goal of equality in a competitive market system is accepted, liberalism's failure to acknowledge human interdependence or to discuss society's reproductive and domestic needs has important practical consequences, for these needs will not simply 'go away' once it is recognised that women have a right to fulfil themselves in other roles. The liberal feminist promise of liberation from domesticity therefore begs the question of who is to care for children and the home; although as we have seen some writers now advocate flexible work arrangements, childcare provision and greater male involvement in the home, it is hard to see why capitalism should accommodate these changes or why a majority of men should willingly embrace activities which feminists have seen as inherently unfulfilling. (Friedan cited as evidence of a change in male attitudes the fact that 'three out of four gourmet dinner parties suddenly seem to be cooked, soup to mousse, by men' [1981:41]; sceptics might find a sudden male enthusiasm for cleaning the lavatory rather more convincing.)

The individualistic assumptions of liberalism, particularly as these have been expressed in the United States, are also difficult to reconcile with collective or state support for caring responsibilities; Flora Davis therefore blames the particularly poor level of provision in the United States on 'the American tradition of extreme individualism, which undercut the commitment to the community, to the common good, and even to the family' (Davis, 1999:307; see also Somerville, 2000). As Selma Sevenhuijsen has pointed out, the damaging effects of applying the discourse of individual rights is particularly clear in child custody cases, where she says it should be replaced by one based on needs and welfare (Sevenhuijsen, 1991). Similar problems arise when abortion is defended in terms of a woman's right to do what she wants with her own body, as this creates an adversarial relationship between a woman and her foetus/unborn child which ignores the considerations of care and responsibility that may influence her decision (see Bryson, 1999, chapter 7 for an exploration of these issues). Some feminists have therefore argued that a less individualistic 'ethic of care', as discussed below, is more appropriate than an individual rights-based approach when discussing reproductive issues.

A final problem arising from the individualistic assumptions of liberalism is the difficulty these may pose for a feminist politics based on recognition of shared gender interests: the liberal belief that it is up to each person to make the best of his or her own life clashes with feminist awareness of group disadvantage and the need for collective action. Arguing from a socialist perspective, Zillah Eisenstein claimed in the early 1980s that this contradiction meant that liberal feminism was constantly threatening to overstep the boundaries of liberalism itself, and that in thus revealing the limitations of liberal thought it had the potential for developing in a truly radical direction (although she did not think this development was inevitable: Eisenstein, 1981 and 1984; see also Cott, 1987:6). In contrast, as we have seen, Joan Scott sees this tension as an essentially unresolvable paradox; rather than trying to move beyond liberalism, she explores the ways that the contradictory 'discourses of liberal individualism' produced feminism, stating that both that feminism has historically depended on liberalism for its existence and that 'there was (is still) no alternative' (Scott, 1996:18).

In practice, although liberal feminism remains based on the assumptions of competition, the pursuit of self-interest and the inherent 'fairness' of western democracies, not all liberal feminists are as rabidly individualistic as some of the above criticisms suggest. In particular, as Jet Bussemaker has argued, it is important to distinguish between the significance of individualism in Anglo-American and in continental European societies. Although she rejects individualism in an egoistic or atomistic sense, Bussemaker argues that in Europe today it provides an important defence against the growth of neo-conservatism, with its stress on traditional family and community responsibilities, so that 'although we should distrust strong vocabularies on individualism, we should not reject the concept of individualism wholesale' (Bussemaker, 1998:23). It is, moreover, far from self-evident that recognition of the values of co-operation, nurturing and love need preclude all ideas of individual responsibility and fulfilment. Such values need not be written off as 'male' or 'bourgeois', but can perhaps be rescued and reconciled with other values; the vision of the creative and fulfilled individual, whose needs and desires are bound up with those of the whole community was central to both Marx and Mill, and it is only a minority of radical feminists who wish to submerge women's personhood in their biological function. Nevertheless, for many critics the liberal feminist view of human nature remains a major theoretical problem: for some, this is also bound up with the liberal stress on *reason*, which has provided a focal point for much recent feminist debate.

Reason, knowledge and ethical thought

Although feminists from at least the seventeenth century have argued for equal rights on the grounds that women are as intelligent and rational as men, some recent critics have rejected the idea that women should conform to male standards. They have questioned the authority of systems of knowledge which exclude the experiences and perspectives of half the human race and a scale of values whereby 'producing a book on childcare earns more respect than producing a happy baby' (Jaggar, 1983:188). Some claim that 'male reason' itself is deeply and inherently flawed and some have also denied the very possibility of objective knowledge.

The partiality of male thought

At a fundamental level, it has been argued that liberalism's insistence on the value of the mind over the body is bound up with a rejection of all things female. In *The Man of Reason* (1984), Genevieve Lloyd argued that 'Reason' in Western philosophy is not, as commonly supposed, sex-neutral, because it has been defined in terms of overcoming nature, emotion and particularity, and these have been identified as essentially female: 'the feminine has been associated with what rational knowledge transcends, dominates or simply leaves behind' (Lloyd, 1984:2). Women have therefore traditionally been excluded from the life of the mind, and it is only by *denying* their female-ness that they have been allowed to enter. Lloyd seemed to think that in principle an objective and sex-neutral form of reason was possible. However, Carole Pateman has argued that 'Reason' cannot be 'disembodied', and that the exclusion of women has been *central* to the concerns of western philosophers (Pateman, 1986b), while Nancy Hirschmann has seen this damaging exclusion as in part the deep-seated and non-accidental product of the female monopoly of childcare which produces 'the male infant's need to objectify the mother and to experience the self–other relationship as a dichotomy' (Hirschmann, 1992:192).

Many recent writers have also drawn on postmodernist ideas to argue not simply that manmade knowledge is incomplete because it excludes women, but that *any* attempt to establish universal principles and objective knowledge is inherently misguided and incapable of realisation. From this perspective, any claim to impartial knowledge is a form of political control, a bid for mastery that seeks to present particular versions of reality as impartial and timeless truths. Such a claim 'acts as a cover for situated judgements', while

> The unified, transcendent, reasoning moral subject is not only an intellectual construct but a political one: the objectivity and impartiality attributed to his reasoning stance is in fact a mark of his political power, constituted and conferred in a concrete situation. (Frazer and Lacey, 1993:64)

From this perspective, the task for feminists is not simply to assert women's equal rationality, but to expose and challenge the particularities, limitations and vested interests involved in male knowledge claims (for further discussion, see Chapter 14 below).

Women's experiences and the 'ethic of care' debate

The claim that male knowledge is limited is not confined to postmodern writers, but has been developed by feminists in a number of ways. Some argue that men and women have different ways of thinking that are a product of biology. A strand within radical feminism has argued that women's reproductive functions give them a better way of apprehending the world based on emotion and intuition rather than cold calculation, and they have rejected 'male logic' as both inappropriate to women's lives and a form of patriarchal domination.

The application of reason and rationality to all areas of life can certainly be problematic. Its application to sexuality may lead to a counter-productively calculating hedonism and an inability to 'switch off' mental processes that limits physical pleasure, and it cannot take into account the power of such 'irrational' emotions as jealousy, which may be easier to ignore in theory than in practice (as earlier feminists such as Wollstonecraft and Goldman discovered; see Chapters 1 and 5 above). Many women have also found that the application of rational principles to childrearing is quite simply inefficient, for the experience of childbirth can generate complex and unpredictable emotions, while the needs of children cannot be neatly packaged into pre-planned slots of 'quality time'. Some therefore argue for the superiority of instinct and intuition over calculation and academic knowledge, although others continue to insist that the intelligent use of reason is the basis of good mothering. Many also agree with Richards that in practice reason need not be in conflict with other modes of knowing, but is frequently based upon them, and that although it may have been misused to dominate women, 'Reason is not the same thing as men's often questionable use of reasoning' (Richards, 1982:41).

Some writers argue that women's typical experiences, rather than innate biological differences, give rise to distinctive ways of thinking. Here the work of Carol Gilligan has been particularly influential. In *In a Different Voice*, first published in 1982, Gilligan argued that women's involvement in caring activities has led to empirically identifiable differences between men and women in the ways in which they think and moralise about the world. She claimed that while male ethical systems are based on individualistic ideas of justice and right, female ones are based on caring and responsibility, and that, unlike men's, women's moral thinking recognises the importance of emotions, intimacy and relationships.

The idea that morality can be based on 'womanly values' of care and a recognition of human connectedness, rather than on cold calculation or 'cool, distanced relations between more or less free and equal adult strangers' (Baier, 1986:248), has proved very attractive to many writers. Others, however, have been much more critical. Dietz has argued that 'maternal thinking' is inherently limited and cannot provide an adequate basis for political theory or citizenship (Dietz, 1985), while Grimshaw reminded those who wish to replace or supplement 'male philosophy' with one based on female experiences that there is no unity of experience shared by all men or by all women (against which Hirschmann argues that mother-only childrearing cuts across cultures to offer at least a 'large historical narrative' of common experiences: Grimshaw, 1986:259 and Hirschmann, 1992:175). Others argue that key features of an 'ethic of care' are not unique to women. Several have identified similarities with the moral theory produced by the male writers of the Scottish Enlightenment (Sevenhuijsen, 1991; Tronto, 1993; Baier, 1987); Patricia Hill Collins argues that its stress on connection and the concrete rather than separation and abstraction is also to be found in African-American thought (Collins, 1990); while Joan Tronto has argued that an ethic of care may be a product of subordination or minority status rather than any essential difference between male and female modes of thought (Tronto, 1993).

Gilligan's work has sometimes been treated as an affirmation of female superiority and essential difference from men. However, she argued that a mature ethical theory would *combine* ideas of responsibility with those of rights, recognising both human interdependence and an individual's sense of self; as such, it would be superior to both the selfish, individualistic male ethic and the self-sacrificing female ethic. Because she saw ways of thinking as a product of experience rather than biology, changing gender roles could in principle facilitate the development of such a mature theory; this ideas has been developed by other writers to argue that men as well as women can and should be involved in the activities that give rise to an ethic of care. Sarah Ruddick, for example, has argued both that the demands of childrearing lead to the development of particular ways of thinking that are opposed to militarism and that, in the interest of world peace, men as well as women must gain these experiences (Ruddick, 1980, 1984 and 1990; see also the excellent discussion in Grimshaw, 1986). As we have seen above, Okin has similarly argued that men should play a greater role in the family, and claims that this would improve their capacity to act morally in public life:

> The experience of *being* a physical and psychological nurturer – whether of a child or of another adult – would increase that capacity to identify with and fully comprehend the viewpoints of others that is important to a sense of justice. (*Justice*:18)

The idea that ethics of responsibility and justice are complementary rather than opposed have become increasingly influential in recent years (Squires, 1999; see also Lister, 1997). More generally, it might be that the dichotomy between man and woman, mind and body, reason and nature may be less clear cut than both traditional theory and some feminist criticism suggests; it may also be that the distinctions are not inherently hierarchical, but may in principle simply represent different and interrelated modes of knowledge and existence.

Feminism, equal rights and liberalism today

In the past, the struggle for legal and political equality was clearly progressive, and was bound up with the achievement of concrete improvements in the lives of women of all classes. Today, in many countries of the world, the legal, political and economic rights demanded by earlier generations of feminists are seen as obvious and uncontested entitlements. At the very least, these equal rights provide us with a better starting-point for future struggle and most feminists agree both that they must be defended against any attempts to remove or weaken them and that we should support women pursuing them in nations where they do not exist.

Public discussion of how western feminists can build upon their rights and translate them into more genuine and inclusive equality generally remains within a liberal paradigm, which has established as 'common sense' a set of assumptions with which feminists have had to engage. As this chapter has shown, however, these assumptions are in significant respects inadequate, and can obscure rather than enhance our understanding. In particular, they are based on concepts which often work to exclude, marginalise or devalue qualities, roles and experiences traditionally associated with women. These concepts can lock us in ways of thinking which treat men as the undisputed measure of what it is to be human and make it difficult to see the complex interrelationships between 'public' and 'private' life and the broader power structures within which rights and responsibilities may be exercised. They may also be based on categories of thought which, while they appear to be impartial, are both an expression of and a means to women's subordination.

In practice, experience (both personal and political) seems to push many feminist campaigners for equal rights into challenging key liberal assumptions, particularly by recognising the shared nature of apparently individual experiences, by calling for a form of equality that recognises the importance of caring responsibilities and by advocating state intervention to promote it. Some of the 'radical feminist' ideas discussed in the following chapters have also been quite widely accepted by 'mainstream' feminists, and the identification of strands of feminism is even more complex than in the past. Nevertheless, liberal concepts of equality and individual rights remain the starting-point for each new feminist generation in the west, the 'default setting' of political thought which continues to structure debates.

10

Radical feminism and the concept of patriarchy

The equal rights feminism discussed in the previous chapter took the 'common sense' values of liberal democracy as its starting-point. In contrast, the radical feminist ideas thrown up by the Women's Liberation Movement (WLM) from the late 1960s produced a challenge to accepted values and life-styles that often seemed both extreme and shocking. Although in practice there was always a significant overlap between the WLM and equal rights feminism in terms of both goals and membership, radical feminism had a theoretical starting-point which clearly distinguished it from other approaches. Firstly, as its name suggests, radical feminism claimed to go to the roots of women's oppression, and it proclaimed itself as a theory of, by and for women; as such, it was based firmly in women's own experiences and perceptions and saw no need to compromise with existing political perspectives and agendas. Secondly, it saw the oppression of women as the most fundamental and universal form of domination, and its aim was to understand and end this; here 'patriarchy' was a key term. From this it followed that, thirdly, women as a group had interests opposed to those of men; these interests united them in a common sisterhood that transcended the division of class or 'race', and meant that women should struggle together to achieve their own liberation. Finally, radical feminist analysis insisted that male power was not confined to the public worlds of politics and paid employment, but that it extended into private life; this meant that traditional concepts of power and politics were challenged and extended to such 'personal' areas of life as the family and sexuality, both of which were seen as instruments of patriarchal domination.

The origins of radical feminism

As we have seen in earlier chapters, such ideas were not new, but it was not until the late 1960s that they began to be formulated as a self-conscious theory. The impetus towards this development came from women's

163

experiences in the Civil Rights, anti-war, New Left and student movements in North America, Europe and Australia. In these, young women were to find that left-wing groups were not immune from the 'feminine mystique' that Betty Friedan had identified in mainstream American life, and that their role was essentially that of secretary, housewife or sex object, servicing the political, domestic and sexual needs of male activists; any attempt at raising the subject of women's exclusion from decision-making was met with silence, ridicule or contempt. Such sexism has by now been well documented (see for example Evans, 1980; and Sargent, 1986); it is perhaps also worth recording that my first sight of a 'Women's Lib' banner was at a student sit-in in 1970, and that it was produced as a reaction to the proposal that the 'girls' clean up while the 'men' discussed strategy. In the United States, the irony of a movement that seemed to promise freedom to black people while denying it to women soon became apparent, symbolised in the often quoted comment of the black leader, Stokely Carmichael, who refused to discuss the position of women in the movement beyond saying that it should be 'prone'. As in the nineteenth century, parallels between the situation of blacks and women were readily drawn (see, for example, Gayle Rubin, 'Woman as Nigger', 1970), and when, after 1964, sections of the black movement shifted away from liberal civil rights ideas to more radical and militant concepts of black power, white imperialism, black separatism and liberation through revolution, some women saw this as a clear model for a female liberation that went far beyond liberal ideas of equal rights. From this new perspective, women were involved in a revolutionary struggle against men that could not be won by polite requests for equal opportunities or changes in the law; far from seeking respectability and acceptance within the system, feminists were now committed to its overthrow.

Despite these origins in black movements, many critics claim that from its inception radical feminism has been rooted in racist assumptions. There had always been social, racial and sexual tensions between black and white women in the civil rights movement and, although black women had been to the forefront of early complaints about sexism, they rapidly became invisible in a movement that contrasted the demands of *blacks* and *women*, as if *black women* did not exist (see Evans, 1980, and Spelman, 1988). Insistence on the oppression shared by all women also obscured the very real differences that existed amongst women, and seemed to deny the possibility that women could oppress each other.

The systematic articulation of a black feminist critique lay however in the future, and in the first heady years of the new movement such problems seemed easily ignored. In 1967, the first radical women's groups were formed in the United States. Influenced by Maoist ideas current in left-wing circles, these used the Chinese communist idea of 'speaking bitterness' to express and share personal experiences so as to bring out their political implications and to develop a political strategy for change. This approach, which also drew on 'Old Left' ideas about enabling workers to recognise their collective oppression and potential power (Weigland, 2001:151), became known as 'consciousness raising' and was of central importance in this period as women broke years of silence to discover the shared nature of problems which they had assumed to be theirs alone. Later, some women tended to use consciousness-raising as a form of therapy which articulated problems to which individualistic solutions could be found; originally, however, it was a self-consciously political strategy, based on the premise that women's problems were shared and that they could only be ended by collective political action (see Morgan, 1970 and Brooke, 1978). As new groups spread rapidly, the key message was that 'the personal is political', and that a new theory and strategy for women's liberation could only be based on women's shared experiences, not on abstract speculation. From this perspective, no aspect of life lacked a political dimension and political struggle could therefore take many new forms; women's struggle could not be postponed until 'after the revolution' but was a matter for immediate political action, and was to be waged against the universal oppressor–man. Such views were epitomised by the New York Redstockings manifesto of 1969:

> Women are an oppressed class. Our oppression is total, affecting every facet of our lives. We are exploited as sex objects, breeders, domestic servants, and cheap labor. We are considered inferior beings whose only purpose is to enhance men's lives ... we have been kept from seeing our personal suffering as a political condition ... the conflicts between individual men and women are political conflicts that can only be solved collectively ... We identify the agents of our oppression as men. Male supremacy is the oldest, most basic form of domination ... *All men* receive economic, sexual, and psychological benefits from male supremacy. *All men* have oppressed women. (in Morgan, 1970:598)

Kate Millett and the theory of patriarchy

By the early 1970s, these new ideas were reflected in a substantial body of literature that included Kate Millett's *Sexual Politics*, Shulamith Firestone's *The Dialectic of Sex*, Germaine Greer's *The Female Eunuch* and Eva Figes' *Patriarchal Attitudes* (all first published in 1970); anthologies of some of the new manifestos, speeches and articles were also published in Betty and Theodore Roszak's *Masculine/Feminine* (1969), Robin Morgan's *Sisterhood is Powerful* (1970), Leslie Tanner's *Voices from Women's Liberation* (1970) and Michelle Wandor's *The Body Politic* (1972). While all of these were important manifestations of the new movement, it is the second chapter of Millett's *Sexual Politics* that was of the most theoretical importance, as it introduced into feminist thought the key concept of *patriarchy*.

The term patriarchy was not of course new to political theory, but the use to which Millett put it certainly was. Derived from the Greek *patriarches*, meaning 'head of the tribe', it was central to seventeenth-century debates over the extent of monarchical power; here supporters of absolute rule claimed that the power of a king over his people was the same as that of a father over his family, and that both were sanctioned by God and nature. Millett seemed to take such familial power as her starting-point, so that 'the principles of patriarchy appear to be twofold: male shall dominate female, elder male shall dominate young' (*Politics*:25). It was, however, only the first of these principles that she explored, and she did not distinguish between male power within the family and in society as whole; despite the efforts of some writers to restrict the term to strictly family-based power (see Randall, 1987:20; and Cocks, 1989), its use as a shorthand for a social system based on male domination and female subordination has become standard amongst feminists.

Millett's central claims were simple, and they essentially represented a formalisation of the ideas that were already current in the new women's movement. She argued that in all known societies relationships between the sexes have been based on power, and that they are therefore political. This power takes the form of male domination over women in all areas of life; sexual domination is so universal, so ubiquitous and so complete that it appears 'natural' and hence becomes invisible, so that it is 'perhaps the most pervasive ideology of our culture and provides its most fundamental concept of power' (*Politics*:25). According to Millett, the patriarchal power of men over women is basic to the functioning of all societies and it extends far beyond formal institutions of power. It overrides class and 'race' divisions, for economic dependency means that women's class identity is a 'tangential, vicarious and temporary matter', while 'sexism may be more endemic in our society than racism' (*Politics*:38 and 39). Patriarchy is primarily maintained by a process of conditioning which starts with childhood socialisation within the family and is reinforced by education, literature and religion to such an extent that its values are internalised by men and women alike; for some women this leads to self-hatred, self-rejection and an acceptance of inferiority. Millett further argued that, despite the success of this 'interior colonisation', patriarchy also rests upon economic exploitation and the use or threat of force. This means that its history is a record of man's inhumanity to woman and that the thousands of women who die in the United States each year as a result of illegal abortion are victims of the same system as the Indian woman forced to die on her husband's funeral pyre, the Chinese woman crippled by foot-binding and the African girl whose clitoris is cut out. In all societies too, patriarchy relies upon sexual violence and rape. In this context, sexual relations between men and women are but an expression of male power, and Millett devoted a large section of her book to 'deconstructing' the portrayal of sex in the work of four major twentieth-century writers (D. H. Lawrence, Henry Miller, Norman Mailer and Jean Genet) so as to reveal the crude sexual domination involved. Love, too, can be but a confidence trick, part of a patriarchal ideology designed to hide the realities of power; not until patriarchy has been overthrown and sexuality radically transformed can men and women relate as equal human beings.

Criticisms of the concept of patriarchy

For many women, Millett's ideas were a revelation, enabling separate pieces of knowledge and experience to 'click' into place, and transforming the way they saw the world (Tobias, 1997:5 and 192). As discussed in the following sections, the radical feminist concept of patriarchy has, however, been heavily criticised by other feminists, and has been accused of being both politically counter-productive and based on sloppy, over-ambitious and dangerously misleading theoretical assumptions (for influential early criticisms, see Rowbotham, 1982 and Beechey, 1979). My own view is that 'patriarchy' can be an illuminating concept, but not a fully-fledged theory, and that if used carefully it can avoid the problems that critics have identified (see Bryson, 1999b).

Politics and personal life

The claim that 'the personal is political' is central to the concept of patriarchy. Some critics say that this has totalitarian implications, for it implies that no area of life can be free from political scrutiny and that feminists are to be held accountable to their 'sisters' for their every aspect of their behaviour; according to Natasha Walter, such a 'politically correct' approach believes that feminism is incompatible with enjoyment of fashion or heterosexuality (Walter, 1998). Other critics argue that the insistence that the personal is political is effectively *de-politicising*, as it can seem to suggest that feminists can never hope to change the world before they have put their own personal houses in impeccable order; as such, it legitimises a privatised and self-indulgent retreat from collective struggle and into the seductive world of open-ended therapy, counselling and 'alternative' healing.

Although some women may have interpreted it in these ways, these criticisms are not true of Millett's original theory, and owe more to media hype than radical feminist analysis. In 1996, a new international collection of essays by sixty-eight self-proclaimed radical feminists, *Radically Speaking*, defended their position against such misinterpretation, and made it clear that they were not demanding that private life should *become* political, but claiming that it *already is*. From this perspective, current notions of privacy conceal many of the ways in which women are oppressed, but the question of whether we should have a right to private life can be left open. Several contributors also explicitly stated that their goal was not individual therapy but collective action (Bell and Klein (eds), 1996).

A merely descriptive approach?

In describing her work as 'notes towards a *theory* of patriarchy' (*Politics*:24), Millett seemed to imply that she was doing much more than simply describing male power; critics, however, say that both she and later feminist writers on patriarchy have confused description with explanation and that, despite their theoretical pretensions, they have provided only the former; they have, in short, both claimed too much and delivered too little (see for example Beechey, 1979; Gardiner, 1997; Whelehan, 1995).

Even at its most basic level, however, the concept of patriarchy was not confined to description; nor could it be. Deciding which 'facts' are politically significant inevitably involves theoretical assumptions; in describing facts that had previously gone unremarked, feminist discussions of patriarchy made these assumptions explicit, and thereby provided a profound challenge to conventional political theory and the definition of politics itself. This may not constitute a fully-fledged theory; but it does provide the basis for analysis and understanding which goes well beyond simple description.

Millett did not claim to provide a theory of the origins of patriarchy, although she was clear that patriarchy must be understood in its own terms rather than as a product of class society. Other writers have, however, been less reticent, and by the late 1980s there seemed to be a fairly widespread consensus that a matriarchy in which women were in positions of power and domination has never existed, but that some very early societies have been much more woman-centred than our own, and that some may have been based on matrilineal descent and a degree of sexual equality (see Lerner, 1986). For some radical feminists, the original shift to patriarchy was simply a consequence of men's greater strength, stemming from women's weakness during pregnancy, childbirth and lactation; for others, it was above all men's ability to rape that enabled them to dominate women (Brownmiller, 1977). Some, however, claimed that it was the discovery of the male role in reproduction that was critical and first led men to seek to control women. Thus Rich wrote that:

> A crucial moment in human consciousness arrives when man discovers that it is he himself, not the moon or the spring rains or the spirits of the dead, who impregnates the woman; that the child she carries and gives birth to is his child, who can make him immortal. (Rich, 1977:60; see also Figes, 1970; O'Brien, 1981)

Yet others saw the development of patriarchy as rooted in the early development of hunting by men, which both gave them a new source of power and led to the development of a value system based on violent conquest (see French, 1985; Collard, 1988; Mies, 1998).

There has therefore been no radical feminist agreement as to the causes or origins of patriarchy, and some see this as a flaw, arguing that if we do not understand the origins of women's oppression we cannot develop a strategy for ending it. Spender, however, did not think this was the case. Like Millett, who refused to become involved in 'the evanescent delights afforded by the game of origins', on the grounds that 'Conjecture about origins is always frustrated by lack of evidence. Speculation about pre-history ... remains nothing but speculation' (*Politics*:28 and 29), she argued that:

> We do not need definite evidence of the first cause to know that men have power, that they have had it for a very long time, that they seem to have had it in every known human society, and that they now use it to keep their power. (Spender, 1985b:42)

From this perspective, what is important is to identify and understand the structures and institutions that maintain patriarchy today in order that these may be overthrown, and this Millett and later writers have attempted to do.

The theoretical stakes are however raised if it is claimed that patriarchy should be defined as a *system* of male domination and female subordination or oppression (see for example, Walby, 1990:20; Cockburn, 1991:6; Rowland and Klein, 1996:15; Tobias, 1997:ix). Here, there is a clear danger of slipping into more ambitious explanatory claims which are based on tautology (men dominate women because they have more power) rather than on the identification of genuine causal relationships. As Anna Pollert has argued, it is not appropriate to treat patriarchy as a system in the same sense as the capitalist market economy, for patriarchy does not have an internal dynamic that is equivalent to the capitalist pursuit of profit: even the most well-intentioned capitalist must exploit his workers or go out of business, but men's relationship with women does not *have* to be exploitative, however deep-seated women's oppression might be

(Pollert, 1996; see also Acker, 1989). Nevertheless, as I have argued elsewhere (Bryson, 1999b), the concept of 'system' can usefully highlight the recurrent and patterned nature of male power, helping to reveal how its different manifestations reinforce each other, so that patriarchy is more than the sum of its parts. This stress on interconnection also suggests that feminist challenges to male power in one area can have knock-on effects in others.

An over-generalised and a-historical account?

For many writers, the task of understanding patriarchy involved the identification of women's oppression across cultures and nations and over time. Thus, for example, Adrienne Rich's account of patriarchy explicitly abstracted the position of women from any social context:

> Under patriarchy, I may live in *purdah* or drive a truck; I may raise my children in a *kibbutz*, or be the sole breadwinner for a fatherless family ... I may serve my husband his early-morning coffee within the clay walls of a Barbar village or march in an academic procession; whatever my status or situation, my derived economic class or my sexual preference, I live under the power of the fathers, and have access only to so much of privilege or influence as the patriarchy is willing to accede to me, and only for so long as I will pay the price for male approval. (Rich, 1977:58)

Similarly, Andrea Dworkin linked the pre-revolutionary Chinese practice of foot-binding to the girdles, high heels and eyebrow plucking dictated by American fashion, claiming that for all women 'Pain is an essential part of the grooming process and that is not accidental ... [it] serves to prepare women for lives of childbearing, self-abnegation and husband-pleasing' (Dworkin, 1974:115). Mary Daly too claimed that such horrors as foot-binding, witch-burning, genital mutilation and modern American gynaecology are all essentially similar manifestations of the universal system of male tyranny, so that the situation of women is basically the same whether they live in Saudi Arabia or Sweden, and 'Even outer space and the future have been colonized' (Daly, 1973, and 1978:1).

At one level, such analyses have an intuitive appeal and contain a kind of truth. It is not necessary to believe in the immutable and biologically based 'badness' of men to agree that women in radically different societies or situations frequently have experiences in common involving sexual exploitation, lack of reproductive freedom and marginalisation or exclusion from 'malestream' economic, social, political and intellectual life; these experiences may reflect the systematic (that is, non-random) exercise of power by men over women. Nevertheless, the idea that all women are united in a common sisterhood that transcends all man-made divisions can be dangerously misleading.

In the first place, a too-easy comparison of women's experiences across the centuries and within and between modern societies may trivialise the depth of suffering experienced by some women. Thus, the oppression experienced by a modern American 'fashion victim' (even one who diets herself to death) is qualitatively different from the suffering of the generations of Chinese women who were from childhood deliberately and systematically crippled in the name of erotic attraction, able only to totter painfully

> on the outside of toes which had been bent under into the sole of the foot. The heel and instep of the foot resembled the sole and heel of a high-heeled boot. Hard callouses formed, toe-nails grew into the skin; the feet were pus-filled and bloody; circulation was virtually stopped. (Dworkin, 1974:101)

Similarly, attempts to compare the experiences of women in very different contemporary societies that are based on the premise that these are essentially 'the same', conceal the vast gap in experience that is involved. For example, lack of reproductive rights has meant something very different to the Romanian woman forced to bear at least six children, the Chinese woman forced by the 'one child' policy to abort her second, the white American career woman whose contraception has failed and the Puerto Rican woman sterilised against her will.

The attempt to universalise women's experience may conceal other forms of oppression based on 'race' or class or belittle their importance, as from the perspective of the global and transhistorical oppression of women, racism, militaristic nationalism and economic exploitation are portrayed as trivial squabbles amongst men. According to some critics, therefore, the feminist assumption that the concerns of white, middle-class Western women can be equated with the experiences of all women everywhere is itself a form of cultural imperialism that seeks to disguise the particularity of its own worldview by the use of spuriously general concepts. This means that 'patriarchy' and 'sisterhood' may be mystifying devices that conceal divisions in society in much the same way as male perspectives have concealed the oppression of women, so that 'There are disturbing parallels between what feminists find disquieting in Western political thought and what many black women have found troubling in much of Western feminism' (Spelman, 1988:6; see also Moraga and Anzaldua, 1983, especially the article by Lorde; Davis, 1982 and 1990; *Feminist Review*, no. 17, 1984; Collins, 1990; Ramazanoglu, 1986).

Such criticisms are extremely serious. However, I would argue that they stem from the use of the concept by some of its less cautious exponents rather than being inherent in it. To use the concept of patriarchy is not necessarily to deny that other forms of oppression are at least as important; rather, it can indicate that a key feminist task is to explore the ways in which oppressions interconnect.

Some writers on patriarchy have seemed to produce an a-historical accumulation of descriptions of men's inhumanity to women which sees women solely as passive victims of male injustice, so that 'Women's powerlessness, victimisation and lack of resources ... constitute women's timeless history' (Segal, 1987:xi). Again, however, the idea that societies are structured by male domination need not in itself preclude the possibility of change or resistance. Millett herself never claimed that patriarchy was an unchanging system of oppression; rather, she argued that as a result of past struggles women had made 'monumental progress' which provided the basis for future change (*Politics*:64); by making patriarchy visible and identifying the battles that have to be fought she saw her own work as itself a part of that struggle.

Later writers have therefore attempted to produce a more sophisticated concept which argues that, far from being unchanging, patriarchal domination takes a number of different forms which are the product of particular historical situations. Thus Ferguson and Walby have both argued that in western societies there has been a general shift away from private patriarchy based on individual control within the household to a public patriarchy based on structures outside the home – although Walby cautions that this is 'a continuum rather than a rigid dichotomy', and has since analysed the complex gains and losses experienced by different groups of women in different areas of their lives (Walby, 1990:180 and 1997; Ferguson, 1989; see also Dahlerup, 1987; Cocks, 1989). Such analysis does not see patriarchy as an unchanging and monolithic structure of oppression, but allows for the possibility that patriarchal power may be challenged and feminist victories won. This means that changes in the nature or degree of patriarchy become visible, as do women's challenges to it.

Women good, men bad: an essentialist view of sex difference?

Although the point was not developed by Millett as much as by some later theorists, a central message of her work must be that it is not unjust laws or economic systems that are responsible for women's oppression but *men*, that men as a group have interests opposed to those of women and that it is therefore against the power of men that the battle must be fought. For many critics such a position is untenable, and is largely responsible for feminism's negative image as a complaining, whining, negative creed, irrelevant to the lives of go-ahead young women (see in particular,

Wolf, 1993 and Walter, 1998, discussed in Chapter 9 above). They point out that many men are not in positions of power over women but may in fact be subordinate to them and that, despite the general imbalance of power, loving and non-exploitative relationships between men and women can and do exist in our society. Men, too, they say, may suffer in a sexist society: for example, they are forced into the role of breadwinner and denied an active role in bringing up their own children and, by having to repress unacceptably 'feminine' aspects of their personality, they are alienated from their own full humanity (for overviews of feminist analyses of men's situation and the ways that they may be damaged by patriarchy, see Bryson 1999a, 2000). Many men, critics say, are willing to help women in their struggle, and their support should not be rejected. Moreover, men cannot be simply 'killed off' in the same way as a class enemy might conceivably be; quite apart from humanitarian considerations, this would be a biological impossibility.

Such criticisms, however, miss the point that the concept of patriarchy does not necessarily imply that all individual men oppress all women, that each and every male person is to be considered an enemy incapable of reform, or that the total elimination of the male sex would be the desired consequence of an improvement in sperm-bank technology. Indeed, an important aspect of the concept is that it enables us to distinguish between the structures of male domination on the one hand and individual men on the other (Dahlerup, 1987; Walby, 1990). This means that the enemy is male *power* in all its manifestations and that, as contributors to *Radically Speaking* make clear, this power is socially constructed and therefore contestable, rather than embodied in all biological males.

It remains true that some radical feminists believe that there are essential and irreducible biological differences that shape men and women's nature, and that women are naturally superior. This view has led some to develop an 'eco-feminist analysis' (see Chapter 11, below), while a small minority have rejected all association with men, whether this be social, sexual or political. Separatist ideas must, however, be disentangled from the original theory of patriarchy; although the concept of patriarchy can be developed in this direction, man-hating and separatism are not inherent in it. Far from seeing all men as an undifferentiated enemy, who can never be trusted as fathers, friends, colleagues, sexual partners or political allies, the concept can in principle be used to explore the possibility of male support and political solidarity, and to analyse ways in which some or all men may themselves be harmed by patriarchy.

For postmodernist critics, the rejection of essentialism goes much further. As we shall see in Chapter 14, postmodernism does not only stress the differences amongst women and the consequent dangers of generalising about their situation, it also questions the underlying assumption (common to all 'modernist' feminists) that it is meaningful to talk about 'women' and 'men' at all. In other words, it destroys the ontological basis of any claims about 'women', for the very terms 'woman' and 'man' are not stable referents to real-world phenomena, but artificial and fluid categories of meaning which should themselves be challenged. The editors of *Radically Speaking* have greeted this kind of analysis with outrage. They claim that postmodernism is a ploy to deny women's collective identity just at a time when they are learning to recognise their shared experiences and act together politically and they proclaim: 'Stubbornly, defiantly, we hold on to that truth. There is such a thing as woman' (Bell and Klein, 1996:xviii). As we shall see, postmodernism may not be as completely incompatible with collective feminist politics as this response suggests. Nevertheless, it is clearly difficult to reconcile a postmodern philosophical stance with the analysis of patriarchy.

The concept of patriarchy today

For some feminists in the 1970s, the beauty of the concept of patriarchy lay in its simplicity, as it seemed to cut through distracting details and irrelevant differences to lay bare the essential, underlying power structure and organising principle of society. Today, partly because of the impact of postmodernism, such simplicity seems much less attractive, and the whole search for an overarching theory feels decidedly old-fashioned. Nevertheless, the concept continues to have widespread currency. At the most general level, it provides a handle on the world which connects different areas of experience, helps make sense of the hostility generated by seemingly moderate feminist demands and enables us to see the extent to which male needs and assumptions are still central to political, cultural and economic life, the norm against which women are measured. Some of the ways in which it has been applied to 'private' and 'public' life are explored in the following chapters.

11

Patriarchy and private life: the family, reproduction and sexuality

In the years immediately following the publication of Millett's *Sexual Politics*, the feminist analysis of patriarchy developed in a very wide range of ways. Different writers focused upon very different aspects and sources of male power, and there were fierce disputes amongst feminists convinced that they alone held the key to unlocking patriarchy. However, if we remember that the concept of patriarchy stresses the interconnections between different areas of life, these apparently competing approaches can also be seen as complementary; this means that theorists working in one area can learn from those working in another, and different forms of political activity can have a cumulative effect.

Although radical feminism peaked as a distinct body of theory and movement of women in the 1970s, many of its ideas have entered more mainstream feminist analysis and political practice. Such developments are discussed in this and the following chapter through an exploration of the main structures that have been seen as important to the workings of patriarchy. This chapter focuses on the 'private' aspects of male power in the family, reproduction, sexuality and violence. Chapter 12 turns to the state, the economic system and male control of language and knowledge. This overlaps with the structures identified by Sylvia Walby in *Theorizing Patriarchy* (1990); like her, I argue that the analysis of patriarchy should not be reduced to an examination of any one structure, but must explore their interrelationships.

Patriarchy and the family

According to Millett, 'Patriarchy's chief institution is the family' (*Sexual Politics*:33), and many other radical feminists have agreed that, contrary to the assumptions of conventional political theory, the family is indeed a central part of society's power structure; as such it both sustains patriarchal power in the 'public' world and is itself a source of women's oppression. Far from being a 'natural' arrangement or individual choice based on mutual love and respect in which the emotional, sexual and domestic needs of adult partners are met and their children cared for, it is a social institution in which women's labour is exploited, male sexual power may be violently expressed and oppressive gender identities and modes of behaviour are learned.

Domestic labour

Like liberal feminists, many early radical feminists saw all domestic work, including childcare, as inherently unfulfilling and degrading; unlike liberal feminists, however, they did not see women's responsibility for the home as a kind of unfortunate accident that could be rectified by an obliging husband and a cleaning lady. With the insights provided by the concept of patriarchy, it was argued that men benefited from present arrangements both in terms of domestic comfort and through disadvantaging women who attempted to compete with them in politics and paid employment. From this perspective, men's resistance to change and their refusal to help with domestic chores which liberal feminists found surprising or 'unfair' were only to be expected, and quarrels about who should do the washing were not individual disagreements but part of a wider power struggle. For a few, the solution was simply to refuse to continue to perform domestic services for men, and this implied separatist women-only households. Others believed that men could be forced or persuaded into accepting domestic responsibilities, but saw that this would not be an automatic consequence of pointing out the injustice of present arrangements, but must be consciously and continuously struggled for. For some, the solution lay not simply in abolishing the division of labour within the family, but in abolishing the family itself; this was bound up with a more widespread countercultural rejection of traditional values and an experimentation with alternative lifestyles. Experience, however, was to show that the sexual division of labour could flourish in communes as well as in the nuclear family; 'progressive' men might pay lip-service to feminist principles, but in practice they too benefited from patriarchy and could dismiss women's complaints as petty and trivial; many feminist women also found that years of training in domestic skills and expectations could be hard to put aside.

The most formal radical feminist analysis of women's domestic work as a source of oppression was provided by the French feminist Christine Delphy, who argued that, because they perform unpaid housework, all women share a common economic position: 'As a group effectively (at any given time) subject to this relation of production they constitute a *class*; as a category of human beings *destined by birth* to become a member of this class, they constitute a *caste'* (Delphy, 1980:35; see also Delphy and Leonard, 1992). Delphy claimed that marriage is a labour contract through which men exploit women's labour and become their economic masters and that, because most women perform this unpaid labour, the position of all women in the employment market is depressed and marriage continues to appear their most viable economic option. This domestic exploitation takes place outside the capitalist mode of production, and she therefore argued that a genuinely materialist analysis of women's oppression shows that this is not simply derived from class struggle and capitalism, but that it has an independent material basis in women's unpaid domestic labour. Delphy's analysis has been heavily criticised by socialist feminists, who accuse her of a woolly misuse of Marxist concepts and of a failure to explore changes in marriage over time and between classes; they also dislike the implication that it is at the level of domestic exploitation rather than paid work or ideology that feminists should be struggling (see Barrett and McIntosh, 1979; Bubeck, 1995). Her approach was also heavily weighted in favour of a now rather dated version of the white western family, and ignored the extent to which some groups of women exploit others as domestic workers (for critical discussion, see Pollert, 1996; Jackson, 1996).

Clearly, there are problems in universalising from a particular historical moment and in seeing domestic labour as the sole or even the prime source of women's oppression, and Delphy's analysis fell short of the claims that she made for it. However, this kind of approach focuses our attention on an important area neglected by earlier feminist theorists; it ties in with Marxist analyses of women's domestic labour discussed in Chapter 13, and there has been a general increase in awareness of the economic and social importance of women's domestic and caring work, and its impact on women's opportunities in the employment market.

Sexual exploitation and violence within the home

For other radical feminists, it was sexual rather than domestic exploitation within the family that was important (although the two were sometimes connected). Later sections explore the related claim that patriarchy is based primarily upon male violence and control of women's sexuality; here it should be noted simply that, for some feminists, high levels of domestic violence and the sexual abuse of both women and children within the home meant that the family was seen as the cutting edge of patriarchal oppression where many women faced male power in its crudest and most aggressive form. From this perspective, individual acts of abuse are linked to wider patterns of power, so that it is unsurprising that authorities have been reluctant to interfere in 'private' domestic affairs or to provide adequate support for women trying to escape domestic violence.

This kind of analysis has had a major impact on public awareness of the extent of abuse within the home. While most public debate still sees this as a product of individual 'badness', important work has been done on the ways in which power and violence have been eroticised and linked with dominant forms of masculinity, and in disentangling this from biological imperatives, so that we can recognise that men's violence is a problem without condemning all men in perpetuity (for an early example of such work, by a man, see Hearn, 1988).

Some early radical feminists argued further that, even for those women lucky enough to escape the worst manifestations of patriarchal aggression, marriage perpetuates a form of domination disguised by love. Thus Shulamith Firestone argued that 'Love, perhaps even more than child-bearing, is the pivot of women's oppression today' (Firestone, 1979:121), and that love in a patriarchal society cannot be based upon equality, but reflects women's economic and social dependency and ensures that they will not challenge their subordinate position. Although contested by many feminists who have (critics would say 'claim to have') loving and equal relationships with men, her argument has affinities with the analyses of William Thompson, Anna Wheeler and John Stuart Mill who had argued a century earlier that men are not content with women's obedience, but demand their love as well.

Psychoanalytic theory: parenting and the acquisition of adult sexual identity

For Millett, the family's main importance was as an agent of socialisation, the primary social institution through which young children learn the values and expectations of their society. Thus, it is within the family that boys and girls first encounter patriarchal power and the sexual division of labour, and it is through the example and admonitions of their parents that they are first taught the roles, temperament and status appropriate to their sex. Such lessons are reinforced by peer groups, schools and the media, and having been learned at such an early age, they are particularly resistant to later challenges.

For some writers, however, the question of sexual identity went even deeper and could only be understood by using insights derived from psychoanalytic theory. Freud has had an extremely hostile feminist press; indeed his whole theory has been ridiculed and seen as a patriarchal tool designed to reconcile women with an oppressive reality. Some more recent feminist writers have, however, attempted to rehabilitate him, and claim that his concepts of the unconscious and of infantile sexuality can be used to understand adult behaviour; for such writers, it is important to understand how infant experiences mould adult attitudes and behaviour if these are to be challenged and changed (for a lucid discussion of such writings, see Sayers, 1986). This means that childrearing practices are seen as having a political dimension; here the work of Nancy Choderow and Dorothy Dinnerstein has been particularly influential.

Although their theoretical starting-points differ, both these writers have concluded that it is the female monopoly of childcare that is at the root of our present problems – indeed Dinnerstein claims that the resulting psychological damage has brought the human race to the very edge of extinction. Their solution is therefore the involvement of men in parenting, which they say will make possible new forms of gender identity freed from ideas of domination and submission and the development of a fully integrated and responsible adult personality for both sexes. The consequences of this will be to end women's exclusion from public power and transform the gender arrangements of society; as discussed in Chapter 9 above, some writers also think that shared parenting will facilitate the development of a mature ethical theory which includes ideas of connectedness as well as rights.

Even if this analysis has some truth, it leaves a number of problems unresolved. In particular, shared parenting would require major changes to work patterns which are unlikely to be compatible with profitability, and it is quite unclear how mother-raised men and women are to break out of the vicious circle of which they are a part. Some critics further complain that, like many radical feminists, these psychoanalytic theorists have generalised from the experiences of white, middle-class Americans (for a defence of the approach against this charge, see Hirschmann, 1992). Their assumptions are also challenged by other schools of psychoanalytic thought which merge with some forms of postmodernism. In particular, the French writers discussed further in Chapter 14 below have linked the acquisition of gender identity to the child's acquisition of language; debates here have involved complex arguments as to whether sex differences are acquired via the Oedipal recognition of sex difference or whether they in fact pre-date it and are essentially rooted in the body, while some query the whole notion of a stable adult identity. These arguments suggest that it is not simply patterns of infant care that are important in forming the (possibly ever-changing) adult psyche, but that this may be rooted in the structures of language and thought processes available to the child, or that (as some claim) it is inescapably linked to biological difference.

Despite these disagreements, the recognition that we are not as rational as we like to think and that sex differences are at least in part unconsciously held has important implications for feminist politics, and may help us to understand why gender relations are so difficult to change. As we shall see, such recognition is an important aspect of postmodernist thought and has also been developed by some Marxist/socialist feminists such as Lynne Segal, who has recently argued that, although it must be combined with analysis of other forms of identity and difference (particularly around ethnicity and class), feminism needs psychoanalysis as this 'provides the fullest account we have of the complex and contradictory nature of subjectivities formed through desire and identification' (Segal, 1999:198).

Pro-family arguments

While early radical feminists were extremely hostile to the family, Choderow and Dinnerstein attacked the current sexual division of labour rather than the family as such. Other feminists from the mid-1980s onwards have positively defended traditional values and roles (see Stacey, 1986 and Somerville, 2000 for critical assessment of such theories). Thus Germaine Greer, whose earlier *The Female Eunuch* (1970) had done much to popularise radical feminist ideas, argued in 1984 in favour of the kind of extended family to be found in southern Italy and India: 'The family offers the paradigm for female collectivity; it shows us women co-operating to dignify their lives, to heighten each other's labour ... growing in real love and sisterhood' (Greer, 1984:241). Elshtain similarly defended traditional 'womanly values' to be found within the family and insisted that stable family life is an essential prerequisite for a civilised society: 'Not every neglected and abused child becomes a Charles Manson [a notorious mass murderer], but every Charles Manson was an abused and neglected child' (Elshtain, 1981b:332). She therefore objected to collective childcare, which she saw as a form of neglect, and to attempts to politicise family life or to devalue nurturing and domestic skills. Others argued that traditional family structures did allow women a certain degree of control and autonomy, but that this was now being eroded and undermined by the state (Stacey and Price, 1981); yet others saw the family as an essential bastion against class or 'race' oppression, a part of life in which non-capitalist relationships survive and emotional needs are met (Humphries, 1982). This last point has been reinforced by black feminists, who have accused white feminists of attacking their one refuge from a racist society and ignoring the way in which immigration laws deny women in some minority ethnic groups the right to family life.

In general, pro-family arguments ignore the power relationships that exist both within the family and in the wider society of which it is a part. They tend to confirm women's confinement to the 'private' realm and hence their economic dependency and exclusion from public decision-making; they ignore the extent to which violence, emotional manipulation and sexual exploitation may be as typical of family life as love and mutual support; and they do not consider the possible negative effects of the traditional female monopoly of parenting. They have the advantage of rejecting the uncritical adoption of male values and the devaluation of skills and attributes traditionally associated with women. There is, however, a danger that this traditional association will be confirmed as 'natural', inevitable and desirable, and that it will be used by anti-feminists as an excuse for a rigid gender division of labour that combines veneration of women's alleged qualities with a refusal to allow these to be 'corrupted' by public power, free choice or financial reward.

Today, although few feminists would accept that it is simply an oppressive institution, the radical feminist approach has helped open up the 'black box' of the family to public scrutiny and shocked society into greater recognition of the abuse and exploitation that it may have concealed. As we saw in Chapter 9, theorists such as Richards and Okin have extended liberal approaches to argue that a just society requires a radical restructuring of domestic and caring responsibilities; men's failure to make a greater contribution to domestic and caring work is also a recurrent theme in much recent feminist writing on public policy, and there is growing understanding that the personal economic dependency and poverty experienced by many women within marriage is incompatible with equal citizenship.

Patriarchy and reproduction

Reproduction has been largely ignored by conventional political theory, because it is seen as both 'natural' and 'private'. A woman's 'right to choose' whether and in what circumstances she gives birth has, however, become a key feminist issue, mobilising millions of women across the world, particularly in demanding or defending access to safe, affordable abortion. Although this often seemed to unite all feminists, radical feminism provided a distinct approach: rather than seeing it as a matter of private, individual choice, it saw campaigns for reproductive rights as part of a collective struggle against men's control over women's bodies; that is, reproduction is a key site of patriarchy, where control over women's bodies is exercised but where it can also be resisted (for overviews of feminist approaches to reproduction, see Bryson, 1999a; Zalewski, 2000). Some radical feminists have also developed a strand of eco-feminist thought which claims that women's life-giving reproductive role gives them a special relationship with the natural world.

Reproductive technology

Although many of her conclusions are out of line with current feminist thinking, the most notorious radical feminist analysis of reproduction remains Shulamith Firestone's *The Dialectic of Sex* (first published 1970, references here to the 1979 edition). In this, Firestone argued that women's role as reproducers handicapped them over the centuries and made possible men's patriarchal power: 'The heart of women's oppression is her childbearing and childrearing role.' It was, she said, this biological reality rather than economic structures that formed the material basis for the most fundamental division in society, that between men and women. She therefore attempted to rewrite the Marxist theory of history, combining it with what she saw as the positive aspects of Freudian analysis, and substituting 'reproduction' for 'production' and 'sex class' for 'economic class', so that the 'sexual-reproductive organisation of society' was the key to economic, legal and political institutions and dominant belief systems. Although she saw it as rooted in nature, Firestone argued that this biological basis was not unchanging, and that the development of effective contraception and new reproductive technology were creating the possibility of breaking the link with biology and freeing women from their reproductive role; in particular, she saw future artificial reproduction outside the womb as the basis for women's liberation. Such liberation would not, however, be the automatic consequence of the new technologies, for men's interest in maintaining patriarchy would continue, and the new technology, especially fertility control, might be used against women to reinforce the entrenched system of exploitation. As an oppressed class, women must therefore rise up and seize control of the 'means of reproduction' (including the social institutions of childbearing and childrearing as well as the new technologies), with the ultimate goal of eliminating not just male privilege but the sex distinction itself. She assumed that this would be accompanied by a proletarian revolution which would eliminate social class and, through the use of cybernetics, make possible the elimination of labour; it was, however, the women's revolution that she saw as the ultimate human revolution, for this would end not just a particular form of power, but the psychology of power itself (*Dialectic*, 1979:73 and 21).

Such sweeping and grandiose proposals were a product of the optimism current in some left-wing and feminist circles at the time, and were clearly inadequate as a political programme. As we shall see, many feminists have also rejected Firestone's negative portrayal of motherhood and her enthusiasm for reproductive technology, and her whole theoretical framework has long been attacked as confused and simplistic (see, in particular, O'Brien, 1981). Nevertheless, the central idea that a feminist theory of women's history and oppression must start with human reproduction and that modern technology may be the basis of liberation, has been shared by a number of writers. For example, Mary O'Brien in *The Politics of Reproduction* (1981) argued that reproduction is not an unchanging biological fact, but a process related to human consciousness and the basis of human society. From this perspective, the two key moments of human history are the first early discovery of paternity, and the modern contraceptive technology which has for the first time made possible the rational control of reproduction. Both of these are 'world historical events', which 'create a transformation in human consciousness of human relations with the natural world' and change the whole structure of society. Most of human history has occurred between these two events, and has been characterised by a male supremacy that is in fact based on men's failure to establish absolute control over reproduction: 'The social relations of reproduction are relations of dominance precisely because at the heart of the doctrine of potency lies the intransigent impotency of uncertainty ...'. Now, however, 'The institutions of patriarchy are vulnerable because the Age of Contraception has changed the process of reproduction, and the social relations of reproduction must therefore undergo transformation' (O'Brien, 1981:189, 22, 121 and 62; for related arguments, see Badinter, 1989).

Other feminists are less inclined to be so positive about historical developments, which some have seen as a process through which reproductive decision-making has shifted from women to men. From this perspective, the medicalisation of childbirth has involved a transfer of power from female friends, relations and midwives to male doctors and gynaecologists, leaving little active role with the birthing mother herself. Similarly, it is argued that contraception and abortion endanger women's health and increase sexual exploitation, and that they have been used to limit the reproductive capacities of women deemed 'unfit' to become mothers (particularly black, poor, third world, unmarried, lesbian or disabled women, who may face forced sterilisation or be the unwitting guinea pigs for contraceptive or reproductive experiments). Many are highly suspicious of recent developments in reproductive technology, and have argued that these are being used against women to consolidate male power and make patriarchy for the first time absolute: 'Here is man's control of the awesome power of woman; the last stronghold of nature which he can finally dominate' (Arditti, 1984:265). Thus access to AID (artificial insemination by donor) or IVF (in vitro fertilisation) programmes may be limited to those the authorities consider 'respectable', and surrogate motherhood involves the exploitation of poor or third world women. Perhaps even more sinisterly, pre-birth diagnosis of sex has led in some circumstances to selective abortion of female foetuses, and Andrea Dworkin has claimed that this and other developments mean that women may ultimately become dispensable, or that 'there will be a new kind of holocaust, as unimaginable now as the Nazi one before it happened ... men will finally have the means to create and control the kind of women they want ... There will be domestics, sex prostitutes, and reproductive prostitutes' (Dworkin, 1983:151). This view of the new technologies as a new male weapon in the battle to maintain or consolidate patriarchal power has led some to organise resistance through the Feminist International Network of Resistance to Reproductive and Genetic Engineering (FINRRAGE); see Rowland, 1992). (For critical accounts of reproductive technology see also Corea, 1985; Stanworth, 1987. For fictional explorations see Fairbairns, 1979; Piercy, 1979.)

All this is a far cry from Firestone's belief in the liberating possibilities of artificial wombs, and suggests that in a patriarchal society 'seizing the means of reproduction' might be a neat reformulation of Marx, but that it can have little practical meaning. It remains true that the ability to plan and control fertility has a potentially liberating effect, and many women have already experienced a kind of freedom undreamed of by earlier generations. However, recent developments in technologies around cloning, genetic engineering and sex-selection are contributing to increasingly widespread unease, and the original radical feminist claim that reproduction can be a site of political power has more resonance than ever before. In this context, it is once again important to understand that reproductive issues are connected to other power structures rather than contested in isolation, and that genuine freedom of reproductive choice would involve major changes in the economic and social circumstances which currently constrain many women's choices.

For some feminists, the central problem with Firestone's analysis was not simply her naïve assumption that reproductive technology could be readily used to benefit women, but the underlying belief that pregnancy, childbirth and childrearing are essentially humiliating and oppressive activities from which women should be liberated. On this Firestone (who was heavily influenced by de Beauvoir) was quite explicit. Pregnancy, she insisted, is *not* a fulfilling and creative experience but 'the temporary deformation of the body of the individual for the sake of the species', while childbirth simply hurts ('like shitting a pumpkin', she was told by a friend), and with its attendant possessiveness and emotional manipulation, it is psychologically damaging to both mother and child (*Dialectic*, p. 189). A problem with this analysis is that it is contradicted by the perceptions and experiences of those many women who have found joy and fulfilment in motherhood, and that, like much liberal feminism, it rested upon an uncritical acceptance of a scale of values which rates traditional male activities above those associated with women. It also failed to distinguish between conditions of mothering as they actually exist and as they might be. This point was elaborated by Adrienne Rich in *Of Woman Born* (1977), in which she argued that it is not the biological fact of giving birth that oppresses women, but the fact that they reproduce in a patriarchal society in which motherhood is seldom freely chosen and is controlled by men. Although she agreed with Firestone's rejection of the current institutions of mothering, she also affirmed the positive values associated with the experience of motherhood, and saw these as a potential source of power for women.

Mothering and eco-feminism

By the 1980s, Rich's ideas had led to a more general re-evaluation of motherhood which Lynne Segal critically labelled 'maternal revivalism' (Segal, 1987:145). This saw motherhood and the care of the young as positive experiences to be celebrated and as giving rise to 'womanly values' to do with nurturing, co-operation and peace, in contrast to male attributes of self-interest, competition and aggression. Such a celebration of 'womanly values' was influential in peace movements, most famously at the women-only peace camp at Greenham Common in Britain.

Such thinking has contributed to the development of 'eco feminist' theory. Such writers as Susan Griffin (*Woman and Nature*, 1984), Andrée Collard (*Rape of the Wild*, 1988) and Caldecott and Leland (eds, *Reclaim the Earth*, 1983) have equated men's treatment of women with their treatment of nature. Claiming that both have been raped, exploited, abused and hated, they assert that it is only women's values that can save the planet from ecological disaster (for good overviews and critical discussion, see Plumwood, 1993; Mellor, 1996).

For some writers, this analysis ties in with a critique of western thought's denigration of all things physical in favour of abstract reason and scientific knowledge. In particular, the Indian writer Vandenna Shiva, has linked environmental destruction with a process of 'maldevelopment', which she sees as a product of both patriarchal and western value systems and patterns of thought:

> modern science and development are projects of male, western origin, both
> historically and ideologically. They are the latest and most brutal expression of a
> patriarchal ideology which is threatening to annihilate nature and the entire human
> species.

She argues that solution lies in developing an 'Indian world view', in which nature is *Prakriti*: 'a living and creative process, the feminine principle from which all life arrives' (Shiva, 1988:xvi and xviii; see also Salleh, 1997; Mies and Shiva, 1993).

For a few feminist writers, alleged gender differences are innate. Thus Rich argued that women see the world differently from men because they experience it in relation to their own physicality. Griffin similarly saw women as closer to nature than men, and therefore more able to express and identify with its needs, while Collard stated that

> Nothing links the human animal and nature so profoundly as woman's reproductive system, which enables her to share the experience of bringing forth and nourishing life with the rest of the living world. Whether or not she personally experiences biological mothering, it is in this that woman is most truly a child of nature and in this natural integrity lies the wellspring of her strength. (Collard, 1988:106)

As Val Plumwood has said, there are clear dangers in this kind of 'good woman' argument (Plumwood, 1993). To the extent that it is based on belief in essential differences between women and men, it runs counter to important trends in contemporary thought, particularly those influenced by postmodernism. It also contradicts current scientific thinking, which undermines the idea of simple sexual dichotomies by showing that there exists a continuum of chromosomal, hormonal, genital and general anatomical differences. It also flies in the face of much historical evidence, for women have frequently supported wars and the despoliation of nature while some men have opposed them. However empowering, it involves 'a-historical abstractions and unreflective celebrations' (Elshtain, 1987:240), and there is a danger that it can lead not to planet-saving action but to fatalism or a retreat into separatism which leaves the structures of patriarchal power intact.

Moreover, while the idea that women and men embody respectively the values of peace and war, nurturing and destruction has been used for centuries by feminists to demand that women's voices be heard, it has also been used by anti-feminists to argue that women's essential purity must not be sullied by the sordid realities of public life. Many contemporary feminists are therefore extremely wary of alleging any natural differences in aptitude or moral outlook between the sexes, fearing that in a patriarchal society this will always be used to the detriment of women. In this context, to say that women's traditional role involves life-enhancing values for which they should demand a public hearing is one thing; to say that women's biological attributes give them a monopoly of such values is quite another, for this would seem to confirm traditional roles and divisions, allowing men to continue to destroy the planet while women celebrate alternative virtues within the home. Some feminists agree that differences do exist, but argue that these are acquired rather than biologically given, and that the solution is to ensure both that positive 'womanly qualities' are properly valued and that men are enabled and encouraged to acquire them too by being involved in childcare. As discussed above and in Chapter 9, other writers have drawn on both psychoanalytic and liberal ideas to reach similar conclusions about the need to break the female monopoly of childcare.

The issue of reproduction is one which profoundly divides radical feminists, and there seems little meeting point between those who see it as a barbaric relic of a lower state of human development and those who insist that it embodies women's superior creativity and virtue. However, these divisions conceal a more general agreement that women's reproductive activities are politically significant and that men's attempts to control them have resulted in a loss of women's freedom which must be resisted. Attempts by women to reassert control over this area of their lives is therefore an agreed radical feminist goal. Those who view motherhood in a negative way may stress the importance of freely available contraception and abortion while others focus on the right of all women to have children if they wish, but both groups are united by the belief that the bearing of children is not a purely private affair, but one which reflects the power relationships between the sexes. This means in turn that the struggle for control over reproduction cannot be divorced from struggle in other areas. As legislative battles over abortion and the uses of new reproductive technology show, it is clearly connected with the control of state power, while economic circumstances and the structure of family life obviously limit or expand women's reproductive choices. The issue is also integrally related to the issues around sexuality.

Patriarchy, sexuality and sexual violence

As with the other aspects of 'private' life discussed in this chapter, the idea that sexuality is not simply an individual matter but one that is bound up with power structures in society is not new to feminist theory, although it is contrary to the assumptions of mainstream political thought. A few earlier writers stressed the liberating effects of a freely expressed sexuality, but most past feminists have held a much more negative view, equating sexuality with male violence, disease, loss of autonomy and 'animal instincts', and advocating chastity for both sexes. Hostility to heterosexual intercourse became an important strand within radical feminist thought from the 1970s; lesbianism rather than chastity was, however, the more commonly preferred solution.

A minority of radical feminists have believed that women have a 'natural' sexuality that is repressed in patriarchal society. Most, however, have agreed that it is socially constructed (see Scott and Jackson, 1996). Either way, existing sexuality has been seen as symptom, product or cause of patriarchal society, part of a world in which men have authority, women are economically dependent, and male needs and desires set the agenda in all spheres. From this perspective, sexual behaviour today is neither 'natural' nor freely chosen, but is bound up with ideas of owner- ship, domination and submission; many have also argued that it is condi- tioned by a manmade culture in which pornography is all-pervasive, sexual violence is tolerated, women are treated as sex objects and different moral codes exist for men and women. In this context, some writers have argued that, in a patriarchal society, sex and love between men and women cannot exist on a basis of equality, for power and eroticism are inextricably entangled; they are therefore likely to involve at worst rape and violent humiliation, at best emotional dependency and the neglect of women's sexual needs. The demand for sexual autonomy and fulfilment has therefore been seen as part of the general political struggle against patriarchy, which current practices both reflect and reinforce. Some writers have gone further, seeing sexuality not just as one aspect of patri- archal domination, but the main political problem confronting feminists (for good overviews of recent feminist debates on sexuality, see Whelehan, 1995 and the collection in Jackson and Scott (eds), 1996).

The attack on heterosexuality

In the 1960s, lesbianism was not a visible option for many feminists, who frequently shared the dominant feelings of suspicion, fear and hostility towards it. Such feminist attitudes have since been radically challenged. In 1970, the publication of Anna Koedt's *The Myth of the Vaginal Orgasm*, which argued that female sexual pleasure was located in the clitoris and that satisfaction did not require penile penetration, created a great stir in some feminist circles. The resulting demand for the 'right to orgasm' led some women to attempt to renegotiate sexual practices with their male partners, but for others it suggested that men could be dispensed with and heterosexual relationships abandoned.

For some, the issue was not simply one of sexual pleasure, for hetero- sexuality itself was declared to be a *political institution* rather than a natu- ral expression of sexual desire (see Rich, 1980). As such, heterosexuality was imposed upon women for the benefit of men, a means of dividing and controlling women and ensuring that they served men domestically and emotionally as well as sexually. From this perspective, 'male domination of the female body is the basic material reality of women's lives; and all struggle for dignity and self-determination is rooted in the struggle for actual control of one's body' (Dworkin, 1981:205); some even argued that all heterosexual intercourse was a form of rape, irretrievably bound up with the system of patriarchal domination and oppression. This view was well illustrated in a pamphlet issued by the Leeds Revolutionary Feminist Group in 1979:

> Only in the system of oppression that is male supremacy does the oppressor actu-
> ally invade and colonise the interior of the body of the oppressed ... Penetration is
> an act of great symbolic significance by which the oppressor enters the body of the
> oppressed ... its function and effect is the punishment and control of
> women ... every act of penetration for a woman is an invasion which undermines
> her confidence and saps her strength. (in Evans, 1982:64–5)

This meant that the rejection of heterosexuality was not just a matter of personal sexual orientation, but a political act that struck at the very heart of patriarchy, while 'Woman-identification is a source of energy, a poten-tial springboard of female power, violently curtailed and wasted under the institution of heterosexuality' (Rich, 1980:657). In this context 'political lesbianism' became a solution for some women who identified emotion-ally and politically with other women and who had withdrawn from men, but who did not engage in actual sexual activity with women, and some even argued that women who continued to have relationships with men were traitors to the feminist cause: 'Men are the enemy. Heterosexual women are collaborators with the enemy' (Leeds Feminist Group, in Evans, 1982:64–5; see also the extract in Evans from Jill Johnson's 1974 *Lesbian Nation*, and Jeffries, 1990).

Many other feminists, however, fiercely rejected the attempt to impose 'politically correct' sexual behaviour, and, although the British 1978 National Women's Liberation Conference in Birmingham passed a resolu-tion making 'the right to define our sexuality' *the* over-riding question of the women's movement, the hostility engendered during this debate meant that this was in fact the last such conference. Unsurprisingly, there was particular opposition to the portrayal of heterosexual intercourse as inherently and inevitably oppressive, as this denied the validity of the experiences of all those women who found it both physically and emo-tionally pleasurable. The equation of all intercourse with rape was seen as particularly dubious, as this not only denied all possibility of reciprocal tenderness, love and desire between men and women, but by classifying all heterosexual acts together it concealed the horror of actual rape. The idea that women can only be the passive victims of male lust was also crit-icised: thus Lynne Segal reported that it certainly did not feel like that to her during the time in the 1960s 'when I rarely slept alone and devoted much of my leisure time to bedding my favourite man of the moment' (although she admitted that her activities earned her more by way of status than physical pleasure, and cautioned that 'seducing one's professor was usually the most boring experience of all, and not to be repeated' [Segal, 1987:77–8]).

Perhaps surprisingly, the accusation that radical feminists want to impose 'politically correct' sexual behaviour has also been made by some lesbians, who have defended sado-masochistic practices and the use of lesbian pornography. Such activities are anathema to those who see them as aping the worst aspects of male sexuality, and the black lesbian writer Audre Lorde argued that they are unacceptable because

> Whatever we do takes place in a social context and has an effect upon other human beings. To degrade someone, even with that person's expressed consent, is to *endorse* the degradation of persons. It is to affirm that the abuse of persons is *acceptable*. (Quoted in Tong, 1989:122; see also Jeffries, 1990; Richardson, 1996)

Against this, some sexual libertarians have argued that because lesbian sex is outside the power structures of patriarchal society, lesbian sado-masochism and pornography are purely about fantasy and private preference, and that women should be enabled to pursue forms of excitement absent from what they describe as 'vanilla sex' (for a classic statement of this, see Califia, 1996, first published in 1981). The very fact that such debates can take place should be evidence of the dangers of a too simplistic celebration of the joys of sisterhood, and suggests that the problems of power cannot be escaped simply by withdrawing from men.

The whole idea that sexuality is the most important problem has been attacked by feminists such as Segal, who asked 'How could such a concrete reductionism, such phallic obsession, have got such a hold on feminism?' (Segal, 1987:97). This 'obsession' has been seen as evidence of radical feminism's narrowly bourgeois horizons and its blindness to other forms of oppression. Marxists and socialists in particular argued that it is only from the perspective of a white middle-class woman that sexual lifestyles and the pursuit of orgasm can appear as central political issues; for women struggling for economic or physical survival, such questions can only be frivolous luxuries which distract energies from the more important issues of economic exploitation and class struggle, while separatism requires a degree of financial independence simply not available to most working-class women. Against this, however, the breakdown in many societies of traditional patterns of marriage means that, for many women, life without a permanent male partner is already a reality, although it is often accompanied by poverty; some ideas of female autonomy and independence may therefore be less utopian or class-biased than socialist criticism suggests.

Today, demands for separatism or warnings of the dangers of sex with men can seem at best old-fashioned and at worst oppressive to those young western women who frequent gay pubs or are highly confident in their sexual behaviour. However, although the silencing of lesbian experience is less absolute than in the recent past, sexual 'choice' remains a political issue, as many lesbians face hostility, abuse and discrimination; indeed, 'accusations' of lesbianism are often used to discredit feminism and deter young women from identifying with it. The analysis of sexual politics can therefore alert us to the ways in which 'forced heterosexuality' may still operate to weaken and manipulate women, while the idea that women can be liberated from the need to please men and should not be judged in terms of their ability to attract them can still be an empowering one. As discussed in Chapter 14 below, it may also be that flamboyantly 'transgressive' forms of sexual behaviour which deliberately flout conventional expectations can help undermine or disrupt restrictive gender identities.

Patriarchy, sexual violence and pornography

The radical ideas discussed above suggested that sex with men is oppressive because it is unfulfilling, it is not freely chosen and it is used as a means of dividing and controlling women. Other feminist writers have more explicitly linked their analysis to male *violence* and the idea that patriarchy, like all other systems of power, rests ultimately on force. Kate Millett said:

> We are not accustomed to associate patriarchy with force. So perfect is its system of socialisation, so complete the general assent to its values, so long and so universally has it prevailed in human society, that it scarcely seems to require violent implementation.

Nevertheless, she argued, 'Control in patriarchal society would be imperfect, even inoperable, unless it had the rule of force to rely upon, both in emergencies and as an ever-present instrument of intimidation' (*Politics*:3); such violence frequently takes the form of sexual violence, particularly rape.

The socially dominant view of rape is that this is an extremely rare act carried out by a tiny minority of abnormal and deviant men, an unfortunate individual experience suffered by a small number of women. Feminists have, however, challenged this orthodoxy by pointing out that clinical tests show that, with rare exceptions, rapists appear to be mentally 'healthy' and normal and that sexual violence in general and rape in particular are far more common than had previously been thought. They point out that, contrary to popular mythology, most rapists are in fact known to their victims. They have helped draw a reluctant public's attention to the scale of sexual abuse of children and they have re-defined sexual violence to include such 'benign' forms as obscene phone calls and sexual harassment in the workplace. This means that rape is not seen as a discrete and isolated experience but as part of a whole culture in which the threat of sexual violence dominates women's lives: thus Catherine MacKinnon has claimed that over 90 per cent of American women have been sexually assaulted or harassed at some point in their lives and that this represents 'the effectively unrestrained and systematic sexual aggression of one-half of the population against the other half' (MacKinnon, 1989a:332; see also Lederer, 1980; Hester, Kelly and Radford (eds), 1996; Corrin (ed.), 1996).

Although MacKinnon argued that in a patriarchal society it is virtually impossible to disentangle 'normal' sex from the violent exercise of power, many feminists have distinguished between them. This has given rise to an 'orthodox' feminist analysis which argues that rape is about power rather than sex, a manifestation of men's hatred and contempt for women rather than of ungovernable lust. Many radical feminists have further argued that the fear which it engenders in women is central to their subordination and control by men, so that rape should be understood as a *political* act. Some have therefore also argued that although not all men actually rape, all men benefit from the sexual violence that curtails women's lives and leads them to seek the protection of one man against all others. The best known statement of this perspective has been provided by Susan Brownmiller, who has notoriously claimed that rape 'is nothing more or less than a conscious process of intimidation by which *all men* keep *all women* in a state of fear' (Brownmiller, 1977:15). Jalna Hanmer has similarly argued that

> The fact that many husbands do not beat their wives, and many men do not attack women on the streets ... is not proof that wife-beating and other assaults are irregular, unsystematic practices ... but merely that it is not necessary to do so in order to maintain the privileges of the superior group. (Hammer, 1978:229)

From this perspective, the current policies and attitudes towards rape and domestic violence which so outrage other feminists are in fact only to be expected; state connivance or indifference, the myth that victims are 'asking for it' and the tendency to treat it as a joke are all seen as evidence of male interest in perpetuating a system of domination based on fear.

Some feminists have argued that pornography is a cornerstone of this system, leading to sexual violence against women, so that 'pornography is the theory; rape is the practice'. They argue not simply that men are led to imitate what they see depicted, but that they are desensitised to acts of violence and that the 'pornographic lie' that women enjoy pain, humiliation and domination is heard while women's voices are silenced; power is therefore eroticised and women too internalise a false view of their own sexuality.

The best known of the anti-pornography campaigners are Andrea Dworkin and Catherine MacKinnon. Dworkin has argued that pornography is both symptom and cause of the male hatred and contempt for women that has led to their systematic abuse over the centuries, and that affects their behaviour and treatment in all areas of life, so that 'at the heart of the female condition is pornography; it is the ideology that is the source of all the rest' (Dworkin, 1983:223). MacKinnon has developed this analysis to argue that the ubiquity of pornography means that the gender identity and sexuality of both men and women are learned in a context of domination and submission from which they become inseparable. Sexual pleasure for women is therefore masochistic, while for men power is eroticised. Indeed, she has suggested that men's prime motive for oppressing women may be the sexual satisfaction derived from domination: 'Part of the male interest in keeping women down is the fact that it gets men up' (MacKinnon, 1989a:335). In this context pornography does not simply create oppressive sexual needs, it reflects them; it gives men what they already want, and this is

> Women bound, women battered, women tortured, women humiliated, women degraded and defiled, women killed – or, to be fair to the soft core – women sexually accessible, have-able, there for them, wanting to be taken and used, with perhaps just a little of light bondage. (MacKinnon, 1989a:326–7; see also MacKinnon, 1983 and 1994; Griffin, 1981; Dworkin, 1981 and 1988; Itzin (ed.), 1992; Russell, 1993; Easton, 1994 and Everywoman, 1988)

MacKinnon and Dworkin succeeded in having anti-pornography ordinances passed in two American cities (Minneapolis and Indianapolis). These would have enabled individual women to bring a legal action against the producers or distributors of pornographic material on a number of grounds, including that of violating their civil rights by degrading women as a group and causing them to be treated as second-class citizens. They were, however, declared unconstitutional by the Supreme Court. They were also vehemently opposed by many other feminists, who argued that such attempts at censorship involved an unhealthy alliance with the right-wing 'moral majority', that they were likely to be used against sexually explicit feminist material, that they involved a dangerous increase in the power of the state and that, because of the problems to do with definition and provability, they would be unworkable. As with the arguments for political lesbianism, many feminists also rejected the hostility to men and heterosexuality that the anti-pornography campaigners seemed to express. (See in particular Strossen, 1996; Segal and McIntosh (eds), 1992; Assiter and Carol (eds), 1993. For an overview of debates around pornography, see Chester and Dickey (eds), 1988; and Bryson, 1999a.)

It is not necessary to accept the most extreme radical feminist claims to agree that sexual violence and pornography may be important aspects of patriarchal power and that women's sexuality has become distorted or curtailed. In this sense, sexuality is indeed a political issue, and contesting the ways in which it is constructed and experienced may sometimes be an important feminist task. To see this as the sole or prime cause of patriarchy is however to be guilty of crude reductionism and an over-general and a-historical approach which obscures changes in the nature of patriarchy and the ways in which it interacts with other forms of oppression. For example, a white student today who is pressured into 'permissive' sexual activity is sexually oppressed in a very different way from a South Asian woman whose chastity is central to her family's honour or an East European woman tricked into prostitution by the promise of employment in the west; in the early nineteenth century, a black female slave could be raped by her owner with impunity, while the sexuality of 'respectable' white women was entirely denied. It may also be that, as Ferguson has argued, the recent increase in pornography in the west reflects 'a shift from private to public patriarchy which requires a more collective, impersonal, male control of women's bodies' (Ferguson, 1989:115; and Chapter 9 above).

It is also important to remember both that women are not simply passive victims and that men are not an undifferentiated group of oppressors. Indeed, women's resistance to sexual exploitation can ignore and add to the oppression experienced by disadvantaged men: thus feminist marches to 'reclaim the streets' at night have been widely criticised for marching through working-class and black areas and reinforcing myths about black male rapists, ignoring the fact that many black men's freedom of movement has been curtailed by racism and police harassment. Although there is quite widespread agreement amongst feminists that sexual violence is related to underlying power structures, most reject the claim that all men consciously collude or participate in sexual violence, that such violence is biologically determined by male hormones or that men can have no motivation for helping to end it. This opens up possibilities of co-operating with men to achieve changes in practices and attitudes (for example by working in schools or improving police treatment of women who report rape).

Whilst the 'private' areas discussed in this chapter can be seen as both interconnected and political, they also have to be understood in their economic and cultural contexts and in relation to politics as more conventionally understood. For example, genuine reproductive choice would mean that no woman ever became pregnant as a result of coercive sex, that no woman would be childless because she could not afford to raise a child and no woman would be denied either safe, affordable, legal abortion or fertility treatment. As such, genuine choice would require not only legislative change, but radical social, cultural and economic transformation as well. Similarly, women's economic dependency upon men may be the cause as well as the consequence of their sexual subordination, while the growth of pornography into a multi-billion dollar industry could only have been possible in a particular economic and cultural context.

12

Patriarchy: the public sphere

Patriarchy and the state

Radical feminist analysis of the state has generally been implicit, rather than fully developed in its own right. However, this neglect itself implies a theory of state power, which it has seen as a product of inequality between women and men rather than either an independent cause of oppression or a neutral tool that feminists can use. This means that, because the structures and institutions of the state and the law have been made by men and protect their interests, the under-representation of women is no unfortunate and easily remedied accident, and its patriarchal nature cannot be overcome simply by getting more women into political office, for political outcomes are structured by society-wide power relations, not by individual decision-makers. From this perspective, feminist demands are unlikely to be conceded by the state, and legislation can do little to improve the real situation of women. Indeed, feminist engagements with the state are likely to be positively damaging when they are not simply ineffective: women can gain power only by playing according to male rules which are stacked against them and which require them to assimilate to the male norms they are supposed to be attacking, apparent legal gains can disguise or legitimate women's oppression by providing a formal equality which again requires them to conform to rules that have been established by men, and welfare benefits may be dependent upon an intrusive regulation or investigation of women's domestic circumstances.

From the late 1960s, such critiques led some radical feminists to be very suspicious of the state and to reject conventional politics and institutions in favour of non-hierarchical and separatist activities and/or local community activism. The identification of patriarchal power within the state can, however, also be used to develop a realistic assessment of political possibilities, without ruling out involvement with formal structures. From this perspective, the state is seen as an arena of conflict which may be systematically biased against women but within which important victories can nevertheless be won; it is essential to understand the power relations that are involved and the tremendous obstacles that women face, but this need not lead to the pessimistic abandonment of conventional

196

politics. Such an approach would support the use of quotas in elected assemblies as a means of ensuring that women's interests are represented and their voices heard (see Chapter 9 above). In principle, it can also recognise the importance of cross-cutting 'race' and class conflicts that will help determine political outcomes and which interact with gender struggles in highly complex ways.

The classic radical feminist approach to the state can give us a simplistic picture of a monolithic institution that can be written off by feminists as an instrument of patriarchal oppression. It can, however, also provide the basis for a more sophisticated approach that allows us to recognise both the importance and the limitations of conventional politics and legislation. For example, a law that gives a woman the right to leave an abusing husband is not in itself enough to protect her from marital violence, for it is likely to be enforced by a sexist police force within a culture in which sexuality and domination are inextricably linked, and she is unlikely to have the economic resources to maintain herself. If, however, the law is passed in the context of feminist struggles to make such violence visible and unacceptable, to increase the accountability of the police, to provide safe houses for battered wives and to improve educational and employment prospects for women, then it can represent a significant victory (for the classic radical feminist analysis of the state see MacKinnon, 1983 and 1989b, for further discussion of feminist approaches to the state, see Bryson, 1999a).

Patriarchy and the economic system

As we have seen in earlier chapters, the classic Marxist position on women's oppression was that this is a product of class society that will disappear with the overthrow of capitalism and the establishment of a classless communist society. For radical feminists, such reductionism was completely unacceptable, for it ignored the non-economic bases and the ubiquity of male power, and it denied the shared experiences of all women and the vested interests of men in maintaining their oppression. This meant that economic change on its own could never change the deeply-rooted structures of patriarchal power, and a socialist revolution 'would be *no* revolution; but only another coup d'état among men' (Morgan, 1970:*xxxvi*); the failure of so-called communist revolutions to liberate women was seen as proof of the hollowness of the Marxist promise.

From the new radical perspective, women were economically exploited *as women*, rather than as gender-neutral members of the proletariat. Poor pay and discrimination in the workplace were seen as both cause and effect of women's economic dependency upon men: forced to work unpaid in the home and to service men's sexual needs, women could not achieve full economic independence and equality in the paid workforce at the same time as running the home and, even when they escaped the worst effects of sexual harassment, they would not be taken seriously as workers in a culture that saw them primarily as sex objects or nurturers. This meant that proposed liberal solutions of equal pay and opportunities legislation would have little effect on workplace inequalities, which could only be understood and contested in the context of wider challenges to patriarchal power.

This kind of analysis can again become very simplistic and over-general, ignoring the diversity of women's situations and the specific forms of economic exploitation experienced by black and third world women. It also ignores the realities of a world in which most men's labour is also exploited and in which many women are themselves exploiters. Nevertheless, the radical approach does offer important insights into the nature of women's economic situation and the ways in which this is con-nected with other areas of life. As we shall see in Chapter 13, it encouraged Marxist feminists to re-examine their assumptions, opening up a whole area of debate as to the relationship between patriarchy and capitalism and making visible the domestic labour performed by women in the home. Its has also fed into more mainstream debates over citizenship and 'work-life balance'.

Patriarchy, 'man-made language' and knowledge

For some radical feminists, the basis of women's oppression lies not in the state or economics, but in a male control of culture, religion, language and knowledge that limits the ways in which we can think and causes patriar-chal assumptions to be internalised by women as well as by men. Millett had argued that education, literature and religion were central to the maintenance of patriarchy and, as we saw in Chapter 9, some feminist have built on this to challenge the claims of philosophy and political theory to embody reason and universality. Here they have argued that these are based on a male paradigm that ignores or devalues experiences and ways of thinking associated with women, so that 'objectivity' in fact means the subjective perception of men. The whole of cultural and aca-demic life has therefore been seen by some feminists as a political arena in which male biases must be exposed and female knowledge asserted: for example, feminist literary criticism reveals the assumptions and power structures embodied in literary texts, while feminist historians have reclaimed women's history in the name of women's right to knowledge of their own past. At first sight, this kind of analysis appears to have much in common with the postmodern approaches discussed in Chapter 14. However, the latter have a very different philosophical starting-point, and do not accept the radical feminist analysis of patriarchy and its underlying assumptions about the nature and meaning of gender difference.

Important pioneering work on language and knowledge was done by the radical feminist Dale Spender, who argued that women's knowledge and understanding of their own situation had been suppressed over the centuries, so that 'every 50 years women have to re-invent the wheel' (Spender, 1983a:13). In *Women of Ideas (and what men have done to them)*, she documented part of the long and forgotten heritage of feminist ideas, arguing that the discovery of our feminist foremothers is both exciting and empowering, and in *For the Record*, she provided an account of recent theories which she saw as part of a feminist struggle to prevent these too from 'disappearing'. In *Man Made Language*, she argued that male control is also exercised at the level of the very language we use, for this is not a neutral medium of communication, but involves a way of structuring our thought that is based on men's perceptions and cannot accommodate women's experiences. Thus, for example, there is no word to describe the activities of the 'non-working' mother whose time- and energy-consuming chores therefore disappear from public consciousness. Further problems arise from the 'male includes female – sometimes' rule in many languages, whereby words such as 'he', 'his' and 'man' can be understood as containing their female equivalent. This reinforces the view that man is the norm and woman a kind of 'optional extra', and there is empirical evidence to suggest that people 'think male' when confronted with such labels as 'economic man', even though this can in principle mean 'economic people'.

Such analysis finds it unsurprising that Friedan could only describe the discontents of American housewives as 'the problem that has no name' (see Chapter 9 above), and *labelling* their situation becomes a vital first step for feminists seeking to understand and change it. Terms like 'sexism' or 'sexual harassment' are therefore not simply 'feminist jargon', but involve a redefinition of reality from a female perspective. For example, many women today will say they dislike pornography because it degrades women; thirty years ago such language was not available, and, as it seemed that pornography could only be opposed from the standpoint of sexual puritanism, much of the unease which it generated went unarticulated.

Other writers have taken the idea of challenging male knowledge and use of language further by creating alternative methodologies and linguistic structures which, they claim, escape the confines of male logic and enable us to reach a higher and fuller understanding of the world. Andrea Dworkin, in an 'Afterword' to her first book, *Woman Hating*, recorded that she had wanted to have the text printed in lower case letters only, in the belief that

> reading a text which violates standard forms forces one to change mental sets in order to read ... to permit writers to use form to violate conventions just might permit writers to develop forms which could teach people to think differently: not to think different things, but to think in different ways. (Dworkin, 1974, p. 202)

Her publisher was, however, unconvinced, and she was not permitted to make this feminist experiment. Robin Morgan also attempted to experiment with new forms: in *The Anatomy of Freedom* she combined conventional academic argument and grammatical forms with poetry, private correspondence, imaginary dialogues and discursive asides. Eschewing the trappings of formal logic and escaping at times into the wilder shores of fantasy, she claimed to be providing an open-ended approach in which the disparate elements are complementary parts of a multidimensional whole.

The most famous of such feminist practitioners of new forms was, however, Mary Daly. In *Beyond God the Father, Gyn/Ecology* and *Pure Lust* she developed a new language and mode of writing and thinking which she saw as leading to a new female consciousness and culture that is remote from and inaccessible to men. Men have, she said, stolen the power of *naming* from women, who must therefore fight against the deceptions of language and logic, the 'gang-rape of minds as well as bodies' (Daly, 1973:9) and, by inventing new words and forms, discover new ways of being. This involved an inversion of dominant values and a dramatic assertion of the power of Hags, Crones, Harpies, Furies, Amazons and Spinsters to resist the power of men by flying above and beyond their understanding. Eisenstein has called *Gyn/Ecology* 'An extraordinary synthesis of poetry, history, philosophy, literary criticism and diatribe' (Eisenstein, 1984, p. 107), and the power, wit and imagination of her work is undeniable. However it rested upon a number of dubious assertions: that women are wholly good while men are wholly bad, that women's energies must be directed towards an inner transformation rather than an engagement with power structures, that most women (including in particular 'successful' feminists) are collaborators with the existing order and that only a small elite can or deserve to be free. Daly has therefore been accused of advocating a withdrawal from all practical struggle into a woman-only culture to which only a few middle-class women could hope to have access. Like the other writers discussed above, but to a greater degree, she is said to want a purely idealist solution which would leave material conditions and bases of power unchanged, and to accept a false dichotomy between male and female culture that ignores shared values, changes over time and divisions between women. Such possible short-comings must be disentangled from the underlying analysis of language and knowledge as sites of political struggle; this need not imply that these are the causes or most important aspects of patriarchy, but simply recognition that, although new ways of thinking may not in themselves end women's oppression, they must constitute an important weapon against it.

Conclusions: the impact of radical feminism

It should by now be clear that radical feminism offered a fundamental challenge to the whole of traditional political theory. As women, their experiences and their way of seeing the world were taken as the starting-point, 'common-sense' assumptions about the scope and nature of politics were shattered, and men's conversation with each other was not only interrupted, but declared partial and irrelevant. It is true that some of the earlier expositions of radical feminism and the concept of patriarchy were characterised by enthusiasm rather than theoretical rigour, and the over-simplifications of some accounts were both deeply distorting and politically counter-productive. Today, writers are much less ready to try to reduce the whole of women's oppression to a single cause, or to generalise about the condition of all women in all societies in all historical epochs. Partly because of the impact of black and postmodern feminisms, they are more likely to explore the relationships of patriarchy to other forms of inequality and to recognise that, although women's struggles may have their own dynamic, they do not exist in isolation, and that ties of 'race' and class may unite women with men, at the same time as their gender interests divide them.

Good use of radical feminist insights facilitates a realistic assessment of power and opportunities, through which the structures of patriarchy can be seen, not as monolithically oppressive, but as interdependent arenas of struggle within which opportunities may exist and gains be won, so that different forms of feminist action can be seen as complementary rather than alternative, as changes in one structure may both affect and be affected by changes in others. In the first edition of this book, I argued that if it developed in this way radical feminism might be synthesised with some other approaches, and provide a starting-point for a theory that would be both more comprehensive than any that had gone before and self-consciously aware of its own inevitable limitations. Such a theory would continue to see women as central, but would explore the interrelationships between class, 'race' and sex oppressions, and although it would be suspicious of liberal and humanitarian values it would not reject these out of hand. It would also recognise the ubiquity of male power and men's

Feminist Political Theory

interests in continuing present arrangements, but in distinguishing between the structures and agents of oppression it would see men as potential allies as well as adversaries.

To some extent this has happened. Some writers have developed increasingly sophisticated approaches, which attempt to analyse changes in the nature of patriarchy over time and the way in which it interacts with other forms of oppression. While important theoretical differences remain, there has also been a tendency for feminists to move beyond their origins in malestream thought, and many of the claims that seemed so startling thirty years ago are now quite widely accepted by writers and activists who would never accept a 'radical feminist' label. As we shall see, the most acute theoretical disagreements amongst feminists in recent years has not been between radical, liberal and Marxist/socialist strands, but between all these 'modernist' approaches and those based in postmodern philosophy.

13

Marxist and socialist feminism from the 1960s

The starting-point of the radical feminist approaches discussed in the last three chapters was the claim that women should develop their own theories, based on their own experiences, rather than relying on ideas that had been developed by men. Some were also particularly hostile to Marxist and socialist theories because of their experience of sexism in left-wing organisations. Nevertheless, many writers continued to find these a source of inspiration and/or aid to feminist understanding, and from the 1970s there were intense theoretical debates, particularly over the use of Marxist concepts. Today, although philosophical and political developments have combined to make all forms of socialist thought much less fashionable, socialist and Marxist analysis continues to play a significant role in feminist theory and practice.

After the 1920s, so-called communist societies had made little contribution to the the development of feminist thought, but generally followed the official Soviet line that the 'Woman Question' was a product of capitalist society which they had therefore solved. As the Soviet Union became more open from the 1960s, it acknowledged that there were still problems facing women, and Soviet sociologists documented at length the tremendous burdens faced by women combining paid work with domestic responsibilities. However, such problems were officially deemed to be 'non-antagonistic contradictions', resolvable within the existing socio-economic system. During the 1980s, the twin policies of *Glasnost* (openness) and *Perestroika* (restructuring) again placed women's issues on the political agenda. By this time, however, the Marxist orthodoxy that women's liberation required economic independence and full participation in the economy was largely rejected in favour of a renewed emphasis on their traditional role within the home. Contrary to the classic Marxist position, it was now argued that women's double burden should not be resolved by collective housework and childcare, but by increasing their opportunity for part-time and flexible working arrangements. The underlying sexual division of labour remained unchallenged; indeed the official Soviet line now emphasised natural differences rather than equality between men and women and argued that, both for their own benefit and for that of society as a whole, women should be enabled to fulfil themselves in the traditional roles of mother, wife and homemaker (see Buckley, 1989; Rosenberg, 1989; Waters, 1989). Although a few Soviet sociologists said that feminists should try to re-examine Marxist concepts and use them in their analysis (see Voronina, 1989), most abandoned any kind of Marxist or socialist approach to women's situation. This retreat from Marxism was completed by the collapse of communism throughout Eastern Europe and the disintegration of the Soviet Union. It is to the west that we must therefore look for any advances in socialist feminist thought.

By the 1960s, the rise of the New Left, associated with the Civil Rights, anti-war and student movements, provided fertile ground for an exploration of socialist ideas which distinguished between 'genuine' socialism and the repression of so-called communist states. Earlier socialist and Marxist feminist analyses had however largely been forgotten in the west too, and left-wing activist men in the late 1960s were quite unprepared for the new radical feminist attack which denounced their political practice as sexist, and claimed that their theories were patriarchal ideologies that served to conceal the reality of women's oppression. Some initially responded with ridicule, or argued that feminism could only be a bourgeois deviation that divides the workers and distracts them from the class struggle; others simply ignored feminism, apparently in the belief that it would somehow 'go away'. However, many women refused to believe that sexism was inherent in socialist principles; rather, they believed that socialist theory could be used to address feminist concerns. Their attempts to develop such theory are the focus of this chapter.

In discussing such approaches, confusion often arises from the number of different ways in which the terms 'socialist feminist' and 'Marxist feminist' have been used. It should by now be clear that, in practice, ideas, institutions and movements cannot be neatly classified, and I am therefore not attempting to establish 'correct' definitions. Throughout this book, I use 'Marxist feminist' fairly loosely to refer to all feminist theories which employ Marxist concepts, even if they develop these in radical ways, and 'socialist feminist' as a more general term that includes all approaches (including Marxist feminist) that see the goals of feminism as inseparable from socialism (however defined). In practice, the lines between Marxist and socialist feminisms are shifting and blurred, and, although this chapter traces a general development from attempts to fit feminist concerns into a Marxist framework and towards more independent and open-ended analysis (at times almost indistinguishable from postmodernism), this should not be seen as a rigid pattern.

The kind of Marxism that western feminists were able to draw on in the 1960s was in many ways much more open to their concerns than in the past. Previously, Marxism had been seen as a rigid theory of economic determinism, but from the 1960s the ideas of the New Left and the rediscovery of the 'young Marx' and his idea of alienation led to a looser interpretation which at times had more affinity with liberal humanitarianism than with Stalinist dogma. There were also attempts to synthesise Marxism with the insights of psychoanalysis (most famously by Wilhelm Reich in the 1930s, and by Herbert Marcuse in the 1960s); these extended Marxist concerns beyond the economic, and identified the importance of sexuality and the workings of the unconscious for any understanding of society and social change. The ideas of the inter-war Italian Marxist Gramsci were developed by writers such as Althusser and Poulantzas to argue for the importance of ideological and political struggle and their relative autonomy from economic determinants, and there was an increasingly widespread move away from an analysis that saw class as central and towards a more pluralistic approach that could encompass other forms of struggle (for an early critique of such 'revisions' of Marxism, see Wood, 1986). Such developments are reflected in some of the discussions below. Some writers, however, drew on more orthodox Marxist economic concepts, which they tried to use to analyse the particular situation of women; here analysis initially focussed on the so-called 'domestic labour debate', to which we now turn.

The domestic labour debate

At first sight the domestic labour debate, much of which was conducted in the pages of the British journal *New Left Review* during the 1970s, might appear to be an example of the tedium and inaccessibility of late twentieth century Marxist thought, involving nit-picking terminological disagreements of interest only to sectarian Marxists and illustrating the futility of trying to apply Marxist concepts to women (Evans, 1995 and Bubeck, 1995). However, as Vogel says, it was not simply 'an obscure exercise in Marxist pedantry' (Vogel, 1983:21), but an attempt to make visible the work done by women within the home and, by exploring its relationship to the capitalist economy, to assess its strategic importance and the possible implications of this in achieving socialist change (for summaries and discussion of the debate see Foreman, 1978; Molyneux, 1979; Burton, 1985; Gardiner, 1997; Bubeck, 1995).

An assumption of classic Marxism was that capitalism's drive for profit was 'sex-blind', and would increasingly draw women and children into the paid labour market; this would represent an increase in exploitation through a depreciation in the value of the male worker's labour power, as he need no longer be paid the cost of maintaining his family as well as himself. Marx never explored the possibility that this process might be reversed and male workers be paid a 'family wage', and he ignored the economic significance of the unpaid work that continued to be done by women at home, whether or not they were in paid employment. The protagonists in the domestic labour debate were agreed both that such omissions were a serious limitation on Marxist understanding and that Marxist concepts could nevertheless be employed to fill the gap. They disagreed, however, as to whether women's domestic work should be seen as some kind of precapitalist mode of production outside of the money economy, whether it is essential to the reproduction of labour power under capitalism and whether it does in fact produce exchange value in the strict Marxist sense (in the form of the labour power of the adult male worker, sold like any other commodity on the market, with his overalls neatly pressed and his sandwiches in his pocket).

Such disagreements were not 'merely academic', for the centrality of domestic labour to capitalism is related to the kind of political action that might be taken by women. Thus, some writers argued that, because domestic labour produces value in the same way as other forms of productive labour, then the unpaid work of the housewife is exploited by capitalism and her role is as strategically important as the factory worker, for 'woman is the slave of a wage-slave, and her slavery ensures the slavery of her man' (James, quoted in Malos, 1980:178; see also Dalla Costa, 1973). From this perspective, women should not enter the paid workforce as earlier Marxist analysis had suggested, but they should demand that housework itself be paid for. The international 'Wages for Housework' campaign was heavily criticised for alleged misunderstanding of Marxist concepts, for perpetuating the assumption that housework is women's responsibility and for the impracticality of its demands. Its proponents, however, argued that it corresponded to the real needs of working-class women who would never be liberated by the kind of paid work available to them, and that to demand that housework be paid for by the capitalist state was both to make visible its importance as part of the class struggle and to challenge the assumption that its performance is some kind of natural attribute of womanhood. Most writers did not go so far, but, as the debate developed, there appeared to be a general agreement that the housework done by women does not simply represent a personal service to individual men, but that it serves the interests of the capitalist economy by reproducing and maintaining the workforce in a particularly cheap and efficient way; this in turn implies that male supremacy within the home is not simply a matter of personal patriarchal oppression, but is embedded in economic structures. Maria Mies has since argued that the insight that capitalism depends upon and exploits western women's unpaid domestic labour can be extended to analyse the ways in which other forms of unpaid work, particularly by third world peasants and homeworkers, are an integral part of the international economy, central to the processes of capital accumulation (Mies, 1998).

The debate drew attention to an important aspect of economic life which had previously been neglected, and meant that domestic labour could not be sidelined as something that would automatically be resolved 'after the revolution'. However, it did not really explore differences in women's situation (particularly across class and ethnic groupings) and it notably failed to ask why it is that domestic labour is overwhelmingly performed by *women* or to explore the pre-existing structures or patriarchal attitudes that produced the present gender division of labour; any idea that men as well as capitalism benefit from present arrangements therefore tended to disappear. It also failed to analyse the dynamic inter-relationship between gender divisions and the capitalist economy, through which the need for domestic services could often conflict with the demand for women's paid labour. Perhaps most fundamentally, the debate was in danger of providing a new form of economic determinism that argued that because present arrangements can be shown to be advantageous to capitalism, they are also somehow caused by it and unchangeable within it. However, the male breadwinner family structure was not simply a product of the abstract 'needs of capitalism'; indeed, forcing workers to live in barracks might have been a more cost-effective, although politically unacceptable alternative. Rather, it resulted from the complex interplay of factors including working-class campaigns and pre-existing gender ideology. This means that the significance of domestic labour cannot be understood in economic terms alone.

Women and the labour market

For some writers, the significance of women's domestic labour lies not so much in the ways in which this serves the needs of capitalism, as in the ways in which it structures women's relationship to the paid economy. This means that, contrary to Engels' prediction that women's employment would end their oppression, women enter the labour market from a position of subordination which is both reflected in and reinforced by their conditions of employment. The arguments involved here are complicated, and at times shift from one explanatory level to another. A central starting-point, however, is that women's assumed dependency on a male breadwinner[8] depresses their wages relative to men's, for employers need not pay them directly either for the entire cost of reproducing their own labour power or for reproducing the next generation; this low pay in turn reinforces both their economic dependency within marriage and the economic necessity of finding a husband. This assumed dependency also means that women can more easily than men be made unemployed at a time of recession, and here writers have used the concept of the *reserve army of labour*, which Marx saw as essential to the workings of the capitalist economy, to analyse women's economic situation. According to Marx, capitalism's need for labour inevitably fluctuated as the economy went through cycles of expansion and recession. It therefore required the existence of a group of workers who could be treated as marginal to the economy and dispensed with at times of recession; although he treated this 'reserve army' as an 'empty' category, some Marxist feminists have argued that it is particularly applicable to the employment of women. While it may be intuitively appealing, this analysis is not however entirely supported by the available empirical evidence. In particular, the relative cheapness of women's labour creates a contrary pressure to employ them in preference to men, while in recent years the shift from manufacturing to service industries in western economies has produced male unemployment and a demand for female workers.

Nevertheless, many women workers still play a marginal role in the paid labour market. They are heavily concentrated in part-time, low-pay occupations, and it seems clear that their domestic roles disadvantage them in a competitive employment market that ignores family responsibilities and makes it difficult for women to defend their own economic interests. Not only do they have less time to attend union meetings or to work the hours that help achieve promotion, but ideological factors mean that their labour is seen as less important than that of men and more likely to be labelled 'unskilled'. Marx had claimed that, as capitalism developed, employers would increasingly seek to simplify the labour processes and replace skilled with unskilled workers, and that the entry of women and children into the workforce was a reflection of this process. However, as Phillips and Taylor have argued, 'skill' is frequently an ideological category, arising from the struggle of men to maintain their dominance in the sexual hierarchy, and enabling men to resist the 'deskilling' process by displacing this onto women (Phillips and Taylor, 1986). From this perspective, women are not paid less simply because they are unskilled, but because working-class men have succeeded in protecting their own interests at women's expense; they have been able to do this because dominant attitudes label any work done by women as inherently inferior to that done by men. This means that there has been conflict between men and women workers, and we must look at least in part to the activities of men, particularly as organised in the trade union movement, if we are to understand the historical reasons for women's lower pay and inferior conditions of employment.

This does not mean that gender struggle is always overt, clear-cut and unambiguous, for prevailing gender ideologies may be accepted by women themselves as well as by both employers and male workers; indeed, such ideologies are likely to be internalised at the deepest emotional and psychological level, so that women's sense of identity and expectations of fulfilment are bound up with family and personal life rather than paid work, and they are likely to welcome forms of employment, particularly part-time working, that do not involve high levels of commitment or time. The demand for the 'family wage' or protective legislation can also be seen as part of a general class struggle to improve working-class standards of living, rather than a move to reinforce male domination (Humphries, 1982; Brenner and Ramas, 1984). It does mean, however, that positions in the labour hierarchy have always reflected the struggle between men and women as well as that between labour and capital, so that capitalism's need for a marginal or reserve army of cheap, docile and unskilled labour has been met in gender-specific ways.

Two systems or one? 'Dual systems' v. 'capitalist patriarchy'

This kind of analysis has suggested to some writers that there are *two* dynamic forces at work in history, which must therefore be understood in terms of patriarchy as well as class. As with the domestic labour debate, the arguments can seem very abstract. They do however have practical implications, for if patriarchy exists independently, rather than as an integral part of capitalism, it may be possible and necessary to challenge it separately, and for women to organise autonomously in defence of their own interests. If, however, what we have is a unified system of capitalist patriarchy, then gender issues can only be tackled as part of a general movement against capitalism, while anti-capitalist struggles cannot ignore or sideline the oppression of women.

In an influential essay, Heidi Hartmann rejected the orthodox Marxist view that class and capitalism are more fundamental than gender and patriarchy. She argued that attempts to combine Marxist and feminist analysis had produced an 'unhappy marriage' based on the same kind of subordination as the marriage of husband and wife in English common law, through which the wife's legal identity became incorporated into that of her husband. To avoid this subordination, she said, 'either we need a healthier marriage or we need a divorce' (Hartmann, 1986:2). She claimed that contemporary society must be understood as both capitalist and patriarchal. Although they have become bound up with each other, neither of these 'dual systems' can, she said, be reduced to the other, and although at times they are mutually reinforcing, they may also come into conflict (most notably when capitalism's need for women's labour power is opposed by the patriarchal demand for personal services within the home). She said that Marxist analysis forgets that men as well as capitalism benefit from present arrangements, and she claimed that, because they 'have a higher standard of living than women in terms of luxury consumption, leisure time and personalised services', men of all classes have at least a short-term material interest in maintaining women's oppression, which pre-dates capitalism and could continue beyond it (Hartmann, 1986:9). Ann Ferguson similarly argued that there is a semi-autonomous system of patriarchy, and that, as traditional Marxism cannot fully understand women's oppression, new concepts derived from radical feminism must be developed. She said that, in addition to its economic mode of production, society is based on a mode of 'sex affective production'. By this somewhat clumsy term she understood the social bonding, the physical and emotional interactions that arise in such areas as sexuality, parenting, family and friendship, and she argued that 'the form of human organisation which a society develops to meet the human material needs for such connection will be as important in understanding these societies as their economic systems' (Ferguson, 1989:83). Like Hartmann, she therefore insisted both that the concept of patriarchy must be given a history and that this is not reducible to economic change as traditionally understood by Marxists. In particular, she argued that contemporary American society must be understood as a public and capitalist patriarchy, but that the contradictions between capitalist and patriarchal interests provide a potential for disruption and the pursuit of both socialist and feminist goals.

Other writers, such as Iris Young, rejected such 'dual systems' approaches, and claimed that what we now have is a unified system of capitalist patriarchy. Young agreed that patriarchy is based on men's control over women's labour, but she argued that this material basis is not separate from the productive process, but an integral part of it. This meant that, although she followed orthodox Marxism in seeing production and class as the sources of women's oppression, these were reconceptualised to include the gender division of labour; from this perspective, the analysis of gender was not some kind of optional extra for Marxists, but central to the understanding of any economic system and hence basic to the whole of society. Young's approach informs Maria Mies' more recent analysis of 'capitalist-patriarchy' as 'an intrinsically interconnected system' in which the gender division of labour and exploitation of women's labour are central to the never-ending, worldwide process of capital accumulation (Mies, 1998:38). Both she and Young identify pre-capitalist forms of patriarchy but, rather than seeing patriarchy as unchanging and autonomous, they see it as evolving with changes in production and class relations. (Young, 1986). Anna Pollert similarly argues that there is a 'fused system of gender and class relations' which can be analysed through the development of a feminist historical materialism, although she dislikes any use of the term 'patriarchy', which she says implies inappropriate theoretical claims (Pollert, 1996:647; see also the discussion in Chapter 10, above).

While earlier Marxist accounts had treated women's oppression simply as a by-product of class society, the analysis of capitalist patriarchy sees it as central. From this reformulated perspective, the analysis of gender inequalities must understand that these are bound up with the economic system, and feminist politics cannot be separated from anti-capitalist struggle (see Brenner, 2000). At the same time, any economic analysis that ignores gender issues will be partial and flawed. For some writers, a key tool in such analysis is the concept of *social reproduction*.

Social reproduction

As discusssed in Chapter 3 above, Marx and Engels recognised in passing that biological reproduction as well as production was a part of the material basis of society. In the *German Ideology* they wrote of 'the production of life, both of one's own in labour and of fresh life in procreation', and Engels stated that

> The social institutions under which the people of a particular historical epoch and a particular country live are conditioned by both kinds of production: by the state of development of labour on the one hand and of the family on the other. (*The Origin*:4)

Neither Marx nor Engels explored the implications of this, and Engels argued that the independent development of the family ceased at a very early stage. Nevertheless, it suggested that in principle there could be reciprocal interaction rather than one-way causation between the two spheres, opening up the possibility that patriarchy may have a material base, rooted in reproduction and the family instead of or as well as in conditions of productive labour.

In 1983, Lise Vogel's *Marxism and the Oppression of Women* provided an early exploration of such ideas. Clearly, any mode of production requires that workers are maintained and reproduced. Although in principle this can be achieved through immigration, the latter is of course normally done through procreation, and Vogel argued that the organisation of such 'generational reproduction' provides the key to understanding the material basis of women's oppression in class society. Most obviously, the biological fact of childbearing imposes a basic division of labour, and means that the economic productivity of reproductively active women is temporarily reduced. Under capitalism, this involves a contradiction for the ruling class, as its interest in extracting the maximum profit from women's labour conflicts with the need for efficient generational replacement and maintenance of the workforce. It resolves this by taking advantage of pre-existing kinship relationships to institutionalise the financial support by working-class men of less productive women, so that although historically conditions of reproduction and forms of the family have varied:

> In virtually all cases, they entail men's greater responsibility for provision of material means of subsistence, women's greater responsibility for the ongoing tasks of necessary labour, and institutionalised forms of male domination over women. (*Marxism*:149)

In other words, in any form of class society, women's biological role as childbearers almost inevitably involves an economic dependency upon men. It also involves an extended division of labour whereby women are disproportionately responsible for the domestic labour necessary to maintain the workforce, and men for that which involves the production of a surplus. Under capitalism, the separation of home and work and the system of wage labour increases and formalises both the distinction between domestic and production work and women's economic dependency. However, Vogel argued that in a socialist society, in which production would be for use rather than profit, the economic imperative to extract a surplus from women's labour would no longer be operative, childcare and domestic labour would be socialised and the biological division of labour would no longer involve an oppressive economic dependency.

It is important to recognise that Vogel was not saying simply that men can exploit women because they have babies, but that their subordination solves an economic problem for the ruling class that stems from their role in the reproduction of labour power; she was therefore arguing that, contrary to the classic Marxist analysis, working-class women do suffer from sex-specific oppression and that Marxist concepts can be used to understand it. Here her argument that oppression constitutes a resolution of contradictions within capitalism itself avoided the need to posit an autonomous system of patriarchy with interests potentially opposed to that of capitalism; working-class women are, she said, oppressed as women, but they are oppressed by capitalism, not by working-class men.

Despite its insights, Vogel's analysis gives rise to problems at a number of levels. Firstly, she made no attempt to substantiate her claims with reference to anthropological evidence or to an examination of precapitalist societies; the whole argument that it is only in class society that the sexual division of labour becomes oppressive therefore remains a theoretical deduction wide open to empirical challenge. Secondly, women's economic dependency on a male breadwinner was not simply imposed upon the working class, but fought for by them (often with the support of working-class women). Thirdly, any attempt to reduce women's oppression to the needs of class society ignores the ways in which it may also benefit men, and fails to understand that even working-class and socialist men may have an interest in maintaining gender inequalities. This meant that Vogel could report that 'existing socialist societies ... have been unable to confront the problems of domestic labour and women's subordination in any systematic way' (*Marxism*:174), without considering whether this 'inability' might in fact be a *refusal* stemming from continued male dominance in all spheres. Similarly, she blithely stated that in the transition to a socialist society domestic work would be both socialised and shared with men, ignoring any likelihood of male opposition. She also failed even to acknowledge the non-economic forms of oppression which radical feminists had identified, such as male violence or cultural control of language and knowledge, while broader issues around biological reproduction (such as abortion, changes in contraceptive knowledge or reproductive technology) were not included in her analysis.

These limitations were at least in part the product of an unhelpfully narrow use of the concept of social reproduction that remained confined by orthodox Marxist perceptions. From this perspective, women's responsibility for social reproduction is unproblematically constant, and changes in the material conditions of reproduction and of social relations based upon them disappear from history. From the 1980s there were, however, some attempts to use Marxist methods to conceptualise biological reproduction, sexuality and the family as more active parts of the material basis of society. This meant that they were given a history of their own, rather than being either the unchanging product of nature, or the inevitable by-product of particular conditions of production. From this perspective, changes in sexual behaviour, changes in the role of women and men within the family and the development of new methods of contraception or reproductive technology can all be seen as real material changes that cannot simply be explained in terms of the needs of the economy. Efforts to change practices in these areas are therefore as important as attempts to change conditions of paid employment, so that if women demand the same sexual freedom as men, or insist that men contribute more to family life or campaign for affordable and legal abortions, these can be seen as basic material demands as well as political and ideological struggles. This means that Marxism's focus on work is not essentially incompatible with a focus on sexuality, reproduction and the family, for all are part of the real material conditions in which we produce and reproduce, and:

> Systems of social reproduction are the historical outcomes of class and gender struggles – struggles that are often about sexuality and emotional relations, as well as political power and economic resources. (Brenner and Laslett 1991:63; see also O'Brien, 1981 and 1989; Jaggar, 1983; Brenner, 2000; Bryson, 1995.)

Ideology, the family and 'structures of oppression'

The above Marxist feminist approaches all sought in various ways to develop a materialist analysis of women's oppression. As discussed at the beginning of this chapter, however, mainstream Marxist thinking became much more open-ended in the second half of the twentieth century, and much more willing to explore non-economic perspectives. Some feminists were able to use such developments to move even further from a purely materialist analysis whilst continuing to draw on Marxist ideas.

Here, a pioneering and influential contribution was made by Juliet Mitchell, whose *Women, The Longest Revolution*, first published in 1966, has been described as 'really the first written text of the British Women's Liberation movement' (Wilson, 1980:196). In this essay and in *Women's Estate* (1971) and *Psychoanalysis and Feminism* (1974), she sought to 'ask the feminist questions, but try to come up with some Marxist answers' (*Estate*:99). She argued that, although earlier generations of Marxists had been correct in seeing women's relation to production as of key importance, their analysis did not go nearly far enough and ignored the crucial ways in which women's subordination is maintained within the family. More specifically, she claimed that four structures are involved in determining women's situation: in addition to the structure of production, traditionally analysed by Marxist theory, feminists must examine the family-based structures of reproduction, sexuality and the socialisation of children. This led her to an analysis of the ways in which subordination is internalised and consent engineered, which in turn involved an examination of the workings of the unconscious and of the ways in which adult identity is learned in our society.

There were two key aspects to Mitchell's theory. Firstly, influenced by the French Marxist Louis Althusser, she argued for the 'relative autonomy' as well as the interdependence of her four structures, and for the importance of ideology in understanding the workings of society; secondly, her exploration of psychoanalytic theory led her to try to rehabilitate Freud and to show that, despite their frequent misuse and the criticisms of feminists, his ideas can be used in feminist analysis. This meant that her concerns overlapped with radical feminist critiques of the family, sexuality and men's control over knowledge, although she attempted to give these a history which was still in the last analysis based upon developments in production. She claimed that her hopes and predictions for the future were based on an analysis of the present in which economic conditions may be fundamental, but in which political and ideological struggles also have a key role. She therefore avoided the kind of crude economic reductionism to which Marxist analysis is prone. Her analysis also led her to advocate autonomous women's organisations, insisting that as an oppressed group women must work for their own liberation and that there will be no automatic dissolution of patriarchy without feminist struggle.

As with the later 'dual systems' theories discussed above, the problem remained as to precisely how Mitchell's four structures interacted, and there was a danger that her analysis could lead to an artificial distinction between economic and ideological struggles, whereby 'Marxism appears as the theory for class struggle, and psychoanalysis the theory for the analysis of patriarchy' (Wilson, 1980:199; see also Foreman, 1978). Nevertheless, as Lynne Segal has recently argued, the principle that different forms of understanding can be complementary is important, and Mitchell's identification of the psychoanalytic bases of gender identity can both help explain why gendered patterns of behaviour are so difficult to change and challenge conventional certainties about the 'naturalness' of gendered behaviour (Segal, 1999).

The idea that gender issues may have a degree of independence from class was also explored by Michelle Barrett. She too was strongly influenced by Althusser, particularly his claim that, contrary to many traditional interpretations of Marx, ideas are not simply determined by economic relationships, but may have a certain independence. In terms of political activity and outcomes, this means that the 'battle of ideas' is important in its own right, and that social arrangements may be a consequence as well as a cause of the dominant ideology.

In *Women's Oppression Today* (first published in 1980), Barrett argued that women's oppression cannot be reduced to the needs of the capitalist economy, but that it is also the product of a specific pre-existing gender ideology; as such it may be extraordinarily useful to capitalism, but it was certainly not caused by it. This means that ideological as well as economic forces helped create women's economic dependency on a male breadwinner. However, this leaves open the question of where the original gender ideology came from, and how this could over-ride the sex-blind operations of capitalism (which treats women and men as disembodied units of production). Although Marx would agree with Barrett that ideology is not mechanically determined by the economy, he did not see socially dominant ideas as 'free-floating' but as reflecting real social relations, albeit in a distorted form. Barrett seemed at times to accept this, but she never really examined the precapitalist conditions that might have given rise to her gender ideology, and she has been accused of treating this as a covenient, but unexplained, *deus ex machina* (Brenner and Ramas, 1984). Related problems arise from her claim that the main significance of the family in late twentieth-century capitalist society is ideological, rather than economic. Much like Robert Owen in the early nineteenth century, she and Mary McIntosh argued in *The Anti-Social Family* that the family is both the product of a selfish, individualistic society and the means by which it is ideologically maintained. As such, its ideology must be challenged by feminists, but as it promises to satisfy real needs for affection and intimacy which are not at present met elsewhere, significant changes can only be achieved through transforming the economic relations of society (Barrett and McIntosh, 1982). As with Mitchell's analysis, this can usefully widen our understanding and open up possibilities for feminist activism. Again, however, it seems to contrast feminist ideological struggle with economic class struggle, with the success of the former ultimately being dependent on the latter.

Such separation can perhaps be avoided if we ally this kind of analysis with the previously discussed idea that social reproduction (including procreation and the physical maintenance of the workforce) must be understood as part of the economic basis of society. From this perspective, ideology is a reflection of material conditions within the family as well as of productive life, and changes in family structure are themselves a form of material change that may not be simply reducible to the needs of the capitalist economy. For example, changes in sexual behaviour may result from increased knowledge and availability of contraception, and also from the spread of AIDS. This means that attempts to change family structures can themselves constitute direct economic as well as political and ideological struggle; such developments as increased male involvement in childcare therefore represent real changes in the conditions of social reproduction which may have an independent effect upon production (for example, by decreasing the attractiveness of overtime working). Therefore, although the family may itself play an important ideological role in providing an appropriately socialised and motivated workforce, it cannot be reduced to this function. At the same time, concentration on the workplace as part of the process of production should not obscure the fact that it too can play an ideological role, reinforcing not only hierarchical productive relationships but sexist attitudes towards women (for example, by the display of pin-up posters or, more subtly, by assuming that women will naturally undertake tea-making or pastoral responsibilities).

Alienation

Some recent feminist theories suggest that the complex interrelationship between family and the paid economy can be further explored by using Marx's concept of *alienation*. As discussed in Chapter 3 above, this was important in Marx's early writings, and it involved a humanitarian critique of conditions of labour under capitalism, arguing that the pursuit of profit and the extreme division of labour meant that work had become an alien activity over which the worker had no control, rather than an expression of human creativity. Both Foreman and Jaggar have extended this idea to argue that, for women, alienation is not confined to the world of paid employment and that it is experienced within the family and private life. Here, it involves a loss of control over reproduction and sexuality and the provision of emotional and material support to men in a form that denies women's own needs. This means that, whereas for the male worker the family is the one area of life where his human needs can be met,

> for women there is no relief. For those intimate relations are the very ones that are the essential structure of her oppression ... while alienation reduces the man to an instrument of labour within industry, it reduces the woman to an instrument for his sexual pleasure within the family. (Foreman, 1978:102 and 151)

From this perspective, women's personal relationships cannot be understood as the freely chosen expression of their own desires, but are imposed upon them. This alienation is, however, disguised, because relationships within the family are not normally mediated by money, and the dominant ideology denies that they are based on anything other than love. Men benefit emotionally, sexually and economically from this concealed alienation; they will therefore resist any attempts to commercialise women's services, for this would represent a final stage of universal alienation and the ultimate denial of their own humanity. Such a stage would, however, be progressive, for Marx did not see alienation as simply negative, but as a necessary stage in human evolution, a precondition for full conscious control and fulfilment and man's mastery over nature. Foreman and Jaggar therefore argued that women's alienation is historically specific rather than an unchanging aspect of gender relations. As such, it is a product of women's economic dependency and the impoverishment of human relationships under capitalism; modern physiological knowledge and reproductive technology are at present used to manipulate women, but they could in the future be used to liberate them, so that for the first time in human history reproduction and sexual activity could be freely chosen.

If, as has been argued, we see reproduction and sexuality as part of the material basis of society, such 'private' alienation and its overcoming must

be as fundamental as that experienced in production and, unlike the
religious and political alienation also identified by Marx, not simply a
reflection of it. This means that areas of life traditionally ignored by political theorists can in fact be integrated into Marx's theory of history using
one of his original concepts, and that 'the patterning of the intimate
relations of men and women is a vital element in completing the Marxist
theory of the development of human consciousness' (Foreman, 1978:110).

Marx's analysis of alienation was tied in with a critique of the division
of labour in society. Under capitalism, he said, specialisation becomes so
extreme that skills are lost and work becomes a denial rather than an
expression of human creativity. However, in future communist society the
positive use of technology to meet human needs will allow the division of
labour to be abolished or at least greatly reduced, with individuals enjoy-
ing an unprecedented opportunity to choose and move between different
occupations; unlike the stunted, impoverished individual of today, the
worker of tomorrow will be able to explore his full potential through productive labour, which will be a means of human fulfilment rather than
degradation. Unlike the earlier utopian socialists, Marx never applied
these ideas to the sexual division of labour. This is, however, central to
much recent feminist analysis, which argues both that women must be
enabled to do 'men's work' and that men should develop their caring and
nurturing qualities through participation in productive life and childrearing; such change is both an important prerequisite of gender equality and
an important goal in itself. This would seem to be a logical extension of
Marx's analysis. Similarly, radical and postmodern feminist demands that
sexuality be liberated from gender stereotypes and polarities can be seen
as the demand for an end to ascribed gender roles; as for Marx, the goal is
the fully rounded individual free to express himself or herself in all
possible ways. A Marxist perspective, however, does not simply endorse
such demands, but gives them a historical context, arguing that they can
only be met at a certain stage of human development. It also means that
they cannot be isolated from other forms of social change, but are part of
a more general social movement. In other words, the ending of women's
sex-specific alienation will never be achieved on its own, as liberal and
radical perspectives might suggest, for it is integrally bound up with the
struggle to end alienation in all its forms.

Feminist standpoint theory

The radical feminist Catherine MacKinnon has argued that feminism
cannot be combined with Marxism, partly because feminist method and
knowledge is based on women's lived experience and a rejection of the

distinction between knowing subject and known object, so that 'women grasp the collective reality of women's condition from within the perspective of that experience, not from outside it'[9] (MacKinnon, 1983:268). However, Marx too argued that good theory cannot be deduced from abstract speculation or outside observation, but can only result from concrete practices which it both reflects and informs. Nancy Harstock has therefore claimed that 'consciousness raising' (see Chapter 10, above) was a re-invention of Marx's original method, and she uses this to argue for the development of a 'feminist standpoint', based on the material reality of women's lives. She claims that this standpoint leads to a form of knowledge superior to that available to men, partly because women's subordinate position gives them a material interest in understanding gender relations, while men's interests lie in ignoring or concealing them. She also claims that its superiority is a consequence of the nature of women's work, which grounds their ideas in physical reality, and means that women would never develop the kind of abstract, disembodied theories that characterise male philosophy. In support of this point she quotes from Marilyn French's feminist novel, *The Woman's Room*:

> Washing the toilet used by three males, and the floor and walls around it, is, Myra thought, coming face to face with necessity. And that is why women were saner than men, did not come up with the mad, absurd schemes men developed: they were in touch with necessity, they had to wash the toilet bowl and floor. (Quoted in Harstock, 1985:236)

Despite the intuitive appeal of such ideas, Harstock has been heavily criticised for failing to recognise that women may be divided as well as united by their experiences: at an obvious level, not every woman does have to clean the toilet, and for the black cleaning woman employed by a wealthy white woman, the experiences of racism and class exploitation may appear more salient than her gender. Here the logic of Harstock's own approach suggests that it is her situation as a white woman privileged by a racist system that has made it difficult for her to see this point.

Later writers have been much more ready to recognise the diversity of women's situations. Nevertheless, Nancy Hirschmann has argued that women's near-universal monopoly of childcare provides a basic commonality of experience which affects our whole sense of being (Hirschmann, 1992), while Sandra Harding argues that women's shared experience of subordination and marginality can provide the basis for an 'oppositional consciousness' and for forms of knowledge that are both different from and superior to the narrow and unreflective standpoints of the dominant male elite (Harding, 1986 and 1991). Although Harding now says that such knowledge may in principle be accessible to men, standpoint theory remains prone to essentialising generalisations. To the extent that it avoids this by recognising a multiplicity of partial and specific viewpoints, it becomes increasingly indistinguishable from some of the ideas of postmodernism.

Recent developments in Marxist feminist thought

As already indicated, the second half of the twentieth century saw a general trend in Marxist thought away from ideas of economic determinism and class conflict as narrowly understood, and towards a more pluralist approach which allows for a greater independence to political and ideological struggle and for the identification of interests not based on class. Some writers have argued that these theoretical developments are themselves a reflection of changes in the technological basis and class structure of advanced capitalist society, in which old economic groupings have become fragmented and the fight for socialism must be seen in terms of multiple struggles rather than straightforward confrontation between opposing classes. In this new context, 'race' and gender become independently important dimensions of struggle, and the fight for ideological domination and control is of central significance (for a particularly clear example of this perspective, see Hall and Jacques (eds), *New Times*, 1989).

Such analysis at times merges with postmodernist approaches. As we shall see in the next chapter, these deny the existence of stable and objectively knowable gender or class interests and identities, claiming that such crude labels conceal the variety and fluidity of human experience and subjectivity and the ways in which meaning and power are constructed through language and knowledge. Although such ideas are clearly incompatible with the assumptions of orthodox Marxism, they mesh neatly with some of the concerns of the new 'revisionists', and postmodernism has been well received by some erstwhile socialist feminists. For example, by 1988 Michelle Barrett (discussed above) had distanced herself from her earlier position to argue that the attempt to construct a Marxist feminist analysis had largely failed, and that 'the arguments of post-modernism already represent, I think, a key position around which feminist theoretical work in the future is likely to revolve' (Barrett, 1988:xxxiv).[10] Postmodernism's focus on the ways in which meanings are constructed has clear links with Barrett's arguments about the independent importance of ideology. More generally, it has supported what Donna Landry and Gerald MacLean have described as a 'materialist analysis of culture informed by and responsive to the concerns of women, as well as people of color and other marginalized groups' (Landry and MacLean, 1993:x).

Critics, however, see this as a poor substitute for a materialist analysis of production and reproduction (Giminez, 2000).

Barrett also says that postmodernism can help avoid the incipient racism of much feminist thought, which has wrongly tended to assume that all women share the same situation. However, because Marxist feminism's starting point is the recognition of more than one form of oppression and the historical specificity of experience, it too should in principle be both open to the analysis of 'race'-based oppression and aware that there is no universal essence to women's oppression. Marxism played a major role in 'black power' politics in the United States from the 1960s and has strongly influenced the black feminist writer Angela Davis. Unlike approaches based in liberal thought, Marxism argues that racism, like sexism, is not simply a question of individual wickedness or injustice, but the product of particular historical situations. In particular, it has roots in colonialism and imperialism, and is now advantageous to capitalism because (like sexism) it divides the working class and provides a marginalised labour force. For feminists, that means that differences between women have to be placed in their global historical context and understood in relation to colonialism, imperialism and nationalistic struggles for independence; in the case of African-American women the legacy of slavery, both economic and psychological, is clearly of pivotal importance.

Despite Marxism's potential, white Marxist feminists have until recently neglected such analysis, and Barrett herself has been robustly criticised, along with her co-author Mary McIntosh, firstly for ignoring black women and then for seeming to treat them as 'different' rather than questioning the 'normality' of white experience (Barrett and McIntosh, 1985; Ramazanoglu, 1986). Recent developments in black feminist thought, discussed in the following chapter, have however had a major impact on white socialist and Marxist feminist thought, and there is growing recognition that black women's experiences must be a central starting-point for feminist analysis (see, for example, Brenner, 2000). The growing interest in 'globalisation' has also increased recognition of the extent to which local experiences fit into an international division of labour (see, for example, Mies, 1998; Ramazanaglu, 1989; Kenway with Langmead, 2000; Ward, 2002).

Socialist feminist strategies

Whilst the kind of theoretical debates discussed in this chapter can at times seem very remote from the everyday concerns of 'real' women, they have practical political implications. In particular, the analysis of the economic importance of women's domestic and caring work suggests both that these should not be seen as simply private responsibilities and that collective solutions will have to be fought for against powerful economic interests. It is also increasingly clear that the gender division of labour occurs on a world scale, and that 'women are central to the compliant, low-paid workforce essential for contemporary capital accumulation' (Ward, 2002:139). This in turn suggests that feminists should work together across national boundaries, while women's situation must be treated as central to any kind of socialist strategy for change.

In the United States, Marxist and socialist analyses were briefly fashionable during the late 1960s and early 1970s, and remain an important strand within academic feminism (see Chinchilla and Gimenez, 1991; Vogel, 1995 and Brenner, 2000); in general, however, liberal and radical feminism have both had more political impact there. In Europe, the greater strength of socialist parties and trade unions has meant that socialist and Marxist feminism has become more integrated into mainstream political life. Although this has frequently been dominated by middleclass 'intellectual socialists', the exclusion of working-class women has been less marked than in the United States; here too, however, black women have often been marginalised or excluded.

In the late 1960s and early 1970s there was quite widespread optimism in left-wing circles about the possibility of revolution in advanced industrial societies. This was soon largely replaced by a more pragmatic approach in which reform 'within the system' and coalitions of 'progressive' groups were preferred to the 'revolutionary overthrow of capitalism' and class struggle. Such changes were reflected in socialist feminist strategies. The immediate political task for socialist feminists in Britain became to challenge sexism within trade unions and left-wing parties, to campaign for the election of a Labour government and to organise around particular class, gender, 'race', community or environmental demands in the belief that these struggles were interconnected and that they could have a cumulative effect upon society. This approach, and the optimism of the time, was epitomised in the widely discussed *Beyond the Fragments* (1979). In this, three leading socialist feminist writers and activists (Hilary Wainwright, Sheila Rowbotham and Lynn Segal) attempted to reformulate the socialist project both by challenging the elitism, sexism and hierarchy of existing left-wing organisations, and by building upon new grass-roots movements in the hope of producing a more democratic and participatory movement against all forms of oppression. They argued in particular that feminist critiques of all forms of power are necessarily central to socialism both as a movement for change and as the future form of society, for

the movement for women's liberation is part of the creation of a new society in which there are no forms of domination. This society cannot be separated from the process of its making. (Rowbotham, in *Fragments*:50)

Such arguments had some effect upon left-wing political organisations, which have taken steps to become more 'woman-friendly' (although this might be seen as a taming of feminism's radical potential rather than a real achievement), During the long years of Conservative rule (1979–97), many pinned their hopes on a Labour government. By 1997, however, the Labour Party seemed to have embraced many of the Thatcherite policies that had done so much to undermine welfare provision and increase inequality. Although socialist feminists could in principle welcome some of the new government's policies, most rejected its reliance on the market, its failure to recognise the full importance of domestic responsibilities and its unwillingness to recognise or tackle structured inequalities or conflicts of interest, so that many soon found their 'initial rising hopes often moving towards despairing resignation' (Segal, 1999:212). In particular, while there is widespread feminist approval of measures to support and encourage working mothers, there is also suspicion that these are intended primarily to cut welfare spending and that the result may be to intensify the double burden of paid and unpaid work (Ward, 2002). Such concerns are particularly acute when extended to lone parents. Although Ruth Lister has offered qualified support for the principle that lone parents should be required to register for at least part-time work when their children reach school age, she therefore insists that 'if the state is going to impose work obligations on a group that also has single-handed care obligations it, too, is under an obligation to provide the necessary social and economic infrastructure' (Lister, 1997:193). This infrastructure would have to include good quality, affordable childcare and the availability of reasonably paid work compatible with family responsibilities. However, as Angela McRobbie has argued, this is unlikely to be provided within the parameters of 'Third Way' and 'New Labour' policies which aim at reducing public spending and reliance on state welfare, while 'The chances of capitalism becoming "more caring and more sharing" are frankly tiny' (McRobbie, 2000:110. See also Franklin, 2000).

This recent experience suggests both that feminists can make tangible gains by working through formal political institutions and that these are likely to be limited. In contrast to the early 1970s, few socialist feminists today would write off legal rights and mainstream politics as 'mere formalities'. Many also work with men in a wide range of local and community organisations and initiatives, and overt sexism in left-wing groups is now much less evident than in the recent past. However, although the theories discussed above agree that working-class women and men have common interests, some also suggest that they may diverge or even conflict, at least in the short term. This lends support to arguments for positive measures to increase the political representation of women, such as the 'all-women shortlist' policy used by the British Labour Party in the run-up to the 1997 election and re-introduced in 2002 (for further discussion, see Chapter 9, above). It also means that women will have to struggle to ensure that their needs are fully recognised in male-dominated trade unions, rather than marginalised as 'different' and that socialist feminists can make demands both as women and as workers: as Jaggar has said, 'When women workers achieve a living wage, they are not just workers winning a concession from capitalism, they are also women winning economic independence from men' (Jaggar, 1983:328).

The Marxist analysis of social reproduction and the sexual division of labour further suggests that economic struggles can include demands for sexual autonomy, 'reproductive rights' and new forms of family organisation. These may in turn involve conflicts with both the state and individual men within the home, and it may at times be necessary for women to organise separately from men. From a socialist feminist perspective, however, such political or 'personal' struggles are not to be approached in isolation, for gains made at these levels are seen to acquire meaning only in a wider social and economic context.

Socialist and Marxist feminism today

Some socialist feminists continue to be active in radical movements, particularly environmental, anti-capitalist and anti-corporatist campaigns (Thomas, 2002; Mies, 1998; Ward, 2002), and Johanna Brenner has recently argued that, because the more equitable organisation of social reproduction would require 'a serious redistribution of wealth', 'feminism's next wave will have to make common cause with and be part of a broad, anticapitalist rainbow movement' (Brenner, 2000:309). In general, however, even moderate forms of socialism are today unpopular in a political environment that has moved sharply to the right and a philosophical environment in which its most fundamental assumptions are widely seen as naïve manifestations of 'modernist' thought. Feminism too is widely perceived as being in crisis or decline, with the certainties, enthusiasm and political activism of the 1970s replaced by apathy, in-fighting and turn-of-the-millenium angst, while the 'f-word' seems old-fashioned and irrelevant to a generation of individualistic, aspirational and assertive young women. In this context, many former activists whose socialist feminism defined them as 'someone who goes to twice as many meetings' are dispirited and exhausted, and socialist feminism is very much on the defensive.

It is, however, certainly not dead, and the theoretical insights of socialist feminism remain of critical importance for any kind of progressive politics. In particular, Marxist concepts can show us that feminist issues have a history, and make us recognise the historical specificity of any situation and the political possibilities to which it may give rise. They also show that any movement to economic justice has to take into account the strategic importance of the unpaid work that is still largely performed by women throughout the world, and forewarn us that even apparently moderate feminist demands are likely to be opposed by powerful economic interests. At the same time, socialist perspectives insist that feminism's focus on gender justice cannot be isolated from its socio-economic context, and that sex equality can have little meaning in a world in which most men as well as most women are exploited. At the very least, the theories discussed in this chapter can provide a useful guard against the kind of individualism that finds it difficult to see collective interests and structural inequalities, the elitism that fails to recognise inequalities of class and 'race' as well as gender, the optimism that thinks that if a cause can be shown to be just it will necessarily be successful, and the ahistorical belief that all women are victims of unchanging male oppression.

14

Black and postmodern feminisms

Although the writers discussed in earlier chapters are often profoundly divided as to the causes of and potential cures for women's subordination, inequality or oppression, they are generally agreed that the task of feminist theory is to contribute to the understanding of women's situation in order that this can be challenged and changed. They therefore rest on the 'common sense' assumption that we know who women are. Some of these writers recognise that there are important differences amongst women. However, they have not usually treated these as central to their analysis, and most have assumed that 'women' are a readily defined and identifiable group of people.

In recent years, these basic assumptions have been profoundly challenged. Black feminists have argued that when white feminists talk about 'women' they tend to think about people like themselves, and that if black women are taken as the starting-point of analysis a very different picture emerges. At the same time, postmodernism has pushed the analysis of differences amongst women much further, and seems to undermine the whole feminist enterprise by denying that the 'common sense' categories of 'women' and 'men' have any inherent meaning at all.

Black feminism

Although black women have contributed to feminist thought and activism from at least the early nineteenth century, they have until recently been marginalised within western feminism, and their insights have been scattered and easily lost. By the closing years of the twentieth century, however, they were developing a more systematic analysis. Today, black feminism is an important, although far from uniform, strand of thought which has moved well beyond a critique of white feminism to the development of original theory. Much as white feminism undermines male political thought and philosophy, this new theory is not simply of relevance to black women, but has profound implications for feminism as a whole.

The critique of white feminism

In the past, a minority of white feminists were overtly racist: for example, some opposed the involvement of black women in the suffrage campaign (see Chapter 4, above). However, many more were involved in the movements against slavery and for civil rights for black people, and today the vast majority would say that they were opposed to racism. Nevertheless, the effects of their feminism has at times been to strengthen racist stereotypes; during the 1970s and 1980s black feminists were particularly angered by *Reclaim the Night* marches which were intended to assert women's right to walk through cities without sexual intimidation, but which often involved white women marching through black and/or working-class neighbourhoods and which seemed to tap into deep-seated assumptions about the threat of black male sexuality. More generally, to the extent that white feminists have recognised the importance of racism, they have tended either to see this in terms of discriminatory laws, 'bad acts' and overt individual prejudice or to treat sex and 'race' as separate systems of oppression. The first perspective fails to see the depth and ubiquity of racism and racist assumptions, and the second contrasts sexism and racism, women and blacks, allowing no space for the experiences of *black women*. Such perspectives forget that the vast majority of women are not white and do not live in the west, and that, even in western nations, women's experiences are far from uniform. They see 'race' as an issue for non-white groups only, failing to see either that white people have an ethnic identity or that they are privileged by it.

A key aspect of white women's privilege has been their ability to assume that when they talked about themselves they were talking about all women, and many white feminists have unthinkingly generalised from their own situation, ignoring the experiences of black women, or treating these as marginal and 'different'. Many have also projected western concerns and priorities onto the rest of the world, measuring 'progress' according to western liberal standards or identifying a global system of patriarchy through which 'differences are treated as local variations on a universal theme' (Liu, 1994:574). Some within the radical feminist tradition have argued that racism is less entrenched than sexism, and Robin Morgan has even claimed that class and 'race' were invented by patriarchy to divide and conquer women (Morgan, 1970:xxxix; see also Millett, 1985:39).

All this means, black feminists say, that white feminists have confirmed and at times even strengthened racist oppression and produced bad and partial theory that misunderstands the world in critically important ways. Such theory silences or marginalises black women's voices and cannot see them as independent actors or explore the ways in which the experience of sex oppression is mediated through 'race' and the experience of racism is gendered. One result is that, as the African-American writer bell hooks has said:

> black women have felt forced to choose between a black movement that primarily serves the interests of black male patriarchs, and a white women's movement which primarily serves the interests of racist white women. (hooks, 1981:9)

Another result is that white feminists have been unable to understand the ways in which racism contributes to their own oppression. (For example, the construction of white femininity as pure and frail, was often bound up with and dependent upon very different assumptions about black womanhood. For critical discussion of the assumptions underlying white feminism, see King, 1988; Aziz, 1997; Spelman, 1988; West and Fenstermaker, 1996.)

Black women: from margin to centre?

Black feminists today are agreed that they do not simply want to be included in white feminism on existing terms, but that they want to de-centre white feminists and challenge the 'normality' of their perspective. This has deep implications for feminist analysis in many areas: for example, white feminist critiques of the public/private distinction look very different from the perspective of women who have always worked outside as well as within the home, whose bodies were historically at the disposal of white slave owners and who today may find their personal lives monitored if they seek welfare benefits or are joined by a spouse from overseas (Crenshaw, 1998; Hall, 2002a). There is however disagreement between those who believe that black women's experience should provide the central starting-point for feminist analysis and those who oppose the idea that any group can constitute a 'centre'.

The arguments of those who believe that black women should be central take a number of forms. Firstly, Angela Davis has argued that a feminist movement which begins with middle-class white women will only change their position at the top of the social pyramid, leaving the lives of other women untouched. If, however, we aim at improving the situation of those at the bottom – that is, working class black women – then the entire oppressive structure of society will have to be transformed; she therefore argues that 'The forward advance of women of color almost always indicates progressive change for all women' (Davis, 1990:31). Some other writers have built on the standpoint theory discussed in the previous chapter. This claims that those who are on the receiving end of oppression are more able to see it than those who are advantaged by it, and suggests to some that, because black women 'occupy a position whereby the inferior half of a series of dichotomies converge', they have a particularly clear view of the world from which we can all learn (Collins, 1990:70). Here it is argued not only that they are inevitably aware of the power relations involved in racism, which white feminists can conveniently forget, but that black women's experience of gender, 'race' and frequently also class oppressions shows that these are not simply separate systems which produce cumulative disadvantage, but that they are dynamically interconnected. This means that systems of oppression are mutually reinforcing, producing experiences of gender which vary with 'race' and experiences of 'race' which vary with gender. It means that the oppression of black women is more than just the sum of racism and sexism, but is qualitatively distinct, while the oppression of white women too is often bound up with racism (on this 'multiplier' effect and the interlocking nature of oppressions, see King, 1988; Collins, 1989, 1990 and 1995; Crenshaw, 1998; Chow *et al.* (eds), 1996; Brah, 1996; Anderson and Collins (eds), 1995; James and Busia (eds), 1993).

The complex nature of such interconnections can be explored if we look at the example of rape, which at first sight appears to be a paradigmatically 'women's issue', but which is often bound up with racism. Most obviously, in the era of slavery in the United States white men were free to exploit female slaves. This abuse of power was also a way of controlling and humiliating black people as a whole, while stereotypes of black male sexuality were used to inflame racial hatred and also to justify restrictions on the freedom of white women, whose supposed 'purity' was contrasted with the 'promiscuity' of black women. Such stereotypings continue today, and mean that if a black woman is raped she is likely to experiences this as a *black woman*: if her rapist is white she is much less likely to be believed by the authorities than if she were white and he were black; if her attacker is also black she is more likely than a white woman to fear that she is 'betraying' her community by reporting him to a racist police authority (see Liu, 1994; Brah, 1993; Crenshaw, 1998 and, for a discussion of the *Southall Black Sisters*, a British group supporting women on domestic violence issues, Siddiqui, 2000). Rape is also a 'natural' weapon in racist, ethnic or nationalistic conflict (Zartov, 1995), where it can be used both to humiliate the enemy and to dilute the 'purity' of its stock, and where fear of rape can be used to justify restrictions on women.

According to Patricia Hill Collins, black feminism's understanding of the interlocking and interdependent nature of oppressions constitutes a paradigm shift in feminist understanding. She is not claiming that black women have discovered 'the truth', but that black feminism's understanding of the multi-facetted and interlocking nature of class, 'race' and gender points the way to awareness of other systems of oppression, such as age, physical ability or sexual orientation, and the ways in which these too have to be understood as part of a larger, interconnected whole. For example, while lesbianism may be a relatively straightforward matter of sexual preference in some communities, lesbians in other groups face particularly acute problems; thus Cherrie Moraga has written that as a lesbian Chicano women, she was not only seen as dividing her own community by rejecting male authority, but also accused of contributing to the 'genocide' of her 'race' (Moraga, 1993; see also Taylor, 1998). According to Collins, opening up feminist concerns in this ways enables us to see that individuals are positioned in a matrix of oppression and privilege, and that they are unlikely to be either oppressed or privileged in every dimension, so that

> Placing African-American women and other excluded groups in the centre of analysis opens up possibilities for a both/and conceptual stance, one in which all groups possess varying amounts of power and privilege in one historically created system. (Collins, 1990:225)

Such an approach aims at exploring the interrelations between different systems in historically specific situations; as such, it rejects the idea that there are 'hierarchies of oppression' and the accompanying debates as to which is the most fundamental. Its claim that different forms of oppression are interconnected and that they reinforce each other means that different forms of resistance are also interconnected. Bell hooks has therefore argued that the idea of *sisterhood*, which implies an oppression shared by all women, should make way for that of *solidarity*. This enables different groups of women to support each other without insisting that their situation is identical; it also enables women to form alliances with oppressed groups of men (hooks, 1984) and to become involved in what Ellen Smith has described as 'a politics of solidarity, which recognizes the multiplicity of oppressions and supports struggles not directly indicated by one's own lived experience' (Smith, 1995:694).

All of this means that exponents of black feminism do not see this simply as a theory of and for feminists who happen to be black. Rather, it is a self-conscious epistemological standpoint which argues that feminist struggles cannot be confined to gender issues and that, if black women's perspectives are excluded from feminist thought, then its attempt to understand even the situation of white women will be seriously flawed. The idea that oppressions interconnect and therefore cannot be challenged in isolation is now widespread amongst black and third world feminist writers (see, for example, the essays in Afshar and Maynard (eds), 1994; Ali, Coate and Goro (eds), 2000). Some white feminists today agree with this analysis, and have attempted to move beyond earlier 'confessions' of shortcomings to a critical awareness of their own ethnicity (see, for example, Ware, 1992; McIntosh, 1995; Jaggar and Rothenberg, 1993b; Frankenberg, 1993a and 1993b and the discussion in Hall, 2002b). Such self-awareness is essential if past errors are not to be repeated in an academic climate in which some fear that 'scholarly spaces' for black women are shrinking (Rooks, 2000 and Painter, 2000; but for more positive assessments, see Ransby, 2000 and Puwar, 2000).

Black women's centrality questioned

Some aspects of these ideas have however been criticised. In the first place, there is a danger of naïve optimism about the likely success of a politics of solidarity, for it is clear that those who are disadvantaged in one system do not automatically empathise with or support other oppressed groups (for sophisticated discussion of issues around solidarity and sisterhood, see Lutz, Anthias and Yuval-Davis, 1995, 1998 and Fester, 2000). Just as white working-class men are capable of the most virulent racism and sexism, and black men can abuse and exploit women, so middle-class white feminists can actively damage the interests of other women; indeed, to the extent that privileges as well as oppressions can be mutually reinforcing, it may be in their interests to do so. Secondly, the approach can sometimes seem to suggest that all oppressions are equal, for although most analyses tend to focus on the 'big three' of class, 'race' and gender oppressions (see for example Chow *et al.* (eds), 1996; Anderson and Collins (eds), 1995) the list in principle seems open-ended, and there can be a danger that localised and personal experiences can be treated as equivalent to those that are related to more structural inequalities of power. This is of course rejected by Marxists, for whom no other system has the same dynamic necessity as capitalist class relations, which *require* the exploitation of workers in order to extract a profit (see Pollert, 1996; Wood, 1995; and the discussion in Chapters 10 and 13 above).

Thirdly, and for many black feminists most critically, any claim that black women have a superior 'standpoint' upon the world is highly suspect. In the first place, it is far from clear who 'black women' are. There is general agreement both that skin colour has no inherent social significance and that it has acquired it in our society, and many use 'black' as an inclusive political term to describe all groups oppressed by white racism. It is however sometimes applied to peoples of African heritage only, and used to distinguish them from other 'non-white' groups such as Asians. This means that, much as the term 'man' marginalised women and the term 'woman' marginalises non-white women, so too the term 'black women' can marginalise some groups. This prioritising of 'African' within black feminist thought is particularly clear in the writing of Collins, who argues that black feminist epistemology is in tune with an Afrocentric way of understanding (Collins, 1990). If the term is used to describe women of colour throughout the world, it can also conceal the extent to which black women in the United States are privileged in comparison with those in many other nations, and may themselves benefit from the exploitation of 'third world' countries (for discussion of issues around terminology and identity, see, for example, Brah, 1996; Afshar and Maynard, 1994; Anderson and Collins, 1995).

Further problems arise if it is assumed that black women necessarily inhabit a standpoint of multiple disadvantage, as this ignores the class divisions and the racism that may exist within and between 'black' groups (see Aziz, 1997). Heidi Mirza, a self-described 'Black British feminist', is particularly concerned about the assumption that there is a fixed identity possessed by all black women, which she rejects as 'a naïve essentialist universal notion of homogenous black womanhood' (Mirza, 1997:5). Like a number of other black feminists, she agrees with Razia Aziz that identity at both individual and group level is not 'neat and coherent, but fluid and fragmented' (Aziz, 1997:75; see also Ransby, 2000; Kanneh, 1998). This means, for example, that a black woman may only be aware of herself as *black, female* or a *black woman* in certain contexts. (If she is with a group of mothers who are all white, she is likely to be self-consciously aware of her 'blackness' but not her gender; if she is with a group of much older people in her own community, her age may seem more significant; if she hears herself described as 'a black bitch', or if she is working with other black women to provide a support network for black female victims of male violence, she is likely to think of herself as a black woman or even a black feminist.) This means that a key role for black feminists is to explore the potential of this fluidity by facilitating the construction and articulation of more positive black female identities than hitherto; black feminists can also use their 'view from the margins' to challenge dominant ways of seeing the world. From this perspective, black feminism is not presupposing any uniform experiences or claiming that black women's experience should be put in the centre of feminist analysis, for it denies that either such experience or a centre exists. Instead, Mirza sees black feminism as 'a spontaneous yet conscious coalition' which recognises, indeed celebrates, differences amongst black women while providing 'a place called home' in which black women 'as racialized, gendered subjects can collectively mark our presence in a world where black women have been so long denied the privilege to speak' (Mirza, 1997:4).

As should become clear in the next sections, these arguments owe much to postmodernism. This too stresses fragmentation and explores the ways in which knowledge and identities are constructed, and it too seeks to articulate marginalised voices while rejecting the idea that there is one discoverably 'correct' way of viewing the world or that politics can be based on more than temporary coalitions. At the same time, it should also become clear that postmodernism has been accused of destroying the very basis of feminist politics by denying the 'reality' of collective identity. It is to this influential and fiercely contested body of thought that we now turn.

Postmodernism

Language, power and identity

There is no general agreement as to the meaning of the term 'postmodern'. Throughout this book I use it as a fairly loose umbrella term to refer to a range of theories which claim to move beyond the 'modernist' belief in reason and human progress by questioning the relationship between what we can know and the world around us. 'Postmodern' is also used as a term to describe today's rapidly changing post-industrial societies in which apparently stable groupings such as class and gender have broken down and everything seems transitory and insecure. (For a recent summary of key themes in postmodernism, see Brown, 2002. For critical discussion and feminist perspectives, see in particular Lovibond, 1989; Nicholson (ed.), 1990; Weedon, 1987; Coole, 1993; Assiter, 1996; Jones, 1993; Segal, 1999; Squires, 1999; and Zalewski, 2000.)

From the seventeenth century, western philosophy was increasingly dominated by the Enlightenment belief that everything is in principle knowable through human reason, and that society can be ordered in accordance with reason, knowledge and justice. As we have seen throughout this book, these 'modern' ideals inspired many earlier generations of feminists and they remain central to equal rights and socialist feminism today. For postmodernists, however, the search for certainty is misguided, for truth, they say, can only be provisional. The very possibility of objectivity is rejected in principle, as is the search for a single all-encompassing theory; here Marxism in particular is accused of making inappropriate and totalitarian claims. From a postmodernist perspective, western philosophy's quest for truth and certainty (sometimes described as logocentricism) is simply the product of a particular historical era that is becoming inappropriate in a postmodern society that is increasingly characterised by fragmentation and diversity in all spheres of life.

This critical position is related to overlapping and interconnected developments in post-structuralist linguistics and psychoanalytic and political theory associated particularly with the male French writers Derrida, Lacan and Foucault. According to Derrida, although objects and individuals may have a material existence, 'reality' does not have an inherent meaning, but is mediated by experience and language. Words themselves only have meaning in relation to other words (so that, for example, to describe someone as a 'woman' may be to distinguish her from a 'man', a 'girl' or a 'lady'); they are also hierarchically ordered (for example, 'man' is usually the standard in relation to which 'woman' gains meaning, rather than vica versa). Although the words available to us determine how we see the world, the meaning of these words is itself always shifting and changing and understood differently by different people and at different times; the process of describing or 'naming' is therefore inherently open-ended rather than closed. This means that 'reality' never has exactly the same meaning for all of us, so that there can be no impersonal, objective 'God's-eye view' of the world, only particular, individual and ever-changing subjectivities. This analysis rules out any theory which seeks or claims to have discovered 'the truth'. It also undermines the binary logic which is basic to western thought; this depends on such fixed dichotomies as truth/falsehood, public/private or man/woman, which themselves assume a stability of meanings.

In this context, the analysis of the ways in which words are used and knowledge, meaning and culture are produced is politically important. Foucault has argued that these are not free-floating and indiscriminately available, but form patterns or 'discourses' which organise our under-standing of society and are bound up with the exercise of power. This means that dominant groups will attempt to impose their way of seeing the world on the whole of society and that their discourses will be privileged, although they can be challenged or subverted by marginal groups. Such resistance can, however, never be total or final, merely fragmented and provisional. To think otherwise is to embrace outdated 'modernist' assumptions about power, progress and certainty in an era in which power is increasingly dispersed throughout society and exercised at micro-level within such apparently non-political institutions as families, schools or hospitals (Foucault, 1980).

Ideas about the instability of meaning and its relationship with power have also combined with post-Freudian psychoanalytic theory to produce arguments about the essentially precarious nature of adult identity, so that it is not only the object of knowing that has been dissolved as a stable entity, but also its knowing subject. According to Lacan and his followers, sexual identity in particular is never secure, and the terms 'woman' and 'man' are not unified or stable categories; to treat them as such is to forget that all women and men have different (and ever-changing) subjectivities and that the categories are linguistically constructed rather than biologically given. Nevertheless, Lacan argues that in all cultures the acquisition of sexual identity is fundamentally different for boys and girls, because this is acquired via a resolution of the Oedipal complex and entry into the 'Symbolic Order' of adult masculine language. The organising principle of the Symbolic Order is the 'phallus'; this metaphor for paternal power is the condition of discourse, which is constituted in binary, either/or terms of presence or lack. Although the phallus cannot be reduced to the penis, its association with the presence or absence of this means that, according to Lacan, 'woman' is constituted in terms of a lack; the feminine is therefore outside of and permanently excluded from 'phallic discourse' and can never be expressed.

Postmodern feminisms

Lacan's ideas seem at first sight particularly inhospitable to feminism. However, as we shall see, some feminists have used these as a basis for their theory. Other aspects of postmodernism seem to have much more in common with some of the feminist ideas discussed in earlier chapters. There are clear affinities between postmodernism's rejection of claims to objectivity and truth and feminist critiques of the partiality of male reason and the limitations of binary thought. Postmodernism's stress on difference and diversity also seems to support those feminists who reject the essentialism of some radical feminist thought and the tendency of white, middle-class feminists to generalise from their own experience. As we have seen, some radical and Marxist feminists agree that language, culture and ideology can play an important political role. Postmodern ideas about the ubiquity of power also sound at first sight very like the claim that patriarchal power is exercised in personal life as well as through formal political institutions, while rejection by some feminists of mainstream politics in favour of small-scale community and/or separatist activity might seem to be in line with Foucauldian notions of resistance by marginalised groups (see Chapters 9–13 and the section on black feminism above).

At this kind of level, postmodernism might seem largely to endorse what many feminists have long being saying, or what they have recently started to argue as a result of their own experience. Other writers, however, argue that postmodernism has much more profound implications for feminist thought; some believe that it is more genuinely subversive than anything that has gone before, but some see it as a threat to everything that feminism has ever stood for.

For a number of writers, postmodernism seems to represent a way of resolving many of the dilemmas that have pre-occupied and divided feminists in the past. In particular, it transforms the terms of debate by rejecting the dichotomous thinking that has trapped and limited feminist thought by presenting 'equality' and 'difference' as hierarchical, immutable and irreconcilable choices, so that feminists have had to argue *either* that women have an equal right to be included in manmade political, economic and philosophical structures *or* that the 'womanly' qualities, perspectives and roles should be properly valued. As Judith Squires puts it, the postmodern strategy of 'displacement' goes beyond strategies based on 'inclusion' or 'reversal':

> The strategy of inclusion seeks gender-neutrality; the strategy of reversal seeks recognition for a specifically female gendered identity; and the strategy of displacement seeks to deconstruct those discursive regimes that engender the subject. (Squires, 1999:3)

Whilst this kind of analysis sounds very abstract, it has clear practical implications. For example, as Joan Scott has argued, it enables feminists to contest the ways in which equal rights employment disputes are framed. These have required women either to claim equality by assimilating to a male norm or to abandon the goal of equality by asserting their 'different' needs, interests and characteristics. Scott, however, says that this apparent choice rests on a false dichotomy which constructs a hierarchical power relationship which privileges men, conceals differences *amongst* women and men and fails to see that 'equality is not the elimination of difference; difference does not preclude equality' (Scott, 1990:138; for related arguments, see Cornell, 1992). She argues that, in a world in which no two people are identical, equality does not mean that they should somehow become 'the same', but that their differences can in some situations be deemed irrelevant; she also says that women can both demand entry into male-dominated areas of employment and insist that their traditional roles are more highly valued. Squires applies a similar refusal to let feminist arguments be 'forced into preexisting categories and ... a dichotomy we did not invent' (Scott, 1990:142) to analyse debates around justice, representation and citizenship as well as equality, and she finds that the general trend in recent feminist thought is to reject either inclusion or reversal in favour of reconceptualising the terms of debate. Such new thinking, she says, 'takes the deconstruction of binary oppositions to be its central task' and means that feminists can at last move beyond 'Wollestonecraft's dilemma' (identified by Carole Pateman and discussed in Chapters 1 and 9 above) by refusing to compare themselves with men. As we shall see, such thinking also dissolves the underlying opposition between 'men' and 'women', and opens up political thought to more open-ended analyses of gender which move beyond feminism's focus on women to 'all theories of corporeal subjectivity' (Squires, 1999:125 and 232).

Diana Coole shares this belief in the subversive implications of post-modernist thought, although she traces a rather different trajectory of a movement from 'modern' feminist debates around 'difference' (whether women are the same as or different from men), to postmodern insistence on 'differences' amongst women (differentiated not only by class, 'race', age, sexuality or physical ability but also by individual subjectivities) to a post-structuralist politics of 'différance' which subverts the very structure of language and meaning and invokes 'the Other of Western culture: that which is so different, it cannot in principle be spoken in its terms' (Coole, 1993:211–12).

As we have seen, Lacanian thought identifies this 'Other' with 'the feminine', which is necessarily excluded from the linguistic structures of phallic discourse (the only discourse which we can have) and which there-fore cannot in principle be articulated. Some French feminists agree that the feminine is outside of male discourse, but argue that it *can* be brought into an existence that subverts the male order and structures of thought (in this context, 'feminine' does not have the negative connotations usually attached to it in feminist theory). Their attempts to 'express the inexpress-ible' have produced works which deliberately subvert all rules of grammar, syntax, form and logic, thus 'disordering the Symbolic order' (Segal, 1999:51). In particular, Julia Kristeva has argued for the disruptive potential of re-envisaging a pre-Oedipal, pre-dualistic, pre-verbal mother–infant communication, a 'rhythmic economy of impulses and drives' to which we can never fully return but which can invoke 'a differ-ent relation to the body and a fluidity immune to the organization of the system' (Coole, 1993:219). While Kristeva sees this as open to either sex, Hélène Cixous and Luce Irigaray argue that specifically feminine ways of thinking that defy the logical forms and binary oppositions of 'phallogo-centric' thought are located in the female body. They claim that such thought is based on women's experience of sexual pleasure (*jouissance*) and that, unlike men, women's sexual pleasure is diffused throughout the body, giving rise to a plurality of experiences and sensations that cannot be comprehended within male discourse. These writers are united by their insistence on the need to develop 'non-phallogocentric' ways of thinking, sharing 'what seems a common desire to think non-binary, non-oppositional thought, the kind that may have existed before Adam was given the power to name the animals' (Tong, 1989:233) and to explore the relationships between language, sexuality and power. They are however divided as to whether there is an essential femininity based in biology and whether only women can in principle express themselves in 'feminine' ways (see Moi (ed.), 1987; Weedon, 1987; and Duchen, 1986).

As Drucilla Cornell has argued, any such essentialism is ruled out by Derrida, whose post-structuralism exposes all dichotomies as constructed and relational, rather than eternally given. This focus on discourse suggests that masculinity and femininity have meaning only in relation to one another and not because of their basis in sexed bodies, so that 'the question of gender then becomes primarily linguistic or discursive rather than material or social' and 'its meaning is generated within linguistic structures' (Squires, 1999:60). If the relationship between gender and bio- logical sex is essentially arbitrary, then there is no need to think in terms of only two genders, and we can explore the ways in which the interaction of biological sex and sexual orientation with other attributes and modes of behaviour throws up a multiplicity of genders rather than a male/female or masculine/feminine dichotomy. (At a fairly obvious level, there may be masculine heterosexual men, feminine heterosexual men, masculine heterosexual women ... and so on. See Carver, 1996.)

Some writers go further and argue that sex itself is a product of society, rather than fixed by nature, for biological differences only acquire signifi- cance if they are identified and labelled by society. In other words, society creates the categories of 'man' and 'woman' by making us aware of, and attaching great importance to, particular features of our anatomy (in much the same way that skin pigmentation is not inherently politically or socially significant, but is made so in some societies). This means that sex is a 'category of meaning' rather than a naturally given 'fact', and that the sex/gender distinction used by earlier feminists to distinguish between the biological characteristics of males and females and the socially pro- duced attributes of masculinity and femininity is invalid (see Riley, 1988 for a sophisticated and influential discussion of the shifting, provisional and discursively constructed nature of 'women'). At a more practical level, a number of writers have pointed out that neither biology nor experience provides the basis for a binary classification, as this ignores the extent to which all our bodies and behaviours display a mix of masculine and feminine characteristics, not to mention the significant number of people whose physical characteristics are a mix of 'normal' male and female anatomies. (Hird quotes evidence suggesting that one in 1,000 births show an 'anomoly' that raises questions about the assignment of sex, and that 1 in 2,000 have some form of 'intersexuality' (Hird, 2000). See also Crawford, 2000 and the discussion in Bryson, 1999a, Chapter 2.)

Such ideas can seem liberating, and Judith Lorber has argued that, because it helps us move beyond seeing gender as normal, natural and binary, postmodernism subverts the legitimacy of the entire gender order (Lorber, 2000). The claim that the meaning of being a woman is constructed rather than inherent in female bodies means that anatomy need not be destiny and that we can intervene in the processes through which sex is constructed; for some writers, this implies that a central task for feminists is to unravel and contest the complex cultural, linguistic and symbolic ways through which this occurs. Such an approach opens up masculinity as well as femininity to scrutiny. It also insists that sexuality too is not naturally given but socially and linguistically created, and analyses its relationship with power (see Carver and Mottier, 1998). This means, for example, that 'Homosexuality is not a natural difference ... but a category that only exists in relation to normative heterosexuality' (Jackson, 1998:73).

While post-structuralists concentrate on discourse, some writers argue that social practices are also important in constructing meanings and gender identities (see for example Connell, 1987). Others have argued that gender is something that one *does*, an *act* that requires repeated performances of gender-appropriate behaviour and that can never be finally secured. Here, the work of Judith Butler has been particularly influential, and her idea of 'gender as performance' (which also ties in with 'queer theory') suggests that oppressive structures of gender and sexuality can be challenged by transgressive forms of behaviour, such as transvestism, which deliberately cross gender lines and flout expectations of gender appropriate behaviour. This opens up the possibility of a society that is no longer organised in terms of the binary opposition between male and female, and in which gender identities could be fluid, freely chosen and multiple rather than the stable core of our identity (Butler, 1990 and 1993; see also West and Zimmerman, 1991 and, for critical discussion, Segal 1999:Chapter 2). According to some writers, gender identities might even disappear; thus Judith Grant has argued that

> The aim of feminist politics is the end of gender and the creation of new human beings who are self-determining and fully participate in the development of their own constantly evolving subjectivity. (Grant, 1993:183)

Feminist criticisms of postmodernism

All this suggests that postmodernism can liberate us from the closed mindset of modernist thought, with its mistaken quest for all-encompassing theory and denial of the inherent messiness, instability and uncertainty of life, and that it can open up a range of exhilarating insights into the construction of identities, culture and knowledge which also throws up new possibilities of resistance. Many 'modern' feminists, however, reject its claims or, to the extent that it support their own position see it as a pretentious irrelevance, which at best dresses up conclusions that feminists have already reached in ridiculous philosophical clothes designed by misogynistic men. Thus, a recent collection claims that radical feminists have always been aware of issues around difference and diversity which postmodernists seem to think they have discovered for themselves (Bell and Klein (eds), 1996), while Sonia Kruks points out that many of postmodernism's apparent insights into the construction of femininity are only 'a series of radical glosses' on points made half a century earlier by Simone de Beauvoir (Kruks, 1992:91); it is perhaps even more irritating for feminists who have exposed the partiality of men's thought to be told that they should express this in terms of new theories which have also been made by men.

To the extent that postmodernism mystifies feminist understanding and makes it inaccessible, it is inimical to the development of feminist politics, as traditionally understood. Depending on which strand is being used, it can also seem to suggest that 'transgressive performances' or textual/cultural analysis should be the primary form of feminist activity.[11] Whilst this may be great fun, and it can usefully politicise the study of literature, film and art, it also de-politicises the study of politics, and seems at best a frivolous luxury when compared to issues of poverty, exploitation and the abuse of women's bodies. Moreover, as Judith Lorber has pointed out, 'trangression' can actually strengthen gender, which it presupposes in order to subvert (Lorber, 1991).

Additional difficulties arise from what Segal has described as 'feminist pirouettes on the Lacanian stage' which she feels have 'served more to exhaust than invigorate radical theorizing' (Segal, 1999:181). Whilst she agrees that language is politically important and that the phallus is privileged in existing discourse, she takes issue with Lacan's underlying claim that subjectivity is constructed solely in and through language, and that the phallus has a transcendental rather than historically constructed primacy (Segal, 1999:184; see also Assiter, 1996). Particular difficulties arise from the 'French feminism' of Kristeva, Cixous and Iragaray, which at times seems to imply not only biological essentialism, but a sexual reductionism that lacks a social context, that ignores the fact that we also experience our bodies in non-sexual ways and that involves some questionable assertions about the inevitably limited nature of male sexuality; it also disregards the ways in which other social groups too may be disadvantaged in language.[12]

A more general and perhaps more dangerous problem arises from postmodernism's stress on differences, shifting subjectivities and the constructed nature of social groups. This makes it difficult to talk about 'women' in any meaningful way, and therefore seems incompatible with the identification and analysis of patriarchy or with collective struggles against it; indeed, radical critics have claimed that postmodernism itself is a patriarchal ploy to deny women's collective identity just at a time when they were learning to act together politically (see Bell and Klein (eds), 1996 and Chapter 10 above).

Other critics claim that postmodernism's extreme relativism and its refusal to ask 'big' questions about the nature or desirability of social arrangements (on the grounds that there can be no objective answers) is politically convenient for those who have already been advantaged by the 'project of modernity', but who now rule all further questions of 'right' and 'justice' out of order. Thus Lovibond asks

> If there can be no systematic political approach to questions of wealth, power and labour, how can there be any effective challenge to a social order which distributes its benefits and burdens in a systematically unequal way between the sexes? (Lovibond, 1989, p. 22)

For such critics, postmodernism is an essentially conservative theory, that turns feminism from a subversive social movement into an inward-looking elite activity, and that, in rejecting the possibility of wholesale transformation, discredits all movements for social change. This means that, to use its own terms, postmodernism itself may be a discourse of power, imposing a particular worldview in the guise of rejecting all (like the Cretan who said 'all Cretans are liars', it seems to insist on the truth of the statement that 'there are no truths').

Feminism and postmodernism today

In 1992, Michelle Barrett and Anne Phillips wrote that the impact of post-structuralism and postmodernism had produced 'an almost paradigmatic shift from 1970s to 1990s feminism', with 'previously shared assumptions and unquestioned orthodoxies relegated almost to history' (Barrett and Phillips, 1992:6 and 2). Since then, postmodernism's forward march seems in many ways to have continued. However, some writers have recently argued that the alleged break in continuity is far from absolute. For example, Segal says that the 1970s feminism of which she was a part was always far richer and more subtle than some recent accounts suggest and the gulf between it and 1990s feminism exaggerated; Diana Coole argues that feminism's 'own inner logic already reconstructs it as postmodern'; while Zalewski points out that the idea of an absolute, binary gulf between modern and postmodern thought is itself at odds with postmod-ernism's own rejection of dichotomous thinking (Segal, 1999; Coole, 1993:3; and Zalewski, 2000).

As discussed in my final chapter, there also seems to be quite a wide-spread sense that the dust is beginning to settle on modern v. postmodern feminist disputes, and a trend towards combining elements of these apparently competing approaches rather than defending entrenched and opposing positions. This trend is exemplified in the recent writings of Segal, Coole and Zalewski mentioned above, and in Judith Squires' *Gender in Political Theory*, in which she argues both that postmodern strategies can usefully contest the reification of gender and that this need not preclude the self-identification of women as a collective group; indeed, she claims that such kind of gender theory can play a vital role in distinguishing between alliances forged with liberatory intent and those imposed upon people and in 'keeping us continually aware of the contingency of claims to group sameness and mindful of the power relations which produced the conditions of identity' (Squires, 1999:74). This kind of approach can allow for the development of a 'strategic sisterhood' (Baden and Goetz, 1997) which builds alliances amongst women without losing sight of the historical and cultural specificities of their experiences and which has much in common with the black feminist concept of 'solidarity' discussed earlier in this chapter.

Taken to an extreme, postmodernism's preoccupation with discourse can become a self-referential end in itself, which produces an elitist, jar-gon-ridden rhetoric of oppression which collapses into a woolly rela-tivism, negates all possibility of collective action and paralyses political will. However, if it is handled with care and if it is combined with the analysis of material conditions, social practices and political possibilities, it can help us to understand and contest the deep-seated nature of gender hierarchies and identities and their roots in language, culture and psychic identity. As such, it can open up possibilities and choices at the level of identity as well as practice. It can also contribute to a movement beyond the adversarial, dichotomous thinking that has trapped feminists in conceptual frameworks not of their own choosing and help them to reconstitute debates in their own terms.

15

Feminist theory in the twenty-first century

Feminism today is widely perceived as being in crisis or decline, with the certainties, enthusiasm and political activism of earlier years replaced by apathy, in-fighting and defensiveness. Not only can it seem old-fashioned and irrelevant now that the rights for which earlier generations had to fight are taken for granted in western societies, but its core assumptions have been challenged by postmodernist thinking, and its intellectual energies sometimes seem to have spiralled away into the elaboration of increasingly impenetrable theories, far from the everyday concerns of 'ordinary women'.

However, the idea that feminism is irrelevant and obsolete can readily be countered. The vast majority of women in the world do not live in the west, and many lack basic rights and legal protection; the impact of global economic forces, ethnic conflict and religious fundamentalism has in recent years produced a deterioration in the situation of many. In the west, there have clearly been enormous practical gains for many women; today, most have a degree of independence and range of choices scarcely dreamed of by their foremothers and a minority have reached elite positions. Even here, however, these gains are not enjoyed equally by all groups of women and major inequalities remain. In general, women remain strikingly under-represented in political elites and legislative bodies; they work much longer hours than men (particularly within the home), but receive far less financial reward and are much more likely to live in poverty; their sexual and reproductive choices are still constrained; and the lives of many are restricted or ruined by the fear or reality of male violence.[13] In this context, the idea that we live in a post-feminist era is nonsense, and feminism is faced with urgent practical tasks. Although there is no longer a mass women's movement, feminist activities continue at all levels from the local to the global in self-help groups, community organisations, pressure groups, trade unions and formal political institutions.[14]

Less tangibly, we live in a world in which the standards for what is 'normal' have been set by men, so that women's priorities, perspectives and practices are marginalised as 'different' and inferior, something to be overcome if women are to be equal as citizens, workers or thinkers. Societies are largely structured around a dichotomous conception of gender which imposes 'appropriate' identities, roles and behaviour upon us, although the nature of such identities, roles and behaviour varies within and between nations. If feminists are to fully understand and overcome practical inequalities and oppressions, they must therefore also both challenge the 'normality' of man-made standards and address the ways in which gender is constructed. These are complex tasks, which have inspired a wide range of new theoretical approaches. Some likely avenues of exploration have turned out to be barren culs-de-sac, and some have produced theories which seem almost wilfully obscure. At their best, however, the new approaches suggest exciting new ways of seeing the world and developing political concepts that are no longer restricted by the partiality and limitations of malestream thought.

In western societies, hegemonic malestream theory is also liberal democratic theory. The rights and opportunities that this promises are significant, and the importance of earlier feminist struggles to achieve them should not be under-estimated. However, they are also in many ways limited, and, as discussed in Chapter 9 above, claims for equal rights for women within a liberal framework have created a range of practical problems. These problems are related to liberalism's underlying assumptions, which lose sight of human interdependence and caring responsibilities and which artificially restrict both the terms in which we think and the choices open to women. This means that, despite its apparent gender-neutrality, a liberal approach cannot fully express women's experiences and needs and that feminists who start with 'common sense' liberal assumptions frequently move to a more radical position.

Today, an increasing number of feminist activists are seeing that meaningful equality has to change the terms on which equality is granted (so that, for example, equal workplace opportunities should start from the understanding that 'normal' employees have caring responsibilities and are not necessarily available for 50 hours a week). Such political perspectives are supported by theoretical developments, as recent writers have moved beyond exposing the shortcomings of old concepts and towards rebuilding them on very different foundations. Particularly important work has been done on citizenship, justice, obligation, and authority (see in particular Lister, 1997; Gilligan, 1982; Hirschmann, 1992; Jones, 1993; and the collection edited by Hirschmann and Di Stefano, 1996). Although these developments do not constitute a unified approach, they generally share a sense that connectedness and interdependence are central to our humanity, and that they must also be a starting-point for political theory. As such, they draw on earlier radical feminist assertions about the value of women's attributes and experiences, particularly in relation to their childbearing and caring roles. At the same time, however, they tend to avoid the kind of generalised and essentialist assumptions about the nature of women that has characterised some strands of radical feminism, and, whilst they seek to de-centre men, they do not necessarily *re*-centre on women.[15] They also recognise that shared experiences of gender are often fractured by class, ethnicity and other social divisions. Whilst socialist feminists have stressed the ways in which women can be divided by class, this more general awareness of differences amongst women owes much to recent developments within black feminism, which has effectively critiqued the universalising pretensions of much white feminist thought and which sees that the analysis of gender cannot be isolated from other dimensions of inequality and oppression. It also reflects the growing influence of postmodernism, with its assertion that knowledge is always provisional and partial and its analysis of the instability of identity and the relativistic nature of all dichotomies.

As we have seen in the previous chapter, postmodernism's stress on differences amongst women and the precarious nature of identity can make it difficult if not impossible to speak of women as a meaningful social group or 'category of analysis'. If we cannot speak about 'women' it is at first sight hard to see how we can recognise or talk about sex-based oppression, let alone organise collectively to combat it. Even if postmodernism's concern with the ways in which gender is constructed does allow a role for feminist analysis and intervention, this seems to be at the level of discourse and culture, rather than social, political and economic practices and institutions. Such analysis can lend itself to intellectual posturing and can seem to deny the 'reality' of obvious, observable injustices and exploitation and undermine the potential for radical political action. However, such outcomes are not an inevitable result of adopting postmodernist perspectives, and some recent writers are suggesting that, far from modern and postmodern feminisms being inherently incompatible and antagonistic, they may be seen as complementary. As we have seen, the history of feminist thought shows that it has always been much more fluid and complex than some attempts to classify it suggest, and it is clear that many postmodernist ideas (particularly the critique of 'objectivity' and binary thinking, the stress on difference and diversity, the analysis of the ubiquity of power and the political role of language, culture and ideology) were anticipated by radical, Marxist and black feminist approaches. As Marysia Zalewski has pointed out, postmodernism's own logic requires it to move beyond dualistic categories to reject any simple modern/postmodern dichotomy in favour of exploring the ambiguities, fragmentation and continuities between apparently antagonistic modes of thinking (Zalewski, 2000).

Today, an increasing number of writers are attempting to do just this, and many agree with Zalewski that there is a place for both modern 'real world politics' and postmodern 'creative intellectual practices' (Zalweski, 2000:141). For example, Diana Coole argues that today's society is not simply either modern or postmodern, and that

> women, especially, occupy a variety of worlds, traditional (as wives and mothers), modern (as workers and citizens) and postmodern (as consumers and participants in contemporary culture), each with its own oppressions, opportunities and politics. (Coole, 1993:222)

Coole argues that, because each of these worlds has its own oppressions and opportunities, different political strategies will be appropriate in different areas of life. This means, she says, that conventional politics can and should coexist with postmodern strategies for restructuring/ transgressing phallocentric reasoning, without which she believes no final emancipation or liberation is possible for women. She therefore defends postmodernism against the charge that it is a-political, insisting rather that postmodern feminists

> participate in a politics and on a terrain that is simply different from those relevant to struggles against domination or exploitation. Women ask: who are we? How might we be constituted as gendered subjects and how might we be different? This cannot be all of politics but without it, women are always in danger of reproducing identities and pursuing interests that are already effects of phallic power. (Coole, 2000:43; see also Coole, 1997)

The leading socialist feminist writer Lynne Segal similarly argues that feminism need not choose between modern and postmodern goals and methods, and that its objectives can be both to work to improve the lives of women and to reinvent the meanings of womanhood (Segal, 1999). Although she insists on the importance of combating socio-economic inequalities and the need to locate feminism within wider movements for economic transformation and social justice, she refuses to reduce women's oppression to socio-economic causes and solutions, and argues that, if we are to begin to understand the multi-layered complexity of gender issues, we must draw on more than one theoretical approach or academic discipline.

To say that modern and postmodern strategies and analyses should complement one another implies more than peaceful coexistence or toler-ation of competing enterprises; rather, it requires us to explore the ways in which these can interact to develop theory which informs and is informed by experience and practice. This means that, although highly abstract fem-inist theory may be needed to help us think outside existing paradigms, this theory should not be seen as an end in itself, and that even the most abstract thinkers should consider their priorities with reference to 'real world' concerns. To some extent this has already happened, and post-modern feminism has helped reinforce and develop existing feminist insights by contributing to a general climate of opinion which both rules out some of the more simplistic arguments which characterised some earlier feminist approaches and helps move our thinking beyond the dichotomies in which it has so often been trapped.

In terms of 'real world' politics, we are likely to continue to talk about 'women' for the foreseeable future, and we are likely to assume that most who fall within this category will have been legally assigned their sex at birth on the basis of biological characteristics. We should however be aware that we are walking a precarious tightrope, as political practicalities run up against awareness of instabilities, complexities and differences. At one level, such tensions may not be a problem for feminist politics if we remember both that gender categories are not inherently meaningful, and that they are made so in contemporary societies. Those, such as transsexuals, who cannot or will not be readily slotted into a binary system of classification, are likely to experience particular difficulties; however, as Judith Butler has argued, the deliberate transgression of gender norms, particularly around sexuality, may help expose the artificial nature of both this binary classification and its supposed biological basis, and open up the way to more fluid gender identities (Butler, 1990). More frequently, feminists are likely to find it politically useful to identify themselves as women in the name of contesting the socio-economic and the cultural practices that create gender identities and roles: as Judith Squires has said: 'A "historically specific *we* of political identity" is liberatory in a way in which a group identity imposed by oppressive power relations is not' (Squires, 1999:73). At the same time, however, it is important that this claim to collective identity is not made by privileged women on behalf of their sex or used to deny the importance of class and ethnicity. Here, black feminist critiques of the universalising pretensions of some white feminism can be strengthened by postmodernism's rejection of *all* totalising theory.

Similar arguments apply to the feminist concept of 'patriarchy'. I believe that it is important to retain this as the one concept which highlights the non-random nature of male privilege and female disadvantage and the extent to which these recur and reinforce each other in different areas of public and private life. The concept also helps us to see the extent to which dominant assumptions and practices throughout society are based on the idea that men are the norm, and women some kind of optional extra. It therefore highlights the need to challenge the underlying 'rules of the game' if there is to be meaningful equality between the sexes. New feminist rules could value both the roles and the ways of thinking traditionally associated with women, without assuming that these are natural attributes of womanhood inaccessible to men. In practical terms, this would mean, for example, that people who bring up the next generation of citizens and workers are not economically punished; in terms of theory, it means developing approaches that treat care and co-operation as normal attributes of human nature which any political theory must take into account. The concept of patriarchy suggests that, although men may have a lot to gain from these changes in the long run, most also have a lot to lose, particularly in the short term, so that feminists should not rely on their support (see Bryson, 2000).

Despite its usefulness, the concept of patriarchy needs to be handled with extreme care if it is to avoid the twin pitfalls of essentialism and false universalism, and its use should not be taken to imply explanatory claims or the possibility of understanding gender in isolation from class, 'race' and other systematic (that is, non-random) inequalities. As with the term 'woman' (which it presupposes), if the concept is to be politically useful we need to be self-consciously aware of its limitations. Postmodernism's stress on the precarious and provisional nature of all categories and identities can enhance such awareness without precluding the strategic use of the concept. Taking black feminist analysis as a central starting-point is also important: not only does this preclude the kind of false universalism to which white feminists have been prone, but it provides important insights into the ways that the meaning of 'being a woman' interacts with other identities and oppressions. Because black feminism shows the importance of 'race' for *all* groups of women, its insights cannot be set aside or treated as a marginal extra if we are to address the complex ways in which gender is constructed.

Until recently, most work on gender has focused on women. However, once we cease to treat men as the unquestioned norm of humanity, masculinity too logically comes up for scrutiny, and recent years have seen a rapid growth in work on men and masculinities, much of which has been inspired by feminism (see, for example, Carver, 1996; Connell, 1995 and 2000; Segal, 1990; and, for overviews, Squires, 1999, and Bryson, 1999a). Writers in this field generally agree that masculinity is, like femininity, socially and culturally produced rather than a simple product of biology; that factors such as age, class, 'race', sexual orientation and (dis)ability interact to affect the meaning of what it is to be a man; and that dominant models of masculinity (often linked to high income, power, strength, exual experience and heterosexuality) may be experienced as oppressive by many men. There is a danger that discussion of masculinity can become a form of 'phallic drift' ('the powerful tendency for public discussion of gender issues to drift, inexorably, back to the male point of view' Bell and Klein, 1996:561), or even that it blames women or feminism for the problems facing many men. However, work on masculinity clearly has the potential to enhance feminist understanding, and could be explored in relation to black feminist analyses of the interlocking nature of oppressions and the possibility of a politics of 'solidarity' between oppressed groups of women and men (see Chapter 14 above). Any questioning of the 'normality' of men also has important practical implications. While changes in women's roles have already had a significant knock-on effect on men's lives, the kinds of changes that feminists are increasingly demanding – that is, radical changes to man-made structures, practices and assumptions rather than slotting women into these – would clearly require more drastic transformations. In this context, a key task for feminists working on masculinity is to identify positive models of masculinity and the kinds of policies that might encourage them (such as the provision of well-paid parental leave for both men and women).

In practical terms, the logic of feminism that pushes it beyond the dichotomous, male-based assumptions of liberal thought also pushes it towards some kind of socialist solution. Whilst women's situation and the gender division of labour cannot be simply explained away in terms of the needs of the capitalist economy, it seems clear that a society based on individualistic assumptions and the pursuit of profit is unlikely to provide the kind of flexible employment conditions or economic recognition of caring responsibilities that a majority of feminist campaigners now advocate, and that the free market will never provide good quality, affordable childcare to all who want it. This means that feminist goals are unlikely to be met without major economic changes, and that they are often likely to be opposed by powerful economic interests. Here, a Marxist perspective can usefully contextualise feminist claims and help assess both the potential for change and the strength of opposing forces. In particular, as discussed in Chapter 13 above, an expanded conception of the Marxist concept of social reproduction can help us see the wider economic significance of women's reproductive and domestic role, and the ways in which this may be related both to global economic forces and international movements of resistance.

Today, practical experience and theoretical developments both clearly indicate that there can be no simple explanation of gender injustices or inequalities and no easy solutions. This means that any one-dimensional theory that claims to have found the key (whether it be the economic system, the family, sexuality, pornography, reproduction, culture or language) cannot be adequate and that the multiple, interconnected forces that maintain present gender inequalities cannot be isolated from other forms of oppression. There is a danger that this recognition will lead to a sense of helplessness and a paralysis of political will. However, it can also show that, although any kind of action or theory will be inadequate in itself, it can gain significance and strength when accompanied by other forms of political engagement or philosophical perspectives. This does not absolve feminists from the need to assess priorities and possibilities or imply that all actions and approaches are equally valid. However, it suggests that our political choices should to a significant extent be context dependent and that there can be no 'one size fits all' approach to feminist political theory or practice. Such flexibility means that feminist theory need not be restricted by the labels which have been used to classify it. By pointing a way forward beyond the modern/postmodern, local/global, theory/practice and academic/real world dichotomies, it also opens up the possibility of more open-minded, generous and inclusive forms of feminist theory and practice than in the recent past.

Notes

1. Putting the term 'race' in quotation marks is commonly used as a way of indicating that this refers to a socially constructed category, rather than one that is inherently meaningful and based in biology.
2. In an 'Introductory Letter', Thompson states that Wheeler was the originator and he the 'interpreter and scribe' of the ideas expressed in the book; he also states that a few pages were written exclusively by her and that the remainder was their 'joint property'. The book has, however, usually been published in his name alone, as is the case with the edition cited here.
3. Although the terms 'suffragist' and 'suffragette' are often confused or used interchangeably, it was only the latter who used violent direct action against property in pursuit of their aims. However, there was often a fluid and overlapping membership between different, apparently rival, organisations, and the militant/consitutional distinction was less rigid than some accounts suggest (Hannan, 2000; Frances, 2000).
4. It has much in common with Judith Squires' recent identification of three key 'archetypal' approaches: 'inclusion' (or liberal feminism), 'reversal' (or radical, maternal or cultural feminism) and 'displacement' (or postmodernist or post-structuralist feminism). However, her approach neglects both socialist/Marxist and black feminist perspectives (Squires, 1999).
5. In 1971 the Equal Rights Amendment (ERA) was passed by both Houses of Congress with huge majorities. However, despite taking up much of the energy of the women's movement in the 1970s, the ERA was never ratified by the necessary number of states; by 1982 it was finally defeated by a loose populist coalition of conservative business interests and the 'Moral Majority'.
6. *Epistemology* concerns theories of knowledge and the way we know things; *ontology* concerns theories of existence and how we conceptualise being.
7. As Judith Squires has pointed out, the apparent binary division is in fact a tripartite one, between state, civil society and personal life (Squires, 1999:24–32).
8. Recent changes in family and employment patterns mean that this is increasingly only an assumption, not a realistic assessment of women's situation. It is, however, an assumption that persists in the west and has been extended to third world women (Mies, 1998).
9. MacKinnon also claims that they have radically different and probably irreconcilable starting-points, as feminism is based on an understanding of sexuality and its exploitation, while Marxism focuses upon work: 'Sexuality is to feminism what work is to Marxism: that which is most one's own yet most taken away' (MacKinnon, 1983:227). However, many feminists would dispute the centrality of sexuality, while the use of Marxist concepts may not preclude the analysis of sexuality.
10. Iris Young, discussed above, has also been strongly influenced by postmodernism. Her recent work focuses on group differences rather than capitalism and class, and Judith Evans has argued that her movement away from 'revolutionary socialist feminism' to 'radical pluralism' symbolises a more general shift away from socialist feminism (Evans, 1995:111–22).
11. However, contrary to the suggestion of some of her critics, Butler does not see performance as sufficient in itself (see Lloyd, 1998).
12. There are, of course, other forms of feminism in France, and other groups were particularly angered by the decision of the Psych et Po (Psychoanalyse et Politique) group with which Kristeva, Cixous and Iragaray have all been associated to register for its own exclusive use the logo MLF (Mouvement de Libération des Femmes [Women's Liberation Movement]; see Duchen, 1986).

13. For a global overview of women's situation, see United Nations, 2002.
14. For a snapshot of feminist activities around the world, see Ali *et al.* (eds), 2000. A quick internet trawl also gives some idea of the range, energy and ubiquity of feminist activities today.
15. As discussed in Chapter 9, Gilligan is much less prone to essentialist generalisations and an uncritical celebration of female qualities than some commentators have suggested.

Bibliography

Abel, E. and Abel, E. (eds) (1983) *The Signs Reader* (Chicago: Chicago University Press).

Ackelsberg, M. and Shanley, M. (1996) 'Privacy, Publicity and Power: A Feminist Rethinking of the Public–Private Distinction', in N. Hirschmann and C. Di Stefano (eds).

Acker, J. (1989) 'The Problem with Patriarchy', *Sociology*, vol. 23, no. 2.

Afshar, H. and Maynard, M. (1994) 'The Dynamics of "Race" and "Gender" ', in H. Afshar and M. Maynard (eds), *The Dynamics of 'Race' and 'Gender': Some Feminist Interventions* (London: Taylor & Francis).

Akkerman, T. (1998) 'Liberalism and feminism in late nineteenth-century Britain', in T. Akkerman and S. Stuurnam (eds).

Akkerman, T. and Stuurnam, S. (eds) (1998a) *Perspectives on Feminist Political Thought in European History: From the Middle Ages to the Present* (London: Routledge).

Akkerman, T. and Stuurnam, S. (eds) (1998b) 'Introduction', in T. Akkerman and S. Stuurnam (eds).

Alberti, J. (2000) ' "A Symbol and a Key": The Suffrage Movement in Britain, 1918–1928', in J. Purvis and S. Holton (eds).

Alcoff, L. (1988) 'Cultural Feminism versus Poststructuralism: The Identity Crisis in Feminist Theory', *Signs*, vol. 13, no. 3.

Alexander, S. (1987) 'Women, Class and Sexual Difference', in A. Phillips (ed.).

Alexander, S. and Taylor, B. (1982) 'In Defence of Patriarchy', in M. Evans (ed.).

Ali, S., Coate, K. and Goro, W. (eds) (2000) *Global Feminist Politics. Identities in a Changing World* (London and New York: Routledge).

Allen, A. (1996) 'Privacy at Home: The Twofold Problem', in N. Hirschmann and C. Di Stefano (eds).

Amos, V. and Parmar, P. (1984) 'Challenging Imperial Feminism', *Feminist Review*, no. 17.

Anderson, B. (1998) 'The Lid Comes Off: International Radical Feminism and the Revolutions of 1848', *NWSA Journal*, no. 10–12 (Bloomington and Indianapolis: Indiana University Press).

Anderson, M. and Collins, P. (eds) (1995) *Race, Class and Gender: An Anthology* (London: Wadsworth).

Annas, J. (1977) 'Mill and the Subjection of Women', *Philosophy*, vol. 52.

Anthony, S. B. (ed.) (1987) *The History of Woman Suffrage*, vol. III (New York: Fowler & Wells).

Anthony, S. B. and Harper, I. H. (eds) (1902) *The History of Woman Suffrage*, vol. IV (New York: Fowler & Wells).

Appignanesi, L. (1988) *Simone de Beauvoir* (Harmondsworth: Penguin).

Arditti, R., Klein, R. and Minden, S. (eds) (1984) *Test-tube Woman* (London: Pandora Press).

Arneil, B. (1999) *Politics and Feminism* (Oxford: Blackwell).

Ashton, F. and Whitting, G. (eds) (1987) *Feminist Theory and Practical Policies: Shifting the Agenda in the 1980s* (Bristol: School for Advanced Urban Studies).

Assiter, A. (1989) *Pornography, Feminism and the Individual* (London: Pluto Press).

Assiter, A. (1996) *Enlightened Women. Modernist Feminism in a Postmodern Age* (London and New York: Routledge).

Astell, M. (1996) *Political Writings*, edited and with an Introduction by P. Springborg (Cambridge: Cambridge University Press).

Attwood, L. (1999) *Creating the New Soviet Woman: Women's Magazines as Engineers of Female Identity, 1922–53* (Basingstoke: Macmillan).

Aziz, R. (1997) 'Feminism and the challenge of racism: Deviance or difference?', in H. Mirza (ed.).

Bacchi, C. (1990) *Same Difference: Feminism and Sexual Difference* (London: Allen & Unwin).

Bacchi, C. (1996) *The Politics of Affirmative Action* (London: Sage).

Baden, S. and Goetz, A. (1997) 'Who Needs [Sex] When You Can Have [Gender]? Conflicting Discussions at Beijing', *Feminist Review*, no. 56.

Badinter, E. (1989) *Man/Woman: The One is the Other* (London: Collins Harvill).

Badran, M. and Cooke, M. (1990) *Opening the Gates: A Century of Arab Feminist Writing* (London: Virago).

Baker, K. (ed.) (1976) *Condorcet: Selected Writings* (Indianapolis: Bobs-Merrill).

Ball, T. (1980) 'Utilitarianism, Feminism and the Franchise: James Mill and his Critics', *History of Political Thought*, vol. 1.

Banaszak, L. (1996) *Why Movements Succeed or Fail: Opportunity, Culture, and the Struggle for Women's Suffrage* (Princeton, New Jersey: Princeton University Press).

Banks, O. (1985) *The Biographical Dictionary of British Feminists*, vol. I: *1800–1930* (Brighton: Harvester Press).

Banks, O. (1986) *Faces of Feminism* (Oxford: Blackwell).

Banks, O. (1993) *The Politics of British Feminism, 1918–1970* (Aldershot: Edward Elgar).

Banner, L. (1980) *Elizabeth Cady Stanton: A Radical for Woman's Rights* (Boston and Toronto: Little, Brown).

Bar On, B. (ed.) (1994) *Modern Engendering: Critical Feminist Readings in Modern Western Philosophy* (Albany: State University of New York).

Barre, F. P. de la (1990) *The Equality of the Sexes*, translated and with an introduction by D. Clarke (Manchester and New York: Manchester University Press).

Barrett, M. (1984) 'Rethinking Women's Oppression: A Reply to Brenner and Ramas', *New Left Review*, no. 146.

Barrett, M. (1985) 'Weir and Wilson on Feminist Politics', *New Left Review*, no. 150.

Barrett, M. (1987) 'Marxist Feminism and the Work of Karl Marx', in A. Phillips (ed.).

Barrett, M. (1988) *Women's Oppression Today: The Marxist/Feminist Encounter* (London: Verso).

Barrett, M. and McIntosh, M. (1979) 'Christian Delphy: Towards a Materialist Feminism?', *Feminist Review*, no. 1.

Barrett, M. and McIntosh, M. (1982) *The Anti-Social Family* (London: Verso).

Barrett, M. and McIntosh, M. (1985) 'Ethnocentricism and Socialist-Feminist Theory', *Feminist Review*, no. 20.

Barrett, M., Campbell, B., Phillips, A., Weir, E. and Wilson, E. (1986) 'Feminism and Class Politics: A Round-Table Discussion', *Feminist Review*, no. 23.

Beauvoir, S. de (1968) *Force of Circumstance* (Harmondsworth: Penguin).

Beauvoir, S. de (1972) *The Second Sex* (Harmondsworth: Penguin).

Beauvoir, S. de (1974) *All Said and Done* (London: André Deutsch and Weidenfeld & Nicolson).

Beauvoir, S. de (1987) 'Women and Creativity', in T. Moi (ed.).

Bebel, A. (1904) *Woman under Socialism*, translated by D. de Leon (New York: New York Labour Press).

Beecher, J. and Bienveneau, R. (1972) *The Utopian Vision of Charles Fourier: Selected Texts on Work, Love and Passionate Attraction* (London: Jonathan Cape).

Beechey, V. (1979) 'On Patriarchy', *Feminist Review*, no. 3.

Beechey, V. (1982) 'Some Notes on Female Wage Labour in Capitalist Production', in M. Evans (ed.).

Beechey, V. and Perkins, T. (1987) *A Matter of Hours: Women, Part-time Work and the Labour Market* (Cambridge: Polity Press).

Bell, D. and Klein, R. (eds) (1996) *Radically Speaking: Feminism Reclaimed* (London: Zed Books).

Benhabib, S. and Cornell, D. (eds) (1987) *Feminism as Critique* (Oxford: Polity Press).

Benston, M. (1969) 'The Political Economy of Women's Liberation', *Monthly Review*, vol. 21, no. 4.

Bernstein, S. (1962) *The First International in America* (New York: Augustus M. Kelly).

Beuchler, S. (1990) *Women's Movements in the United States: Woman Suffrage, Equal Rights, and Beyond* (New Brunswick and London: Rutgers University Press).

Bhavnani, K. and Coulson, M. (1986) 'Transforming Socialist Feminism: The Challenge of Racism', *Feminist Review*, no. 23.

Bhavnani, R. (1987) 'Race, Women and Class: Integrating Theory and Practice', in F. Ashton and G. Whitting (eds).

Bland, L. (1987) 'The Married Woman, the "New Woman" and Femininity: Sexual Politics in the 1890s', in J. Rendall (ed.).

Bland, L. (1995) *Banishing the Beast: English Feminism and Sexual Morality 1885–1914* (London: Penguin Books).

Bolt, C. (1995) *Feminist Ferment: 'The Woman Question' in the USA and England, 1870–1940* (London: UCL Press).

Bolt, C. (2000) 'The Ideas of British Suffragism', in J. Purvis and S. Holton (eds).

Boralevi, L. (1987) 'Utilitarianism and Feminism', in E. Kennedy and S. Mendus (eds).

Borchorst, A. and Siim, B. (1987) 'Women and the Advanced Welfare State – A New Kind of Patriarchal Power?', in A. S. Sassoon (ed.).

Bordo, S. (1994) 'The Cartesian Masculinization of Thought and the Seventeenth-Century Flight from the Feminine', in B. Bar On (ed.).

Bouchier, D. (1983) *The Feminist Challenge* (London: Macmillan).

Boxer, M. and Quataert, J. (eds) (1978) *Socialist Women: European Socialist Feminism in the Nineteenth and Early Twentieth Centuries* (New York: Elsevier North-Holland).

Brah, A. (1996) *Cartographies of Diaspora* (London: Routledge).

Braidotti, R. (1986) 'Ethics Revisited: Women and/in Philosophy', in C. Pateman (ed.).

Braun, L. (1987) *Selected Writings on Feminism and Socialism*, translated and edited by G. Meyer (Bloomington and Indianapolis: Indiana University Press).

Brennan, T. and Pateman, C. (1979) 'Mere Auxiliaries to the Commonwealth: Women and the Origins of Liberalism', *Political Studies*, vol. 27.

Brenner, J. (2000) *Women and the Politics of Class* (New York: Monthly Review Press).

Brenner, J. and Laslett, B. (1991) 'Gender, Social Reproduction and Women's Self-Organization: Considering the US Welfare State', *Gender and Society*, vol. 5, no. 3.

Brenner, J. and Ramas, M. (1984) 'Rethinking Women's Oppression', *New Left Review*, no. 144.

Brittan, A. and Maynard, M. (1984) *Sexism, Racism and Oppression* (Oxford: Basil Blackwell).

Brody, M. (1983) 'Mary Wollstonecraft: Sexuality and Women's Rights', in D. Spender (ed.).

Brooke, C. (1978) 'The Retreat to Cultural Feminism', in Redstockings (ed.).

Brown, L. (1993) *The Politics of Individualism: Liberalism, Liberal Feminism and Anarchism* (Montreal and London: Black Rose).

Brown, S. (2002) 'Postmodernism', in G. Blakeley and V. Bryson (eds), *Contemporary Political Concepts: A Critical Introduction* (London: Pluto Press).

Browne, A. (1987) *The Eighteenth-Century Feminist Mind* (Brighton: Harvester Press).

Brownmiller, S. (1977) *Against Our Will* (Harmondsworth: Penguin).

Bruley, S. (1999) *Women in Britain since 1900* (Basingstoke: Macmillan).

Bryson, V. (1995) 'Adjusting the Lenses: Feminist Analyses and Marxism at the End of the Twentieth Century', *Contemporary Politics*, vol. 1, no. 1.

Bryson, V. (1999a) *Feminist Debates: Issues of Theory and Political Practice* (Basingstoke: Macmillan).

Bryson, V. (1999b) ' "Patriarchy": A Concept Too Useful to Lose', *Contemporary Politics*, vol. 5, no. 4.

Bryson, V. (2000) 'Men and Sex Equality', *Politics*, vol. 20, no.1.

Bubeck, D. (1995) *Care, Gender and Justice* (Oxford: Clarendon Press).

Buckley, M. (1989) *Women and Ideology in the Soviet Union* (New York and London: Harvester Wheatsheaf).

Buhle, M. (1981) *Women and American Socialism 1870–1920* (Urbana, Chicago and London: University of Illinois Press).

Buhle, M. and Buhle, P. (eds) (1978) *The Concise History of Woman Suffrage. Selections from the Classic Works of Stanton, Anthony, Gage and Harper* (Urbana, Chicago and London: University of Illinois Press).

Bulbeck, C. (1988) *One World Women's Movement* (London: Pluto Press).

Burton, C. (1985) *Subordination: Feminism and Social Theory* (London: Allen & Unwin).

Bussemaker, J. (1998) 'Contemporary Feminism between Individualism and Community', in T. Akkerman and S. Sturman (eds).

Bussey, G. and Tims, M. (1980) *Pioneers for Peace: Women's International League for Peace and Freedom* (London: WILPF British Section).

Butler, J. (1990) *Gender Trouble: Feminism and the Subversion of Identity* (London: Routledge).

Butler, J. (1993) *Bodies that Matter: On the Discursive Limits of 'Sex'* (London: Routledge).

Butler, J. (1998) 'Sex and Gender in Simone de Beauvoir's *Second Sex*', in E. Fallaize (ed.), *Simone de Beauvoir: A Critical Reader* (London and New York: Routledge).

Bynum, V. (1992) *Unruly Women: The Politics of Social and Sexual Control in the Old South* (Chapel Hill and London: University of North Carolina Press).

Caine, B. (1982) 'Feminism, Suffrage and the Nineteenth-Century Women's Movement', *Women's Studies International Forum*, vol. 5, no. 6.

Caine, B. (1993) *Victorian Feminists* (Oxford and New York: Oxford University Press).

Caine, B. (1997) *English Feminism 1780–1980* (Oxford: Oxford University Press).

Caldecott, L. and Leland, S. (eds) (1983) *Reclaim the Earth: Women Speak Out for Life on Earth* (London: Women's Press).

Califia, P. (1996) 'Feminism and Sadomasochism', in S. Jackson and S. Scott (eds).

Cambridge Women's Peace Collective (1984) *My Country is the Whole World: Art Anthology of Women's Work on Peace and War* (London: Pandora Press).

Cameron, D. (1985) *Feminism and Linguistic Theory* (London: Macmillan).

Cameron, D. (ed.) (1990) *The Feminist Critique of Language* (London: Routledge).

Cannon, K. (1996) *Katie's Canon: Womanism and the Soul of the Black Community* (New York: Continuum).

Canovan, M. (1987) 'Rousseau's Two Concepts of Citizenship', in E. Kennedy and S. Mendus (eds).

Carter, A. (1988) *The Politics of Women's Rights* (London and New York: Longman).

Carver, T. (1985) 'Engels' Feminism', *History of Political Thought*, vol. 6.

Carver, T. (1996) *Gender is Not a Synonym for Women* (Colorado: Lynne Rienner).

Carver, T. and Mottier, V. (1998) (eds) *Politics of Sexuality: Identity, Gender, Citizenship* (London and New York: Routledge).

Charvet, J. (1982) *Feminism* (London: Dent).

Cheatham, A. and Powell, M. (1986) *This Way Daybreak Comes: Women's Values and the Future* (Philadelphia: New Society Publishers).

Chester, G. and Dickey, J. (eds) (1988) *Feminism and Censorship: The Current Debate* (Bridport, Dorset: Prism Press).

Chinchilla, S. and Gimenez, M. (1991) 'Guest Editors' Introduction', *Gender and Society*, vol. 5, no. 3.

Chodorow, N. (1978) *The Reproduction of Mothering: Psychoanalysis and the Sociology of Gender* (Berkeley, Los Angeles and London: University of California Press).

Chow, E., Wilkinson, D. and Zinn, M. (eds) (1996) *Race, Class and Gender: Common Bonds, Different Voices* (London: Sage).

Cixous, H. (1981) 'The Laugh of the Medusa', in E. Marks and I. de Courtrivon (eds).

Clark, L. and Lange, L. (1979) *The Sexism of Social and Political Theory: Women and Reproduction from Plato to Nietzsche* (London, Ontario: University of Toronto Press).

Clements, B. (1979) *Bolshevik Feminist: The Life of Alexander Kollontai* (Bloomington and London: Indiana University Press).

Clements, B. (1997) *Bolshevik Women* (Cambridge: Cambridge University Press).

Cliff, T. (1987) *Class Struggle and Women's Liberation* (London: Bookmarks).

Coates, J. (1986) *Women, Men and Language* (London and New York: Longman).

Cockburn, C. (1991) *In the Way of Women: Men's Resistance to Sex Equality in Organizations* (Basingstoke: Macmillan).

Cocks, J. (1989) *The Oppositional Imagination* (London: Routledge).

Cole, A. (2000) 'Victims No More?', *Feminist Review*, no. 64.

Collard, A. with Contrussi, J. (1988) *Rape of the Wild: Man's Violence against Animals and the Earth* (London: Women's Press).

Collins, P. (1989) 'The Social Construction of Black Feminist Thought', *Signs*, vol. 14, no. 4.

Collins, P. (1990) *Black Feminist Thought* (London, Sydney and Wellington: Unwin Hyman).

Collins, P. (1995) 'Symposium on West and Fenstermaker's "Doing Difference"', *Gender and Society*, vol. 9, no. 4.

Condorcet (1976) *Selected Writings*, edited and with an introduction by K. Barker (Indianapolis: Bobs-Merrill).

Connell, R. (1995) *Masculinities* (Cambridge: Polity).

Connell, R. (2000) *The Men and the Boys* (Cambridge: Polity).

Connell, R. W. (1987) *Gender and Power* (Cambridge: Polity).

Cook, B. W. (ed.) (1978) *Crystal Eastman on Women and Revolution* (Oxford: Oxford University Press).

Coole, D. (1993) *Women in Political Theory* (London: Harvester Wheatsheaf).

Coole, D. (1997) 'Feminism without nostalgia', *Radical Philosophy*, no. 83.

Coole, D. (2000) 'Threads and plaits or an unfinished project? Feminism(s) through the twentieth century', *Journal of Political Ideologies*, vol. 5, no. 1.

Cooper, J. (1988) *A Voice from the South*, with an 'Introduction' by M. H. Washington (New York and Oxford: Oxford University Press).

Coote, A. and Campbell, B. (1982) *Sweet Freedom* (London: Picador).

Coote, A. and Patullo, P. (1990) *Power and Prejudice: Women and Politics* (London: Weidenfeld & Nicolson).

Corea, G. *et al.* (1985) *Man-made Woman: How New Reproductive Technologies Affect Women* (London: Hutchinson).

Corrin, C. (ed.) (1996) *Women in A Violent World: Feminist Analyses and Resistance Across 'Europe'* (Edinburgh: Edinburgh University Press).

Cott, N. (1987) *The Grounding of Modern Feminism* (New Haven and London: Yale University Press).

Cottrell, R. (1975) *Simone de Beauvoir* (New York: Frederick Ungar).

Coulson, M., Magas, B. and Wainwright, H. (1979) 'The Housewife and her Labour under Capitalism: A Critique', *New Left Review*, no. 89.

Coward, R. (1983) *Patriarchal Precedents* (London: Routledge & Kegan Paul).

Crawford, M. (2000) 'A Reappraisal of Gender: An Ethnomethodological Approach', *Feminism and Psychology*, vol. 10, no. 1.

Crenshaw, K. (1998) 'Demarginalizing the Intersection of Race and Sex: A Black Feminist Critique of Antidiscrimination Doctrine, Feminist Theory, and Antiracist Politics', in A. Phillips (ed.), *Feminism and Politics* (Oxford: Oxford University Press).

Cross, M. (1996) 'Mary Wollstonecraft and Flora Tristan; One Pariah Redeems Another', in C. Orr (ed.).

Dahlerup, D. (1986) *The New Woman's Movement: Feminism and Political Power in Europe and the USA* (London: Sage).

Dahlerup, D. (1987) 'Confusing Concepts – Confusing Reality: A Theoretical Discussion of the Patriarchal State', in A. S. Sassoon (ed.).

Dale, J. and Foster, P. (1986) *Feminists and State Welfare* (London: Routledge & Kegan Paul).

Dalla Costa, M. (1973) *The Power of Women and the Subversion of the Community* (Bristol: Falling Wall Press).

Daly, M. (1973) *Beyond God the Father: Towards a Philosophy of Women's Liberation* (Boston: Beacon Press).

Daly, M. (1978) *Gyn/Ecology: The Metaethics of Radical Feminism* (Boston: Beacon Press).

Daly, M. (1984) *Pure Lust: Elemental Feminist Philosophy* (London: Women's Press).

Davies, M. (ed.) (1978) *Maternity: Letters from Working Women* (London: Virago).

Davies, S. (1998) *Unbridled Spirits: Women of the English Revolution 1640–1660* (London: The Women's Press Ltd).

Davis, A. (1982) *Women, Race and Class* (London: Women's Press).

Davis, A. (1990) *Women, Culture and Politics* (London: Women's Press).

Davis, F. (1999) *Moving the Mountain: The Women's Movement in America since 1960* (Urbana and Chicago: University of Illinois Press).

Davis, M. (1999) *Sylvia Pankhurst: A Life in Radical Politics* (London: Pluto Press).

Degler, C. (1966) 'Introduction' to C. P. Gilman, *Women and Economics* (New York: Torchbook).

Delmar, R. (1976) 'Looking Again at Engels' "Origin of the Family, Private Property and the State" ', in J. Mitchell and A. Oakley (eds).

Delmar, R. (1986) 'What is Feminism?' in J. Mitchell and A. Oakley (eds).

Delphy, C. (1977) *The Main Enemy* (London: Women's Research and Resources Centre).

Delphy, C. (1980) 'A Materialist Feminism is Possible', *Feminist Review*, no. 4.

Delphy, C. (1981) 'For a Materialist Feminism', *Feminist Studies*, no. 2.

Delphy, C. (1984) *Close to Home: A Materialist Analysis of Women's Oppression* (London: Hutchinson).

Delphy, C. and Leonard, D. (1992) *Familiar Exploitation: A New Analysis of Marriage in Contemporary Western Societies* (Cambridge: Polity).

Dietz, M. (1985) 'Citizenship with a Feminist Face: The Problem with Maternal Thinking'. *Political Theory*, vol. 13.

Dietz, M. (1992) 'Introduction: Debating Simone de Beauvoir', *Signs*, vol. 18, no. 1.

Dinnerstein, D. (1987) *The Rocking of the Cradle and the Ruling of the World* (London: Women's Press).

Dodd, K. (ed.) (1993) *A Sylvia Pankhurst Reader* (Manchester: Manchester University Press).

Draper, H. (1972) 'Marx and Engels on Women's Liberation', in R. Salper (ed.).

Draper, H. and Lipow, A. (1976) 'Marxist Women versus Bourgeois Feminism', in *Socialist Register*, ed. R. Miliband (London: Merlin).

Dubois, E. (1979) 'The Nineteenth-century Woman Suffrage Movement and the Analysis of Women's Oppression', in Z. Eisenstein (ed.).

Dubois, E. (1981) *Elizabeth Cady Stanton and Susan B. Anthony: Correspondence, Writings, Speeches*, with a critical commentary by E. Dubois (New York: Schocken Books).

Dubois, E. (1987) 'The Radicalisation of the Woman Suffrage Movement', in A. Phillips (ed.).

Dubois, E. (1994) 'Working Women, Class Relations, and Suffrage Militance: Harriet Stanton Blatch and the New York Woman Suffrage Movement, 1894–1909', in V. Ruiz and E. Dubois (eds).

Duchen, C. (1986) *Feminism in France* (London: Routledge & Kegan Paul).

Dworkin, A. (1974) *Woman Hating* (New York: E. P. Dutton).

Dworkin, A. (1981) *Pornography: Men Possessing Women* (London: Women's Press).

Dworkin, A. (1982) *Our Blood: Prophecies and Discourses on Sexual Politics* (London: Women's Press).

Dworkin, A. (1983) *Right-Wing Women: The Politics of Domesticated Females* (London: Women's Press).

Dworkin, A. (1988) *Letters from a War Zone* (London: Secker & Warburg).

Eastman, C. (1978) *Crystal Eastman on Women and Revolution*, edited by B. Cook (Oxford: Oxford University Press).

Eckhart, C. (1984) *Fanny Wright: Rebel in America* (Cambridge, Mass. and London: Harvard University Press).

Edmondson, L. (1981) 'Sylvia Pankhurst: Suffragist, Feminist or Socialist?', in J. Slaughter and R. Kern (eds).

Edmondson, L. (1984) *Feminism in Russia 1900–1917* (London: Heinemann Educational).

Eisenstein, H. (1984) *Contemporary Feminist Thought* (London: Unwin Paperbacks).

Eisenstein, Z. (1981) *The Radical Future of Liberal Feminism* (New York and London: Longman).

Eisenstein, Z. (1984) *Feminism and Sexual Equality* (New York: Monthly Review Press).

Eisenstein, Z. (1994) *The Color of Gender* (London: University of California Press).

Eisenstein, Z. (1996) 'Equalizing Privacy and Specifying Equality', in N. Hirschmann and C. Di Stefano (eds).

Eisenstein, Z. (ed.) (1979) *Capitalist Patriarch, and the Case for Socialist Feminism* (New York and London: Monthly Review Press).

Elshtain, J. (1981a) 'Against Androgyny', *Telos*, no. 47.

Elshtain, J. (1981b) *Public Man, Private Woman* (Oxford: Martin Robertson).

Elshtain, J. (1987) *Women and War* (Brighton: Harvester Press).

Elshtain, J. (ed.) (1982) *The Family in Political Thought* (Brighton: Harvester Press).

Elwood, R. C. (1992) *Inessa Armand: Revolutionary and Feminist* (Cambridge: Cambridge University Press).

Engel, B. (1978) 'From Separatism to Socialism: Women in the Russian Revolutionary Movement of the 1870s', in M. Boxer and J. Quataert (eds).

Engels, F. (1973) *The Condition of the Working Class in England* (Moscow: Progress Publishers).

Engels, F. (1978) *The Origin of the Family, Private Property and the State* (Peking: Foreign Languages Press).

Ericson, Y. and Jacobsson, R. (eds) (1985) *Side by Side: A Report on Equality between Women and Men in Sweden* (Stockholm: Gotab).

Evans, J. (1995) *Feminist Theory Today: An Introduction to Second-Wave Feminism* (London: Sage).

Evans, J. et al. (1986) *Feminism and Political Theory* (London: Sage).

Evans, M. (1985) *Simone de Beauvoir: A Feminist Mandarin* (London and New York: Tavistock).

Evans, M. (1987) 'Engels: Materialism and Morality', in J. Sayers, M. Evans and N. Redclift (eds).

Evans, M. (1996) *Simone de Beauvoir* (London: Sage Publications).

Evans, M. (ed.) (1982) *The Woman Question: Readings on the Subordination of Women* (London: Fontana).

Evans, R. (1977) *The Feminists: Women's Emancipation Movements in Europe, America and Australasia 1840–1920* (London: Croom Helm).

Evans, R. (1980) 'Bourgeois Feminists and Women Socialists in Germany 1894–1914: Lost Opportunity or Inevitable Conflict?', *Women's Studies International Quarterly*, vol. 3.

Evans, R. (1987) *Comrades and Sisters. Feminism, Socialism and Pacifism in Europe, 1870–1945* (Sussex: Wheatsheaf Books).

Evans, R. (ed.) (1998) *Simone de Beauvoir's The Second Sex: New Interdisciplinary Essays* (Manchester: Manchester University Press).

Evans, S. (1980) *Personal Politics: The Roots of Women's Liberation in the Civil Rights Movement and the New Left* (New York: Vintage Books).

Fairbairns, Z. (1979) *Benefits* (New York: Avon).

Faludi, S. (1992) *Backlash: The Undeclared War against Women* (London: Chatto & Windus).

Farnsworth, B. (1978) 'Bolshevism, the Woman Question and Alexandra Kollontai', in M. Boxer and J. Quataert (eds).

Feminist Review (1984) 'Many Voices, One Chant. Black Feminist Perspectives', *Feminist Review*, no. 17.

Feminist Review (ed.) (1986) *Waged Work: A Reader* (London: Virago).

Ferguson, A. (1981) 'Androgyny as an Ideal for Human Development', in M. Vetterling-Braggin, F. Elliston and J. English (eds).

Ferguson, A. (1989) *Blood at the Root* (London: Pandora Press).

Ferguson, K. (1980) *Self, Society and Womankind: The Dialectics of Liberation* (Westport, Conn.: Greenwood Press).

Ferguson, M. (ed.) (1985) *First Feminists. British Women Writers 1578–1799* (Bloomington: Indiana University Press).

Ferguson, M. and Todd, J. (1984) *Mary Wollstonecraft* (Boston: Twayne Publishers).

Fester, G. (2000) 'Despite Diversity: Women's Unity in Western Cape, South Africa (1980–94)', in S. Ali, K. Coate and W. Goro (eds).

Figes, E. (1978) *Patriarchal Attitudes* (London: Virago).

Firestone, S. (1979) *The Dialectic of Sex* (London: Women's Press).

First, R. and Scott, A. (1980) *Olive Schreiner: A Biography* (London: André Deutsch).

Flax, J. (1981) 'Do Feminists Need Marxism?', in *Building Feminist Theory: Essays from Quest* (London: Longman).

Flax, J. (1987) 'Postmodernism and Gender Relations', *Signs*, vol. 12, no. 4.

Flax, J. (1990) *Thinking Fragments* (Berkeley, California: University of California Press).

Fletcher, I., Mayhall, L. and Levine, P. (eds) (2000) *Women's Suffrage in the British Empire: Citizenship, Nation and Race'* (London and New York: Routledge).

Flexner, E. (1959) *Century of Struggle: The Women's Rights Movement in the United States* (Cambridge, Mass.: Harvard University Press).

Florence, M. *et al.* (1987) *Militarism versus Feminism: Writings on Women and War*, edited by M. Kamester and J. Vellacott (London: Virago).

Florent, S. (1988) 'Women and Politics 1830–1850', unpublished MA dissertation, Manchester Polytechnic.

Foner, P. (1984) *Clara Zetkin: Selected Writings* (New York: International Publishers).

Foreman, A. (1978) *Femininity as Alienation* (London: Pluto Press).

Forster, M. (1984) *Significant Sisters: The Grassroots of Active Feminism 1839–1939* (Harmondsworth: Penguin).

Forster, P. and Sutton, I. (eds) (1989) *Daughters of de Beauvoir* (London: Women's Press).

Foucault, M. (1980) *Power/Knowledge: Selected Interviews and Other Writings 1972–1977* edited by C. Gordon (London: Harvester Wheatsheaf).

Frances, H. (2000) ' "Dare to be free!" The Women's Freedom League and its Legacy', in J. Purvis and S. Holton (eds).

Frankenberg, R. (1993a) 'Growing up White: Feminism, Racism and the Social Geography of Childhood', *Feminist Review*, no. 45.

Frankenberg, R. (1993b) *White Women, Race Matters: The Social Construction of Whiteness* (Minneapolis: University of Minnesota Press).

Franklin, J. (2000) 'What's Wrong with New Labour Politics?', *Feminist Review*, no. 64.
Fraser, N. (1998) 'Sex, Lies and the Public Sphere: Reflections on the Confirmation of Clarence Thomas', in J. Landes (ed.).
Frazer, E. and Lacey, N. (1993) *The Politics of Community: A Feminist Critique of the Liberal-Communitarian Debate* (New York and London: Harvester Wheatsheaf).
Freeman, J. (1975) *The Politics of Women's Liberation* (New York and London: Longman).
French, M. (1985) *Beyond Power: Women, Men and Morals* (London: Jonathan Cape).
Friedan, B. (1970) 'Our Revolution is Unique', in M. L. Thompson (ed.).
Friedan, B. (1977) *It Changed My Life: Writings on the Women's Movement* (London: Victor Gollancz).
Friedan, B. (1981) *The Second Stage* (London: Michael Joseph).
Friedan, B. (1986) *The Feminine Mystique* (Harmondsworth: Penguin Books).
Friedan, B. (1997) *Beyond Gender: The New Politics of Work and Family* (Washington: Woodrow Wilson Center Press).
Gardiner, J. (1975) 'Women's Domestic Labour', *New Left Review*, no. 89.
Gardiner, J. (1997) *Gender, Care and Economics* (Basingstoke: Macmillan).
Garnett, R. G. (1972) *Co-operation and the Owenite Socialist Communities in Britain 1825–45* (Manchester: Manchester University Press).
Garry, A. and Pearsall, M. (eds) (1989) *Women, Knowledge and Reality. Explorations in Feminist Philosophy* (Boston and London: Unwin Hyman).
Gaspard, F. (2001) 'The French Parity Movement', in J. Klausen and C. Maier (eds).
Gender and Society (1991) 'Special Issue on Marxism and Feminism', *Gender and Society*, vol. 5, no. 3.
George, M. (1970) *One Woman's 'Situation': A Study of Mary Wollstonecraft* (Urbana, Chicago, London: University of Illinois Press).
German, L. (1989) *Sex, Class and Socialism* (London: Bookmarks).
Giddings, P. (1984) *When and Where I Enter: The Impact of Black Women on Race and Sex in America* (New York: William Morrow).
Gilligan, C. (1982) *In a Different Voice: Psychological Theory and Women's Development* (Cambridge, Mass and London: Harvard University Press).
Gilman, C. P. (1904) *Human Work* (New York: McClare, Phillips).
Gilman, C. P. (1906) *Women and Economics* (London: Putnam, and Boston: Small, Maynard).
Gilman, C. P. (1911) *The Man Made World* (London: T. Fisher Unwin).
Gilmore, G. (1996) *Gender and Jim Crow: Women and the Politics of White Supremacy in North Carolina 1896–1920* (Chapel Hill and London: University of North Carolina Press).
Gimenez, M. (2000) 'What's Materialist about Materialist Feminism? A Marxist Feminist Critique', *Radical Philosophy*, no. 101.
Gleadle, K. (1995) *The Early Feminists: Radical Unitarians and the Emergence of the Women's Rights Movement, 1831–51* (Basingstoke: Macmillan).
Gleadle, K. (2000a) *British Women in the Nineteenth Century* (Basingstoke: Palgrave).
Gleadle, K. (2000b) ' "Our Several Spheres": Middle-class Women and the Feminisms of Early Victorian Radical Politics', in K. Gleadle and S. Richardson (eds).
Gleadle, K. and Richardson, S. (eds) (2000) *Women in British Politics, 1760–1860. The Power of the Petticoat* (Basingstoke: Macmillan and New York: St Martin's Press).
Gluck, S. (1987) 'Socialist Feminism Between Two World Wars: Insights from Oral History', in C. Scharf and J. Jenson (eds).
Goldman, E. (1979) *Red Emma Speaks: The Selected Speeches and Writings of the Anarchist and Feminist Emma Goldman* edited by A. K. Shulman (London: Wildwood House).
Goldstein, L. (1980) 'Mill, Marx and Women's Liberation', *Journal of the Philosophy of History*, vol. 18.
Goldstein, L. (1982) 'Early Themes in French Utopian Socialism: the St Simonians and Fourier', *Journal of the History of Ideas*, no. 43.
Gordon, L. (1994) 'Black and White Visions of Welfare: Women's Welfare Activism, 1890–1945', in V. Ruiz and E. Dubois (eds).
Gordon, L. (ed.) (1990) *Women, the State, and Welfare* (Madison, Wisconsin: University of Wisconsin Press).
Goreau, A. (1983) 'Aphra Benn: A Scandal to Modesty', in D. Spender (ed.).
Gouges, O. de (1980) 'Declaration of the Rights of Woman', in E. Reimar and J. Fout (eds).

Graham, S. (1998) *Woman Suffrage and the New Democracy* (New York: Yale University Press).

Grant, J. (1993) *Fundamental Feminism: Contesting the Core Concepts of Feminist Theory* (London: Routledge).

Greer, G. (1979) *The Female Eunuch* (London: Paladin).

Greer, G. (1984) *Sex and Destiny: The Politics of Human Fertility* (London: Seker & Warburg).

Grewal, S. *et al.* (1988) *Charting the Journey: Writings by Black and Third World Women* (London: Sheba).

Griffin, S. (1981) *Pornography and Silence: Culture's Revenge against Nature* (London: Women's Press).

Griffin, S. (1984) *Woman and Nature: The Roaring Inside Her* (London: Women's Press).

Griffith, E. (1984) *In Her Own Right: The Life of Elizabeth Cady Stanton* (New York and Oxford: Oxford University Press).

Griffiths, M. and Whitford, M. (eds) (1988) *Feminist Perspectives in Philosophy* (Basingstoke: Macmillan).

Grimshaw, J. (1982) 'Feminism: History and Morality', *Radical Philosphy*, no. 30.

Grimshaw, J. (1986) *Feminist Philosophers: Women's Perspectives on Philosophical Traditions* (Brighton: Wheatsheaf).

Grimshaw, J. (1989) 'Mary Wollstonecraft and the Tensions in Feminist Philosophy', *Radical Philosophy*, no. 52.

Grogan, S. (1992) *French Socialism and Sexual Difference: Women and the New Society, 1803–44* (London: Macmillan).

Gross, E. (1986a) 'Philosophy, Subjectivity and the Body: Kristeva and Irigaray', in C. Pateman and E. Gross (eds).

Gross, E. (1986b) 'What is Feminist Theory?', in C. Pateman and E. Gross (eds).

Grosz, E. (1990) *Jacques Lacan: A Feminist Introduction* (London and New York: Routledge).

Gruber, H. and Graves, P. (eds) (1998) *Women and Socialism/Socialism and Women: Europe Between the Two World Wars* (New York and Oxford: Berghahn Books).

Guettel, C. (1974) *Marxism and Feminism* (Ontario: Canadian Women's Educational Press).

Gunew, S. (ed.) (1991) *A Reader in Feminist Knowledge* (London: Routledge).

Hall, R. (2002) 'When is a Wife not a Wife? Some Observations on the Immigration Experiences of South Asian Women in West Yorkshire', *Contemporary Politics*, vol. 8, no. 1.

Hall, R. (forthcoming) 'Inside Out: Some Notes on Carrying Out Feminist Research in Cross-cultural Interviews with South Asian Women Immigration Applicants', *International Journal of Social Research Methodology Theory & Practice*.

Hall, S. and Jacques, M. (eds) (1989) *New Times: The Changing Face of Politics in the 1990s* (London: Lawrence & Wishart).

Hanmer, J. (1978) 'Violence and the Social Control of Women', in G. Littlejohn *et al. Power and the State* (London: Croom Helm).

Hannan, J. (2000) ' "I had not been to London": Women's Suffrage – A View from the Regions', in J. Purvis and S. Holton (eds).

Harding, S. (1986) *The Science Question in Feminism* (Ithaca: Cornell University Press).

Harding, S. (1991) *Whose Science? Whose Knowledge? Thinking from Women's Lives* (Ithaca: Cornell University Press).

Hardy, D. (1979) *Alternative Communities in Nineteenth-Century England* (London and New York: Longman).

Harrison, J. (1969) *Robert Owen and the Owenites in Britain and America* (London: Routledge & Kegan Paul).

Harstock, N. (1979) 'Feminist Theory and the Development of Revolutionary Strategy', in Z. Eisenstein (ed.).

Harstock, N. (1985) *Money, Sex and Power: Towards a Feminist Historical Materialism* (Boston: Northeastern University Press).

Hartmann, H. (1983) 'Capitalism: Patriarchy and Job Segregation by Sex', in E. Abel and E. Abel (eds).

Hartmann, H. (1986) 'The Unhappy Marriage of Marxism and Feminism: Towards a More Progressive Union', in L. Sargent (ed.).

Hawkesworth, M. (1988) 'Feminist Rhetoric. Discourses on the Male Monopoly of Thought', *Political Theory*, vol. 16.

Hawkesworth, M. E. (1990) *Beyond Oppression* (New York: Continnuum).

Hayek, F. A. (ed.) (1951) *John Stuart Mill and Harriet Taylor: Their Friendship and Subsequent Marriage* (London: Routledge & Kegan Paul).

Hearn, J. (1988) 'Commentary, Child Abuse: Violence and Sexualities Towards Young Children', *Sociology*, vol. 22, no. 4.

Heath, J. (1989) *Simone de Beauvoir* (New York and London: Harvester Wheatsheaf).

Hedman, C. (1990) 'The Artificial Womb', *Radical Philosophy*, no. 56.

Heinen, J. (1978) 'Kollontai and the History of Women's Oppression', *New Left Review*, no. 110.

Hernes, H. (1988) 'The Welfare State, Citizenship and Scandinavian Women', in K. Jones and A. Jonasdottir (eds).

Herstein, S. R. (1985) *A Mid-Victorian Feminist: Barbara Leigh-Smith Bodichon* (London and New Haven: Yale University Press).

Hester, M., Kelly, L. and Radford, J. (1996) *Women, Violence and Male Power* (Buckingham: Open University Press).

Hewlett, S. A. (1988) *A Lesser Life: The Myth of Women's Liberation* (London: Sphere).

Hill, B. (1986) *The First English Feminist: Reflections upon Marriage and other Writings by Mary Astell*, edited and with an Introduction by B. Hill (Aldershot: Gower).

Hill, M. A. (1980) *Charlotte Perkins Gilman: The Making of a Radical Feminist 1860–1896* (Philadelphia: Temple University Press).

Hills, J. *et al.* (1986) *Feminism and Political Theory* (London: Sage).

Hird, M. (2000) 'Intersexuality, transsexualism and the "sex"/"gender" binary', *Feminist Theory*, vol. 1, no. 3.

Hirsch, P. (1996) 'Mary Wollstonecraft: A Problematic Legacy', in C. Orr (ed.).

Hirschmann, N. (1992) *Rethinking Obligation: A Feminist Method for Political Theory* (Ithaca and London: Cornell University Press).

Hirschmann, N. and Di Stefano, C. (eds) (1996) *Revisioning the Political: Feminist Reconstructions of Traditional Concepts in Western Political Theory* (Boulder, Colorado and Oxford: Westview Press).

Holland, B. (ed.) (1985) *Soviet Sisterhood* (Bloomington: Indiana University Press).

Holt, A. (1977) *Alexandra Kollontai: Selected Writings* (London: Allison & Busby).

Holton, S. (1994) 'To Educate Women into Rebellion: Elizabeth Cady Stanton and the Creation of a Transatlantic Network of Radical Suffragists', *American Historical Review*, vol. 74, no. 1.

Honeycut, K. (1981) 'Clara Zetkin: A Socialist Approach to the Problem of Women's Oppression', in J. Slaughter and R. Kern (eds).

hooks, b. (1981) *Ain't I a Woman: Black Women and Feminism* (Boston: South End Press).

hooks, b. (1984) *Feminist Theory: From Margin to Center* (Boston: South End Press).

hooks, b. (1991) *Yearning, Race, Gender and Cultural Politics* (London: Turnaround).

Horowitz, D. (1998) *Betty Friedan and the Making of 'The Feminine Mystique'* (Amherst: University of Massachusetts Press).

Howarth, J. (2000) 'Mrs Henry Fawcett (1847–1929): The Widow as a Problem in Feminist Biography', in J. Purvis and S. Holton (eds).

Hull, G. Scott, P. and Smith, B. (eds) (1982) *But Some of Us Are Brave: Black Women's Studies* (New York: Feminist Press).

Humphries, J. (1982) 'The Working-Class Family: A Marxist Perspective', in J. Elshtain (ed.).

Humphries, J. (1987) 'The Origin of the Family: Born Out of Scarcity, not Wealth', in J. Sayers, M. Evans and N. Redclift (eds).

Hunt, K. (1986) 'Crossing the River of Fire: The Socialist Construction of Women's Politicization', in J. Evans (ed.).

Hunt, K. (1988) 'Equivocal Feminists: The Social Democratic Federation and the Woman Question 1884–1911', unpublished PhD thesis, University of Manchester.

Inman, M. (1936) *In Woman's Defence* (Los Angeles: Mercury Printing).

Irigaray, L. (1991) 'This Sex Which Is Not One' in S. Gunew (ed.).

Isenberg, N. (1998) *Sex and Citizenship in Antebellum America* (Chapel Hill and London: University of North Carolina Press).

Jackson, S. (1996) *Christine Delphy* (London: Sage).

Jackson, S. (1998) 'Sexual Politics, Feminist Politics, Gay Politics and the Problem of Heterosexuality', in T. Carver and V. Mottier (eds).

Jackson, S. and Jones, J. (eds) (1998) *Contemporary Feminist Theories* (Edinburgh: Edinburgh University Press).

Jackson, S. and Scott, S. (eds) (1996) *Feminism and Sexuality: A Reader* (Edinburgh: Edinburgh University Press).

Jaggar, A. (1983) *Feminist Politics and Human Nature* (Brighton: Harvester).

Jaggar, A. (1994) 'Introduction: Living with Contradictions', in A. Jaggar (ed.).

Jaggar, A. (ed.) (1994) *Living with Contradictions: Controversies in Feminist Social Ethics* (Boulder: Westview Press).

Jaggar, A. and Rothenberg, P. (eds) (1993a) *Feminist Frameworks: Alternative Theoretical Accounts of the Relations between Women and Men* (New York: McGraw-Hill).

Jaggar, A. and Rothenberg, P. (1993b) 'Introduction', in A. Jaggar and P. Rothenberg (eds).

James, S. (1980) Introduction to 'The Power of Women and the Subversion of the Community', in E. Malos (ed.).

James, S. and Busia, A. (eds) (1993) *Theorizing Black Feminisms: The Visionary Pragmatism of Black Women* (London: Routledge).

Janeway, E. (1972) *Man's World, Woman's Place: A Study in Social Mythology* (London: Michael Joseph).

Jebb, C. (ed.) (1912) *Mary Wollstonecroft* (London: Herbert & Daniel).

Jeffries, S. (1982) 'Free From All Uninvited Touch of Man: Women's Campaigns Around Sexuality 1880–1914', *Women's Studies International Forum*, vol. 5, no. 6.

Jeffries, S. (1985) *The Spinster and Her Enemies: Feminism and Sexuality 1880–1930* (London and New York: Pandora).

Jeffries, S. (1990) *Anticlimax* (London: Women's Press).

Johnston, J. (1982) 'Lesbian Nation: The Feminist Solution', in M. Evans (ed.).

Jones, K. (1993) *Compassionate Authority: Democracy and the Representation of Women* (London: Routledge).

Jones, K. and Jonasdottir, A. (eds) (1988) *The Political Interests of Gender: Developing Theory, and Research with a Human Face* (London: Sage).

Joseph, G. (1986) 'The Incompatible *Ménage à Trois*: Marxism, Feminism and Racism', in L. Sargent (ed.).

Kamm, J. (1966) *Rapiers and Battleaxes: The Women's Movement and its Aftermath* (London: Allen & Unwin).

Kamm, J. (1977) *John Stuart Mill in Love* (London: Gordon & Cremonesi).

Kanneh, K. (1998) 'Black Feminisms', in S. Jackson and J. Jones (eds).

Kanter, S., Lefanu, S., Shah, S. and Spedding, C. (eds) (1984) *Sweeping Statements: Writings from the Women's Liberation Movement 1981–83* (London: Women's Press).

Kauffman, L. (ed.) (1989) *Feminism and Institutions* (Oxford: Basil Blackwell).

Kazi, H. (1986) 'The Beginning of a Debate Long Due: Some Observations on "Ethnocentricism in Socialist Feminist Theory" ', *Feminist Review*, no. 22.

Keefe, T. (1983) *Simone de Beauvoir: A Study of Her Writings* (London: Harrap).

Kelly, G. (1992) *Revolutionary Feminism: The Mind and Career of Mary Wollstonecraft* (Basingstoke: Macmillan).

Kelly, J. (1984) 'Early feminist theory and the *Querelle des femmes* 1400–1789', in *Women, History and Theory: The Essays of Joan Kelly* (Chicago: University of Chicago Press).

Kelly, L. (1987) *Women of the French Revolution* (London: Hamish Hamilton).

Kennedy, E. and Mendus, S. (eds) (1987) *Women in Western Political Philosophy: Kant to Nietzsche* (Brighton: Wheatsheaf Books).

Kent, S. (1990) *Sex and Suffrage in Britain* (London: Routledge).

Kent, S. (1993) *Making Peace: The Reconstruction of Gender in Interwar Britain* (Princeton, New Jersey: Princeton University Press).

Kent, S. (1999) *Gender and Power in Britain, 1640–1990* (London: Routledge).

Kenway, J. with Langmead, D. (2000) 'Fast Capitalism, Fast Feminism and Some Fast Food for Thought', in S. Ali, K. Coate and W. Goro (eds).

King, D. (1988) 'Multiple Jeopardy, Multiple Consciousness: The Context of a Black Feminist Ideology', *Signs*, vol. 14, no. 1.

King, M. (1997) 'Introduction to the Series', in L. Careta, *Collected Letters of a Renaissance Feminist*, translated and edited by Diana Robin (Chicago and London: University of Chicago Press).

King, Y. (1983) 'The Eco-feminist Imperative', in L. Caldecott and S. Leland (eds).

Kinnard, J. (1983) 'Mary Astell: Inspired by Ideas', in D. Spender (ed.).

Klausen, J. and Maier, C. (eds) (2001) *Has Liberalism Failed Women? Assuring Equal Representation in Europe and the United States* (New York and Basingstoke: Palgrave).

Klein, V. (1946) *The Feminine Character: History of an Ideology* (London: Routledge & Kegan Paul).

Kleinberg, S. (1999) *Women in the United States, 1830–1945* (Basingstoke: Macmillan).

Koedt, A. (1970) 'The Myth of the Vaginal Orgasm', in L. Tanner (ed.).

Kollontai, A. (1977) *Selected Writings,* translated and with an introduction and commentary by A. Holt (London: Allison & Busby).

Komisar, L. (1971) *The New Feminism* (London and New York: Franklin Watts).

Koonz, C. (1987) *Mothers in the Fatherland: Women, The Family and Nazi Politics* (London: Jonathan Cape).

Kraditor, A. S. (1965) *The Ideas of the Woman Suffrage Movement 1890–1920* (New York and London: Columbia University Press).

Kramnick, M. (1978) 'Introduction' to Mary Wollstonecraft's *Vindication of the Rights of Woman* (Harmondsworth: Penguin).

Kristeva, J. (1981) 'Woman Can Never Be Defined', in E. Marks and I. de Courtrivon (eds).

Kruks, S. (1992) 'Gender and Subjectivity: Simone de Beauvoir and Contemporary Feminism', *Signs,* vol. 18, no. 1.

Kuhn, A. and Wolpe, A. (eds) (1978) *Feminism and Materialism: Women and Modes of Production* (London: Routledge & Kegan Paul).

Lambert, C. (May 2001) 'French Women in Politics: The Long Road to Parity', *US–France Analysis* (Washington DC: Brookings Institution Center on the United States and France).

Land, H. (1980) 'The Family Wage', *Feminist Review,* no. 6.

Land, H. (1984) 'The Introduction of Family Allowances' in C. Ungerson (ed.).

Landes, J. (1988) *Women and the Public Sphere in the Age of the French Revolution* (Ithaca and London: Cornell University Press).

Landes, J. (ed.) (1998) *Feminism, the Public and the Private* (Oxford and New York: Oxford University Press).

Landry, D. and Maclean, G. (1993) *Materialist Feminisms* (Oxford: Blackwell).

Landy, A. (1943) *Marxism and the Woman Question* (New York: New York Workers Library).

Lane, A. (1976) 'Women in Society: A Critique of Frederick Engels', in B. Carroll (ed.). *Liberating Women's History* (Urbana, Chicago and London: University of Chicago Press).

Lane, A. (1983) 'Charlotte Perkins Gilman: The Personal Is Political', in D. Spender (ed.).

Lean, P. (1986) 'The Role of "The Family" in Recent Feminist Thought', unpublished MA dissertation, University of Manchester.

Lederer, L. (ed.) (1980) *Take Back the Night* (New York: William Morrow).

Leeds Revolutionary Feminist Group (1982) 'Political Lesbianism: The Case Against Heterosexuality', in M. Evans (ed.).

Lee-Lampshire, W. (1994) 'Marx and the Ideology of Gender: A Paradox of Praxis and Nature', in B. Bar On (ed.).

Lees, S. (1986) 'Sex, Race and Culture: Feminism and the Limits of Cultural Pluralism', *Feminist Review,* no. 22.

Leighton, J. (1975) *Simone de Beauvoir on Women* (London: Associated University Press).

Lenin, V. (1977) *On the Emancipation of Women* (Moscow: Progress Publishers).

Lerner, G. (1986) *The Creation of Patriarchy* (Oxford and New York: Oxford University Press).

Lerner, G. (1993) *The Creation of Feminist Consciousness: From the Middle Ages to Eighteen-seventy* (Oxford: Oxford University Press).

Levin, M. (1987) *Feminism and Freedom* (New Brunswick and Oxford: Transaction Books).

Levine, P. (1987) *Victorian Feminism 1850–1900* (London: Hutchinson).

Levitas, R. (1998) 'Equality and Difference. Utopian Feminism in Britain', in T. Akkerman and S. Stuurnam (eds).

Lewis, J. (1985) 'The Debate on Sex and Class', *New Left Review,* no. 149.

Lewis, J. (ed.) (1983) *Women's Welfare, Women's Rights* (London and Canberra: Croom Helm).

Liddington, J. (1984) *The Life and Times of a Respectable Rebel: Selina Cooper 1864–1946* (London: Virago).

Liddington, J. and Norris, J. (1978) *One Hand Tied Behind Us: The Rise of the Women's Suffrage Movement* (London: Virago).

Lister, R. (1997) *Citizenship: Feminist Perspectives* (Basingstoke: Macmillan).

Lister, R. (2000) 'Dilemmas in Engendering Citizenship', in B. Hobson (ed.) *Gender and Citizenship in Transition* (Basingstoke: Macmillan).

Litwack, L. and Meier, A. (eds) (1998) *Black Leaders of the Nineteenth Century* (Urbana and Chicago; University of Illinois Press).

Liu, T. (1994) 'Teaching the Differences Among Women from a Historical Perspective: Rethinking Race and Gender as Social Categories', in V. Ruiz and E. Dubois (eds).

Lloyd, G. (1984) *The Man of Reason: 'Male' and 'Female' in Western Philosophy* (London: Methuen).

Lloyd, M. (1998) 'Sexual politics, performance, parody: Judith Butler', in T. Carver and V. Mottier (eds).

Lockwood, G. (1971) *The New Harmony Movement* (New York: Dover).

Lorber, J. (1991) 'Dismantling the Noah's Ark', in J. Lorber and S. Farrell (eds).

Lorber, J. (2000) 'Using Gender to Undo Gender: A Feminist Degendering Movement', *Feminist Theory*, vol. 1, no. 1.

Lorber, J. and Farrell, S. (eds) (1991) *The Social Construction of Gender* (London: Sage).

Lorde, A. (1984) *Sister Outsider: Essays and Speeches* (New York: Crossing Press).

Lovell, T. (ed.) (1990) *British Feminist Thought: A Reader* (Oxford: Blackwell).

Lovenduski, J. (1988) 'Feminism in the 1980s', *Politics*, vol. 8, no. 1.

Lovibond, S. (1989) 'Feminism and Postmodernism', *New Left Review*, no. 178.

Lutz, A. (1944) *Created Equal: A Biography of Elizabeth Cady Stanton* (New York: John Day).

Lutz, A., Phoenix, A. and Yuval-Davis, N. (1995) 'Introduction, Nationalism, Racism and Gender: European Crossfires', in H. Lutz, A. Phoenix and N. Yuval-Davis (eds) *Crossfires: Nationalism, Racism and Gender in Europe* (London: Pluto Press).

Luxemburg, R. (1971) *Selected Political Writings*, edited and with an introduction by D. Howard (New York and London: Monthly Review Press).

MacKinnon, C. (1983) 'Feminism, Marxism, Method, and the State: An Agenda for Theory', in E. Abel and E. Abel (eds).

MacKinnon, C. (1989a) 'Sexuality, Pornography and Method: Pleasure under Patriarchy', *Ethics*, vol. 99, no. 2.

MacKinnon, C. (1989b) *Towards a Feminist Theory of the State* (London: Harvard University Press).

Maconachie, M. (1987) 'Engels, Sexual Divisions and the Family', in J. Sayers, M. Evans and N. Redclift (eds).

Malmgreen, G. (1978) *Neither Bread nor Roses: Utopian Feminists and the English Working Class* (Brighton: John L. Noyce).

Malos, E. (1980) *The Politics of Housework* (London: Allison & Busby).

Mansbridge, J. (1986) *Why We Lost The ERA* (Chicago and London: University of Chicago Press).

Mansbridge, J. (2001) 'The Descriptive Political Representation of Gender: An Anti-Essentialist Argument', in J. Klausen and C. Maier (eds).

Marcus, J. (ed.) (1987) *Suffrage and the Pankhursts* (London and New York: Routledge & Kegan Paul).

Marks, E. and de Courtrivon, I. (eds) (1981) *New French Feminisms* (Brighton: Harvester Press).

Marsh, S. M. (1981) *Anarchist Women 1870–1920* (Philadelphia: Temple University Press).

Marx, K. (1963) *Early Writings*, translated and edited by T. B. Bottomore (London: Watts).

Marx, K. (1972) *Critique of the Gotha Programme* (Peking: Foreign Languages Press).

Marx, K. and Engels, F. (1968) *Selected Works* (London: Lawrence & Wishart).

Marx, K. and Engels, F. (1982) *The German Ideology* (London: Lawrence & Wishart).

Marx, K., Engels, F., Lenin, V., and Stalin, J. (1975) *Women and Communism: Selections from the Writings of Marx, Engels, Lenin and Stalin* (Westport, Conn.: Greenwood Press).

Mason, M. (1988) *The Equality Trap* (New York: Simon & Schuster).

Maynard, M. (1989) 'Privilege and Patriarchy: Feminist Thought in the Nineteenth Century', in S. Mendus and J. Rendall (eds).

McDermid, J. and Hillyar, A. (1999) *Midwives of the Revolution: Female Bolsheviks and Women Workers in 1917* (London: UCL Press).

McIntosh, P. (1995) 'White Privilege and Male Privilege: A Personal Account of Coming to See Correspondence Through Work in Women's Studies', in M. Anderson and P. Collins (eds).

McLaren, A. (1991) *A History of Contraception* (Oxford: Blackwell).

McMillan, C. (1982) *Women, Reason and Nature: Some Philosophical Problems with Feminism* (Oxford: Blackwell).

McMillan, J. (1981) *Housewife or Harlot: The Place of Women in French Society 1870–1940* (Brighton: Harvester Press).

McRobbie, A. (2000) 'Feminism and the Third Way', *Feminist Review*, no. 64.

Meehan, E. and Sevenhuijsen, S. (eds) (1991) *Equality Principles and Politics* (London: Sage).

Mellor, M. (1996) 'The Politics of Women and Nature: Affinity, Contingency or Material Relation?', *Journal of Political Ideologies*, vol. 1, no. 2.

Mendus, S. (1989) 'The Marriage of True Minds: The Ideal of Marriage in the Philosophy of John Stuart Mill', in S. Mendus and J. Rendall (eds).

Mendus, S. and Rendall, J. (eds) (1989) *Sexuality and Subordination* (London: Routledge & Kegan Paul).

Michels, R. (1962) *Political Parties*, translated by E. Paul and C. Paul (New York: Free Press).

Midgley, C. (1995) *Women Against Slavery: The British Campaigns 1780–1870* (London and New York: Routledge).

Midgley, M. and Hughes, J. (1983) *Women's Choices: Philosophical Problems Facing Feminism* (London: Weidenfeld & Nicolson).

Mies, M. (1998) *Capitalism and Accumulation on a World Scale: Women in the International Division of Labour* (London and New York: Zed Books).

Mies, M. and Shiva, V. (1993) *Ecofeminism* (London and New Jersey: Zed Books).

Mill, J. S. (1900) *Principles of Political Economy* (London: Longmans, Green).

Mill, J. S. (1971) *Autobiography*, edited by J. Stillinger (Oxford: Oxford University Press).

Mill, J. S. (1983) *The Subjection of Women* (London: Virago).

Mill, J. S. (1985) *John Stuart Mill on Politics and Society* edited by G. Williams (Glasgow: Fontana).

Miller, D. (1990) 'The Resurgence of Political Theory', *Political Studies*, vol. 38.

Millett, K. (1985) *Sexual Politics* (London: Virago).

Mills, H. (1996) ' "Saintes soeurs" and "femmes fortes": Alternative Accounts of the Routes to Womanly Civic Virtue, and the History of French Feminism', in C. Orr (ed.).

Mink, G. (1995) *The Wages of Motherhood: Inequality in the Welfare State, 1917–1942* (Ithaca and London: Cornell University Press).

Mirza, H. (1986) 'The Dilemma of Socialist Feminism: A Case for Black Feminism', *Feminist Review*, no. 22.

Mirza, H. (1997) 'Introduction: Mapping a Genealogy of Black British Feminism', in H. Mirza (ed.).

Mirza, H. (ed.) (1997) *Black British Feminism: A Reader* (London and New York: Routledge).

Mitchell, C. (1989) 'Madame Pelletier (1874–1939): The Politics of Sexual Oppression', *Feminist Review*, no. 33.

Mitchell, H. (1977) *The Hard Way Up* (London: Virago).

Mitchell, J. (1971) *Woman's Estate* (Harmondsworth: Penguin).

Mitchell, J. (1974) *Psychoanalysis and Feminism* (London: Allen Lane).

Mitchell, J. (1984) *Women: The Longest Revolution* (London: Virago).

Mitchell, J. and Oakley, A. (eds) (1979) *The Rights and Wrongs of Women* (Harmondsworth: Penguin).

Mitchell, J. and Oakley, A. (eds) (1986) *What is Feminism?* (Oxford: Blackwell).

Moi, T. (1990) *Feminist Theory and Simone de Beauvoir* (Oxford: Blackwell).

Moi, T. (1994) *Simone de Beauvoir: The Making of an Intellectual Woman* (Oxford: Blackwell).

Moi, T. (ed.) (1987) *French Feminist Thought: A Reader* (Oxford: Blackwell).

Molyneux. M. (1979) 'Beyond the Domestic Labour Debate', *New Left Review*, no. 116.

Moon, S. (1978) 'Feminism and Socialism: The Utopian Synthesis of Flora Tristan', in M. Boxer and J. Quataert (eds).

Moore, J. (1999) *Mary Wollstonecraft* (Plymouth: Northcote House).

Moraga, C. (1993) 'From a Long Line of Vendidas: Chicanas and Feminism', in A. Jaggar and P. Rothenberg (eds).

Moraga, C. and Anzaldua, G. (eds) (1983) *This Bridge Called My Back: Writings by Radical Women of Color* (New York: Kitchen Table, Women of Color Press).

Morewedge, R. (ed.) (1975) *The Role of Women in the Middle Ages* (London: Hodder & Stoughton).

Morgan, R. (1978) *Going Too Far. The Personal Chronicle of a Feminist* (New York: Vintage).

Morgan, R. (1982) *The Anatomy of Freedom* (Oxford: Martin Robertson).

Morgan, R. (1984) *Sisterhood is Global: The International Women's Movement Anthology* (Harmondsworth: Penguin).

Morgan, R. (ed.) (1970) *Sisterhood is Powerful: An Anthology of Writings from the Women's Liberation Movement* (New York: Vintage).

Morrell, C. (1980) ' "Black Friday": Violence Against Women in the Suffragette Movement', *Explorations in Feminism*, no. 9 (London: Women's Research and Resources Centre).

Morton, M. (2001) 'Review of Kate Weigland's "Red Feminism: American Communism and the Making of Women's Liberation" ', *American Historical Review*, vol. 106, no. 5.

Moses, C. (1998) 'French Utopians: The Word and the Act', in T. Akkerman and S. Stuurnam (eds).

Moses, C. and Rabine, L. (1993) *Feminism Socialism, and French Romaniticism* (Bloomington and Indianapolis: Indiana University Press).

Muncy, R. (1973) *Sex and Marriage in Utopian Communities* (London and Bloomington: Indiana University Press).

Myers, M. (1982) 'Reform or Ruin: "A Revolution in Female Manners" ', in H. Payne (ed.) *Studies in Eighteenth-century Culture* (Wisconsin and London: University of Wisconsin Press).

Myers, M. (1986) 'Hannah More's Tracts for the Times: Social Fiction and Female Ideology', in M. Schofield and C. Macheski (eds) *Fettered or Free? British Women Novelists, 1670–1815* (Ohio and London: Ohio University Press).

Nicholson, L. J. (ed.) (1990) *Feminism/Postmodernism* (New York and London: Routledge).

Nye, A. (1990a) *Feminist Theory and the Philosophies of Man* (London: Routledge).

Nye, A. (1990b) *Words of Power: A Feminist Reading of the History of Logic* (London: Routledge).

O'Brien, M. (1979) 'Reproducing Marxist Man', in L. Clark and L. Lange (eds).

O'Brien, M. (1981) *The Politics of Reproduction* (London: Routledge & Kegan Paul).

O'Brien, M. (1989) *Reproducing the World: Essays in Feminist Theory* (London: Westview Press).

O'Neil, W. (1969) *The Woman Movement: Feminism in the United States and England* (London: Allen & Unwin).

Oakley, A. (1972) *Sex, Gender and Society* (London: Maurice Temple Smith).

Oakley, A. (1979) 'Wisewoman and Medicine Man: Changes in the Management of Childbirth', in J. Mitchell and A. Oakley (eds).

Oakley, A. (1983) 'Millicent Garrett Fawcett: Duty and Determination', in D. Spender (ed.).

Offen, K. (1998) 'Reclaiming the European Enlightenment for Feminism: or Prologomena to any Future History of Eighteenth-century Europe', in T. Akkerman and S. Stuurnam (eds).

Offen, K. (2000) *European Feminisms 1700–1950: A Political History* (Stanford, California: Stanford University Press).

Okely, J. (1986) *Simone de Beauvoir: A Re-Reading* (London: Virago).

Okin, S. M. (1980) *Women in Western Political Thought* (London: Virago).

Okin, S. M. (1987) 'Justice and Gender', *Philosophy and Public Affairs*, vol. 16, no. 1.

Okin, S. M. (1989) 'Reason and Feeling in Thinking about Justice', *Ethics*, vol. 99, no. 2.

Okin, S. M. (1990) *Justice, Gender and the Family* (New York: Basic Books).

Orr, C. (ed.) (1996) *Wollstonecraft's Daughters: Womanhood in England and France 1780–1920* (Manchester: Manchester University Press).

Owen, R. (1972) *A New View of Society and Other Writings*, introduced by J. Butt (London: David).

Owens, R. (1984) *Smashing Times: A History of the Irish Women's Suffrage Movement 1889–1922* (Dublin: Attic Press).

Paglia, C. (1992) *Sex, Art, and American Culture: Essays* (New York: Vintage Books).

Paine, T. (1894) 'An Occasional Letter on the Female Sex', in *The Writings of Tom Paine*, vol. I, collected and edited by M. D. Conway (New York and London: Putnam).

Painter, N. (2000) 'Regrets', *Signs*, vol. 25, no. 4.

Pankhurst, C. (1987) 'The Great Scourge and How to End It', in J. Marcus (ed.).

Pankhurst, S. (1977) *The Suffragette Movement* (London: Virago).

Pateman, C. (1986a) 'The Theoretical Subversiveness of Feminism', in C. Pateman and E. Gross (eds).

Pateman, C. (1986b) 'Review of Genevieve Lloyd's "The Man of Reason" ', *Political Theory*, vol. 14.

Pateman, C. (1987) 'Feminist Critiques of the Public/Private Dichotomy', in A. Phillips (ed.).

Pateman, C. (1988a) *The Sexual Contract* (Cambridge: Polity Press).

Pateman, C. (1988b) 'The Patriarchal Welfare State', in A. Gutmann (ed.) *Democracy and the Welfare State* (Princeton: Princeton University Press).

Pateman, C. (1989) *The Disorder of Women* (Cambridge: Polity).

Pateman, C. and Gross, E. (eds) (1986) *Feminist Challenges: Social and Political Theory* (London: Allen & Unwin).

Perry, R. (1986) *The Celebrated Mary Astell* (Chicago and London: University of Chicago Press).

Phelps, L. (1981) 'Patriarchy and Capitalism', in *Building Feminist Theory: Essays from Quest* (London: Longman).

Phillips, A. (1983) *Hidden Hands: Women and Economic Policies* (London: Pluto Press).

Phillips, A. (1987a) *Divided Loyalties: Dilemmas of Sex and Class* (London: Virago).

Phillips, A. (1991) *Engendering Democracy* (Cambridge: Polity Press).

Phillips, A. (1993) *Democracy and Difference* (Cambridge: Polity Press).

Phillips, A. (1995) *The Politics of Presence* (Oxford: Clarendon Press).

Phillips, A. (1999) *Which Equalities Matter?* (Cambridge: Polity Press).

Phillips, A. (ed.) (1987b) *Feminism and Equality* (Oxford: Blackwell).

Phillips, A. and Taylor, B. (1986) 'Sex and Skill', in Feminist Review (ed.) *Waged Work: A Reader* (London: Virago).

Piercy, M. (1979) *Woman on the Edge of Time* (London: Women's Press).

Pilardi, J. (1995) 'Feminists Read the Second Sex', in M. Simons (ed.).

Plumwood, V. (1993) *Feminism and the Mastery of Nature* (London and New York: Routledge).

Pollard, S. and Scott, J (eds) (1971) *Robert Owen, Prophet of the Poor* (London: Macmillan).

Pollert, A. (1996) 'Gender and Class Revisited; or, The Poverty of "Patriarchy" ', *Sociology*, vol. 30, no. 4.

Pornography and Sexual Violence. Evidence of the Links: The complete transcript of Public Hearings on Ordinances to Add Pornography as Discrimination Against Women. Minneapolis City Council, Government Operations Committee. Dec. 72 and 73, 1983 (London: Everywoman).

Power, E. (1975) *Medieval Women* (Cambridge: Cambridge University Press).

Pugh, M. (2000) *Women and the Women's Movement in Britain, 1914–1999* (Basingstoke: Macmillan).

Purvis, J. and Holton, S. (eds) (2000) *Votes for Women* (London and New York: Routledge).

Puwar, N. (2000) 'Making Spaces for South Asian Women: What Has Changed Since Feminist Review Issue 17?', *Feminist Review*, no. 66.

Quataert, J. (1978) 'Unequal Partners in an Uneasy Alliance: Women and the Working Class in Imperial Germany', in M. Boxer and J. Quataert (eds).

Quataert, J. (1979) *Reluctant Feminists in German Social Democracy 1885–1917* (Princeton, NJ: Princeton University Press).

Ragland-Sullivan, E. (1991) 'Jacques Lacan. Feminism and the Problem of Gender Identity', in S. Gunew (ed.).

Ramazanoglu, C. (1986) 'Ethnocentricity and Socialist–Feminist Theory: A Response to Barrett and McIntosh', *Feminist Review*, no. 22.

Ramazanoglu, C. (1989) *Feminism and the Contradictions of Oppression* (London: Routledge).

Ramelson, M. (1967) *The Petticoat Rebellion: A Century of Struggle for Women's Rights* (London: Lawrence & Wishart).

Randall, V. (1987) *Women and Politics* (Basingstoke: Macmillan).

Rang, B. (1998) 'A "learned wave": Women of Letters and Science from the Renaissance to the Enlightenment', in T. Akkerman and S. Stuurnam (eds).

Ransby, B. (2000) 'Black Feminism at Twenty-One: Reflections on the Evolution of a National Community', *Signs*, vol. 25, no. 4.

Rathbone, E. (1927) *The Disinherited Family: A Plea for Direct Provision for the Costs of Child Maintenance through Family Allowances* (London: Allen & Unwin).

Rauschenbusch-Clough, E. (1898) *A Study of Mary Wollstonecraft* (London, New York and Bloomsbury: Longman Green).

Rawls, J. (1971) *A Theory of Justice* (Oxford: Oxford University Press).

Redstockings (1970) 'Manifesto', in R. Morgan (ed.).

Redstockings (1978) *Feminist Revolution. An Abridged Edition with Additional Writings* (New York: Random House).

Reeves, M. (1979) *Round About a Pound a Week* (London: Virago).

Reid, M. (1988) *A Plea for Women*, introduced by S. Ferguson (Edinburgh: Polygon).

Bibliography

Rendall, J. (1985) *The Origins of Modern Feminism: Women in Britain, France and the United States 1780–1860* (London: Macmillan).

Rendall, J. (ed.) (1987) *Equal or Different: Women's Politics 1800–1914* (Oxford: Blackwell).

Rich, A. (1977) *Of Woman Born: Motherhood as Experience and Institution* (London: Virago).

Rich, A. (1980) 'Compulsory Heterosexuality and Lesbian Existence', *Signs*, vol. 5, no. 4.

Richards, J. R. (1982) 'Reply to Grimshaw: Philosophy and Feminism', *Radical Philosophy*, no. 32.

Richards, J. R. (1982) *The Sceptical Feminist* (Harmondsworth: Penguin).

Richardson, D. (1996) 'Constructing Lesbian Sexualities', in S. Jackson and S. Scott (eds).

Richardson, M. (1987) 'Introduction' to M. W. Stewart.

Richardson, S. (2000) ' "Well-neighboured Houses": The Political Networks of Elite Women, 1760–1860', in K. Gleadle and S. Richardson (eds).

Riemar, E. and Fout, J. (eds) (1980) *European Women: A Documentary History 1789–1945* (Brighton: Harvester Press).

Riley, D. (1988) *'Am I That Name?' Feminism and the Category of 'Women' in History* (Basingstoke: Macmillan).

Robertson, P. (1982) *An Experience of Women: Pattern and Change in Nineteenth-century Europe* (Philadelphia: Temple University Press).

Robnett, B. (1997) *How Long? How Long? African-American Women in the Struggle for Civil Rights* (New York and Oxford: Oxford University Press).

Rogers, K. M. (1982) *Feminism in Eighteenth-century England* (Brighton: Harvester Press).

Roiphe, K. (1993) *The Morning After: Sex, Fear and Feminism* (London: Hamish Hamilton).

Romero, P. (1987) *Sylvia Pankhurst: Portrait of a Radical.* (New Haven and London: Yale University Press).

Rooks, N. (2000) 'Like Canaries in the Mines: Black Women's Studies at the Millenium', *Signs*, vol. 25, no. 4.

Rose, H. (1986) 'Women's Work: Women's Knowledge', in J. Mitchell and A. Oakley (eds).

Rosen, A. (1974) *Rise Up Women! The Militant Campaign of the Women's Social and Political Union 1903–1914* (London and Boston: Routledge & Kegan Paul).

Rosenberg, C. (1989) *Women and Perestroika: Present, Past and Future for Women in Russia* (London: Bookmarks).

Ross, L. (1993) 'African-American Women and Abortion: 1800–1970', in S. James and A. Busia (eds).

Rossi, A. (ed.) (1970) *Essays on Sex Equality: John Stuart Mill and Harriet Taylor* (Chicago and London: University of Chicago Press).

Rossi, A. S. (ed.) (1973) *The Feminist Papers from Adams to de Beauvoir* (New York and London: Columbia University Press).

Roszak, B. and Roszak, T. (eds) (1969) *Masculine/Feminine: Readings in Sexual Mythology and the Liberation of Women* (New York: Harper Colophon Books).

Rousseau, J. J. (1955) *Emile*, translated by B. Foxley (London: Dent).

Rover, C. (1967) *Women's Suffrage and Party Politics in England 1866–1914* (London: Routledge & Kegan Paul).

Rover, C. (1970) *Love, Morals and the Feminists* (London: Routledge & Kegan Paul).

Rowan, C. (1982) ' "Mothers, Vote Labour!" The State, the Labour Movement and Working-class Mothers, 1900–1918', in R. Brunt and C. Rowan (eds) *Feminism, Culture and Politics* (London: Lawrence & Wishart).

Rowbotham, S. (1972) *Women, Resistance and Revolution* (Harmondsworth: Penguin).

Rowbotham, S. (1973a) *Hidden from History* (London: Pluto Press).

Rowbotham, S. (1973b) *Women's Consciousness, Man's World* (Harmondsworth: Penguin).

Rowbotham, S. (1977) *A New World for Women: Stella Browne – Socialist Feminist* (London: Pluto Press).

Rowbotham, S. (1982) 'The Trouble with Patriarchy', in M. Evans (ed.).

Rowbotham, S. (1983) *Dreams and Dilemmas* (London: Virago).

Rowbotham, S. (1989) *The Past is Before Us: Feminism in Action since the 1960s* (London: Pandora Press).

Rowbotham, S. (1996), 'Forward', to B. Winslow (1996).

Rowbotham, S. and Weeks, J. (1977) *Socialism and the New Life: The Personal and Sexual Politics of Edward Carpenter and Havelock Ellis* (London: Pluto Press).

Rowbotham, S., Segal, L. and Wainwright, H. (1979) *Beyond the Fragments* (London: Merlin Press).

Rowland, R. (1992) *Living Laboratories: Women and Reproductive Technologies* (Bloomington and Indianapolis: Indiana University Press).

Rubin, G. (1970) 'Woman as Nigger', in L. Tanner (ed.).

Rubin, M. (1998) 'The Languages of Late-Medieval Feminism', in T. Akkerman and S. Stuurnam (eds).

Rubinstein, D. (1986) *Before the Suffragettes* (Brighton: Harvester Press).

Ruddick, S. (1980) 'Maternal Thinking', *Feminist Studies*, vol. 6 no. 1.

Ruddick, S. (1984) 'Preservative Love and Military Destruction: Some Reflections on Mothering and Peace', in J. Trebilcot (ed.).

Ruddick, S. (1990) *Maternal Thinking: Towards a Politics of Peace* (London: Women's Press).

Ruiz, V. and Dubois, E. (1994) 'Introduction', in V. Ruiz and E. Dubois (eds).

Ruiz, V. and Dubois, E. (eds) (1994) *Unequal Sisters: A Multi-Cultural Reader in US Women's History* (London and New York: Routledge).

Sabrovsky, J. A. (1979) *From Rationality to Liberation: The Evolution of Feminist Ideology* (Westport Conn. and London: Greenwood Press).

Salleh, A. (1997) *Ecofeminism as Politics: Nature, Marx and the Postmodern* (London and New York: Zed Books).

Salper, R. (1972) *Female Liberation: History and Current Politics* (New York: Knopf).

Sapiro, V. (1992) *A Vindication of Political Virtue: The Political Theory of Mary Wollstonecraft* (London: University of Chicago Press).

Sapiro, V. (1998) 'A Woman's Struggle for a Language of Enlightenment and Virtue: Mary Wollstonecraft and Enlightenment "Feminism" ', in T. Akkerman and S. Stuurnam (eds).

Sarah, E. (1983) 'Christabel Pankhurst: Reclaiming her Power', in D. Spender (ed.).

Sargent, L. (1986) (ed.) *The Unhappy Marriage of Marxism and Feminism: A Debate on Class and Patriarchy* (London: Pluto Press).

Sassoon, A. S. (1987) *Women and the State: The Shifting Boundaries between Public and Private* (London: Hutchinson).

Sawicki, J. (1991) 'Foucault and Feminism: Towards a Politics of Difference', in M. Shanley and C. Pateman (eds).

Sayers, J. (1982) *Biological Politics: Feminist and Anti-Feminist Perspectives* (London and New York: 1982).

Sayers, J. (1986) *Sexual Contradictions: Psychology, Psychoanalysis and Feminism* (London and New York: Tavistock).

Sayers, J., Evans, M. and Redclift, N. (eds) (1987) *Engels Revisited: New Feminist Essays* (London and New York: Tavistock).

Schapiro, J. S. (1978) *Condorcet and the Rise of Liberalism* (New York: Octagon Books).

Scharfe, L. (1980) *To Work and To Wed: Female Employment, Feminism and the Great Depression* (Westport, Conn. and London: Greenwood Press).

Scharfe, L. and Jensen, J. M. (eds) (1978) *Decades of Discontent: The Women's Movement 1920–1940* (Boston: Northeastern University Press).

Schneewind, J. (ed.) (1965) *J. S. Mill; Essays on Literature and Society* (London: Collier-Macmillan).

Schneir, M. (ed.) (1972) *Feminism: The Essential Historical Writings* (New York: Vintage).

Schwarzer, A. (1984) *Simone de Beauvoir Today: Conversations 1972–1982*, translated from the French by M. Howarth (London: Chatto & Windus).

Scott, A. (1992) *Natural Allies: Women's Associations in American History* (Urbana and Chicago: University of Illinois Press).

Scott, H. (1982) *Sweden's Right to be Human* (London: Allison & Busby).

Scott, J. (1989) 'French Feminists and the Rights of "Man": Olympe de Gouge's Declarations', *History Workshop*, no. 28.

Scott, J. (1990) 'Deconstructing Equality-Versus-Difference: Or, the Uses of Poststructuralist Theory for Feminism', in M. Hirsch and E. Keller (eds) *Conflicts in Feminism* (New York and London: Routledge).

Scott, J. (1996) *Only Paradoxes to Offer: French Feminists and the Rights of Man* (Cambridge, MA, and London: Harvard University Press).

Scott, S. and Jackson, S. (1996) 'Sexual Skirmishes and Feminist Factions: Twenty-five Years of Debate on Women and Sexuality', in S. Jackson and S. Scott (eds).

Seccombe, W. (1974) 'The Housewife and her Labour under Capitalism', *New Left Review*, no. 83.
Seccombe, W. (1975) 'Domestic Labour: Reply to Critics', *New Left Review*, no. 74.
Segal, L. (1987) *Is the Future Female? Troubled Thoughts on Contemporary Feminism* (London: Virago).
Segal, L. (1990) *Slow Motion: Changing Masculinities and Changing Men* (London: Virago).
Segal, L. (1999) *Why Feminism?* (Cambridge: Polity Press).
Sevenhuijsen, S. (1991) 'Justice, Moral Reasoning and the Politics of Child Custody', in E. Meehan and S. Sevenhuijsen (eds).
Shaffer, R. (1979) 'Women and the Communist Party USA 1930–1940', *Socialist Review*, vol. 9, no. 3.
Shahar, S. (1983) *The Fourth Estate: A History of Women in the Middle Ages*, translated by C. Galai (London and New York: Methuen).
Shanley, M. L. and Pateman, C. (eds) (1991) *Feminist Interpretations and Political Theory* (London: Polity Press).
Shiva, V. (1988) *Staying Alive: Women, Ecology and Development* (London and New Delhi: Zed Books).
Shulman, A. K. (1983) 'Emma Goldman: "Anarchist Queen" (1869–1940)', in D. Spender (ed.).
Shulman, A. K. (ed.) (1979) *Red Emma Speaks: The Selected Speeches and Writings of the Anarchist and Feminist Emma Goldman* (London: Wildwood House).
Sichterman, B. (1983) *Femininity: The Politics of the Personal* (Oxford: Polity Press).
Siddiqui, H. (2000) 'Black Women's Activism: Coming of Age?', *Feminist Review*, no. 64.
Signs (1981) 'Special edition on French Feminist Theory' *Signs*, vol. 7, no. 1.
Siim, B. (1991) 'Welfare State, Gender Politics and Equality Principles – Women's Citizenship in the Scandinavian Welfare State', in E. Meehan and S. Sevenhuijsen (eds).
Simons, M. (1992) 'Lesbian Connections: Simone de Beauvoir and Feminism', *Signs*, vol. 18, no. 1.
Simons, M. (1995) 'The Second Sex: From Marxism to Radical Feminism', in M. Simons (ed.).
Simons, M. (ed.) (1995) *Feminist Interpretations of Simone de Beauvoir* (Pennsylvania: Pennsylvania State University Press).
Slaughter, J. and Kern, R. (eds) (1981) *European Women on the Left: Socialism, Feminism and the Problems Faced by Political Women 1880 to the Present* (Westport, Conn. and London: Greenwood Press).
Smart, C. (1989) *Feminism and the Power of Law* (London and New York: Routledge).
Smart, C. and Smart, B. (1978) *Women, Sexuality and Social Control* (London: Routledge & Kegan Paul).
Smith, B. (1995) 'Crossing the Great Divide: Race, Class and Gender in Southern Women's Organizing, 1979–1991', *Gender and Society*, vol. 9, no. 6.
Smith, H. (1998) *The British Women's Suffrage Campaign 1866–1928* (Harlow: Pearson Education).
Smith, H. L. (1982) *Reason's Disciples: Seventeenth-century English Feminists* (Urbana, Chicago and London: University of Illinois Press).
Smith, H. L. (ed.) (1990) *British Feminism in the Twentieth Century* (Aldershot: Edward Elgar).
Solaris, V. (1970) 'Excerpts from the SCUM Manifesto', in R. Morgan (ed.).
Somerville, J. (2000) *Feminism and the Family* (Basingstoke: Palgrave).
Sowerwine, C. (1982) *Sisters or Citizens? Women and Socialism in France since 1876* (Cambridge: Cambridge University Press).
Spelman, E. (1988) *Inessential Woman: Problems of Exclusion in Feminist Thought* (Boston: Beacon Press).
Spender, D. (1983a) *Women of Ideas (and What Men Have Done to Them)* (London: Ark).
Spender, D. (1985a) *Man Made Language* (London: Routledge & Kegan Paul).
Spender, D. (1985b) *For the Record: The Making and Meaning of Feminist Knowledge* (London: Women's Press).
Spender, D. (ed.) (1983b) *Feminist Theorists: Three Centuries of Women's Intellectual Traditions* (London: Women's Press).
Springborg, P. (1996) 'Introduction', in M. Astell.
Squires, J. (1999) *Gender in Political Theory* (Cambridge: Polity Press).
Stacey, J. (1986) 'Are Feminists Afraid to Leave Home? The Challenge of Pro-Family Feminism', in J. Mitchell and A. Oakley (eds).
Stacey, M. and Price, M. (1981) *Women, Power and Politics* (London and New York: Tavistock).
Stafford, W. (1998) *John Stuart Mill* (Basingstoke: Macmillan).

Staggenborg, S. (1998) *Gender, Family and Social Movements* (Thousand Oaks, California: Pine Forge Press).

Stanley, L. (1983) 'Olive Schreiner: New Women, Free Women, All Women' in D. Spender (ed.).

Stanton, E. C. and Anthony, S. B. (1981) *Correspondence, Writings, Speeches*, edited and with a critical commentary by E. C. Dubois (New York: Schocken).

Stanton, E. C., Anthony, S. B. and Gage, M. (eds) (1881 and 1882) *The History of Woman Suffrage*, vols I and II (New York: Fowler & Wells).

Stanworth, M. (ed.) (1987) *Reproductive Technologies* (Oxford: Polity Press).

Steinem, G. (1984) *Outrageous Acts and Everyday Rebellions* (London: Fontana).

Stenton, M. (1957) *The English Woman in History* (London: Allen & Unwin).

Stewart, M. W. (1987) *America's First Black Woman Political Writer: Essays and Speeches*, edited and with an Introduction by M. Richardson (Bloomington and Indianapolis: Indiana University Press).

Stites, R. (1978) *The Women's Liberation Movement in Russia: Feminism, Nihilism and Bolshevism 1860–1930* (Princeton, New Jersey: Princeton University Press).

Stites, R. (1981) 'Alexandra Kollontai and the Russian Revolution', in J. Slaughter and R. Kern (eds).

Stone, L. (1979) *The Family, Sex and Marriage in England 1500–1800* (Harmondsworth: Penguin).

Stott, A. (2000) 'Patriotism and Providence: The Politics of Hannah More', in K. Gleadle and S. Richardson (eds).

Strachey, R. (1974) *The Cause: A Short History of the Women's Movement in Great Britain* (Bath: Cedric Chivers).

Strange, P. (1983) *It'll Make a Man of You – A Feminist View of the Arms Race* (Nottingham: A Peace News/Mushroom pamphlet).

Stuurnam, S. (1998) *'L'égalité des sexes qui ne se conteste plus en France*: Feminism in the Seventeenth Century', in T. Akkerman and S. Stuurnam (eds).

Tanner, L. (ed.) (1970) *Voices from Women's Liberation* (New York: Mentor).

Taylor, B. (1983) *Eve and the New Jerusalem: Socialism and Feminism in the Nineteenth Century* (London: Virago).

Taylor, D. *et al.* (1985) *Women: A World Report* (London: Methuen).

Taylor, H. (1983) *The Enfranchisement of Women* (London: Virago).

Taylor, U. (1998) 'The Historical Evolution of Black Feminist Theory and Praxis', *Journal of Black Studies*, vol. 29, no. 2.

Terborg-Penn, R. (1998) *African-American Women in the Struggle for the Vote, 1850–1920* (Bloomington and Indianapolis: Indiana University Press).

Thatcher, M. (1954) Article in *Onward*, a Conservative Party publication, April 1954. Reprinted in *The Guardian*, 21 March 1990.

Thompson, D (1987) 'Women, Work and Politics in Nineteenth-century England: The Problem of Authority', in J. Rendall (ed.).

Thompson, D. (ed.) (1983) *Over Our Dead Bodies: Women Against the Bomb* (London: Virago).

Thompson, M. L. (ed.) (1970) *Voices of the New Feminism* (Boston: Beacon Press).

Thompson, R. (1974) *Women in Stuart England and America* (London: Routledge & Kegan Paul).

Thompson, W. (1983) *Appeal of one Half of the Human Race, Women against the Pretensions of the Other Half, Men, to retain them in Political, and Thence in Civil and Domestic Slavery* (London: Virago).

Thonnessen, W. (1973) *The Emancipation of Women: The Rise and Decline of the Women's Movement in German Social Democracy 1863–1963*, translated by J. de Bres (Bristol: Pluto Press).

Thornton, M. (1986) 'Sex Equality is not enough for Feminism', in C. Pateman and E. Gross (eds).

Tobias, S. (1997) *Faces of Feminism: An Activist's Reflections on the Women's Movement* (Boulder, Colorado: Westview Press).

Todd, J. M. (ed.) (1977) *A Wollstonecraft Anthology* (Bloomington and London: Indiana University Press).

Tomalin, C. (1974) *The Life and Death of Mary Wollstonecraft* (London: Weidenfeld & Nicolson).

Tong, R. (1989) *Feminist Thought: A Comprehensive Introduction* (London: Unwin Hyman).

Tovey, B. and Tovey, G. (1974) 'Women's Philosophical Friends and Enemies', *Social Science Quarterly*, vol. 55.

Treblicot, J. (ed.) (1984) *Mothering: Essays in Feminist Theory* (New York: Rowman & Littlefield).

Tress, D. (1988) 'Comment on Flax's "Postmodernism and Gender Relations in Feminist Theory', *Signs*, vol. 14, no. 1.

Tronto, J. (1993) 'Beyond Gender Difference to a Theory of Care', in J. Larrabee (ed.) *An Ethic of Care* (London: Routledge).

Trotsky, L. (1924) *Problems of Life*, translated by Z. Venerora, with an introduction by N. Minsky (London: Methuen).

Trotsky, L. (1970) *Women and the Family* (New York: Pathfinder).

Tulloch, G. (1989) *Mill and Sexual Equality* (Hemel Hempstead: Harvester Wheatsheaf).

Ungerson, C. (ed.) (1985) *Women and Social Policy: A Reader* (Basingstoke: Macmillan).

United Nations (2002) *The World's Women 2000: Trends and Statistics* (New York: United Nations Department of Economic and Social Affairs, Statistical Division).

Urbanski, M. (1983) 'Margaret Fuller: Feminist Writer and Revolutionary', in D. Spender (ed.).

Vetterling-Braggin, M., Elliston, F. and English, J. (eds) (1981) *Feminism and Philosophy* (Totowa, NJ: Littlefield, Adams).

Viner, K. (2001) 'Stitched Up', *The Guardian*, 1 September.

Vintges, K. (1998) 'Beauvoir's Philosophy as the Hidden Paradigm of Contemporary Feminism', in Akkerman and Stuurman (eds).

Vogel, L. (1983) *Marxism and the Oppression of Women* (London: Pluto Press).

Vogel, L. (1995) *Woman Questions: Essays for a Materialist Feminism* (London: Pluto Press).

Vogel, U. (1986) 'Rationalism and Romanticism: Two Strategies for Women's Liberation', in J. Evans *et al.*

Vogel, U. (1989) 'Is Citizenship Gender Specific?', unpublished paper presented to the Political Studies Association Annual Conference.

Voronina, O. (1989) 'Women in a "Man's Society" ', *Soviet Sociology*, vol. 28, no. 2.

Walby, S. (1990) *Theorizing Patriarchy* (Oxford: Blackwell).

Walby, S. (1997) *Gender Transformations* (London: Routledge).

Walker L. (1984 *The Women's Movement in England in the Late Nineteenth and Early Twentieth Centuries*, unpublished PhD thesis, University of Manchester.

Walter, N. (1998) *The New Feminism* (London: Little, Brown).

Walter, N. (ed.) (1999) *On the Move: Feminism for a New Generation* (London: Virago).

Walters, M. (1979) 'The Rights and Wrongs of Women: Mary Wollstonecraft, Harriet Martineau, Simone de Beauvoir', in J. Mitchell and A. Oakley (eds).

Waltzer, M. (1983) *Spheres of Justice: A Defense of Pluralism and Equality* (New York: Basic Books).

Wandor, M. (ed.) (1972) *The Body Politic: Women's Liberation in Britain* (London: Stage 1).

Wandor, M. (ed.) (1990) *Once a Feminist: Stories of a Generation* (London: Virago).

Ward, L. (2002) ' "Globalization" and the "Third Way": A Feminist Reponse', *Feminist Review*, no. 70.

Wardle, R. (1951) *Mary Wollstonecraft: A Critical Study* (London: Richards Press).

Ware, S. (1981) *Beyond Suffrage: Women in the New Deal* (Cambridge, Mass.: Harvard University Press).

Ware, V. (1992) *Beyond the Pale: White Women, Racism and History* (London: Verso).

Warnock, M. (ed.) (1966) *Utilitarianism* (London: Collins).

Washington, M. (1988) 'Intoduction' to J. Cooper.

Waters, E. (1989) 'Restructuring the "Woman Question": Perestroika and Prostitution', *Feminist Review*, no. 32.

Waters, K. (ed.) (2000) *Women and Men Political Theorists: Enlightened Conversations* (Oxford: Blackwell).

Watts, R. (1998) *Gender, Power and the Unitarians in England 1760–1860* (London and New York: Longman).

Weedon, C. (1987) *Feminist Practice and Poststructuralist Theory* (Oxford: Blackwell).

Weigland, K. (2001) *Red Feminism, American Communism and the Making of Women's Liberation* (Baltimore and London: John Hopkins University Press).

Weiner, G. (1983) 'Harriet Martineau: A Reassessment', in D. Spender (ed.).

Weir, A. and Wilson, E. (1984) 'The British Women's Movement', *New Left Review*, no. 148.

Wenzel, H. (1986) 'Interview with Simone de Beauvoir', in *Simone de Beauvoir: Witness to a Century* (New Haven, Conn.: Yale University Press).

West, C. and Fenstermaker, S. (1996), 'Doing Difference', in E. Chow, D. Wilkinson and M. Zinn (eds).

West, C. and Zimmerman, D. (1991) 'Doing Gender', in J. Lorber and S. Farrell (eds).

Wexler, A. (1984) *Emma Goldman: An Intimate Life* (London: Virago).

Wheeler, L. (1983) 'Lucy Stone: Radical Beginnings 1818–93', in D. Spender (ed.).

Whelehan, I. (1995) *Modern Feminist Thought: From Second Wave to 'Post-Feminism'* (Edinburgh: Edinburgh University Press).

Whitelegg, E. *et al.* (1982) *The Changing Experience of Women* (Oxford: Martin Robertson).

Willard, C. (1975) 'A Fifteenth-century View of Woman's Role in Medieval Society: Christine de Pizan's "Livre des Trois Vertus" ', in R. Morewedge (ed.).

Williams, G. (ed.) (1985) *John Stuart Mill on Politics and Society* (Glasgow: Collins Fontana).

Wilson, E. (1980) *Only Halfway to Paradise: Women in Postwar Britain 1945–1968* (London and New York: Tavistock).

Wilson, E. with Weir, E. (1986) *Hidden Agendas: Theory, Politics and Experience in the Women's Movement* (London: Tavistock).

Wiltsher, A. (1985) *Most Dangerous Women: Feminist Peace Campaigners of the Great War* (London: Pandora Press).

Winegarten, R. (1988) *Simone de Beauvoir: A Critical View* (Oxford: Berg).

Wingerden, S. van (1999) *The Women's Suffrage Movement in Britain, 1866–1928* (Basingstoke: Macmillan).

Winslow, B. (1996) *Sylvia Pankhurst: Sexual Politics and Political Activism* (London: UCL Press).

Wittig, M. (1981) 'One is Not Born a Woman', *Feminist Issues*, vol. 1, no. 1.

Wolf, N. (1993) *Fire with Fire: The New Female Power and How It Will Change the 21st Century* (London: Chatto & Windus).

Wolf, N. (2001) *Misconceptions: Truth, Lies, and the Unexpected on the Journey to Motherhood* (London: Chatto & Windus).

Wolgast, E. (1980) *Equality and the Rights of Women* (Ithaca and London: Cornell University Press).

Wollstonecraft, M. (1792) *Vindication of the Rights of Woman* (Harmondsworth: Penguin, 1978).

Wood, E. (1995) *Democracy Against Capitalism: Renewing Historical Materialism* (Cambridge: Cambridge University Press).

Wood, E. M. (1986) *The Retreat from Class: A New, 'True' Socialism* (London: Verso).

Yellin, J. (1989) *Women and Sisters: The Antislavery Feminists in American Culture* (New Haven and London: Yale University Press).

Yeo, E. (1998) *Radical Femininity: Women's Self-representation in the Public Sphere* (Manchester and New York: Manchester University Press).

Young, I. (1986) 'Beyond the Unhappy Marriage: A Critique of the Dual Systems Theory', in L. Sargent (ed.).

Young, I. (1989) 'Polity and Group Difference: A Critique of the Ideal of Universal Citizenship', *Ethics*, vol. 99, no. 2.

Young, I. (1990) *Justice and the Politics of Difference* (Princeton: Princeton University Press).

Yuval-Davis, N. (1998) 'Beyond Differences: Women, Empowerment and Coalition Politics', in N. Charles and H. Hintjens (eds) *Gender, Ethnicity and Political Ideologies* (London and New York: Routledge).

Zalewski, M. (2000) *Feminism after Postmodernism: Theorising through practice* (London and New York: Routledge).

Zartov, D. (1995) 'Gender, Orientalism and the History of Ethnic Hatred in the Former Yugoslavia', in H. Lutz, A. Phoenix and N. Yuval-Davis (eds).

Zetkin, C. (1984) *Selected Writings*, edited by P. Foner (New York: International Publishers).

Index

solidarity   230, 231, 242
Sommers, Christina Hoff   145
Spender, Dale   102–3, 169, 199
Squires, Judith   236, 242, 247, 251
St Simon, H. de   20, 24
 see also St Simoniennes
St Simoniennes   24, 25
Stalin, J.   119, 123, 125
standpoint theory   11, 65, 218–20, 229, 231–2
Stanton, Elizabeth Cady   2, 29–30, 31, 32–41, 45, 52, 53, 74, 76, 77, 78
state
 anarchist views of   101, 102
 liberal/liberal feminist views of   86, 90, 101, 151, 153–5
 and patriarchy   93, 196–7
 and promotion of gender equality   145, 153–5
 socialist/Marxist views of   68, 93, 97
 and welfare provision   88–91, 92–3, 107, 118, 126, 141, 223
Stewart, Maria   29–31, 34, 39, 72, 74
Stone, Lucy   36
Stopes, Marie   91
Stuurman, S.   6
suffrage movement   40–1, 44, 73–83
 see also political rights

Tanner, Leslie   165
Taylor, Barbara   23,
Taylor, Harriet   42, 45, 48, 49, 51, 53, 54
temperance movement   12, 30–1, 73, 84
Tennyson, Alfred   42
Thatcher, Margaret   141, 145
 Thatcherite   223
Third Way   223
Thomas, Clarence   156
Thompson, William   21, 25–7, 42, 50, 53, 54, 178, 251
trade unions   73, 95, 112, 208, 222, 224
transsexuals   247
transvestism   239
Tristan, Flora   21, 24
Tronto, Joan   161
Trotsky, L.   116–17, 122–3
Truth, Sojourner   39–40

Unitarians   14
United Nations   252
utilitarianism   27, 49–51, 75

Victoria, Queen   55
Vintges, Karen   133
violence, male   43, 52, 62, 144, 166–7, 175, 177–8, 187–8, 191–5, 243
Vogel, Lise   65, 116, 205, 211–13
Voltaire, F.   13

Wages for Housework   91, 206
Wainwright, Hilary   222
Walby, Sylvia   172, 175
Walter, Natasha   145, 146, 167
Walters, M.   11
Wandor, Michelle   165
war, women's opposition to   74, 83, 84–5, 111, 161
 see also eco-feminism
Ware, S.   88
Washington, George   14
Weigland, Kate   104
welfare feminism   87–91, 95, 107, 126
Wheeler, Anna   21, 25–7, 42, 50, 53, 54, 178, 251
Willard, Frances   98
Wilson, E.   128
Wolf, Naomi   144–5, 146, 152, 154
Wolgast, E.   146
Wollstonecraft, Mary   2, 9, 13, 14, 15, 16–20, 21, 25, 26, 32, 34, 38, 42, 48, 70, 73, 74, 102, 160
'Wollstonecraft's dilemma'   18, 148, 236–7
Woman's Bible, the   37–8
'womanly qualities', 'womanly virtues'   5, 12, 40, 43, 44, 46–7, 74–5, 99, 100–1, 149, 181, 185–7
 see also female superiority
Women's Co-operative Guild   73, 88
Women's International League for Peace and Freedom   84–5
Women's Party (British)   80, 82
Women's Party (United States)   80, 86
Women's Property Committee   43
Women's Social and Political Union (WSPU)   76
Woodhull, Victoria   35, 38
Wright, Frances   21, 23, 24

Young, Iris   150, 210–11, 251

Zalewski, Marysia   241–2, 245–6
Zetkin, Clara   107–13, 114, 116, 117, 118, 122
Zhenotdel (Women's Department)   116, 117, 118–19